British Politics in the Age of Holmes

Geoffrey Holmes's *British Politics in the Age of Anne*
40 Years On

Edited by

Clyve Jones

Wiley-Blackwell

for

The Parliamentary History Yearbook Trust

© 2009 The Parliamentary History Yearbook Trust

Blackwell Publishing was acquired by John Wiley & Sons in February 2007. Blackwell's publishing programme has been merged with Wiley's global Scientific, Technical, and Medical business to form Wiley-Blackwell.

Registered Office
John Wiley & Sons Ltd, The Atrium, Southern Gate, Chichester, West Sussex, PO19 8SQ, United Kingdom

Editorial Offices
350 Main Street, Malden, MA 02148-5020, USA
9600 Garsington Road, Oxford, OX4 2DQ, UK
The Atrium, Southern Gate, Chichester, West Sussex, PO19 8SQ, UK

For details of our global editorial offices, for customer services, and for information about how to apply for permission to reuse the copyright material in this book please see our website at
http://www.wiley.com/wiley-blackwell

The right of Clyve Jones to be identified as the author of the editorial material in this work has been asserted in accordance with the Copyright, Designs and Patents Act 1988.

All rights reserved. No part of this publication may be reproduced, stored in a retrieval system, or transmitted, in any form or by any means, electronic, mechanical, photocopying, recording or otherwise, except as permitted by the UK Copyright, Designs and Patents Act 1988, without the prior permission of the publisher.

Wiley also publishes its books in a variety of electronic formats. Some content that appears in print may not be available in electronic books.

Library of Congress Cataloging-in-Publication Data
British politics in the age of Holmes : Geoffrey Holme's British politics in the age of Anne : 40 years on / edited by Clyve Jones.
    p. cm.
    Includes bibliographical references and index.
    ISBN 978-1-4051-9334-4 (alk. paper)
    1. Holmes, Geoffrey S., 1928–British politics in the age of Anne. 2. Great Britain–Politics and government–1702–1714. 3. Anne, Queen of Great Britain, 1665–1714. 4. Holmes, Geoffrey S., 1928–Political and social views. 5. Holmes, Geoffrey S., 1928–Influence. 6. Great Britain–Politics and   government–1702–1714–Historiography. 7. Great   Britain.   Parliament–Historiography. 8. Jacobites–Historiography. 9. Women in politics–Great Britain–Historiography. 10. Political parties–Great Britain–Historiography. I. Jones, Clyve, 1944–
    DA495.B69 2009
    941.06'9–dc22

                                                                    2008052092

ISBN 978-1-4051-9334-4

Geoffrey Holmes, 1928–1993.

CONTENTS

Foreword

ALAN MARSHALL

In the revised edition of *British Politics in the Age of Anne* (1987), Geoffrey Holmes noted that 'twenty years . . . [was] a long time in the bustling, hyper-professional world of late 20th century scholarship', and to produce a 'revised edition' of a work first published in 1967 was, in many ways, to 'attempt the impossible'.

Yet 2007 saw the 40th anniversary of the publication of *British Politics in the Age of Anne* and stood 20 years on from the publication of the revised edition, whose brilliant introduction belies the author's comments. It seemed pertinent to find out how this major work of research had fared in the interim of an even more 'bustling' world of historical scholarship.

With this in mind it was suggested that perhaps a gathering of scholars in a symposium on the work (not excluding Geoffrey Holmes's other major writings), would be timely. In addition, the private circulation by Ella Holmes of the 'missing', incomplete volume on the 'Great Ministry' of Robert Harley made it an opportune time to revisit the era.

The results of this symposium (organised by myself and Clyve Jones), arising from its debates, papers, and discussions within the History of Parliament building on 8 December 2007 are now placed before you.

The day proved to be illuminating and revealing. If the historical academic world has moved on very quickly and books in it, not to mention their ideas, are all too often ephemeral, it was soon clear that here was work which had stood the test of time. What was also clear throughout the day was that even after 40 years, Geoffrey Holmes's ideas as a historian of the reign of Anne were still very much live ones and still providing a foundation for further research. Such lacunae as were noted were rare and the work of Holmes stood up to scrutiny.

In this volume, therefore, are some aspects of the age of Anne seen through the eyes of some of the major scholars of the era in 2007; that their scholarship is also seen to be through the filter of what has come to be called 'British Politics in the Age of Holmes' is perhaps a still more fitting tribute to a very remarkable historian.

Dr Jones and I would like to thank Ella Holmes for supplying the photograph of Geoffrey and for allowing us to publish for the first time Geoffrey's lecture on Lord Wharton. Our thanks are also due to Bath Spa University and the History of Parliament for financially supporting the symposium on which this volume is based, and particularly to Professor Fiona Montgomery (head of the School of Historical and Cultural Studies at Bath Spa University) and to Dr Paul Seaward (director of the History of Parliament) for their support of the project. Finally we would like to thank Alasdair Hawkyard for compiling the index.

LIST OF CONTRIBUTORS

Peter Borsay was an undergraduate and postgraduate student of Geoffrey Holmes at Lancaster University. He is currently professor of history at Aberystwyth University, a member of the international advisory board of *Urban History*, and a committee member of the British Pre-Modern Towns Group. His books include *The English Urban Renaissance: Culture and Society in the Provincial Town, 1660–1770* (Oxford, 1989); *The Image of Georgian Bath, 1700–2000: Towns, Heritage and History* (Oxford, 2000); editor with L. Proudfoot, *Provincial Towns in Early Modern England and Ireland: Change, Convergence and Divergence* (Proceedings of the British Academy, cviii, Oxford, 2002); and *A History of Leisure: The British Experience Since 1500* (2006). He is currently engaged in research on various aspects of 17th- and 18th-century British towns; on the history of Welsh seaside resorts 1750–1914; on heritage and history; and is preparing a book on *The Discovery of England*.

Elaine Chalus is a senior lecturer in history at Bath Spa University and the editor of the 'Parliamentary History Texts & Studies Series'. She is particularly interested in the interplay of gender and politics in the long 18th century. Electoral history, political ritual and the use of the social arena for political ends all feature extensively in her research. Her publications include *Elite Women in English Political Life, c.1754–1790* (Oxford, 2005).

Richard Connors is a member of the History Department at the University of Ottawa. His scholarly interests include the political, constitutional and legal history of Britain and its colonies during the long 18th century. He has taught history at the University of Essex (1992–3), University of Alberta (1994–2002), University of Ottawa (2002–present), and legal history in the Faculty of Law, University of Alberta (2000–2). He has co-edited a number of books and published numerous articles on British, imperial and legal history.

Brian Cowan holds the Canada research chair in early modern British history at McGill University in Montreal, Canada, where he is also an associate professor of history. His monograph, *The Social Life of Coffee: The Emergence of the British Coffeehouse* (2005) was awarded the Wallace K. Ferguson prize by the Canadian Historical Association in 2006. He is a co-investigator with the 'Making Publics in Early Modern Europe. 1500–1700' project supported by a Major Collaborative Research Initiative grant from Canada's Social Sciences and Humanities Research Council, and is also editing *The State Trial of Dr Henry Sacheverell* for the 'Parliamentary History Texts & Studies Series'.

Robin Eagles is a senior research fellow in the House of Lords 1660–1832 section of the History of Parliament. Previous publications include *Francophilia in English Society 1748–1815* (2000), entries in the *Oxford Dictionary of National Biography* and 'Unnatural Allies? The Oxfordshire *Elite* from the Exclusion Crisis to the Overthrow of James II', *Parliamentary History*, xxvi (2007).

Perry Gauci is the current V.H.H. Green fellow in history at Lincoln College, Oxford. His core interests rest with the political, social and commercial development of Britain in the long 18th century. In this field he has published *The Politics of Trade: The Overseas Merchant in State and Society, 1660–1720* (Oxford, 2001), and *Emporium of the World: The Merchants of London 1660–1800* (2007).

D.W. Hayton is professor of early modern Irish and British history and head of the School of History and Anthropology at Queen's University, Belfast. He was formerly on the staff of the History of Parliament Trust, and was one of the editors of the *The History of Parliament: The House of Commons, 1690–1715* (5 vols, Cambridge, 2002), for which he wrote the introductory survey. He has written extensively on British and Irish political history of the late 17th and early 18th centuries, and a collection of his essays on Irish history, *Ruling Ireland 1685–1742* was published in 2004. He was elected a member of the Royal Irish Academy in 2008.

Geoffrey Holmes, FBA, taught at the University of Glasgow, 1952–69, before becoming reader in history in 1969 and professor in 1973 at the University of Lancaster. Besides *British Politics in the Age of Anne* (1967, rev. edn 1987), his major publications were: *The Divided Society* (with W.A. Speck, 1967); *Britain after the Glorious Revolution* (jointly edited, 1969); *The Trial of Doctor Sacheverell* (1973); *Augustan England: Professions, State and Society, 1680–1730* (1982); *The London Diaries of William Nicolson, Bishop of Carlisle, 1702–1718* (jointly edited with Clyve Jones, Oxford, 1985); *The Making of a Great Power: Later Stuart and Early Georgian Britain* (1993); and *The Age of Oligarchy: Pre-Industrial Britain* (with Daniel Szechi, 1993). He died in 1993.

Clyve Jones is an honorary fellow of the Institute of Historical Research and has been the editor of the journal *Parliamentary History* since 1986. Previously he was reader in modern history in the University of London and collection development librarian in the Institute of Historical Research. He has published extensively on the history of the house of lords and of the peerage in the early 18th century. His main publications are editions of *The London Diaries of William Nicolson, Bishop of Carlisle, 1702–1718*, with Geoffrey Holmes (Oxford, 1985), and *Tory and Whig: The Parliamentary Papers of Edward Harley, Third Earl of Oxford, and William Hay, M.P. for Seaford, 1715–1754*, with Stephen Taylor (Woodbridge, 1998). He has also edited a *festschrift* for his mentor Geoffrey Holmes (1987), and essays in memory of his friends Philip Lawson (Woodbridge, 1998), John A. Phillips (Edinburgh, 2005) and, again, Geoffrey Holmes (Oxford, 2009).

Mark Knights is professor of history at Warwick University. His last book was *Representation and Misrepresentation in Later Stuart Britain: Partisanship and Political Culture* (Oxford, 2005). He is currently writing what he hopes will be an accessible introduction to the later Stuart period.

Alan Marshall was supervised by Geoffrey Holmes for his PhD, which was completed in 1991 and was subsequently published as *Intelligence and Espionage in the Reign of Charles II, 1660–1685* (Cambridge, 1994). Since then he has written a number of books and articles on the early modern period. They include: *Oliver Cromwell, Soldier: The Military*

Life of a Revolutionary at War (2004); *The Strange Death of Edmund Godfrey* (Sutton, 1999); *The Age of Faction: Court Politics, 1660–1702* (Manchester, 1999) and '"Mechanic Tyranny": Anthony Ashley Cooper and the English Republic', in *Shaftesbury*, ed. J. Spurr (2009). His current research is on the Leveller assassination plots to kill Oliver Cromwell in the 1650s and the 17th century volume in the *Palgrave History of Britain*.

Hannah Smith is a tutorial fellow and university lecturer in history at St Hilda's College, Oxford. She is the author of *Georgian Monarchy: Politics and Culture, 1714–60* (Cambridge, 2006).

W.A. Speck is emeritus professor of history at Leeds University and special professor in the School of English Studies at Nottingham University. His DPhil thesis on 'The House of Commons 1702–1714: A Study in Political Organisation' (Oxford, 1966) owed much to the advice and inspiration of Geoffrey Holmes, with whom he co-edited *The Divided Society: Party Conflict in England 1694–1716* (1967). He was also heavily indebted to Holmes while writing *Tory and Whig: The Struggle in the Constituencies 1701–1715* (1970) and *The Birth of Britain: A New Nation 1701–1710* (1994). His most recent publications include *Colonial America from Jamestown to Yorktown* with Mary Geiter (2002) and *Robert Southey: Entire Man of Letters* (2006).

Daniel Szechi is a graduate of the University of Sheffield and St Antony's College, Oxford, and was appointed professor of early modern history at the University of Manchester in 2006. He is a fellow of the Royal Society of Edinburgh and the Royal Historical Society. His books include: *1715: The Great Jacobite Rebellion* (New Haven, 2006); *George Lockhart of Carnwath 1689–1727: A Study in Jacobitism* (East Lothian, 2002); *The Jacobites: Britain and Europe, 1688–1788* (Manchester, 1994); with Geoffrey Holmes, *The Age of Oligarchy: Pre-Industrial Britain 1722–1783* (1993); and *Jacobitism and Tory Politics, 1710–14* (Edinburgh, 1984). He has also published articles in *Past and Present, English Historical Review, Scottish Historical Review, Journal of British Studies, Historical Journal, Catholic Historical Review, Parliamentary History* and *Studies in Church History*, and a number of essays in collective works.

Graham Townend was educated at Huddersfield Polytechnic and Edinburgh University, and was awarded a PhD at the latter for a dissertation on the political career of the 3rd earl of Sunderland. He worked as a library assistant at Napier University, Edinburgh, and since 2003 has been self-employed as a researcher and writer. At present he is researching and writing the biographies of the Scottish representative peers for the House of Lords 1660–1832 section of the History of Parliament.

In No One's Shadow: *British Politics in the Age of Anne* and the Writing of the History of the House of Commons

D.W. HAYTON

with a postscript by W.A. SPECK

The publication in 1967 of Geoffrey Holmes's masterpiece, *British Politics in the Age of Anne*, effectively demolished the interpretation of the 'political structure' of early 18th-century England that had been advanced by the American historian R.R. Walcott as a conscious imitation of Sir Lewis Namier. But to understand the significance of Holmes's work solely in an anti-Namierite context is misleading. For one thing, his book only completed a process of reaction against Walcott's work that was already under way in unpublished theses and scholarly articles (some by Holmes himself). Second, Holmes's approach was not simplistically anti-Namierist, as some (though not all) of Namier's followers recognized. Indeed, he was strongly sympathetic to the biographical approach, while acknowledging its limitations. The significance of Holmes's book to the study of the house of commons 1702–14 (and of the unpublished study of 'the Great Ministry' of 1710–14 to which it had originally been intended as a long introduction), was in fact much broader than the restoration of party divisions as central to political conflict. It was the re-creation of a political world, not merely the delineations of political allegiances, that made *British Politics in the Age of Anne* such a landmark in writing on this period.

Keywords: Queen Anne; politics; parliament; house of commons; historiography; Geoffrey Holmes; Sir Lewis Namier

During the reign of Queen Anne the Dutch artist Peter Tillemans painted two interior scenes of the Palace of Westminster, one of the house of commons in session, and one of the house of lords. It was his picture of the lower House that appeared on the dust jacket of the first edition of Geoffrey Holmes's masterpiece, *British Politics in the Age of Anne*. This could be understood as a reference both to the importance of the Commons in British political life in the period, and even more crucially, its importance in the historiography. There was irony here, since a major element in Holmes's reconstruction of the world of Augustan politics – and one he developed in his subsequent writings – was the demonstrable fact that in this period the upper House had not yet been eclipsed by the lower. Indeed, he argued that in many respects Anne's reign was a 'golden age' for the house of lords. The party leaders were to be found there and the crucial parliamentary dramas – over occasional conformity, the Sacheverell impeachment and the peace – were played out by its members. This assertion offered a different perspective on parliamentary history than was to be found in most histories of the British 18th century, which were dominated by the study of the Commons. But despite Holmes's achievement in restoring the Lords to its rightful place in the political narrative, academic readers and reviewers of his book still concentrated on what he had to say about the political allegiances and political behaviour in the lower House. This was because they regarded *British Politics in the Age of Anne* – rightly or wrongly – as an attack on Sir Lewis Namier and his self-appointed disciple Robert Walcott, whose own contributions to the literature had focused on the lower House. As Holmes himself noted, in the very first sentence of the book (which itself says a great deal about the place Namier still enjoyed in 1967 at the centre of historiographical debate)[1] Namier's great works, *The Structure of Politics at the Accession of George III* and *England in the Age of the American Revolution*, cast a deep shadow over the century as a whole, and within that shadow lay the book that *British Politics in the Age of Anne* was and is still popularly understood to have directly controverted: Walcott's *English Politics in the Eighteenth Century*.[2]

Walcott's book, though relatively short, and lacking the depth of documentary research, intellectual subtlety, and literary style to be found in Namier, had enjoyed, for a brief time, a success out of proportion to its merits. Historians who soon came to know better were initially impressed by the way in which it had apparently translated Namier's conclusions about the meaninglessness of whig and tory party labels in the 1760s, in terms of political practice, into what had previously been regarded as the heyday of party politics in the first decade of the century. But there was a crucial difference between Walcott's work and that of his master: Namier had combined biographical research with a close scrutiny of surviving political correspondence, much of it excavated from the muniment rooms of grand houses during his 'paper chases' across the English countryside; Walcott, by contrast, had accumulated a wealth of detail about the family backgrounds of members of parliament but had largely neglected their letters, papers and speeches.[3] When other historians began to undertake this kind of manuscript research a very different picture emerged.

Although Walcott's book had been well reviewed on its appearance in 1956 – a point at which Namier's historiographical revolution was only beginning to come under serious criticism – and could be said to have 'held the field for over ten years',[4] its foundations had been undermined before the appearance of *British Politics in the Age of Anne*. Some of the most comprehensive sapping had been undertaken in unpublished doctoral theses, by B.W. Hill, Angus McInnes, E.L. Ellis, Henry Horwitz and W.A. Speck, while in the Ford Lectures of 1965 J.H. Plumb had signalled a willingness to express more forcibly than before his own deep suspicions of the Walcott thesis.[5] In print, there

[1] Linda Colley, *Lewis Namier* (1989), 94–5.

[2] R.R. Walcott, *English Politics in the Early Eighteenth Century* (Oxford, 1956).

[3] Microfilm copies of the index cards compiled by Walcott during the course of his research were deposited with the History of Parliament Trust, and remain in its archives.

[4] Holmes's own phrase, in a letter published in *The Listener*, 23 May 1968 (see below, n. 26).

[5] B.W. Hill, 'The Career of Robert Harley, Earl of Oxford, from 1702 to 1714', University of Cambridge PhD, 1961; A.J.D.M. McInnes, 'Robert Harley, Secretary of State', University of Wales MA, 1961; E.L. Ellis, 'The Whig Junto in Relation to the Development of Party Politics and Party Organization from its Inception to 1714', Oxford University DPhil, 1962; Henry Horwitz, 'The Political Career of Daniel Finch, Second Earl of Nottingham (1647–1730)', Oxford University DPhil, 1963; W.A. Speck, 'The House of Commons 1702–14: A Study in Political Organization', Oxford University DPhil, 1965. I am greatly indebted to Bill Speck for his comments on this article, and for the 'postscript' which he has added.

had been a number of preliminary sorties into Walcott's defences in the form of articles in learned journals. In particular several historians, beginning with Holmes himself, had published analyses of some of the more important of the parliamentary lists which had been discovered for Anne's reign, which were to prove the most compelling evidence for the reality of party divisions in day-to-day parliamentary politics, determining votes on minor as well as major issues.[6] *British Politics* was thus far from being a bolt from the blue. Nor was it the only frontal assault that Walcott had to face in 1967, since Plumb's Ford Lectures were also published in that year as *The Growth of Political Stability in England, 1675–1725*.[7] However, the thrust of *British Politics* was not polemical. True, the introduction began with a reference to the author writing (inevitably) in the shadow of Namier, and spent a few pages discussing different interpretations of political 'structure' in the period, but thereafter Walcott as prey almost disappeared from the scene. Only twice in the body of the text did Holmes engage directly with his work: in a brief passage in which he dissected the most absurd of Walcott's spurious family-based 'connections', the supposed 'Newcastle–Pelham–Walpole–Townshend' group, and at slightly greater length in his chapter on 'power-groups and pressure-groups', which of necessity included some discussion of familial and patron–client relationships.[8]

Most reviewers, however, concentrated their attention on the arguments *contra* Walcott, despite the fact that Holmes's own forensic researches, and those of a generation of younger scholars, had already rendered the non-party or anti-party interpretation of Augustan politics distinctly shaky in specialist academic circles; and despite the fact that a careful reading of *British Politics* offered a great deal more that was new about the way members of parliament understood and operated their political system, about the dominant ideologies of this political world, and about the continuing constitutional importance of the monarchy and the house of lords. Established 18th-century historians like Plumb,[9] J.M. Beattie,[10] K.G. Davies,[11] and P.D.G. Thomas,[12] writing in academic journals, or in the heavyweight weekly magazines, took as their starting point the restoration of party and often did not get much further.[13] Stephen Saunders Webb, reviewing both *British Politics* and Plumb's *Growth of Political Stability* for the *William and Mary Quarterly*, and with the implications for American colonial history to the forefront of his mind, emphasized the challenge both books posed to 'Walcott's application of Namierist

---

[6] Geoffrey Holmes, 'The Commons' Division on "No Peace Without Spain", 7 December 1711', *Bulletin of the Institute of Historical Research*, xxxiii (1960), 223–4; J.G. Sperling, 'The Division of 25 May 1711, on an Amendment to the South Sea Bill: A Note on the Reality of Parties in the Age of Anne', *Historical Journal*, iv (1961), 191–202; W.A. Speck, 'The Choice of a Speaker in 1705', *Bulletin of the Institute of Historical Research*, xxvii (1964), 20–46; Henry Horwitz, 'Parties, Connections and Parliamentary Politics, 1689–1714: Review and Revision', *Journal of British Studies*, vi (1966), 45–69. Ironically, Walcott himself had been one of the first historians to point to division lists as a significant historical source: R.R. Walcott, 'Division-Lists of the House of Commons, 1689–1715', *Bulletin of the Institute of Historical Research*, xiv (1936), 25–36.

[7] *The Growth of Political Stability in England, 1675–1725* (Harmondsworth, 1967).

[8] Geoffrey Holmes, *British Politics in the Age of Anne* (1967), 230, 327–34.

[9] In the *Spectator*, 25 Aug. 1967. Copies of this and other reviews are preserved in an album of cuttings in the possession of Mrs Ella Holmes. I am grateful to Mrs Holmes for making this available to me.

[10] In *Canadian Journal of History*, iii (1968), 104–5.

[11] In the *New Statesman*, 22 Sept. 1967.

[12] In *Révue Historique*, ccxlii (1970), 134–5.

[13] Notable exceptions were G.V. Bennett's long review in *English Historical Review*, lxxxiv (1969), 358–62; and Caroline Robbins's short notice in *American Historical Review*, lxxiv (1969), 1625–6.

© *The Parliamentary History Yearbook Trust 2009*

themes to British politics in the Age of Anne'.[14] Newspaper reviewers focused even more closely on the implicit challenge to Namier's 'revisionist' picture of 18th-century politics, since this added fuel to the controversy which was still simmering over Namier's stature as a historian and the influence of 'Namierism' over academic history.[15] In the *Daily Telegraph* Maurice Ashley wrote[16] that Holmes 'aims to discredit a newer interpretation of political history in Anne's reign put forward by pupils [sic] of the late Lewis Namier'. He added rather tartly, 'While Namier lived, few British historians had the temerity to challenge his authority. Now that he is dead, the so-called Namierites are being severely criticised', thus placing *British Politics* firmly, though quite unjustifiably, in a line of criticism of Namier's work that had begun with Sir Herbert Butterfield, and had become much more pronounced with bitter reviews (by A.J.P. Taylor and others) of the *History of Parliament* volumes for 1754–90, edited by Namier and John Brooke, that had been published in 1964.

The general tenor of reviews of *British Politics* was highly favourable, and rightly so, since, as J.P. Kenyon wrote, in a review of the revised edition, *British Politics* was 'a major contribution to our understanding of eighteenth-century political history, and one of the most significant products of post-war historical scholarship'.[17] Undoubtedly, however, the fact that the book constituted a firm rebuttal of Walcott's thesis, and did so in such a way as could effectively command assent, because of the vast array of sources, both printed and manuscript, on which it was based, was an additional attraction for those wishing to pick over the bones of Namier's reputation. To attack Namier's achievement was far from Holmes's intention. The single paragraph that he devoted in his introduction to an explicit discussion of Namier's influence on the writing of 18th-century history, was measured and even-handed. He acknowledged that Namier's techniques 'are an indispensable aid to the study of politics in . . . any period of modern British history', but warned of the law of diminishing returns, and stressed that:

> biographical evidence has to become the historian's servant and not his master; it has, after all, no inherent superiority over other types of evidence, and it carries the dangerous liability that by focussing attention exclusively on the trees it can easily persuade us that it is they and not the wood which really matter.[18]

His most serious criticisms were levelled at Walcott rather than at Namier himself, and at least one reviewer who was 'himself a pupil of Namier' found the arguments of the book 'very convincing'.[19] Another, no less a figure than Dame Lucy Sutherland, contributed anonymously a subtle and perceptive review to the *Times Literary Supplement* in which she acknowledged as justified the rejection of the Walcott thesis, which had only ever been 'accepted in principle rather than in detail by those who found the old

[14] *William and Mary Quarterly*, 3rd ser., xxv (1968), 635.

[15] See, e.g., *Birmingham Post* (T.W. Hutton), 19 Aug. 1967; *The Scotsman* (Grant G. Simpson), 16 Sept. 1967; *Glasgow Herald* ('R.E.D.'), 3 Feb. 1968.

[16] *Daily Telegraph*, 5 Oct. 1967. Walcott was never, of course, strictly speaking, a *pupil* of Namier.

[17] *Times Literary Supplement*, 4–10 Mar. 1988.

[18] Holmes, *British Politics*, 6–7.

[19] Thomas, in *Révue Historique*, ccxlii (1970), 135 (English translation taken from typescript of review in album in the possession of Mrs Ella Holmes).

interpretation less than satisfactory', and emphasized instead the ways in which Holmes had carefully qualified an exclusively two-party model of political conflict: the extent to which each of the two parties were themselves 'confederacies rather than unions', the activities of pressure groups, the survival of the 'country' tradition, and, especially, the role of the court manager as broker between the crown and the party leaders, which ensured that although a two-party structure might have prevailed, there was no two-party *system*, but rather, as Namier had argued, a 'mixed government'.[20]

Not all 'Namierites' took the same generous view, however; in part, perhaps, because of the understandable desire to come to the defence of Walcott, as a friend who was being assailed by a barrage of criticism from all sides; and in part because Walcott had himself taken up the cudgels only a few years previously in a public defence of Namier's reputation.[21] The most vigorous response came from the Johnson scholar Donald Greene, who in an intemperate and almost wholly negative review of *British Politics* in the *Philological Quarterly*, began by describing the book as 'a usefully detailed, if sometimes rather tedious narrative', went on to cast some doubt, in passing, on Holmes's accuracy ('there are little slips and solecisms here and there that make one wonder whether Holmes is as completely and intimately familiar with his material as the author of such a work needs to be'), and finally claimed to have exposed him as a historiographical throwback; 'This is the "Whig Interpretation" with a vengeance!':[22]

> This work is in good part polemics, preaching a return to the pleasant pre-Namierian days when history could be written by facilely juggling two nicely balanced entities known as 'Whiggism' and 'Toryism' – entities seldom defined, or, if defined on one page, undergoing protean changes in subsequent ones.

Despite its excessive vehemence (or perhaps because of it, who knows?) this review did not provoke a response. But Holmes's anger was aroused by a hostile review in *The Listener* by another Namierite, Betty Kemp, which focused entirely on the issue of party structure, and accused the author of *British Politics* of manifesting an almost obsessive need to revise the work of other historians, including Trevelyan, Namier, Feiling, and even Plumb, alongside Walcott.[23] Indeed, Walcott scarcely figured in Miss Kemp's remarks, which were principally intended as a defence of Namier. Holmes was said to dislike the Namier method, and much play was made with Lord Treasurer Godolphin's contemporary description of the Commons in the 1705 parliament as divided between tories, whigs, and queen's servants, which, it was argued, bore out Namier's view of political structure, even though W.A. Speck's article on the Speakership election, published in 1965, had effectively corrected this erroneous inference.[24] The conclusion struck a patronising tone, wishing that:

---

[20] *Times Literary Supplement*, 18 Jan. 1956, 56. The review is unsigned, but may be identified through the electronic database, 'TLS Centenary Archive'. Available at *http://www.tls.psmedia.com* (accessed 9 Oct. 2008).

[21] Harvey C. Mansfield, jr, 'Sir Lewis Namier Considered', *Journal of British Studies*, ii (1962), 28–55; Robert Walcott, ' "Sir Lewis Namier Considered" Considered', *Journal of British Studies*, iii (1964), 85–108; Harvey C. Mansfield, jr, 'Sir Lewis Namier Again Considered', *Journal of British Studies*, iii (1964), 109–19.

[22] *Philological Quarterly*, xlvii (1968), 303–4.

[23] *The Listener*, 29 Feb. 1968.

[24] Speck, 'Choice of a Speaker in 1705'.

© *The Parliamentary History Yearbook Trust 2009*

Mr Holmes had been more willing to let the book stand on its own feet. As it is, it risks being judged not on its merits but on the extent to which its author succeeds in his difficult, but self-imposed, task of defining a position different from that of 'the older historians'.

So annoyed was Holmes by this example of what he considered to be misdirected criticism that he took the unusual step of sending a private letter to the reviewer.[25] 'I am bound to say', he wrote of the review,

> I found it pretty extraordinary, and the more often I read it since the more astonished I become. Please don't misunderstand me. The cause of the incredulity is not the receipt of one brickbat after so many bouquets; this in itself would be salutary. It is rather the fact that the missile appears to have been aimed at a non-existent target. The book you were criticizing has not been written; or if it has, I most certainly have not written it.

He did not deny that he taken issue with pre-existing interpretations of the politics of his period, which was, after all, perfectly reasonable, especially in the case of Walcott's contentious thesis, but although 'from time to time . . . I had to step aside for a moment to do a demolition job . . . I don't think I can fairly be accused of keeping my finger permanently on the detonator.' Only seven out of over 400 pages of text, he said, addressed these issues. No one reading the book could possibly conclude that its prime concern, as Miss Kemp had alleged, was the contradiction of other historians. And he was emphatic that his comments about Namier in particular had been misconstrued. He quoted Miss Kemp's criticism of his own opening line: 'Why . . . need a historian writing about Anne's reign feel oppressed . . . by the shadow of Namier?':

> I thought this opening remark, which you appear to have taken in a derogatory sense though it was intended to be quite the opposite, was both intelligible and unexceptionable. A scholar of Namier's stature casts a long shadow both before him and behind him, whatever the limits of his own particular period. Moreover, since the appearance of Walcott's book in 1956 how could anyone possibly not be conscious of the influence of Namier's ideas on the interpretation of early eighteenth-century politics?

There was no reply, nor to the published letter to the editor of *The Listener* in which the same points were made more tersely.[26]

The sharpness of this exchange, and the focus of other reviews on the destruction of the Walcott thesis, over which, in truth, *British Politics* did not so much perform the *coup de grâce* as conduct the final obsequies, may create a misleading impression, namely that Holmes's work was central to the broader reaction against 'Namierism' that was already under way in 1968 and gathered greater impetus in the 1970s through the work of a younger generation of scholars. However, unlike J.H. Plumb, for example, Holmes never

[25] Geoffrey Holmes to Betty Kemp, 13 Mar. 1968 (copy in the possession of Mrs Ella Holmes). Again, I owe a debt of gratitude to Mrs Holmes for permission to consult, and to quote from, materials in her possession.

[26] Geoffrey Holmes, private letter to the editor of *The Listener*, 29 Apr. 1968 (copy in the possession of Mrs Ella Holmes); *The Listener*, 23 May 1968.

© *The Parliamentary History Yearbook Trust 2009*

made dismissive remarks about Namier in print.[27] As is clear from his own writings, he did not himself reject the Namier method, except in his scepticism of an excessive devotion to the small change of biographical evidence at the expense of other, richer sources. Indeed – again unlike Plumb[28] – he was a strong supporter of the work of the 1690–1715 section of the History of Parliament, to which in due course his own notes and transcripts of original sources, both printed and manuscript, were made available. Its biographical approach, combined with detailed research into individual constituencies, was one he endorsed rather than rejected. Holmes was as anxious as any of the research staff employed on the project to find out 'who the chaps were', as Namier had put it.[29] In some key respects his scholarship resembles Namier's, most notably in the attention paid to individuals, and the way in which he lets the protagonists in the political quarrels of Anne's reign, personal or national, speak for themselves. Indeed, as a working historian, Holmes may have followed Namier's example more closely than Walcott; for example, in the enthusiasm for, and use of, contemporary correspondence and diaries. There is little evidence in either Walcott's book, or the index cards on which he based his conclusions (copies of which are preserved at the History of Parliament Trust), of documents unearthed in the kind of 'paper chases' so beloved of Namier, while Holmes's work is suffused with this kind of reference. The backbone of *British Politics* is provided by its detailed knowledge of the personnel of both Commons and Lords, whom the author is able not merely to identify but in many cases to bring to life for the reader with a few well-chosen words. The book is full of striking vignettes of individual MPs, enhanced by the apt use of quotations from contemporary sources. The way, for example, in which Holmes lists and analyses the followers of Robert Harley in 1704–8, the 'country whigs' and 'court whigs' of 1705–8, or the jacobite and Hanoverian tories of 1713–14 are not only examples of masterly historical writing, but a manifestation of a deep knowledge about a very large number of individual MPs.[30] There is a world of difference between this very serious attempt to understand the character and motivation of individuals, and the desiccated tables of family groups and connections produced by Walcott, which simply assume motivation from circumstances – at best a form of 'vulgar Namierism' in which the disciple has failed to understand the thinking of the master. Holmes's commitment to finding out as much as could be found, about everyone involved in the political processes he was describing and discussing, was much nearer to Namier's psychology as a historian than it was to Namier's more virulent critics.

In other respects, of course, there were considerable differences between Geoffrey Holmes's history and that of the man whose 'shadow' he acknowledged falling across his

---

[27] See, e.g., J.H. Plumb, *The Making of an Historian: The Collected Essays of J. H. Plumb* (Hemel Hempstead, 1988), 10–19. But note the unusually sharp comment in Holmes's introduction to the revised edition of *British Politics*, published in 1987, that it had been important 'at a time when "Namierism" was rampant simply to demonstrate the reality of a two-party division in Augustan politics', p. xxii.

[28] See, e.g., Plumb, *Making of an Historian*, 97–100.

[29] Compare the reported comments of Holmes and J.H. Plumb at a colloquium on the parliamentary lists of the late 17th and early 18th centuries held at Leicester University in 1970. Holmes: 'considered it important to begin research with a study of elections and of politicians at Westminster, in order to build up the corpus of information about people'; Plumb: 'replied that . . . it was not vitally important what, for example, was the conduct of Morgan of Tredegar so long as one knew what the major issues were and how they were settled': *The Parliamentary Lists of the Early Eighteenth Century, Their Compilation and Use . . .* , ed. A.N. Newman (Leicester, 1973), 83–5.

[30] Holmes, *British Politics*, 222–34, 263–4, 279–84.

© *The Parliamentary History Yearbook Trust 2009*

period of study. One obvious difference is that while Namier's parliamentary research focused exclusively on the Commons, *British Politics* examined the political life of both Houses. This is unsurprising given the greater political weight carried by the Lords in Anne's reign than in the first decade of George III's and is thus not especially significant. A second contrast, Namier's critics would have argued, was that while Namier's studies of English politics were essentially static, cross-sections of the political nation taken at particular stages in its development, Holmes's work showed a much greater concern with narrative and change over time. There is something here, but perhaps not as much as might at first appear. Holmes's studies of the house of commons were concerned with 'structural analysis', though it is true that he was more inclined to explore the ways in which the structure shifted. More important, is the emphasis that he placed on political ideas, and the language in which they were expressed. While Namier notoriously disparaged the influence of ideas on political consciousness and political conduct, the first substantive chapter of *British Politics* began with a statement of the importance of studying 'the vocabulary which contemporaries used to describe the political attitudes and questions of their own age'.[31] This, rather more than the careful recovery of the party-dominated structure of politics, constituted a frontal challenge to the Namier legacy, and it was followed through in the chapters on 'The Substance of Conflict: Old Issues and New' and 'The "Country" Tradition'. In analysing the mainsprings of political action, for parties and for individuals, Holmes paid close attention to what members of parliament said, as well as what they did. He was not starry-eyed about their characters, as is evident from his discussions of the behaviour of ambitious opportunists like the tory earl of Anglesey, and he was willing to accept that some postures of principle, for example, among the small country whig remnant, were dictated by ulterior motives.[32] But he was unsympathetic to what he considered to be exaggerated exercises in cynicism, which denied any role for principle in the mentality of leading politicians. Some of his stiffest criticism – and he was not naturally given to sharpness of comment in relation to other historians – was directed at Patrick Riley's analysis of the making of the Anglo-Scottish union of 1707, which removed from the members of the whig junto perhaps their most credible claim to statesmanship.[33]

Holmes's interest in the role of ideas in politics was not in itself pioneering. Caroline Robbins's *The Eighteenth-Century Commonwealthman* (1959) may fairly be said to have blazed the trail, and others, most importantly J.G.A. Pocock, were following, and would in their work discuss both whig and tory political ideas to a much greater degree of theoretical sophistication. But the importance of *British Politics* in this context rests with the way in which Holmes integrated the development of party ideology with the development of party structure, and the narrative of parliamentary and governmental politics. Those who followed after him would have to deal with the ideological as well as the practical side of political life, and would have to take the language of debate as seriously as the names on division lists.

---

[31] Holmes, *British Politics*, 134.

[32] Holmes, *British Politics*, 223, 278–9; Holmes, *British Politics*, (rev. edn, 1987), p. xl.

[33] P.W.J. Riley, 'The Union of 1707 as an Episode in English Politics', *English Historical Review*, lxxxiv (1969), 498–527; P.W.J. Riley, *The Union of England and Scotland: A Study in Anglo-Scottish Politics of the Eighteenth Century* (Manchester, 1978); Holmes, *British Politics* (rev. edn), pp. xxxiv–xxxv.

© *The Parliamentary History Yearbook Trust 2009*

The publication of *British Politics in the Age of Anne* in 1967 had an immediate impact: the authority of its judgments, the artistry of its prose, and the vividness of its characterisations exercised the same spellbinding quality on students of the period that Namier's *Structure of Politics* had done 40 years earlier,[34] with the additional piquancy that *British Politics* seemed to be turning on its head the revisionism of that previous generation. Its longer-term impact is more difficult to determine. Certainly it completed the work that Holmes himself, and other scholars, had carried through during the previous decade, in destroying the credibility of the 'Walcott thesis' and restoring the centrality of party to early 18th-century English politics. Walcott's ideas were never taken seriously again by those working on the period. In retrospect, this may look like a small victory, but its importance at the time should not be underestimated. But like many other great books, *British Politics* did not inspire emulation. The very sureness of its judgments, and the forensic skill it demonstrated, may even be said to have acted as a deterrent. In the 40 years since publication the most substantial study of the house of commons between 1702 and 1714 has been that undertaken by the History of Parliament Trust, whose programme of research was dictated by broader institutional considerations.[35] Other historians have nibbled around the edges of Geoffrey Holmes's work, so to speak, picking at details. More substantially, there have been a number of excellent and well-researched biographies of major politicians,[36] and several syntheses of work on the political history of the period,[37] that have engaged with the issue of 'party', but none has attempted a refutation of the 'Holmes thesis' of early 18th-century politics in the way that Holmes refuted Walcott. Rather, those studying the period have operated within the paradigms set by *British Politics*. What is more, the accuracy of Holmes's judgments on points of detail has been confirmed in the vast majority of cases. The 1690–1715 section of the History of Parliament, employing a battery of research staff over a 30-year period, and looking at a range of manuscript collections and other sources unavailable in the 1960s, was able to offer only a few corrections to the picture he had drawn so fully and effectively.

Two of the original reviewers did, however, point to areas of weakness in the book's architecture, which have subsequently been attended to. They are implicit in the title. Curiously for a book entitled *British Politics in the Age of Anne*, there is relatively little discussion of Scottish politics, and nothing before the union, as Patrick Riley pointed out at the time in the *Scottish Historical Review*.[38] Holmes's focus is very much on the world

[34] Compare Angus McInnes's recollection of his first encounter with *British Politics* (review of *Britain in the First Age of Party, 1680–1750*, ed. Clyve Jones (1987), in *British Journal for Eighteenth-Century Studies*, xii (1989), 101), with Richard Cobb's account of having fallen, as a schoolboy, under the spell of Namier (Richard Cobb, *A Sense of Place* (1975), 43).

[35] *The History of Parliament: The House of Commons, 1690–1715*, ed. Eveline Cruickshanks, Stuart Handley and D.W. Hayton (5 vols, Cambridge, 2002). Note also Daniel Szechi, *Jacobitism and Tory Politics 1710–1714* (Edinburgh, 1984).

[36] See H.T. Dickinson, *Bolingbroke* (1970); Angus McInnes, *Robert Harley: Puritan Politician* (1970); W.L. Sachse, *Lord Somers: A Political Portrait* (Manchester, 1975); B.W. Hill, *Robert Harley: Speaker, Secretary of State and Premier Minister* (1988); C.A. Robbins, *The Earl of Wharton and Whig Party Politics, 1679–1715* (Lewiston, New York, 1992); Roy A. Sundstrom, *Sidney Godolphin: Servant of the State* (Newark, New Jersey, 1992).

[37] B.W. Hill, *The Growth of Parliamentary Parties, 1689–1742* (1976); Tim Harris, *Politics under the Later Stuarts: Party Conflict in a Divided Society, 1660–1715* (1993); W.A. Speck, *The Birth of Britain: A New Nation 1700–1710* (Oxford, 1994).

[38] *Scottish Historical Review*, xlvii (1968), 172–3.

© *The Parliamentary History Yearbook Trust 2009*

of Westminster, and it is really only when the Scots enter upon the Commons stage in 1707 that they also enter into his field of vision. So he has brief sections on episcopal tories, and on the *Squadrone* and its factional alliance with the whigs, but nothing more generally on the complex, and changing structure of Scottish political organisation. Certainly he looked at materials in Scotland (the book was, after all, researched and written while he was on the staff of Glasgow University), such as the Dalhousie Papers (at Register House) and the Montrose Papers (then still in private hands), and it would be only fair to point out that many more collections have become publicly available since.[39] It remains a pity, however, that he was not able to engage more fully with the Scottish dimension to Commons politics, which would have offered more grist to many of his arguments: about pressure groups and power groups, for example, and about the ideological dimension to party politics. Riley's own work, and that of other historians, has shown what might have been done.[40]

The second point relates to the time frame of the book. Holmes called his period 'the age of Anne' and the chronology included in the book carefully conformed to the years of her reign. Yet, despite the firmness of the authorial hand, the text does, on occasion, inevitably stray back before 1702 and forward beyond 1714. It has to be said that the construction of *British Politics* begs two important questions: when did the 'age of party' begin, and when did it end? Both have been hotly debated. The case for making a sharp division with the Hanoverian succession and the collapse of the tory party in the Commons at the 1715 election has been challenged by Linda Colley, to a degree that clearly made some impression on Holmes's later thinking.[41] The point at which a two-party political structure may be said to have begun has proved equally contentious. Henry Horwitz's original review of *British Politics*, raised the important question: 'How different were the conditions of William's and Anne's reigns?'[42] and J.H. Plumb made a similar point in his review, expressing the hope that 'one day Dr Holmes will turn his attention to a larger canvass', namely 'the grass roots of party conflict in the seventeenth century'.[43] Subsequently Horwitz has himself gone on to establish the essential continuity of whig and tory party divisions from 1689 through to Anne's reign, despite the efforts of others, notably Dennis Rubini, to argue for the greater importance of the court–country polarity.[44] Horwitz's case has been supported by a battery of parliamentary lists, the kind of evidence that had earlier subverted Walcott's 'connections',[45] and by

---

[39] See Holmes, *British Politics* (rev. edn), pp. lxiv–lxvi; *House of Commons, 1690–1715*, ed. Cruickshanks et al., i, 843–53, 856–8.

[40] P.W.J. Riley, 'The Scottish Parliament of 1703', *Scottish Historical Review*, xlvii (1968), 129–50; Riley, *Union of England and Scotland*; P.W.J. Riley, 'The Abjuration Vote of 27 June 1702 in the Scottish Parliament', *Parliamentary History*, ii (1983), 175–90; Daniel Szechi, 'Some Insights on the Scottish MPs and Peers Returned in the 1710 Election', *Scottish Historical Review*, lx (1981), 61–8; Szechi, *Jacobitism and Tory Politics*; D.W. Hayton, 'Traces of Party Politics in Early Eighteenth-Century Scottish Elections', *Parliamentary History*, xv (1995), 74–99; *House of Commons, 1690–1715*, ed. Cruickshanks et al., i, 505–25.

[41] Linda Colley, *In Defiance of Oligarchy* (Cambridge, 1982); Holmes, *British Politics* (rev. edn), pp. xiv–xv.

[42] In *Journal of Modern History*, xli (1969), 94.

[43] *Spectator*, 25 Aug. 1967.

[44] Dennis Rubini, *Court and Country, 1688–1702* (1968); Henry Horwitz, *Parliament, Policy and Politics in the Reign of William III* (Manchester, 1977).

[45] Horwitz, 'Parties, Connections and Parliamentary Politics', 62–9; I.F. Burton, P.W.J. Riley and Edward Rowlands, *Political Parties in the Reigns of William III and Anne: The Evidence of Division Lists* (*Bulletin of the Institute of Historical Research*, Special Supplement No.7, 1968); Horwitz, *Parliament, Policy and Politics*, 338–57;

the detailed biographical evidence accumulated by the History of Parliament. It would be fair to say that Holmes was always uneasy about the significance as a turning point of 1702, or even 1701, which made more sense in that it could be argued that the political violence of that year, manifest most destructively in the attempts to impeach the leading whig ministers, revived party sentiment and caused allegiances to coalesce.[46] Certainly in relation to the broader public debate about politics, in the press or at elections, he recognized that the division between whig and tory was of prime importance from at least the middle of William's reign, and the edited volume of illustrative documents he published with W.A. Speck in 1967, entitled *The Divided Society*, took as its terminal dates 1694–1716.[47]

When himself reviewing the literature on early 18th-century politics and its contexts that had been published in the 20 years since 1967, for his introduction to the revised edition of *British Politics*, Holmes could take comfort in the fact that while 'a great deal of fresh manuscript material dating from the late seventeenth and early eighteenth centuries has been unearthed, including some collections which I could have used with much profit had I known of their existence in the 1950s and 1960s', and a great deal had been written about the period, the essential structure of his own *magnum opus* remained intact. Much of what had been written – including the work of his research pupils – had illuminated the social background of politics, and especially the workings of the electoral system, which he had deliberately omitted from *British Politics* in order to leave a space for W.A. Speck to publish the findings of his own doctoral research.[48] There had also been a flourishing of interest in the history of political ideas. But the only advances of any significance in relation to house of commons politics had been in relation to the behaviour of the Scottish members – advances that he himself had been a party to[49] – and in the elucidation of the 'country' interest, a key area in which political beliefs and political actions intersected.[50] The situation a further 20 years on is not all that different:

---

[45] *(continued)* D.W. Hayton, 'The Country Party in the House of Commons, 1698–1699: A Forecast of the Opposition to a Standing Army?', *Parliamentary History*, vi (1987), 141–63; *The Parliamentary Diary of Sir Richard Cocks, 1698–1702*, ed. D.W. Hayton (Oxford, 1996), 310–19; *House of Commons, 1690–1715*, ed. Cruickshanks *et al.*, i, 835–7.

[46] Geoffrey Holmes and W.A. Speck, *The Divided Society: Party Conflict in England, 1694–1716* (1967), 3. This volume appeared with the working subtitle provided by the editors when it was commissioned; 'Parties and Politics in England 1694–1716'. They had subsequently changed it to 'Party Conflict in England 1694–1716' which they thought more accurately defined its scope. The publishers, Edward Arnold, accepted the alteration, but the change was not communicated to the printers. Arnold took the unusual step of issuing a correction slip pointing out the correct subtitle. Unfortunately this was not seen by many librarians, who catalogued the book with the working rather than the final subtitle, giving rise to some confusion. (Information from Bill Speck.)

[47] Holmes and Speck, *The Divided Society, passim*. See also, Geoffrey Holmes, 'Introduction', in *Britain after the Glorious Revolution, 1689–1714*, ed. Geoffrey Holmes (1969), 14; and the pamphlet *Religion and Party in Late Stuart England* (Historical Association, 1975), reprinted in Geoffrey Holmes, *Politics, Religion and Society in England, 1672–1742* (1986), 181–215, which in respect of the importance of party in English political culture, treats the period 1689–1714 as a continuum.

[48] Published as *Tory and Whig: The Struggle in the Constituencies, 1701–15* (1970).

[49] Geoffrey Holmes and Clyve Jones, 'Trade, the Scots and the Parliamentary Crisis of 1713', *Parliamentary History*, i (1982), 47–77.

[50] H.T. Dickinson, *Liberty and Property: Political Ideology in Eighteenth-Century Britain* (1977), ch. 3; Colin Brooks, 'The Country Persuasion and Political Responsibility in England in the 1690s', *Parliaments, Estates and Representation*, iv (1984), 135–46; D.W. Hayton, 'The "Country" Interest and the Party System, c.1689–1720', in *Party and Management in Parliament 1660–1784*, ed. Clyve Jones (Leicester, 1984), 37–85; D.W. Hayton,

© *The Parliamentary History Yearbook Trust 2009*

much has been written on Augustan society, on the press, on ideas, and on parliamentary elections, but except for the publication of the 1690–1715 volumes of the History of Parliament relatively little has appeared in print on the specifics of Commons' politics, and even within the several million words of the History's volumes, relatively little that significantly changes the scheme Holmes had drawn up.

In retrospect, what reviewers saw as particularly striking and important about *British Politics in the Age of Anne*, the demolition of Walcott, seems now to be far less important than the creation of Geoffrey Holmes's own perspective on early 18th-century politics, one that still dominates our views of this particular landscape. But then Holmes never intended his book to be a polemic against Walcott, whom, in fact, he always treated in print with exemplary courtesy. Still less did he intend it as a polemic against Namier, whose historical intelligence he admired, whose methods he respected (though not to the point of idolatry), and some of whose characteristics as a historian he shared. The book, like its author, was essentially constructive rather than destructive, and for that reason remains inspirational.

Postscript

British Politics in the Age of Anne was originally intended to be a mere introductory chapter or two to provide the political context for a narrative of the ministry of Robert Harley, earl of Oxford, from 1710 to 1714. In the event it grew into a complete monograph on its own, while the study of the Harley ministry was put on the back burner. Although Holmes wrote a narrative which effectively covered the last four years of the reign of Queen Anne he never completed the task to his own satisfaction. Several chapters were drafted before the appearance of *British Politics in the Age of Anne*. For instance, drafts of those covering the ministerial crisis of 1710 circulated among his friends and colleagues at least as early as 1962. His absorbing narrative of Sacheverell's trial and its aftermath in 1710[51] might be regarded as preparing the ground for the story of the Harley ministry. But that work was laid aside as he became more involved in other projects. The shift of historical interest from high politics to social history is one which can be detected among several leading historians active in the 1960s and 1970s, and Holmes went along with this trend.[52] While he never lost his enthusiasm for political history he did not get round to completing his study of *The Great Ministry*. Although he had broken the back of it by the time of his death in 1993 he himself was not sufficiently satisfied with it to encourage its publication. On the contrary he felt that some parts of it, particularly those dealing with the diplomatic aspects of the Treaty of Utrecht, had not taken on board scholarly contributions made since they had been written. Since he never found the time to bring them up-to-date he made it clear that he did not wish the book to be published.

[50] (*continued*) 'Moral Reform and Country Politics in the Late Seventeenth-Century House of Commons', *Past and Present*, no. 128 (1990), 48–91; Holmes, *British Politics* (rev. edn), pp. xxxviii–xli.

[51] Geoffrey Holmes, *The Trial of Dr Sacheverell* (1973).

[52] See Geoffrey Holmes, 'Gregory King and the Social Structure of Pre-Industrial England', *Transactions of the Royal Historical Society*, ser. 5, xxvii (1977), 41–68; Geoffrey Holmes, 'The Professions and Social Change in England, 1680–1730', *Proceedings of the British Academy*, lxv (1979), 313–54; Geoffrey Holmes, 'The Achievement of Stability: The Social Context of Politics from the 1680s to the Age of Walpole'; in *The Whig Ascendancy: Colloquies on Hanoverian England*, ed. John Cannon (1981), 1–27; Geoffrey Holmes, *Augustan England: Professions, Status and Society, 1680–1730* (1982).

This was a great disappointment to those of his colleagues who had read drafts of the work. The chapters dealing with the ministerial revolution of 1710 alone presented a novel and convincing thesis which they felt deserved to see the light of day. Holmes's explanation of Harley's strategy throughout the changes which were to sweep Lord Treasurer Godolphin and the whig junto from power and to install himself at the head of a largely tory ministry totally replaced previous accounts. For many historians had made the categorical error of deducing Harley's intentions from the results of the political machinations of the months between the Sacheverell trial and the general election of 1710. Holmes, exploiting his unique insight into the workings of politics in the reign, based on a quite unprecedented grasp of the original sources, was able to show that Harley did not, at first, want either a complete change of ministry or an election. On the contrary, he hoped to replace the treasurer and a handful of his immediate supporters, but to retain the services of at least some of the junto and to go on with the parliament elected in 1708. Circumstances made it impossible for him to retain control of this agenda. One of the more important was the attitude of Queen Anne herself. Having persuaded her that the whigs were intent on undermining her prerogative, and that she should assert her authority over them, Harley was in no position to appear to dictate ministerial changes to her. As in the analysis in *British Politics in the Age of Anne*, so in the unpublished narrative of 'The Great Ministry' Holmes put the queen back in the centre of the political system. Party loyalties also played a role. Although some whigs were prepared to play ball with 'Robin the trickster' as they dubbed him, in the end, upbraided by Lord Wharton, the junto responded to appeals to party unity and broke off negotiations. The crunch came when Harley refused to commit himself to postponing a general election until 1711, when one was due to be held under the Triennial Act of 1694. In part his reluctance to give the whigs such a guarantee was to preserve his bargaining position. But it also stemmed from his awareness that it would compromise the royal prerogative. Again the role of the queen was crucial. The tories benefited from Anne's political influence, since she was known to prefer them. When she indicated this preference by making her uncle, the earl of Rochester, lord president of the council, Harley's initial intentions were confounded. This necessitated a general election which the new prime minister had been anxious to avoid,[53] not least because the tories, helped by the backlash against the whigs which resulted from their prosecution of Sacheverell, were returned in greater numbers than he wished.

Harley nevertheless demonstrated his unrivalled political dexterity by staying in power for the next four years, as Holmes indicated by choosing the title *The Great Ministry*. Until the weeks before his dismissal in the summer of 1714 Harley was the prime minister, and it was his administration. His mastery of the political game kept all rivals at bay, including Henry St John. Historians who refer to the Harley–St John ministry in these years are shown to have been mistaken. Only when he lost the confidence of the queen, again a central consideration, did Harley lose power

These conclusions, as fresh and convincing today as they were when Holmes first reached them, would have been left out of the public domain owing to his insistence that they remained unpublished. So would a host of similarly original and authoritative

---

[53] The propriety of applying the term 'prime minister' to Robert Harley is discussed in Holmes, *British Politics*, 440–2; and Holmes, *Politics, Religion and Society*, 163–4.

© *The Parliamentary History Yearbook Trust 2009*

interpretations of the high politics of the last four years of Anne's reign. Those of his colleagues who had collaborated with him were aware that he was a perfectionist. His meticulous and copious comments on their contributions immeasurably improved them. His own concern for accuracy in the smallest details is also manifest from any perusal of his prose in print. Such considerations presumably lay behind his reluctance to publish the narrative of the Harley ministry. He did not wish its unfinished state to detract from his reputation. Those who were acquainted with the scholarly significance of his narrative were convinced that its dissemination could only add to his already unassailable stature as *the* historian of the age of Anne. Fortunately a way out of the predicament was found. Holmes's widow, Ella, undertook what was truly a labour of love when she transformed the minutely written and sometimes cryptically-documented narrative, which occasionally took the form of almost indecipherable notes, into a coherent typescript. Eventually this was copied and bound into a very limited number of copies thanks to the efforts of Clyve Jones and Stephen Taylor and his colleagues at Reading University. Two copies were deposited in repositories accessible to the scholarly community,[54] though not by the general public, which limited access falls sufficiently short of normal publication to respect Holmes's wishes, and at the same time to make his monumental achievement more widely known to historians.

---

[54] The library of the Institute of Historical Research, University of London, and the offices of the History of Parliament Trust.

© *The Parliamentary History Yearbook Trust 2009*

Geoffrey Holmes and the House of Lords Reconsidered

ROBIN EAGLES

The publication of Geoffrey Holmes's *British Politics in the Age of Anne*, arguably, did more than any other volume of the period to reinvigorate interest in the house of lords in the Augustan period. The upper chamber, which had been largely overlooked by historians such as Sir Lewis Namier and Robert Walcott, had come to be regarded as a very inferior partner to the house of commons, populated by great landowners whose principal interest was to see the furtherance of their kinship networks. Holmes's work demonstrated clearly the central role of the Lords in British political life and revised radically the accepted orthodoxy that family predominated over ideology in the early 18th century. This article seeks to reassess Holmes's contribution to the study of the Lords in the light of research undertaken since the publication of *British Politics* and to suggest some ways in which Holmes's model, which remains broadly unassailable, might be reshaped.

Keywords: house of lords; honour; privilege; kinship; party; court; courtier; Namier; peers; peerage

Forty years on from its first publication, it is still difficult to find fault with much of the detail, let alone the overall argument, of Geoffrey Holmes's *British Politics in the Age of Anne*. While the scope and achievement of the whole volume is magisterial, chapter 12, in particular, 'the court and parties in the House of Lords' is especially noteworthy for having done more than almost any other study of the time to revive interest in the upper chamber in the early 18th century. Before then, studies of the Lords in the period were few and far between, despite the publication in the 18th and 19th centuries of a variety of diaries, memoirs and correspondence of major figures, such as those of Gilbert Burnet,[1] Henry, 2nd earl of Clarendon[2] and Charles, duke of Shrewsbury,[3] and perhaps most significantly, Ebenezer Timberland's edition of the proceedings of the House from the Restoration to his own time,[4] offering an insight into the importance of the Lords from the revolution to the accession of the house of Hanover. A.S. Turberville's studies of *The House of Lords in the Reign of William III* (1913) and *The House of Lords in the Eighteenth Century* (1927) are exceptions, but besides these, the most significant studies of

---

[1] Gilbert Burnet, *A History of my Own Time*, ed. M.J. Routh (6 vols, Oxford, 1823).

[2] *The Correspondence of Henry Hyde, Earl of Clarendon, and of His Brother, Lawrence Hyde, Earl of Rochester, with the Diary of Lord Clarendon from 1687 to 1690*, ed. S.W. Singer (2 vols, 1828).

[3] *Private and Original Correspondence of Charles Talbot, Duke of Shrewsbury, with King William, the Leaders of the Whig Party, and Other Distinguished Statesmen*, ed. William Coxe (1821); *Letters Illustrative of the Reign of William III from 1696 to 1708 Addressed to the Duke of Shrewsbury by James Vernon, Esq., Secretary of State*, ed. G.P.R. James (3 vols, 1841).

[4] *The History and Proceedings of the House of Lords from the Restoration in 1660, to the Present Time*, [ed. Ebenezer Timberland] (8 vols, 1742).

© *The Parliamentary History Yearbook Trust 2009*

the upper chamber undertaken in the 20th century have been confined to Turberville's two articles in the *English Historical Review* charting politics in the Lords under Charles II[5] and more closely focused pieces such as E.S. de Beer's article examining the House in the parliament of 1680, published in *Bulletin of the Institute of Historical Research*,[6] and Kenneth Haley's examination of a 1687 'list of English peers' in the *English Historical Review*.[7] All of these (with the exception of Turberville's now largely-outdated general study) stop well short of the reign of Anne leaving a vacuum, which, as Holmes points out would have left an Englishman of the period 'utterly incredulous':

> To him the House of Lords seemed to be gaining rather than declining in impor-
> tance . . . Its prestige was already high in 1702, and it was higher still in 1714.[8]

G.M. Trevelyan's three-volume study of *England under Queen Anne* makes several references to the Lords, notably their involvement in the Sacheverell trial,[9] the debate over occasional conformity[10] and the creation of 'Oxford's dozen' new peers,[11] but his coverage remains a far cry from Holmes's recognition of the Lords' significance. Subsequent studies of the House have supported his conclusion,[12] and the discovery of division lists and lists of peers' likely sympathies unearthed since the publication of *British Politics* have further emphasized Holmes's justification in turning attention back to the upper chamber.[13] As Clyve Jones and John Beckett argued in their introduction to *A Pillar of the Constitution*:

> From 1689 the Lords were arguably the most formidable member of the parliamen-
> tary triumvirate. Although the 1689 Revolution Settlement and the 1701 Act of
> Settlement left the monarch with considerable powers, and by the end of the
> seventeenth century the Commons had laid an unchallengable [*sic*] claim to control
> the raising of finance, the Lords . . . became the dominant partner in the constitution
> for more than a hundred years.[14]

Given this, how did the Lords under Anne (not to mention under William III and Mary II) come to be so grossly overlooked? Undoubtedly, the interpretation of the later 18th century as laid down by Sir Lewis Namier is at the heart of the problem. For Namier, the Lords by the 18th century was of marginal importance: an institution populated by those whose careers were all but over and, lacking the Commons' financial muscle,

---

[5] A.S. Turberville, 'The House of Lords under Charles II', *English Historical Review*, xviv (1929); xlv (1930).

[6] E.S. de Beer, 'The House of Lords in the Parliament of 1680', *Bulletin of the Institute of Historical Research*, xx (1946 for 1943).

[7] Kenneth Haley, 'A List of the English Peers, c. May 1687', *English Historical Review*, lxix (1954).

[8] Geoffrey Holmes, *British Politics in the Age of Anne* (1967, rev. edn 1987), 383.

[9] G.M. Trevelyan, *England under Queen Anne: The Peace and the Protestant Succession* (1934), 57.

[10] Trevelyan, *England under Queen Anne*, 195.

[11] Trevelyan, *England under Queen Anne*, 197–8.

[12] J.V. Beckett and Clyve Jones, 'The Peerage and the House of Lords in the Seventeenth and Eighteenth Centuries', in *A Pillar of the Constitution*, ed. Clyve Jones (1989), 1.

[13] *British Parliamentary Lists, 1660–1800: A Register*, ed. G.M. Ditchfield, David Hayton and Clyve Jones (1995).

[14] *A Pillar of the Constitution*, ed. Jones, 18.

effectively redundant. John Cannon drew attention to Namier's interpretation of those peers in the mid 18th century who received pensions, or what Namier preferred to call their 'aristocratic dole', as being merely the recipients of monarchical generosity rather than suborned figures of real political value.[15] Namier may have found some support for this interpretation from one of the central figures of the later 18th century, Lord Shelburne, who in 1787 commented witheringly that, 'Parliament is unfortunately too much hackney'd to be of the use it ought to be'.[16] Indeed, Shelburne seems to have held this view of parliament as a whole, which was reflected in a pamphlet of 1783 in his possession, decrying the spectre of a house of commons, 'filled with men in trade, greedy of contracts, jobs, and subscriptions' and calling out for:

> everyone who wishes well to his country . . . [to] turn his eyes on the country gentlemen of England . . . and call upon them to exert themselves with vigour to wrest the honour of being representatives of the people, from a set of men who have either no property at all, or such a sort of property as bears no share in the expenses of the state.[17]

Although, as John Cannon has pointed out, Shelburne has 'never been celebrated for his grasp of political reality',[18] his was a cry that the duke of Shrewsbury might well have recognized on his return to England in 1706, dismayed at the way in which the landowners bore the brunt of the wartime taxation while the moneyed men benefited from the spoils of conflict.[19] But while Namier's model still has merits in terms of a consideration of the state of the Lords at the close of the 18th century, it fits much less well with the world of Augustan politics dominated as it was by political figures for whom parliament was the principal stage, and so many of whom were based in the Lords: Thomas, Lord Wharton, Charles, earl of Sunderland, Charles, Lord Halifax, Daniel, earl of Nottingham, and latterly Robert Harley, earl of Oxford and Henry St John, Viscount Bolingbroke, to name but some, many of whom have since Namier's time become the subjects of political biographies and academic theses.[20]

Holmes's recognition of the whig party's understanding of the importance of the Lords, in particular, and especially at times when their strength in the Commons was severely depleted, underscores the centrality of the upper chamber in the first decade of the 18th century.[21] While political ascendancy veered from the uncomfortable coalitions of the first half of Anne's reign, which were cast aside in 1708 by the advent of an almost entirely whig ministry and replaced two years later by Robert Harley's association, which then held sway until Anne's death, it was the Lords that dominated many of the great questions of the day. For most of the reign Britain was at war, and its principal

---

[15] John Cannon, *Aristocratic Century: The Peerage of Eighteenth-Century England* (Cambridge, 1984), 97.

[16] Bodl., MS Film 1996, Bowood MSS, box 24, ff. 119–22.

[17] Bodl., MS Film 994, Bowood MSS, box 109: anon, *Reflections on our Present Political State and General Situation*, 2 Apr. 1783.

[18] Cannon, *Aristocratic Century*, 94.

[19] Edward Gregg, *Queen Anne* (2nd edn, New Haven, 2001), 255.

[20] Henry Horwitz, *Revolution Politicks: The Career of Daniel Finch Second Earl of Nottingham 1647–1730* (Cambridge, 1968); Sheila Biddle, *Bolingbroke and Harley* (1975); Christopher Robbins, *The Earl of Wharton and Whig Party Politics, 1679–1715* (New York, 1992).

[21] Holmes, *British Politics*, 383.

generals, Marlborough, Peterborough and Ormond, were prominent members of the House. In 1707 the Lords was at the forefront of the process that altered the very constitution of the kingdoms of England, Scotland and Ireland with the union of the first two, bringing to Westminster 45 Scots MPs and 16 elected representative peers.[22] In the midst of all this, the trial of Henry Sacheverell in 1710 for high crimes and misdemeanours,[23] examinations into military disasters such as Toulon and Almanza, and consideration of the earl of Nottingham's efforts to secure a bill forbidding the practice of occasional conformity were all played out before the Lords.[24]

Despite this, the progress of whig historiography, ironically, tended to underplay the Lords' role and imposed on the early 18th century the Commons' later dominance as part of the inevitable forward march of democracy. John Cannon suggested that this was 'in part, because piety persuaded many historians to devote their energies to tracing the development of the constitution'.[25] Namier's conception that the Commons was the key compounded this interpretation. Yet while his omission was crucial for understanding why subsequent scholars also tended to downplay the Lords' importance in the period, it remains something of a mystery why a scholar who believed so very definitely in the dominance of elites chose to ignore that ultimate elite: the house of lords.

Namier's influence is blamed squarely by Holmes for the failure of scholars of the mid 20th century to pay the Lords their due,[26] but he reserved his most stringent (though measured) criticism for the work of Robert Walcott, whose general survey of the period, *English Politics in the Early Eighteenth Century* (1956) as Holmes puts it, 'virtually ignores the House of Lords, except as a collection of individual magnates whose real political importance . . . lay in their ability to command followings of varying sizes in the Commons'.[27] Equally scathing is Holmes's appraisal of Walcott's thesis that the period is largely to be understood in terms of 'organised connections' devoid of principle and motivated either by clan loyalty or a grubby desire for material gain.[28] While there were, no doubt, politicians of the reign of Anne who were eager to feather their own nests or were seduced by power, it is foolhardy to assume that such raw ambitions were the driving forces behind all the political events of the period. Principle, as Holmes stressed, was still of arch importance and, against Walcott's vision, he hoped 'by the end of this volume, to leave the reader in no reasonable doubt that whatever the complexities of the body politic in the early years of the eighteenth century, its life-blood was the existence and conflict of two major parties'.[29]

In the remainder of this article what I hope to do is to re-examine Holmes's argument against that of Walcott in greater detail and to suggest some ways in which subsequent studies of the Lords, not least the ongoing work of the House of Lords section of the History of Parliament, something which Holmes and subsequently Professor John

[22] P.W.J. Riley, *The Union of England and Scotland: A Study in Anglo-Scottish Politics of the Eighteenth Century* (Manchester, 1978), *passim*.

[23] Holmes, *The Trial of Doctor Sacheverell* (1973).

[24] Horwitz, *Revolution Politicks*, 90–1, 185–7, 189, 197, 200–3, 231–3, 248, 254–6, 269.

[25] Cannon, *Aristocratic Century*, 5.

[26] Holmes, *British Politics*, 382 n.

[27] Holmes, *British Politics*, 382 n.

[28] Holmes, *British Politics*, 2.

[29] Holmes, *British Politics*, 6.

Cannon bemoaned the lack of, has served to illustrate and, in some instances, revise Holmes's findings.[30] By making use of the longer perspective of the Lords from the Restoration to the end of Queen Anne's reign it may be seen that not only was the Lords of central importance to British politics in the period with which Holmes was particularly engaged, but that many of the themes Holmes considered had their origin in the restoration of the upper chamber in the middle of the previous century.

1

Principled politics may appear to be something of a luxury in the early 21st century, but in the first decade of the 18th century (and beyond) principle was quite as important as short-term political gain. It can be no coincidence that it is precisely those who were perceived to be opportunist in their behaviour, the 2nd earl of Sunderland or Thomas, Lord Wharton, for example, who were singled out for attention.[31] Much more in keeping with the mode of the time was Queen Anne's stolid consort, Prince George of Denmark who, although he may have been obliged to divide against his conscience on the question of occasional conformity, made it plain to his natural allies that his heart was 'vid you'.[32] Seeking to transpose later sensibilities onto the earlier period, though, Robert Walcott attempted to find the opposite and even in his later revised publications stressed that although there may have been certain questions of principle upon which people divided fairly clearly along 'tory' or 'whig' lines:

> within the walls of Parliament as it concerned itself with the day-to-day work of government in the intervals between controversy over the great issues (most of them religious) the apparent division into two national parties dissolves into the multi-party structure normally associated with the reign of George III.[33]

Holmes rightly took issue with this assessment, questioning the extent to which the great divisions of the day really reflected Walcott's vision of politics based on connection. For Walcott:

> The 22 titles, together with the 73 baronetcies held by members of the House of Commons in 1701, tell us something of the social composition of that body; but little about the influence of the House of Lords. More significant is another figure – 97: the number of members nearly related to men sitting in the upper house.[34]

More recent research supports Holmes's conclusion that Walcott made use of kinship in far too cavalier a fashion here and, while kinship may well have been a factor in securing

---

[30] Holmes, *British Politics*, 382 n.; Cannon, *Aristocratic Century*, 5 n. As Professor Cannon points out, hitherto 'the volumes of the *History of Parliament* . . . are something of a misnomer since they concentrate exclusively on the Commons'.

[31] John Kenyon quotes Queen Anne's famous appraisal of Sunderland as 'the subtillest, workingest villain that is on the face of the earth': *Robert Spencer, Earl of Sunderland, 1641–1702* (1958), 329.

[32] Edward Gregg, *Queen Anne* (1984), 163.

[33] Quoted in Holmes, *British Politics*, 38.

[34] Robert Walcott, *English Politics in the Early Eighteenth Century* (Oxford, 1956), 32.

© *The Parliamentary History Yearbook Trust 2009*

loyalty it is foolhardy in the absence of any other material to assume that kinship alone necessarily resulted in long-standing political allegiance.[35] While Holmes recognized that the groupings, 'which attached themselves to Godolphin and Marlborough, to Rochester, Nottingham and Seymour, to Harley and Anglesey, and to the Junto lords all contained a nucleus of relatives', he also argued persuasively that what united these associations was as much political ideology as ties of blood.[36] In supporting this notion and demonstrating the weakness of Walcott's case, Holmes made use of the examples of the Annesleys, Berties and Comptons.[37] He might just as easily have pointed to the Coventry family, the 2nd and 4th earls being inveterate political foes, despite being brothers, and thus according to Walcott's model, likely associates. Indeed, the 2nd earl found it hard to respond to his brother's provocations 'without falling into Billingsgate'.[38] Similarly one might consider the Hyde family: the brothers Clarendon and Rochester, the one a non-juror, the other a pragmatic officeholder under Queen Anne. Walcott did consider the Hydes, particularly Rochester, as one of the clearest examples of connection in the period, but in doing so he made several errors. Minor discrepancies such as mistaking the year of Rochester's elevation to his earldom were of less consequence than Walcott's mistaken belief that after 1689 Clarendon took no further part in politics.[39] Had he appreciated that Clarendon remained active as the principal patron at Christchurch and as the holder of significant interest at Reading, Oxford and in Wiltshire while a non-juror, he may have been able to portray a stronger connection still, though he would then have been left to grapple with the unpalatable reality that the brothers came to very different principled positions following the overthrow of James II and were rarely in accord politically.[40] Another family in which Walcott placed much of his faith was the Finches, led by old 'Dismal' Daniel, earl of Nottingham, an influential family in its own right, whose interest was extended by its connection with the Saviles.[41] But where Walcott may have been correct to assume a degree of reciprocity between Nottingham and Halifax, the suggestion that kinship was the key to their alliance falls down with the example of Robert Spencer, 2nd earl of Sunderland. Sunderland was a kinsman of the catholic Digby family, of the former Cromwellian, Shaftesbury and the trimmer Halifax, with the last of whom he was permanently on disastrous terms, brother-in-law or not.[42] The example of the Berties, noted by Holmes, and their extensive kinship network is also most apt as an example of the way in which kinship alone fails pointedly to provide much insight into political association. While James Bertie, 1st earl of Abingdon, was indeed a close political adherent of his kinsman by marriage, Thomas Osborne, earl of Danby, he was an implacable foe of his brother-in-law Thomas Wharton. At the revolution, Abingdon rallied to William of Orange (in common with both Danby and

[35] Holmes, *British Politics*, 328–9.

[36] Holmes, *British Politics*, 328.

[37] Holmes, *British Politics*, 281–2, 330–1.

[38] Antony MSS (Sir Richard Carew Pole, bt, Antony House, Cornwall) CVC/Z/20: Thomas Coventry to Gilbert Coventry, 13 Feb. 1695.

[39] Walcott, *English Politics*, 60–1.

[40] *The History of Parliament: The House of Commons, 1690–1715*, ed. Eveline Cruickshanks, Stuart Handley and D.W. Hayton (5 vols, Cambridge, 2002), ii, 12–13 n.

[41] Walcott, *English Politics*, 54.

[42] Kenyon, *Sunderland, passim*.

Wharton) in opposition to his other near-kinsman, Edward Henry Lee, earl of Lichfield, who remained loyal to James II. Yet, following the revolution, while Danby was promoted to the marquessate of Carmarthen and Wharton to the office of comptroller of the household, Abingdon found himself so disgruntled with the effects of William's takeover that he contemplated emulating Lichfield and his Oxfordshire neighbour Clarendon and retiring from politics altogether. In the event it was only on account of his friend Clarendon's plea that he agreed to remain in office to protect his non-juring acquaintance from his likely successor, Lord Lovelace.[43]

Having said that, there are certainly examples in the period where blood ties or ties of friendship do appear to have mattered more than strict political principle and although some kinsmen were political adversaries they proved to be sufficiently good friends not to allow such petty divisions to stand in the way of real crises. The duke of Shrewsbury remained puzzlingly loyal to his jacobite connections, particularly the Middletons, in spite of the damage they did him under William III and progressed, with no perceptible alteration of his essential principles, from being the darling of the whigs under William III and an intimate friend of Wharton, to being Harley's partner in an essentially tory ministry in the latter days of Queen Anne.[44] Some great patrons possessed such varied interests that they were compelled to treat each separately, apparently in contradiction to the way they behaved elsewhere. An example of this was the 2nd duke of Bedford, to all intents and purposes a whig, yet a good friend of the ultra-tory 1st Lord Gower, and who therefore found himself in the midst of a cautious balancing act during the 1705 election. While he would not espouse the whig candidates in Middlesex, where he enjoyed considerable authority as lord lieutenant, to Gower's detriment, neither was he prepared to back his friend openly for fear of offending his whig friends in Bedfordshire.[45] Just as curious was Hugh, 1st earl of Cholmondeley, also to all intents and purposes a whig, but a supporter of tories in his native Cheshire, where the whig baton was grasped firmly by his local rival, Warrington.[46]

2

While connection may not have been all, the parties were definitely complicated by the influence of such great patrons, who were able to command a greater or lesser degree of loyalty from members of both Houses. Holmes mentions the earls of Anglesey and (the 2nd) earl of Abingdon, adherents of Nottingham, both peers in the Hanoverian tory interest, but who between them could expect the loyalty of a substantial clutch of followers and were able to operate with a greater or lesser degree of independence.[47]

In this sense, it is perhaps revealing to consider such loose associations from a longer perspective. The example of the 2nd earl of Sunderland, the notoriously amoral premier

[43] Robin Eagles, 'Unnatural Allies? The Oxfordshire *Elite* from the Exclusion Crisis to the Overthrow of James II', *Parliamentary History*, xxvi (2007), 362.
[44] Dorothy Somerville, *The King of Hearts: Charles Talbot, Duke of Shrewsbury* (1962), 78–9.
[45] *House of Commons, 1690–1715*, ed. Cruickshanks *et al.*, ii, 372.
[46] *House of Commons, 1690–1715*, ed. Cruickshanks *et al.*, ii, 58–9.
[47] Holmes, *British Politics*, 273, 282.

© *The Parliamentary History Yearbook Trust 2009*

minister under James II and adviser behind the curtain under William III is perhaps apt.
Sunderland is usually viewed as being wholly without principle, a survivor who shamelessly sought power, but it is possible to regard him as a man of some principle, a courtier
through and through whose primary consideration, next to his own aggrandisement,
granted, was service of the king. The much-employed example of his peculiar, Spencer-
drawl emphasizes this: 'Whaat . . . if his Majesty taarn out faarty of us, may not he have
faarty athors to saarve him as well? And whaat maater who saarves his Majesty, so lang
as his Majesty is saarved?'[48] Sunderland was prepared to work with anybody in return for
influence and security and to see the king's policies enacted. This flexible political
outlook effectively made him the natural head of a court party and it is no coincidence
that one of the rising stars he attempted to attract to his colours was Robert Harley, who
would, under Queen Anne, assemble a similarly rugged association of country whigs and
tories of all kinds as a court interest.[49] Just as Sunderland's return to the House after his
self-imposed exile at the time of the revolution signalled his return to front-line politics,
so Harley's assumption of a place in the Lords demonstrated his continuing supremacy
and was in no manner a signal of his intention to set aside power and cultivate his
garden.

However, while contemporaries undoubtedly viewed the Lords as a far more important body than Namier's (or Walcott's) assessments would allow, there were undoubtedly
peers and bishops who were more than eager to bury themselves in their respective
horticultural endeavours and for whom membership of the House was a burden. There
were others who queried whether the House was really as important as the party
managers asserted it was. By the late 1670s, some peers believed that they could already
detect the steady rise of the Commons. In February 1677, the duke of Buckingham, in
the midst of his speech arguing that parliament was *de facto* dissolved by its long
prorogation, warned of the encroaching power of the Commons:

> I have often wondered how it should come to pass, that this house of commons, in
> which are so many worthy gentlemen, should [. . .] be less respectful to your lordships
> (as certainly they have been) than any house of commons that ever were chosen in
> England. And yet if the matter be a little enquired into, the reason of it will plainly
> appear, for my lords the very nature of the house of commons is changed: they do not
> now think they are an assembly that are to return to their own homes, and become
> private men again, as by the laws of the land and the ancient constitution of
> parliaments they ought to do, but they look upon themselves as a standing senate and
> as a number of men pick'd out to be legislators for the rest of their whole lives: and
> if that be the case my lords they have reason to believe themselves our equals.[50]

Of course, by the reign of Anne, some of Buckingham's concerns had been answered by
the passage of the Triennial Bill in 1694. The bill was championed in the Lords by
Shrewsbury, who had earlier pushed for a bill requiring annual parliaments.[51] The

---

[48] Roger North, quoted in Kenyon, *Sunderland*, 330 n.

[49] Kenyon, *Sunderland*, 317–19.

[50] A speech made by the duke of Buckingham, the first day of the session of parliament, namely Thursday
15 Feb. 1676.

[51] Henry Horwitz, *Parliament, Policy and Politics in the Reign of William III* (Manchester, 1977), 110, 128, 138.

© *The Parliamentary History Yearbook Trust 2009*

Triennial Bill was thus a compromise, but it ensured regular elections and thus obviated Buckingham's fears of a standing senate rivalling the authority of the Lords; though it might be argued that the passage of the later Septennial Bill went some way towards undoing this and assisted in the gradual marginalisation of the Lords in the later 18th century, in spite of the best efforts of peers such as Gilbert, 4th earl of Coventry, who entrusted his proxy to the duke of Buckingham specifying that he employ it to safeguard an act that, 'I always took to be one of the greatest securities our laws afford'.[52]

Besides the encroachments on the Lords from a resurgent Commons, many peers and bishops were reluctant to disturb their repose in the country with an unwelcome journey to London and long service in the House. In 1679 Bishop Fell congratulated his friend, Viscount Hatton, for acting 'more prudently' and remaining in the country rather than beating up to town in time for the opening of the session. With the Commons engaged in electing a Speaker, Fell found so little to do that he resolved to 'steal down to Oxford; where I hope to remain towards the end of this month'.[53] Eleven years later, the earl of Lindsey found the hiatus in proceedings occasioned by the Commons' deliberations useful in view of his uncertain health. Writing to his kinsman, Carmarthen, he explained:

> I am so weakened with the gout that I dare not venture to appear at the opening of the session my physician advising a week's stay to purge and clear the relics of that distemper that so I may be freed from the danger of relapse. I have ordered the black rod how to act in my absence, and if your lordship should be disposed to excuse me to the king, which I hope will not be the case. I am confident to be in Parliament before anything of moment can be transacted considering the House commonly adjourns and that the choice of the Speaker takes up some time.[54]

Two years later Viscount Weymouth had other reasons for wishing to stay at home, citing 'private affairs' and how 'the slender consideration is had of the House of Lords, or that they have indeed for themselves, makes home and quiet very desirable'.[55] Thomas Coventry bemoaned his succession to the earldom of Coventry in 1699, pointing out that:

> I doubt not but I am sufficiently envied for what is fallen to me, though without reason, by such who don't consider the disadvantages I come to the estate with and nothing I am satisfied, will gratify the ambition, and malice, of some people unless, Esau-like, a man will sell his birth-right for a mess of potage.[56]

Under Queen Anne, it remained for managers of all parties a regular challenge to rouse some of the backwoods' peers from their rural hibernation, even if it was only to wrest a proxy from their grasps. In December 1707, it fell to the duke of Somerset to enquire of his friend, Thomas, 2nd earl of Coventry:

[52] Antony House MSS, CVC/V/3/68.

[53] BL, Add. MS 29583, f. 281.

[54] BL, Egerton MS 3337, ff. 175–6.

[55] BL, Add. MS 75363: Weymouth to Halifax, 10 Oct. 1692.

[56] Antony House MSS, CVC/Y/1/60.

© *The Parliamentary History Yearbook Trust 2009*

whether there be any hopes of having the honour soon to see your lordship in parliament at this time a more necessary journey you can never undertake to be more for the service of the queen and for the service of our country too, though your lordship stayed no longer than to take the oaths &c thereby to qualify yourself to make a proxy . . .[57]

Contrary to Walcott's vision of great aristocratic patrons concentrating their interest on the Commons, the example of Warwickshire appears to show quite the opposite, where it was to William Bromley that a number of junior peers looked for guidance. Writing to Oxford, Bromley sought direction on what he should do about two local noblemen with whom he held some influence:

I am consulted by Lord Denbigh as to his coming to parliament. It will be most suitable to his unhappy circumstances to stay as long as he can in the country, but he desires that your lordship may know, that if you think it necessary, he will be here at the opening of the session. I saw such an appearance on Tuesday in the House of Lords, that it seems necessary to me to have all our friends in town. But your lordship is the best judge; and I only mention this because if your lordship is of the same opinion, I believe I can bring up my kinsman and neighbour my Lord Leigh, who is a young man of good understanding and very well inclined, but did not intend coming till after Christmas.[58]

This is not to say that an individual peer or lord of parliament's interest was of no consequence. For the duke of Shrewsbury, the prospect of promoting John Robinson, bishop of Bristol, within government, while 'very reasonable' on the grounds of his abilities, had its own distinct drawbacks as Robinson had, 'passed most of his life abroad, and having . . . not many relations of much figure at home, the bringing him into such a post adds no interest in either House towards carrying her Majesty's business in Parliament'.[59] On occasion and over certain issues, the political world of the Augustan house of lords proved to be a more subtle entity than a simple yin and yang of whig and tory. Given his political proclivities, one might have thought that the extreme whig Lord Mohun, indicted for murder on two occasions in the 1690s, would have attracted little sympathy from the tories in the House and yet following his first trial he was acquitted by an overwhelming majority embracing peers of all shades of opinion.[60] Privilege and pride of caste were important facets of the noble world and quite capable of overturning what might otherwise have been employed for narrow party ends. From the Restoration onwards, the Lords proved to be zealous defenders of its rights and perquisites, which was reflected in such things as Mohun's acquittal and in the cross-party disquiet at the prospect of the admission of Scots peers to the House following the union. In this matter neither party loyalty nor connection serves adequately to explain the peers' voting

[57] Coventry Papers (duke of Beaufort, Badminton House, Gloucester), FMT/A4/3/30.

[58] BL, Add. MS 70214: William Bromley to Oxford, 15 Nov. 1711.

[59] HMC, *Bath*, i, 207.

[60] *A Complete Collection of State Trials* (34 vols, 1816–28), xii, 1048–9.

© *The Parliamentary History Yearbook Trust 2009*

behaviour. Defence of the peerage and raw xenophobia rather than any other issue proved paramount in assuring that the House was protected from the infiltration of penniless North British nobles.[61]

Privilege and suitability also serve to explain more completely a phenomenon mentioned by Holmes: the issue of the acceptance or rejection of peerages by would-be members of the Lords. While Holmes is quite right to stress that admission to the House by no means signalled the end of a political career, the example of George Granville demonstrates clearly that some, invited to accept peerages, rejected them not so much because they wished to be permitted respite from politics (as might have been the case of Sir Michael Warton, who refused to become one of Oxford's dozen 'on the grounds of age and infirmity')[62] but because they were conscious that they lacked the qualifications to maintain the dignity. On being offered a barony in the winter of 1711, Granville, mindful of the cost of accepting his new dignity, at once requested funds to help pay for his immediate expenses.[63] Contrariwise, when Henry St John was promoted to the viscountcy of Bolingbroke, he was tempted to reject the peerage altogether, insulted that he had not been offered the superior earldom of Bolingbroke, to which he had some claim as a cousin of the last holder of the title. He also dismissed Jonathan Swift's suggestion that he ask to be created Viscount Pomfret instead, explaining that it was 'in Yorkshire where he has no estate'.[64] In the event it was with a singularly ill grace that he accepted the proffered title and he made no secret of the fact that the queen could have offered him no lesser title, 'or I must have come in the rear of several whom I was not born to follow'.[65]

In the previous reign, John Sheffield, earl of Mulgrave, had demonstrated similar pride, holding out against being promoted to the marquessate of Normanby as part of a 'general creation' as he wished it to be apparent that he was being honoured in particular and not as part of a group.[66] The acceptance of one of Oxford's peerages by Thomas, Viscount Windsor caused comment on similar grounds as it was thought unlikely that Windsor would wish to be elevated as part of a 'job lot'. Lord Berkeley of Stratton certainly marvelled 'how a man of his singularity likes coming in with soe much company'.[67] Ralph Montagu, who, from his inheritance of the comparatively recent barony of Montagu of Boughton, in time rose to become the 1st duke of Montagu, was utterly shameless in his ambition to rise to the very top of the noble tree, taking what awards he could and immediately pressing for more, both for himself and his family.[68] Similar naked ambition was apparent in Thomas, Lord Raby, whose desire to be restored

---

[61] BL, Add. MSS 40776, f. 9.

[62] Clyve Jones, 'Lord Oxford's Jury: The Political and Social Context of the Creation of the Twelve Peers, 1711–12', in *Partisan Politics, Principle and Reform in Parliament and the Constituencies, 1689–1880: Essays in Memory of John A. Phillips*, ed. Clyve Jones, Philip Salmon and Richard W. Davis (Edinburgh, 2005), 20.

[63] Jones, 'Lord Oxford's Jury', 20.

[64] Jonathan Swift, *Journal to Stella*, ed. H. Williams (Oxford, 2 vols, 1974), ii, 545.

[65] *Letters and Correspondence, Public and Private of the Right Honourable Henry St. John, Lord Viscount Bolingbroke*, ed. Gilbert Parke (4 vols, 1798), ii, 484–5.

[66] University of Nottingham Library, Portland MS, PwA 1217/1.

[67] *The Wentworth Papers, 1705–1739: Selected from the Private and Family Correspondence of Thomas Wentworth, Lord Raby, Created in 1711 Earl of Strafford*, ed. J. Cartwright (1883), 242.

[68] BL, Add. MS 61450, f. 199; HMC, *Buccleuch*, i, 356.

to the earldom of Strafford and subsequent efforts to secure what further emoluments he could, persuaded Holmes to describe him (not without reason) as 'the most persistent and shameless go-getter of his day'.[69] One of the few things that was capable of rousing the reluctant 2nd earl of Coventry from his country pursuits was the need to save his family's reputation from the wanton aggrandisement of his stepmother, Elizabeth Grimes. Coventry was responding to a situation created by his father, the first earl, who in his dotage had made the unforgivable social blunder of marrying his housekeeper. The new countess was quick to make the most of her improved station and with the assistance of the Lancaster Herald, Gregory King, set about devising a more suitable genealogy for herself. Instead of Grimes she insisted that she was a poor relation of the more respectable Graham family and with King's assistance, she commissioned a gaudy monument to her late husband, incorporating the Graham arms impaling those of her late husband's family.[70] Coventry was successful in barring the erection of this from the family church at Croome d'Abitot but was still compelled to engage in lengthy legal actions against Grimes, her second husband, Thomas Savage, and King.[71] Although he found the affair wearisome, he explained to his countess that he would 'with more satisfaction undergo the toil since I have the promises of a great many lords that they will be present at the hearing' and he hoped to persuade still more to turn out for him to oppose the dowager countess's machinations.[72]

Despite the reluctant shouldering of their burden by men like Weymouth and Coventry, by the death of Anne in 1714, there seemed every reason to assume that the Lords' predominance would endure. Pride of caste, which had been demonstrated by the disgust at Oxford's mass promotion, and jealous defence of their privileges was added to the chamber's institutional importance as the final determiner of legal issues and the home of many of the most significant political managers of the day. At the accession of George I this state of affairs appeared to be unchanged. If the Lords did come to be marginalised after 1714 it was on account of the changed circumstances of tory pro-scription and the emergence of new political heavyweights in the Commons such as Walpole, who eschewed transference to the Lords until their careers were all but over. Certainly, at the accession of George I there seemed no inevitability about the Lords' decline and though it undoubtedly did do so during the century, the Lords maintained a central role in British political life far beyond the confines of the reign of the last Stuart monarch.

[69] Holmes, *British Politics*, 386.
[70] *VCH Worcestershire*, iii, 344–5.
[71] The National Archives, Del 1/312.
[72] HMC, *Beaufort*, 96.

The Nature of Stability in the Augustan Age

RICHARD CONNORS

This article seeks to synthesise aspects of recent research on the Augustan age and consider the longevity of the interpretations of the period provided in the late 1960s by Geoffrey Holmes and Jack Plumb. More particularly, it reconsiders the nature of political and social instability in the late 17th and early 18th centuries and examines the arguments historians now offer to account for the diminution of the strife and discord that characterised the rage of party under Queen Anne and the difference between that late Stuart polity and the seemingly more stable and politically placid Georgian period. Furthermore, it considers the broader social and economic conditions of the Augustan age and seeks to show the importance contemporary debates over moral reform, poverty and poor relief had for social stability in the decades after the Glorious Revolution.

Keywords: political instability; social policy; Poor Law; Plumb thesis; bills; acts; parliament; Augustan England; continuity and change; rage of party; social stability; moral reform

The poor are a burthen to the rich a charge and damage to the nation a scandal to the [Christ]ian religion: wherefore I desire you will appoynt a committee to consider of what laws we have proper and of what Laws are wanting with a power to repeale all the old laws and to make one Law in the place of them and that we may send for persons papers and records.[1]

Like many of his counterparts in the late 17th century house of commons, Sir Richard Cocks, MP for Gloucester from 1698 to 1702, vigorously supported 'revolution principles', the reformation of manners movement, and vociferously objected to divisive party politics, fiscal corruption, popery, priestcraft and jacobitism. Regarded by some of his parliamentary colleagues as 'a self-opinionated eccentric', 'a whimsical crazed man' and a 'peevish elf', he was perhaps most clearly recognized by them as a country whig with deep-seated interests in moral reform, social policy and poverty.[2] Cocks embraced and embodied the enthusiastic movement for a 'new reformation' in the late 17th century, a broad movement which in the wake of the Glorious Revolution was 'transmuted into a negative and repressive impulse through a fear of the immanence of providential judgment'.[3] Motivated by these convictions and by a desire to reform public

---

[1] *The Parliamentary Diary of Sir Richard Cocks, 1698–1702*, ed. D. Hayton (Oxford, 1996), 26.

[2] D.W. Hayton, 'Sir Richard Cocks: The Political Anatomy of a Country Whig', *Albion*, xx (1988), 221–46.

[3] *Parliamentary Diary of Sir Richard Cocks*, ed. Hayton, pp. xxix–xxx; see also, J. Spurr, 'The Church, the Societies and the Moral Reformation of 1688', in *The Church of England c.1689–c.1833: From Toleration to Tractarianism*, ed. J. Walsh, C. Haydon and S. Taylor (Cambridge, 1993), 127–41; C. Rose, 'Providence, Protestant

© *The Parliamentary History Yearbook Trust 2009*

morality and to confront vice and corruption in all its guises, Cocks appealed in print[4] and, despite the fact that he considered it 'the most Corrupt Court in [Christ]tendom nay in the world', in parliament too.[5] In his pamphlets and in charges to grand juries Cocks railed against blasphemy and sabbath-breaking, and against profanity and drunkenness.[6] Here Cocks echoed the concerns of many about the perceived moral degeneracy of the age. What was required to set England, and later Britannia, on the path of righteousness was not only a godly reformation in manners, but also for civil officials – at every level from overseer of the poor to member of parliament – to take their responsibilities seriously and impose discipline upon those under their authority. As Cocks noted, magistracy 'signifies command and authority over others moving in lesser stations . . . it intends that a man should like a schoolmaster correct faults, punish idleness and instruct all under our care'.[7] All around him, Cocks feared, those in positions of 'command and authority' were negligent and, as a result, the country was governed by factious politicians bought by places, preferment and patronage.

As David Hayton has shown, Cocks moved in moral reformist circles and though his anti-clericalism prevented him from joining the Society for Promoting Christian Knowledge (SPCK), he counted amongst his friends and associates, Maynard Colchester, MP for Gloucestershire, Peter King, the lord chancellor between 1725 and 1733, Thomas Jervoise, a godly Hampshire gentleman and, Grey Neville, his nephew.[8] To those, like Sir Richard Cocks, who were convinced, during the decades after the Glorious Revolution, of the need for moral reformation, poverty was inextricably connected to the profanity and immorality of the lower sorts. Immiseration and idleness fostered dependence and despair, but more worrisome they also encouraged crime and corruption. Often, therefore, the problems of poverty and the poor cast a long shadow over England as they undermined the economy, distorted social relations and tore asunder the godliness of the kingdom.[9]

---

[3] *(continued)* Union and Godly Reformation in the 1690s', *Transactions of the Royal Historical Society*, 6th ser., iii (1993), 151–69; T. Isaacs, 'The Anglican Hierarchy and the Reformation of Manners, 1688–1738', *Journal of Ecclesiastical History*, xxxiii (1982), 391–411.

[4] Richard Cocks, *The Church of England Secur'd; the Toleration-Act Enervated; and the Dissenters Ruin'd and Undone* (1722); Richard Cocks, *Over Shoes, Over Boots; Being a Second Part of the Church of England Secur'd; the Toleration Enervated; and the Dissenters Ruin'd and Undone* (1722); Richard Cocks, *Sir Richard Cocks his Farewell Sermon; Shewing the Christian Religion was not Introduced by Power and Force, nor Established by Violence* (1722); Richard Cocks, *A True and Impartial Inquiry Made into the Late Bloody Execution at Thorn: or, a Challenge to the Jesuits* (1727).

[5] *Parliamentary Diary of Sir Richard Cocks*, ed. Hayton, 225.

[6] Richard Cocks, *Sir Richard Cocks his Charge to the Grand-Jury of the County of Gloucester, at the General Quarter-Sessions held for that County, April the 30th, 1717* (1717); *A Charge Given to the Grand-Jury of the County of Gloucester, at the Midsummer-Sessions, 1722* (1722), in *Charges to the Grand Jury 1689–1803*, ed. G. Lamoine (1992), on 81–8 and 175–82 respectively.

[7] Bodl., MS Eng. Hist. b. 209, f. 39v, as cited in Hayton, 'Sir Richard Cocks', 240.

[8] *Parliamentary Diary of Sir Richard Cocks*, ed. Hayton, pp. xxx–xxxi; Hayton, 'Sir Richard Cocks', 236–7. On Peter King also see his biography in *The History of Parliament: The House of Commons, 1690–1715*, ed. Eveline Cruickshanks, Stuart Handley and D.W. Hayton (5 vols, Cambridge, 2002), iv, 555–67.

[9] E. Duffy, 'Primitive Christianity Revived: Religious Renewal in Augustan England', *Studies in Church History*, xiv (1977), 287–300; Spurr, 'The Church, the Societies and the Moral Revolution of 1688', 127–42; J. Spurr, *The Post-Reformation 1603–1714: Religion, Politics and Society in Britain* (2006), 193–220.

© *The Parliamentary History Yearbook Trust 2009*

In such a highly-charged political and religious climate, issues of poverty and poor relief received considerable attention by parliamentarians and public authorities alike from the Glorious Revolution onwards. From the outset of William and Mary's reign until the accession of George II in 1727, numerous statutes were passed dealing with settlement, vagrancy, poor laws and workhouses, while 14 acts of parliament established corporations of the poor for towns and urban centres which gave them the authority over parishes and the powers to build workhouses. However, these well-known successful legislative initiatives were but the visible and tangible manifestations of much more energy and effort on the part of late 17th and early 18th century members of parliament since they also proposed, drafted, scrutinised and ultimately rejected a further 40 bills which sought, amongst other things, to better employ, relieve and house the poor. Such proposals failed because they often planned to radically alter the nature of parochial relief established, experienced and expected since their consolidation and reconfiguration by Elizabeth's parliament of 1601. An examination of these unsuccessful initiatives reveals the extent of time, thought and effort to which the later Stuarts were willing to go to address the intertwined issues of moral reformation and poverty. These legislative efforts are instructive too, for they help historians to appreciate the degree to which Augustan social problems were seen as disruptive to a providential social order and social stability.

This article seeks to synthesise aspects of recent research on the Augustan age and consider the longevity of the interpretations of the period provided in the late 1960s by Geoffrey Holmes and Jack Plumb. It contributes to a steady, though hardly torrential, stream of works which have evaluated and re-evaluated the thorny issue of stability and instability in a period aptly called 'the age of Holmes'.[10] For political and social historians toiling in the fields of Augustan England, the scholarship of J.H. Plumb and G. Holmes loom large. Decades after Plumb's *The Growth of Political Stability in England, 1675–1725* and Holmes's *British Politics in the Age of Anne* were published, the arguments and interpretations they offered still have considerable significance for our understanding of the formative period in English and British constitutional and political development.[11] For J.H. Plumb, the emergence of political stability in the second and third decades of the 18th century was of crucial importance for England, and for English men and women, and it distinguished in dramatic fashion their experiences from those of their 17th-century forebears – forebears who had endured under the Stuarts, two revolutions, three civil wars, provincial rebellions and numerous local risings.[12]

In the seventeenth century men killed, tortured, and executed each other for their political beliefs; they sacked towns and brutalized the countryside. They were

[10] See, e.g., D. Cannadine, 'Historians in "the Liberal Hour": Lawrence Stone and J. H. Plumb Re-visited', *Historical Research*, lxxv (2002), 316–54; and the roundtable discussion by Clayton Roberts, Stephen Baxter and Norma Landau in *Albion* in 1993, particularly, C. Roberts, 'The Growth of Political Stability Reconsidered', *Albion*, xxv (1993), 237–56.

[11] J.H. Plumb, The *Growth of Political Stability in England, 1675–1725* (1967); G. Holmes, *British Politics in the Age of Anne* (1967).

[12] On aspects of these subjects see M. Kishlansky, *A Monarchy Transformed: Britain 1603–1714* (1996); D. Underdown, *A Freeborn People: Politics and the Nation in Seventeenth-Century England* (Oxford, 1996); J. Scott, *England's Troubles: Seventeenth-Century English Political Instability in European Context* (Cambridge, 2000). On local risings and violence see A. Wood, *Riot, Rebellion and Popular Politics in Early Modern England* (2002); J. Walter, *Crowds and Popular Politics in Early Modern England* (Manchester, 2006).

© *The Parliamentary History Yearbook Trust 2009*

subjected to conspiracy, plot and invasion. This uncertain political world lasted until 1715, and then began rapidly to vanish. By comparison, the political structure of eighteenth century England possesses adamantine strength and profound inertia.[13]

Plumb is careful to add that other parts of the British Isles, Ireland, Scotland and the American colonies were not so fortunate and continued to experience instability and turbulence long after political conflict had been effaced and institutionalised in England. Plumb's stability thesis rested on three mutually-reinforcing pillars which all took shape in the early 1720s under the watchful eye of their principal architect, Robert Walpole. Hanoverian stability was based upon three factors: the ascendancy of single party government; parliament fell firmly under executive control; and a sense of common identity developed amongst those who wielded economic, social and political power.[14]

For Plumb, these factors accelerated the diminution of political strife which had reached its apogee during 'the rage of party' (1688–1715). Moreover, these developments became increasingly influential after the death of Queen Anne and were reinforced by whig legislative initiatives, such as the passage of the Septennial Act in 1716, an act which, in turn, assisted in the establishment of the executive and in the triumph of a 'Venetian oligarchy', organised and orchestrated by a handful of whig families, who came to govern parliament and the provinces without the partisan dissent and discord that had dominated the polity since the Glorious Revolution.

These short-term processes were underpinned by a number of long-term factors which, between 1675 and 1725, helped unify the political and constitutional structure under the control of a powerful and efficient executive.[15] First, and paradoxically, throughout the 1670s and 1680s 'the core of government was growing both stronger and more efficient in spite of the wild conflicts of political life'. While party conflict raged in every corner of urban and rural England, and with William's and later Anne's wars raging in Europe, England's 'fiscal-military state' necessarily took shape.[16] Inspired, in part, by a financial revolution in government credit and debt,[17] and by a 'widespread attitude among royal officials that sound government required a deeper knowledge of political arithmetic, a more intellectual and systematic approach to administration, steadily strengthened the sinews of the state'.[18] Furthermore, growing commercial trade

---

[13] Plumb, *Stability*, p. xviii.

[14] Plumb, *Stability*, p. xviii.

[15] For Plumb the growth of an efficient executive was crucial to his thesis, for he argues it 'was more important in the development of political stability than the resolution of the arguments between Whig and Tory, or the crushing of the electorate which is a marked feature of politics between 1689 and 1729': Plumb, *Stability*, 13. The following quotation is also drawn from this page.

[16] See J. Brewer, *The Sinews of Power: War, Money and the English State, 1688–1783* (1989); D.W. Jones, *War and Economy in the Age of William III and Marlborough* (Oxford, 1988); M. Braddick, *The Nerves of State: Taxation and the Financing of the English State, 1558–1714* (1996); the essays in *An Imperial State at War*, ed. L. Stone (1994); and in *Rethinking Leviathan: The Eighteenth-Century State in Britain and Germany*, ed. J. Brewer and E. Hellmuth (Oxford, 1999).

[17] D. Stasavage, 'Partisan Politics and Public Debt: The Importance of the "Whig Supremacy" for Britain's Financial Revolution', *European Review of Economic History*, xi (2007), 123–53; G. Holmes, 'Revolution, War and Politics, 1689–1714', in *Stuart England*, ed. B. Worden (Oxford, 1986), 199–221; H. Roseveare, *The Financial Revolution, 1660–1760* (1991); P.G.M. Dickson, *The Financial Revolution in England: A Study in the Development of Public Credit, 1688–1756* (1967).

[18] Plumb, *Stability*, 12–13.

© *The Parliamentary History Yearbook Trust 2009*

and a consumer revolution in England,[19] encouraged by an increasing and insatiable domestic desire for the fruits of empire and a world of imperial goods,[20] accompanied what some have called an 'urban renaissance' that gripped Britain between the Restoration and the age of revolutions in the later 18th century.[21] Put simply, these developments ensured the expansion and emergence of a national – as opposed to local and regional – English economy and a period of relative prosperity at the turn of the century. These themes, first echoed by Plumb in his Ford Lectures, have in the last three decades, been elaborated upon and thoroughly established by a generation of historians as essential characteristics of the economy and society of late Stuart and Georgian England.[22]

Similarly, and even more forcefully than the elegant interpretive essay offered by Plumb, the salient aspects of Geoffrey Holmes's seminal work have stood the test of time, and a generation after *British Politics in the Age of Anne* was published, the contour lines of the Augustan political landscape look very much like those Holmes laid down in that work in 1967. Recent work by Gary De Krey, Tim Harris, David Hayton and Peter Jupp all confirm to a greater and lesser degree, through their own independent researches, an image of the later Stuart political world Holmes established in his writings.[23] Now, as in 1967, we are left with the thoroughly convincing Holmesian interpretation of a period riven by party – rather than Namierite factional – politics where religious and political hostilities and divisions coursed through almost every city, town, and parish.[24] Within this divided society whigs confronted tories, anglicans confronted dissenters and catholics, and English men and women disagreed over the conduct of war and foreign policy, over governance and administration, over financial and commercial practices, over charity schools, and over the dispensation of poor relief.[25] Imbided in coffee houses, taverns and clubs, enflamed by pamphlets and periodicals, encouraged from the pulpit and the press, endorsed by polemicists and politicians, and embraced by the electorate, the 'conflict of

---

[19] N. Glaisyer, *The Culture of Commerce in England, 1660–1720* (2006); K. Wrightson, *Earthly Necessities: Economic Lives in Early Modern Britain* (New Haven, 2000), 227–336; N. Mckendrick, J. Brewer and J.H. Plumb, *The Birth of a Consumer Society: The Commercialization of Eighteenth-Century England* (1982).

[20] P. Gauci, *Emporium of the World: The Merchants of London 1660–1800* (2007); J. Walvin, *Fruits of Empire: Exotic Produce and British Taste, 1660–1800* (New York, 1997); *Consumption and the World of Goods*, ed. J. Brewer and R. Porter (1989).

[21] P. Borsay, *The English Urban Renaissance: Culture and Society in the Provincial Town, 1660–1770* (1989); *The Eighteenth Century Town: A Reader in English Urban History 1688–1820*, ed. P. Borsay (1990); *The Cambridge Urban History of Britain. 1540–1840*, ed. P. Clark (Cambridge, 2000).

[22] See, e.g., the overall image presented in J. Hoppit, *A Land of Liberty? England 1689–1727* (Oxford, 2000) and G. Holmes, *The Making of a Great Power: Late Stuart and Early Georgian Britain 1660–1722* (1993). For an alternative interpretation that downplays the importance of economic and social change in the period see J.C.D. Clark, *English Society 1660–1832: Religion, Ideology and Politics during the Ancient Regime* (Cambridge, 2000).

[23] G. De Krey, *Restoration and Revolution in Britain* (2007); T. Harris, *Politics under the Later Stuarts: Party Conflict in a Divided Society 1660–1715* (1993); T. Harris, *Revolution: The Great Crisis of the British Monarchy, 1685–1720* (2006); D.W. Hayton, *The History of Parliament: The House of Commons 1690–1715, Introductory Survey* (2002); P. Jupp, *The Governing of Britain 1688–1848* (2006). Also see the essays in *Britain in the First Age of Party 1680–1750: Essays Presented to Geoffrey Holmes*, ed. C. Jones (1987).

[24] P. Halliday, *Dismembering the Body Politic: Partisan Politics in England's Towns 1650–1730* (Cambridge, 1998).

[25] G.S. De Krey, *A Fractured Society: The Politics of London in the First Age of Party, 1688–1715* (Oxford, 1985); *The Divided Society: Parties and Politics in England, 1694–1716*, ed. G. Holmes and W.A. Speck (1967); W.A. Speck, *Tory and Whig: The Struggle in the Constituencies, 1701–1715* (1970); and for a broader transnational discussion of political instability, consult Scott, *England's Troubles*.

party in the age of Anne was [as Holmes categorically proved] a conflict over policy and principles'.[26] Furthermore, 'the most extraordinary feature of the age of Anne was the unprecedented extent to which party strife, the inescapable and all-pervading distinction between Tory and Whig, invaded and finally took possession of the very lives of the politically conscious'.[27] *British Politics in the Age of Anne* manifestly revealed in meticulously researched detail the political and social instability identified by J.H. Plumb too.

Symptomatic, for example, of the instability that gripped post-revolutionary England was the challenge that William and Mary and later Anne faced in creating durable ministries. Between 1689 and 1702 William employed half a dozen first lords of the treasury, and of the admiralty too, and issued over a dozen different treasury commissions. Under Anne and until the early 1720s Holmes argues 'the whole political scene none the less remained in a state of flux, as first the Tory party, then their rivals, gained the upper hand at Court and in Parliament'.[28] But, paradoxically as Holmes also notes, at the same time that the hostilities between whig and tory raged, and

> in the passionate closeness of their political involvement, the men of the day could not always appreciate the underlying strength of some of the cements which held together the shot-torn fabric of their society. Without the elements of restraint and cohesion they supplied, it would have been impossible for social stability to be restored as quickly as it was under the Whig oligarchy in the 1720s and 1730s.[29]

And, just as J.H. Plumb traced the realization of political stability to a reconfiguration of politics in the 1720s, so, too, did Geoffrey Holmes. The age of party in Augustan England reached its zenith during Anne's reign and by the first septennial election the political climate and forecast had changed. '1722 marks the line at which the last vestiges of the politics of party, in the clear cut form that had characterized the age of Anne, disappeared and the politics of oligarchy, which recognized and incorporated the divisions between Whigs and Tories without being dictated by them, became firmly established as the dominant pattern for the future.'[30] Put a different way, and reflecting an Englishman's preoccupation with the weather, Holmes also noted: 'the politics of oligarchy and connexion, so appropriate to the temperate air of mid-Georgian Britain, could never have flourished in the hot and highly-charged atmosphere of the early eighteenth century. These were the conditions for the politics of party.'[31]

Scholars have questioned aspects of the overlapping interpretations of political instability and stability in the Augustan age provided by Plumb and Holmes and they have qualified the degree to which stability was achieved under the first two Hanoverian

---

[26] Holmes, *British Politics*, 410. On these themes and on the emergence of a public sphere and a national political culture in Augustan Britain, see M. Knights, *Representation and Misrepresentation in Later Stuart Britain: Partisanship and Political Culture* (Oxford, 2005).

[27] Knights, *Representation and Misrepresentation*, pp. xv, 20–1.

[28] Holmes, *Making of a Great Power*, 384, but also see 322–48; see also, R. McJimsey, 'Crisis Management: Parliament and Political Stability, 1692–1719', *Albion*, xxxi (1999), 559–88.

[29] Holmes, *Making of a Greak Power*, 335.

[30] Holmes, *British Politics*, p. xv.

[31] Holmes, *British Politics*, 406. These convictions are driven home by the fact that G. Holmes's co-authored textbook, with D. Szechi, on the mid to late 18th century is titled *The Age of Oligarchy: Pre-Industrial Britain, 1722–1783* (1993).

monarchs. Linda Colley, for example, has convincingly argued that the tory party defied the inertia of oligarchy and remained an active and viable alternative to the whigs in the 1730s and 1740s.[32] They survived and maintained ideological, electoral and organisational cohesion within parliament and the provinces until the accession of George III reconfigured, yet again, British politics.[33] Other historians have also argued that 'the rage of party' endured into the reign of George I, and observe that jacobitism further complicated political ideologies and that tensions over the Hanoverian succession reveal a polity that had hardly escaped division and discord.[34] However, the fact that tories and jacobites existed and persevered, and were appealing to, and supported by, some – perhaps, even many – Britons during the first half of the 18th century does not negate two basic elements of Plumb's thesis: 'a sense of common identity among those who wielded economic, social and political power', and 'the acceptance by society of its political institutions, and of those classes of men or officials who control them'.[35]

Moreover, there was more to the realization of stability in the 18th century than the pacification of partisan politicians. An important aspect of Geoffrey Holmes's researches was his analysis of the 'social contexts of politics' during the Augustan period. In a number of important publications that followed *British Politics in the Age of Anne*, he suggested, amongst other things, that political stability owed much to a number of broader social and cultural changes that had been developing since the Restoration. The emergence of the professions (lawyers, doctors, military officers, civil servants and the clergy) offered status, wealth and the opportunity for advancement to many who had been excluded from political society in the mid to late 17th century.[36] These people found additional career possibilities in the offices of an expanding state too. War, trade and imperial conquest in the decades following the Glorious Revolution stimulated long-term administrative expansion and the reorganisation of government and finance to meet the needs of what Lawrence Stone described as a 'warfare-welfare state'[37] created a new breed of civil servant with a perennial interest in maintaining efficient government. The emergence of these new servants of state necessarily provided a new and impressively large number of offices and, therefore, a pool of patronage that could be

---

[32] L. Colley, *In Defiance of Oligarchy: The Tory Party, 1714–1760* (Cambridge, 1982).

[33] On this subject see W.A. Speck, 'Whigs and Tories Dim their Glories: English Political Parties under the First Two Georges', in *The Whig Ascendancy: Colloquies on Hanoverian History*, ed. J. Cannon (1981), 51–70; I.R. Christie, 'The Changing Nature of Parliamentary Politics, 1742–1789', in *British Politics and Society from Walpole to Pitt, 1742–1789*, ed. J. Black (1990), 101–22.

[34] On this subject see B.W. Hill, *The Growth of Political Parties, 1689–1742* (1976); E. Cruickshanks, *Political Untouchables: The Tories and the '45* (1979); P. Monod, *Jacobitism and the English People 1688–1788* (Cambridge, 1989); *The Jacobite Challenge*, ed. E. Cruickshanks and J. Black (Edinburgh, 1988); J.C.D. Clark, *English Society 1688–1832: Ideology, Social Structure and Political Practice during the Ancient Regime* (Cambridge, 1985), 119–98.

[35] Plumb, *Stability*, pp. xvi, xviii. For a spirited critique of recent scholarship on the tory party and on jacobite studies, see P.D.G. Thomas, 'Party Politics in Eighteenth Century Britain: Some Myths and a Touch of Reality', *British Journal of Eighteenth Century Studies*, x (1987), 201–10.

[36] This thesis is fully articulated in G. Holmes, *Augustan England: Professions, State and Society, 1680–1730* (1982); G. Holmes, 'The Professions and Social Change in England, 1680–1730', *Proceedings of the British Academy*, lxv (1979), 313–54; see also, P. Corfield, *Power and the Professions in Britain 1700–1850* (1995).

[37] L. Stone, 'The New Eighteenth Century', in *The Past and Present Revisited*, ed. L. Stone (1987), 240; see also, L. Stone, 'Introduction', in *An Imperial State at War: Britain from 1689–1815*, ed. L. Stone (1994), 21.

© *The Parliamentary History Yearbook Trust 2009*

drawn upon to quench the thirst of those clamouring middling and upper sorts who might otherwise precipitate instability by militating against officeholders and government alike.[38]

Furthermore, the growth of the state and state-inspired institutions were reinforced by the commercial and financial revolution, which not only helped redefine and expand Hanoverian conceptions of property during the 18th century, it provided new opportunities for both individual and national wealth. Yet, as Holmes noted, business and commercial interests may have been willing to take risks on trade ventures but they 'placed a high premium on a stable constitutional and political system as a necessary guarantee of the preservation of these coveted benefits'.[39] In addition to the aforementioned trends, Holmes agreed with Plumb that the long-term inclination towards electoral oligarchy (the process by which power was increasingly concentrated in the hands of fewer and fewer political families or individuals) was taking place in the 1720s and 1730s, but suggested that this process likely began during the 1680s and 1690s.

But what of broader Augustan social and economic processes which affected all Britons? Here, too, Geoffrey Holmes provided instructive insights. In an important essay on the achievement of stability he confirmed the importance of a number of factors which contributed to a stable Hanoverian society first alluded to by J.H. Plumb in his Ford Lectures.[40] Along with the effective reduction in sectarian and spiritual tensions brought about by even modest measures of religious toleration,[41] stability was, in part, achieved in the early 18th century by demographic stagnation, improved agricultural production, social mobility, and the potential for greater prosperity for a greater percentage of Britons from the turn of the century onwards.

Recent research has built upon the foundations of social stability established by Geoffrey Holmes by re-emphasizing and re-confirming the explanations he provided historians in the 1970s and 1980s. For instance, well-established demographic findings now note that after a century (1550–1650) of rapid population growth, the period from roughly 1660 until 1740 experienced stable and slow population expansion.[42] In turn, this slow growth alleviated pressure on the standards of living of many middling and plebeian English men and women. Second, the English also witnessed a marked decline in the price of corn which fell by more than 10% between the Restoration and the fall of Robert Walpole in the early 1740s.[43] Occasional years of scarcity and dearth in the

---

[38] Holmes, *Making of a Great Power*, 387.

[39] Holmes, *Making of a Great Power*, 388. The following discussion of electoral oligarchy is also drawn from this source.

[40] G. Holmes, 'The Achievement of Stability: The Social Context of Politics from the 1680s to the Age of Walpole', in *The Whig Ascendancy*, ed. Cannon, 1–22. Information in the following paragraph is drawn from this source.

[41] Holmes, *Making of a Great Power*, 350–65; see also, T. Harris, 'From Rage of Party to Age of Oligarchy? Rethinking the Later Stuart and Early Hanoverian Period', *Journal of Modern History*, lxiv (1992), 700–20.

[42] E.A Wrigley and R.S. Schofield, *The Population History of England 1541–1871: A Reconstruction* (Cambridge, 1981), 532–3, notes that in 1660 in England the population was 5.12 million while in 1690 that number stood at 4.98 million and in 1725 at 5.40 million.

[43] See P.J. Bowden, 'Agricultural Prices, Wages, Farm Profits and Rents, 1640–1750', in *Economic Change*, ed. P.J. Bowden (Cambridge, 1990), 189, 320–1; Wrightson, *Earthly Necessities*, 269–330.

1690s were offset by a modest increase in real wages and by the fact that between 1679 and 1742 English men and women were in no real danger of famine.[44]

Moreover, scholarship on late 17th-century land rent, tenancy, estate management and on agricultural practice have shown that agricultural service emerged from the turmoil of the mid-century civil wars with what might be characterised as a 'new paternalism'. This paternalism revealed itself in agreements by which landowners and landlords 'drew up leases which specified that they would maintain and repair buildings but also engaged in other practices – financial forebearance in times of trouble, positive action to support the rental, the creation of employment opportunities on their estates – which lay beyond the terms of the formal agreement'.[45]

While there can be no doubt that benevolent paternalism, employment opportunities and economic benefits presented themselves in the later Stuart and early Hanoverian period, they were hardly experienced by all. For many 'the life of man [was as Thomas Hobbes had noted] solitary, poor, nasty, brutish, and short'.[46] And for many commentators in Augustan England, questions of prosperity and poverty went hand-in-hand, as did the need for stability and moral reformation.

Contemporaries, like Sir Richard Cocks, spent much time and energy not only pondering the condition of the poor, but actively seeking legislative solutions to eradicate poverty. Cocks was convinced that the root cause of poverty was idleness and: 'The reason of the great charge of the poor is first the negligent way of living of the poor families, their wakes, their frequ[ent ho]lidays, their fiddlers, their debaucheries, their liberalities to their children with no other intent [than to] become chargeable themselves.'[47]

These sentiments were also echoed by Daniel Defoe in his famous pamphlet, *Giving Alms No Charity*, when he repeatedly noted that the root cause of poverty was not the want of work, but the sloth and luxury of the English poor.[48] Debate on how best to deal with the poor reflected the paradoxes found in most contentious issues during 'the rage of party'. In the later 17th century, and after decades of discussion over the most effective ways of addressing poverty, a number of initiatives – public and private – were seized upon to both alleviate and eliminate poverty. Ironically, at the same time, the state opted to abandon paternal mechanisms of the Elizabethan and Caroline periods such as the books of orders which offered instructions to justices of the peace on how to deal with plague, famine and dearth, and how to regulate the corn trade and the sale of grain in times of shortage. The books derived their strength from the royal prerogative and sought to provide support in times of crises and maintain the

---

[44] On this subject see R.B. Outhwaite, *Dearth, Public Policy and Social Disturbance in England, 1550–1800* (1991); R.B. Outhwaite, 'Dearth and Government Intervention in English Grain Markets, 1590–1700', *Economic History Review*, xxxiii (1981), 389–406; W.G. Hoskins, 'Harvest Fluctuations and English Economic History, 1620–1759', *Agricultural History Review*, xvi (1968), 19; Holmes, *Making of a Great Power*, 293–306.

[45] S. Hindle, 'The Growth of Social Stability in Restoration England', *The European Legacy*, v (2000), 565; see also, K. Wrightson, *English Society 1580–1680* (2nd edn, 2003), 65–73.

[46] T. Hobbes, *Leviathan* (1651), pt. 1, ch. 13. On this theme consult, R. Porter, *English Society in the Eighteenth Century* (rev. edn, 1990), 127–42, 290–301; R. Connors, *State and Welfare in Hanoverian England* (forthcoming).

[47] Bodl., MS Cocks 2, f. 60, as cited in Hayton, 'Sir Richard Cocks', 241.

[48] D. Defoe, *Giving Alms No Charity* (1704).

© *The Parliamentary History Yearbook Trust 2009*

public order.[49] In place of these paternalist measures the late Stuart state sought instead to control the corn market, grain trade and the practices of middlemen, badgers, regrators and forestallers.[50] For example, between 1689 and 1699 parliament considered bills that aimed to settle measures of corn and grain, regulate the trade weights of butter and cheese, control the activities of forestallers of corn, and on three separate occasions draw up legislation to make more effective the assize of bread.[51] Throughout much of the 18th century successive monarchs and ministries adopted this lightly-perhaps invisibly-handed paternalist approach to the grain trade, though in times of scarcity or dearth the crown retained the right to embargo exports of corn and continued to exercise that prerogative into the reign of George III.[52]

On the broader challenges presented by poverty and the condition of the poor, the late Stuart state also drew upon parliamentary legislation. In the wake of the Glorious Revolution and with the routinisation of annual meetings, parliament increasingly became the arena within which reform and redress of grievances were contested and conducted.[53] Social welfare initiatives such as those which dealt with the poor law could be national or local in content and context. Proposals of a regional or local nature were far more likely to succeed as wide-ranging and sweeping national initiatives which dealt with the poor and the administration of poor relief proved more likely to fail. Thus, between the mid 1690s and 1712, parliament passed statutes creating 14 corporations of the poor in provincial towns.[54] Inspired, in part, by societies for the reformation of manners, which endeavoured to suppress vice and anti-social behaviour with a puritanical zeal, the 14 corporations established workhouses in towns such as Bristol, Norwich, Colchester, Hereford and Gloucester.

Apart from various uniquely local expectations, and wishing to set the underemployed and unemployed to work, the corporations established workhouses with the ambitious goal of repressing ' "idleness, theft, debauchery, prophaneness and other immoralities in children", to sow "the early seeds of industry, honesty, sobriety, piety and virtue in them", and to achieve "the reformation, happiness and welfare of the nation" '.[55] In his *Essay on the State of England* (1695), John Cary added that the Bristol corporation of the poor

---

[49] P. Slack, 'Books of Orders: The Making of English Social Policy, 1577–1631', *Transactions of the Royal Historical Society*, 5th ser., xxx (1980), 1–22; J. Walter and K. Wrightson, 'Dearth and the Social Order in Early Modern England', *Past and Present*, no. 71 (1976), 22–44.

[50] On this subject see E.P. Thompson, 'The Moral Economy of the English Crowd in the Eighteenth Century', *Past and Present*, no. 50 (1971), 76–136; J. Walter, 'The Social Economy of Dearth in Early Modern England', in *Famine, Disease and the Social Order in Early Modern Society*, ed. J. Walter and R. Schofield (Cambridge, 1989), 75–128.

[51] This information is drawn from *Failed Legislation 1660–1800: Extracted from the Commons and Lords Journals*, ed. J. Hoppit and J. Innes (1997), 160–223.

[52] P. Lawson, 'Parliament, the Constitution and Corn: The Embargo Crisis of 1766', *Parliamentary History*, v (1986), 17–37; R. Connors, 'Parliament and Poverty in Mid-Eighteenth-Century England', *Parliamentary History*, xxi (2002), 207–31.

[53] R. Connors, ' "The Grand Inquest of the Nation": Parliamentary Committees and Social Policy in Mid-Eighteenth Century England', *Parliamentary History*, xiv (1995), 285–313; J. Innes, 'Parliament and the Shaping of Eighteenth-Century English Social Policy', *Transactions of the Royal Historical Society*, 5th ser., xl (1990), 63–92.

[54] On this subject see P. Slack, *Poverty and Policy in Tudor and Stuart England* (1988), 195–200.

[55] F.T. Melton, *Sir Robert Clayton and the Origins of English Deposit Banking* (Cambridge, 1986), 4, as cited in Slack, *Poverty and Policy*, 197.

would effectively find work for the poor, and through the corporation much more could be accomplished for the 'public good' than merely relying on inadequately small parishes.[56] Consolidation and collaborative efforts were needed to overcome the perennial problems of poverty and immorality. In a polity torn by religious fervour and party political animosities this was a tall order and often such tensions within the corporations and communities they oversaw made non-partisan co-operation virtually impossible. However, as Paul Halliday has skilfully shown, urban and corporate instability did not mean that Restoration and revolutionary England were ungovernable. As he suggests, the paradox of partisan politics during the rage of party was that it compelled the mutually antagonistic Augustan English to use courts of law and the laws of parliament to fight their fights and, therefore, and in due course, 'the divided society of the early eighteenth century was also a dynamic, stable one'.[57]

In their desire to contribute to the public good, and their own municipal interests, the corporations were assisted in the 1690s by the newly established board of trade whose job it was to inquire into ways of employing the poor and clearly it took that task seriously. In 1696 and 1697, the commissioners of trade and plantations, including John Locke, took testimony from overseers and experts – John Cary and Thomas Firmin amongst them – inquired into poor rates in parishes, and drafted legislative proposals. When the commissioners reported their findings they chose not to 'recommend wholesale reform of the poor laws, but devoted their proposals instead to ways in which existing provisions to employ the poor could be more strictly enforced'.[58] Subsequent parliamentary initiatives that sought to enact these suggestions were introduced in the house of commons in early 1698 but failed. In fact, these discussions in the board of trade on the poor precipitated a protracted discussion on the poor laws which continued almost unabated among political arithmeticians, polemicists and parliamentarians until the passage of Knatchbull's Workhouse Act in 1723.

Thus, from the mid 1690s until the ascendancy of Robert Walpole, MPs routinely investigated the formal and informal mechanisms of poor relief in England. Between 1689 and 1723, and alongside the establishment of the 14 corporations of the poor, parliament enacted four statutes dealing with matters of poverty and social welfare. One addressed questions of settlement law (1692), another, in 1697, dealt with defects in the poor laws, while a third passed in 1714 consolidated the laws relating to rogues and vagrants into one statute (13 Anne c. 26). Finally, in 1723, legislation 'For Amending the Laws relating to the Settlement, Employment and Relief of the Poor' – the Workhouse Test Act (Knatchbull's Workhouse Act) allowed authorities to refuse relief to those poor who chose not to enter the workhouse. In addition to these successful legislative ventures, the committees of the houses of common and lords also wrote, revised and ultimately rejected between 1689 and 1723, another 40 parliamentary bills on the interconnected issues of the employment of the poor and their relief. Moreover, these parliamentary debates do not include those that addressed the issue of vagrancy which regularly appeared as a contentious issue for MPs, especially those who lived in large

[56] J. Cary, *An Essay on the State of England in Relation to its Trade* (Bristol, 1695), 151–67.

[57] Halliday, *Dismembering the Body Politic*, 341.

[58] S. Macfarlane, 'Social Policy and the Poor in the Later Seventeenth Century', in *London 1500–1700: The Making of the Metropolis*, ed. A.L. Beier and R. Finlay (1986), 252–77, at 261.

© *The Parliamentary History Yearbook Trust 2009*

urban centres and in London in particular.[59] Therefore, it is abundantly clear that this scale of legislative enquiry and energy ensured that the timeless issues of the poor were never far from the surface in late Stuart and early Hanoverian English parliaments.

Sir Richard Cocks's request, with which this article began, called for the complete overhaul and consolidation of poor law legislation. His goal was to make the poor personally responsible for not only their poverty, but their attendant moral failings as well. Going far beyond measures embodied in legislation in 1697, which required that recipients of parish relief be badged – thereby reinforcing the stigma of the dole through shame sanctions,[60] Cocks advocated that both female and male vagrant poor be punished harshly through flogging, imprisonment and transportation. The legislation dealing with the relief of the poor in 1697 went some way to ratcheting down discipline by making the wearing of badges mandatory for all relief recipients, and recent research reveals that the use of badges was far more prevalent than we once assumed.[61] In 1714, the legislation that reduced laws relating to rogues and vagrants into an omnibus act allowed for increasingly harsh corporeal treatment, such as whipping, for those deemed vagabonds or dangerous or incorrigible. Furthermore, certain vagrants could, according to the 1714 law, be bound to service for seven years at home or overseas.[62]

While parliament saw fit to consolidate legislation dealing with rogues and vagrants, it did not do the same for the poor laws. Calls for the complete overhaul of the poor laws echoed throughout the 17th century, and though many attempts were made to accomplish such a task, none succeeded in the Augustan period – or, in fact, until 1834. However, in 1704–5, parliament nearly accomplished this task when the house of commons passed a bill drafted and driven by Humphrey Mackworth, one of the original subscribers to the SPCK and MP for Cardiganshire (1701–5 and 1710–13) and for Totnes (1705–8).[63] Politically Mackworth was a tory, enthusiastically anti-whig and anti-court, and held strong views about public debt and economic reform and local development. He was a staunch social and moral reformer and he believed in legislating against social ills, but his most memorable campaigns on these themes came with his attempts to reform the statutes seeking to usefully employ the poor.

Between 1703 and 1707, Humphrey Mackworth presented several bills to parliament. None passed the house of lords. Most famously, and in light of the fact that the house of commons had debated 'its reform on at least thirteen occasions between 1694 and 1704, the poor law of Elizabeth was not replaced by the poor law of Anne'.[64] In March of 1705 the bill he sponsored to consolidate and amend the poor laws failed to gain

---

[59] Connors, 'Grand Inquest' and 'Parliament and Poverty' drive home similar findings for the mid to late 18th century too.

[60] Consult S. Hindle, *On the Parish? The Micro-Politics of Poor Relief in Rural England c. 1550–1750* (Oxford, 2004), 433–45.

[61] S. Hindle, 'Dependency, Shame and Belonging: Badging the Deserving Poor, c.1550–1750', *Cultural and Social History*, i (2004), 29–58.

[62] 13 Anne c. 26. This statute is summarized in P. Slack, *The English Poor Law 1531–1782* (1990), 62.

[63] On Humphrey Mackworth see *House of Commons, 1690–1715*, ed. Cruickshanks *et al.*, iv, 724–35. The following information is also drawn from his entry in the *Oxford Dictionary of National Biography*. On the SPCK see T. Hitchcock, 'Paupers and Preachers: The SPCK and the Parochial Workhouse Movement', in *Stilling the Grumbling Hive: The Response to Social and Economic Problems in England, 1689–1750*, ed. L. Davison, T. Hitchcock, T. Keirn and R.B. Shoemaker (1992), 145–66.

[64] P. Slack, *From Reformation to Improvement: Public Welfare in Early Modern England* (Oxford, 1999), 117.

approval in the upper House and died on the table when parliament was prorogued. The bill seemed well-conceived and this point is, perhaps, best illustrated by the fact that it – unlike many others – passed the house of commons. Amongst other things it allowed parishes to combine to employ their poor, to appoint paid assistant overseers, and it permitted the incorporation of donors to charity schools and of churchwardens too. It reinforced aspects of the settlement laws and made provision for the badging of the poor.[65] Why such a bill failed twice in the Lords, since it was introduced yet again in the autumn of 1705, owes something to the fact that it dealt with a complicated subject and one that crucially touched on the lives of all rate-paying and rate-receiving English men and women. That it did not succeed in a revised form in subsequent sessions is equally instructive for real issues were at stake here. Writing in the early 20th century, Sidney and Beatrice Webb argued that Mackworth's initiative failed because it met with strident opposition outside parliament from a chief critic of the bill, Daniel Defoe, who strenuously objected to the centrality of the workhouse in schemes to deal with the poor.[66] Secondly, and more recently, Joanna Innes notes that 'the Lords, while not averse to any measure of reform, none the less set their faces against that part of the plan that would have provided for local authority supervision of charities – perhaps because the judiciary objected to any encroachment upon Chancery's supervisory powers'.[67] Finally, Paul Slack reminds us that workhouses were 'vulnerable to the accusation that they increased rather than reduced the charge of the poor, with their huge capital outlays and heavy running costs'.[68] Moreover, he points to a fundamental issue that dogged not only parliamentary attempts at reforming morality or the poor laws, but challenged virtually every assumption about public life and political culture in Augustan England.[69]

For Slack, 'the various critics of reformation threw down intellectual challenges which did as much as the rage of party to undermine any public consensus there might have been behind [Mackworth's scheme]'.[70] Indeed, until that strident, confrontational and partisan political world view was tempered, until its political atmosphere and climate, identified by Geoffrey Holmes, moderated and became more tolerable if not tepid, the political landscape would, in the heat of the midday sun (Anne's reign), remain in the hands of mad dogs and Englishmen. Put another way, reconfiguring issues of such importance as moral reform and the poor laws was impossible until the eclipse of the rage of party. It may, therefore, be more than mere coincidence that the passage of Knatchbull's Workhouse Test Act (1723) came only after the emergence of oligarchy and political stability so carefully charted by both Geoffrey Holmes and J.H. Plumb to the temperate early 1720s. Knatchbull's act went some way to fulfilling some of the

---

[65] HMC, *Lords MSS*, new ser., vi, 273–87; see also, M. Ransome, 'The Parliamentary Career of Sir Humphrey Mackworth, 1701–1713', *University of Birmingham Historical Journal*, i (1948), 232–54, particularly 244–7.

[66] S. and B. Webb, *English Poor Law History. Part I: The Old Poor Law* (1927), 113–16.

[67] J. Innes, 'The "Mixed Economy of Welfare" in Early Modern England: Assessments of the Options from Hale to Malthus (c.1683–1803)', in *Charity, Self-Interest and Welfare in the English Past*, ed. M. Daunton (1996), 152.

[68] Slack, *From Reformation to Improvement*, 118.

[69] M. Knights, *Representation and Misrepresentation*, 1–66, particularly 18–41.

[70] Slack, *From Reformation to Improvement*, 119.

© *The Parliamentary History Yearbook Trust 2009*

expectations Sir Richard Cocks had of parliament in March 1699. Yet, when faced with the righteous, earnest and dogged enthusiasm of Sir Richard Cocks and those like him who sought to regiment, recast and reform the lives of the lower sorts and the labouring poor, one cannot help but recall E.P. Thompson's chilling observation that in our analysis, and discussion of, stability and instability in Augustan England, we would also do well to remember 'that stability, no less than revolution, may have its own kind of Terror'.[71]

[71] E.P. Thompson, *Whigs and Hunters: The Origin of the Black Act* (1975), 253.

© *The Parliamentary History Yearbook Trust 2009*

Jacobite Politics in the Age of Anne

DANIEL SZECHI

Every political movement has watershed moments when decisions are taken with very long-term consequences. This article explores one such moment with respect to the jacobite movement during the reign of Queen Anne. Implicitly building on Geoffrey Holmes's model of the workings of the whig and tory parties in the age of Anne, the article analyses the turn to the Scots that took place within jacobite politics between 1702 and 1710. Throughout the 1690s the English jacobites had dominated the politics of the jacobite movement. Cementing their hold on the jacobite court's outlook and policies there was, too, an intrinsic anglocentrism at royal and ministerial level. Yet by 1715 the Scots jacobites were clearly equal partners with the English within the movement, and this parity was to shape the entire subsequent history of the jacobite cause. This shift within the politics of the movement was, moreover, not simply a corollary of the union. This article argues that the shift to the Scots was far more fundamental in terms of the outlook and policies of the movement, and ultimately did not depend on the immediate military utility of the Scots jacobites, but on a new perception of them as a uniquely important resource.

Keywords: Scotland; England; Ireland; France; jacobite court; jacobitism; jacobites; James Stuart (the old pretender); Queen Mary of Modena; Charles Middleton, earl of Middleton; War of Spanish Succession (1702–13); 1708 jacobite invasion attempt

It is a truism to say that all historians working on early 18th-century Britain are now working in the age of Holmes, and have been for 40 years. Geoff Holmes's influence touches all aspects of our understanding of social and political life from the 1690s to at least the 1720s, and the implications of his interpretation reverberate throughout our vision of the entire 18th century. Speaking personally, I can attest that Geoff Holmes was one of the most profound influences on my own metamorphosis from undergraduate to historian, and hence what follows is more than just the *hommage* suggested by the title of this article. Learning from Geoff, I now see the dynamics of political life through a particular lens, and following his lead I will explore the structure of jacobite politics at its broadest in pursuit of the significance of the age of Anne.

1

There were two strands to jacobite politics throughout the history of the movement, but nowhere more clearly than in the reign of Anne. One strand was internal: jacobite groups interacting with each other within the movement in pursuit of various agendas.[1] The other was external: jacobites as individuals and as a group interacting with individuals and other political groups operating within conventional, legal politics. I have explored the jacobites' interaction with conventional politics after 1710 elsewhere; what I propose to do here is to look at the pre-history of the jacobite politics of the era of Harley's 'Great Ministry', focusing particularly on the processes that predisposed them to embrace Harley's secret initiative after 1711.[2]

First, however, it is necessary to put the jacobites' behaviour and responses in internal, jacobite political context. The political dynamics of the jacobite movement sprang from the conciliarist approach imposed on the exiled royal family by their political and economic circumstances. Bluntly put, the Stuarts at St Germain had little they could offer their adherents. The usual tools of political management: money, place and power, were in very short supply at St Germain. Aside from a few positions at the jacobite court, the ability to ennoble exiled jacobites and some influence with the French and other governments, there was very little James, the old pretender, or Queen Mary of Modena, could do for their friends.[3] Their authority within the movement was thus primarily moral and ideological. In essence, jacobites obeyed the royal family and its ministers because they believed in the righteousness of the cause and accepted the necessity of their own subordination to the court's policies in order to achieve their common goal: the restoration of the main line of the Stuart dynasty.[4] In practice this meant that the government-in-exile had to work by persuasion and moral pressure. If a jacobite did not like the current ministers at St Germain, or thought the policies being pursued by James or Mary were wrongheaded, he or she always had the option of withdrawing into passivity. Withdrawal, moreover, had very few consequences for the individual concerned. They could remain privately, or even semi-publicly, committed to the cause, and thus refusal to co-operate with the exiled court did not even mean they had to sever their ties with the jacobite communities of the British Isles or overseas. Thomas Bruce, earl of Ailesbury, is a case in point. Though he remained in touch with the jacobite court after he went into exile in 1697 and retained his network of jacobite and tory connections within the British Isles, he chose not to participate in further jacobite initiatives and there was nothing the exiled Stuarts could do about it. Yet his reputation as a die-hard jacobite rightly stayed with him to his death.[5]

[1] Daniel Szechi, 'The Jacobite Revolution Settlement, 1689–1696', *English Historical Review*, cviii (1993), 610–28; Edward Gregg, 'The Jacobite Career of John, Earl of Mar', in *Ideology and Conspiracy: Aspects of Jacobitism, 1689–1759*, ed. E. Cruickshanks (Edinburgh, 1982), 183–4; Doron Zimmerman, *The Jacobite Movement in Scotland and in Exile, 1746–1759* (Basingstoke, 2003), 113–14.

[2] Daniel Szechi, *Jacobitism and Tory Politics, 1710–14* (Edinburgh, 1984); see also, Daniel Szechi, *George Lockhart of Carnwath, 1689–1727: A Study in Jacobitism* (East Linton, 2002), 46–72, 127–31.

[3] Éamonn Ó Ciardha, *Ireland and the Jacobite Cause, 1685–1766: A Fatal Attachment* (Dublin, 2002), 222, 350–1.

[4] Westminster Diocesan Archive, Old Brotherhood MSS, iii, pt 3, ep. 259: Sir Edward Hales's memorandum of a conversation with James II, [St Germain], 2 June 1693 ns (all Old Brotherhood material is published with the permission of 'the Old Brotherhood' collection held at the Westminster Diocesan Archives, to whom I am grateful); Henrietta Tayler, *The Jacobite Court at Rome in 1719: From Original Documents at Fettercairn House and at Windsor Castle* (Scottish History Society, 3rd ser., xxxi, Edinburgh, 1938), 57, 80, 106–7; *A Short Account of the Affairs of Scotland in the Years 1744, 1745, 1746: By David, Lord Elcho*, ed. E. Charteris (Edinburgh, 1907), 148–9.

[5] *http://www.oxforddnb.com/view/article/3758?docPos=2*: Thomas Bruce, earl of Ailesbury, by Victor Stater (accessed 15 Apr. 2007); see also, *http://www.oxforddnb.com/view/article/14329?docPos=3*: Henry Hyde, earl of

The upshot was that if the Stuarts wanted their followers on board they had to consult their wishes and, at least to some extent, accommodate their agendas.[6] Theoretically, James and Mary could have negotiated a massive French invasion which could conquer the British Isles without the need for any input from the jacobite underground. In practice, of course, this was simply unattainable at any time during the War of the Spanish Succession. So the exiled Stuarts were always implicitly negotiating with their putative adherents. *Prima facie* this should not have been a problem. There was, after all, a central core of agreement between all jacobites: they wanted the main line of Stuarts back on the thrones of the three kingdoms. In fact, however, there were effectively three national parties, plus a court interest, whose aspirations had to be taken into account for purely practical reasons. These reasons centred on the plain fact that a jacobite uprising in just one part of the British Isles was likely to be vulnerable to military counter-measures by the government, whereas a rebellion in all three kingdoms would be more difficult to suppress. The jacobite court, therefore, always sought to negotiate three simultaneous rebellions. It is a measure of the inherent difficulty of doing so that not once in the history of the jacobite movement was this ever achieved. The best the jacobites ever did was to have two rebellions on the go, 1689–91, and a third (in England) under discussion.[7]

Further to complicate matters, all parties to these internal jacobite negotiations agreed that they needed an infusion of regular troops to bolster the mobs of rebels they hoped would muster for the Stuart cause. The British army developed into a formidable opponent under William and Anne, and only French professional soldiers, the jacobites believed, could adequately protect the rebels while they trained and equipped to confront it. The French could also supply the money and *materiél* the rebels were certain to lack.[8] The problem was that the French government had its own agenda. Louis's key concern by the middle of the war was not whether a jacobite rebellion was well timed and viable, but whether it would disrupt the British war effort on the continent. He and his ministers were, accordingly, interested in achieving maximum dislocation for minimum investment in terms of military resources.[9] From the French point of view, if a rebellion succeeded and put the Stuarts back on the throne, that was wonderful; if it failed but seriously dislocated the allied war effort, that was almost as good. This was not, of course, acceptable as far as the jacobites resident in the three kingdoms were concerned, and thus the court had to play what was, in essence, a double game: promising the French what they wanted, and thus getting them on board, while

[5] *(continued)* Clarendon, by William A. Speck (accessed 15 Apr. 2007); *http://www.oxforddnb.com/view/article/9813?docPos=1*: Alexander Forbes, Lord Forbes of Pitsligo, by Murray G.H. Pittock (accessed 15 Apr. 2007).

[6] Daniel Szechi, 'The Image of the Court: Idealism, Politics and the Evolution of the Stuart Court, 1689–1730', in *The Stuart Court in Rome: The Legacy of Exile*, ed. Edward Corp (Aldershot, 2003), 49–64.

[7] Daniel Szechi, *The Jacobites: Britain and Europe 1688–1788* (Manchester, 1994), 41–50, 54–5.

[8] *Original Papers; Containing the Secret History of Great Britain, from the Restoration to the Accession of the House of Hanover*, ed. James Macpherson (2 vols, 1775), i, 464: Sir George Barclay's memorial to James II and VII, 28 Dec. 1693; Daniel Szechi, *1715: The Great Jacobite Rebellion* (2006), 82–5; Auburn University, Ralph Brown Draughon Library, microfilm Stuart Papers 257/55: [Charles Stuart to James, old pretender], [Gravelines] 22 May 1744 ns (I am grateful to Her Majesty The Queen for permission to cite from the Stuart Papers).

[9] *Original Papers*, ed. Macpherson, ii, 80: Colonel Nathaniel Hooke's instructions from Secretary at War Michel Chamillart, Feb. 1707. The same objective governed French involvement in previous invasion attempts as early as 1691, for which see, *Original Papers*, ed. Macpherson, i, 395: James II and VII to Louis XIV, c.Dec. 1691.

© *The Parliamentary History Yearbook Trust 2009*

reassuring the English, Scots and Irish parties that Louis XIV and his ministers were absolutely committed to jacobite success.[10]

None of the three national parties that dominated the internal politics of the movement had any kind of formal existence, or was ever publicly acknowledged as a political entity, yet the politics of the movement consistently revolved around the attitudes and responses of the 'English', 'Scots' and 'Irish' to the court's directions and initiatives. It must be emphasized that these parties never subsumed all the jacobites of their nationality and had no institutional existence at St Germain. They were also subject to the same kind of factional divisions as were to be found in the whig and tory parties, and hence, like their peers, the jacobite parties rarely acted in a wholly united fashion. They nonetheless had recognized groups of leaders who were accepted as representing a constituency in the British Isles and within the movement, and it was with these cliques of leading men – and occasionally women – that the jacobite court negotiated.[11] There was also a court interest, composed of deracinated servants of the jacobite shadow-state, which, like the court parties of the British Isles, acted as the agent of the monarchy and specifically sought to realize the exiled royal family's agenda within and without the movement. Like the court parties of the three kingdoms, too, the jacobite court interest was divided. Though Charles Middleton, earl of Middleton, was the dominant minister at the exiled court, the adherents of his ousted rival, John Drummond, earl of Melfort, continued throughout the period to intrigue against his hegemony in order to replace him with Melfort's brother, James Drummond, earl of Perth.[12] On occasion the court interest was also assailed by the national party leaders, who tended to see the courtiers as parasites and obstacles and were, accordingly, impatient with the organisation and procedures necessary to maintain a publicly credible government in exile.[13] To further complicate matters, there were also two alignments which episodically overlay the national parties in the same way as court and country did the parties in Westminster, Edinburgh and Dublin. These were the protestant and catholic axes. In the period under consideration here these only operated in the background, but occasionally they could move jacobites from more than one of the national parties briefly to unite in support of a particular confessional objective.[14]

Jacobitism was strongest in Ireland, where it probably had the support of the majority of the population, and it was powerful, too, in Scotland, where in the early 18th century the episcopal church (the bedrock of Scottish jacobitism) commanded the allegiance of

---

[10] *Original Papers*, ed. Macpherson, ii, 101–2: instructions for Charles Farquharson, St Germain, 25 Apr. 1708 ns; *Original Papers*, ed. Macpherson, ii, 102–3: memorandum for the French government re. Farquharson's instructions, Apr. 1708.

[11] Szechi, *Jacobitism and Tory Politics*, 20–5, 124–5, 158–9; Szechi, *George Lockhart*, 125–7; Eveline Cruickshanks, *Political Untouchables: The Tories and the '45* (1979), 38–51.

[12] George H. Jones, *The Mainstream of Jacobitism* (Cambridge, MA, 1954), 28–37; *Correspondence of Colonel N. Hooke, Agent from the Court of France to the Scottish Jacobites, in the Years 1703–7*, ed. W.D. Macray (2 vols, Roxburghe Club, 1870), i, 179: Colonel Nathaniel Hooke to Jean Baptiste Colbert de Croissy, marquis de Torcy, St Germain, 19 May 1705 ns; i, 236: Perth to Anne Drummond, countess of Erroll, 7 July 1705 ns; i, 256–7: Sir Adam Blair to Carron (copy), Paris, 20 June 1705 ns.

[13] Edward Corp with Edward Gregg, Howard Erskine-Hill and Geoffrey Scott, *A Court in Exile: The Stuarts in France, 1689–1718* (2004), 104–36, 180–214; Szechi, 'Image of the Court', 52, 57, 60; *Correspondence of Colonel N. Hooke*, ed. Macray, i, 63: 'Premier Memoire de Monsieur Leviston', 1704.

[14] See, e.g., Szechi, *Jacobitism and Tory Politics*, 20–4.

25%–30% of the Scottish people.[15] Yet, paradoxically, the English were, in essence, the default position within the jacobite cause; whenever the Scots or Irish parties could not offer specific hope of a restoration, it was to the English that the Stuarts turned.[16] This obviously stemmed from the plain fact that England was the largest, most populous and wealthiest of the three kingdoms. Control of England was thus the key to controlling the rest of the British Isles, and since, too, it would have to be reconquered at some point and in the hands of the Stuarts' enemies would make sustaining jacobite control of Scotland or Ireland very difficult, there was a clear advantage – at least theoretically – in tackling it first.[17]

The problem was that the movement was weakest in England. Indeed, up to 1714 – in other words, as long as the piously anglican Anne was on the throne – the jacobites' reliable constituency there was very small indeed, probably no more than 2%–3% of the population.[18] As long as the tories had Anne, very, very few of them were going to turn to James. The upshot of which is that the politics of the jacobite movement should have been relatively lightly, or not at all, influenced by the English party. What, after all, could they certainly deliver? The English party's power to shape the direction of jacobite politics, however, was not set by the number of men they could very likely raise in the event of an uprising, but by the golden promise of their potential power in England as a whole (where tories were probably the natural majority of the population into the mid 18th century) and the personal dynamics of the jacobite court.[19]

The court in exile was always subject to strong English cultural influence. From the outset, and despite his Scottish ancestry, James II and VII saw himself, and was seen by his subjects, as thoroughly English in his tastes, prejudices and sensibilities. He personally favoured English, or at least anglicised, servants and ministers, warned his son against dealing with the 'Macks and Os' of Ireland and even had his overwhelmingly Irish army in exile in France dressed in English livery and equipped with standards sporting the cross of St George.[20] Such strongly anglocentric inclinations were also reflected in the bent of his policies, and through his appointment of ministers and court officials was perpetuated into his son's reign over the jacobite movement.[21] James, the old pretender, was less obviously politically anglocentric, yet he was portrayed as plain English in his personal tastes by jacobite propaganda and when the time came to set up suitable arrangements for the care and education of his own son, Charles Edward, he went out

[15] Ó Ciardha, *Ireland and the Jacobite Cause, passim*; Murray Pittock, *The Myth of the Jacobite Clans* (Edinburgh, 1997), 47; Bruce Lenman, 'The Scottish Episcopal Clergy and the Ideology of Jacobitism', in *Ideology and Conspiracy*, ed. Cruickshanks, 36–48.

[16] Szechi, *Jacobites*, 54–6, 92–5, 105–6, 114–16.

[17] *Original Papers*, ed. Macpherson, i, 682: Macpherson's summary and extracts of a jacobite memorandum proposing an invasion [22 June 1704 ns]; Eveline Cruickshanks, 'Lord Cornbury, Bolingbroke and a Plan to Restore the Stuarts, 1731–1735', *Royal Stuart Papers*, xxvii (1986) 1–12; Zimmerman, *Jacobite Movement*, 62.

[18] Paul Kléber Monod, *Jacobitism and the English People, 1688–1788* (1989), 95–160, 270–1.

[19] Geoffrey Holmes, *British Politics in the Age of Anne* (1967, rev. edn 1987), 248.

[20] *The Life of James the Second, King of England, &c, Collected out of Memoirs Writ of his own Hand, Together with the King's Advice to his Son and his Majesty's Will*, ed. J.S. Clarke (2 vols, 1816), ii, 637; Ó Ciardha, *Ireland and the Jacobite Cause*, 259; Harman Murtagh, 'Irish Soldiers Abroad, 1600–1800', in *A Military History of Ireland*, ed. Thomas Bartlett and Keith Jeffery (Cambridge, 1996), 298.

[21] *Life of James the Second*, ed. Clarke, 608 n; Francis C. Turner, *James II* (1950), 467; *Correspondence of Colonel N. Hooke*, ed. Macray, i, 62: 'Premier memoire de Monsieur Leviston', 1704; i, 152: Hooke to M. de Callieres, Bruxelles, 27 May 1704; i, 195: Hooke to Torcy, St Germain, 10 June 1705 ns.

© *The Parliamentary History Yearbook Trust 2009*

of his way to arrange for the child to be looked after by English nursemaids, so he would learn English as his mother tongue and English ways as young as possible.[22] Allied with the lure of England's manifest economic superiority within the British Isles, this innate anglocentricity at the heart of the jacobite movement was more than enough to make the English party the natural – and naturally resented, as far as the Scots and Irish were concerned – party of government at the jacobite court and the predominant voice in jacobite politics.[23]

2

These internal political dynamics were to be of profound importance in shaping jacobite responses to political developments during the reign of Queen Anne. At the start of her reign the jacobite movement as a whole was virtually inert. The leading activists in England under William had been eliminated in the aftermath of the assassination plot of 1696, Ailesbury by exile and Sir John Fenwick by the headsman's axe, and the survivors of their networks sought to avoid harassment by ostentatiously reverting to passivity.[24] This withdrawal apparently became ingrained as time went on and the movement's prospects remained bleak. Thus at the time of the queen's accession the English jacobites were effectively leaderless. Individuals like John Sheffield, earl of Mulgrave, and Edward Villiers, earl of Jersey, quietly maintained a sympathetic connection to St Germain, and, in due course, returned exiles like James Radcliffe, earl of Derwentwater, became the foci of local jacobite connections in remote rural areas such as Northumberland, but there was no generally acknowledged leader and no evidence survives of any effort to tie together these loose strands to make a coherent, potentially activist, underground.[25] It is a token of the dearth of potential leaders that when the jacobite court secretly contacted one of the duumvirs, Sidney Godolphin, Lord (from 1706, earl of) Godolphin, managing English politics for the queen in 1702, to sound him out on prospects for the restoration of the main line (itself a demonstration – given his record of duplicity with respect to the jacobite cause – of the low ebb to which the movement had been reduced), they had to use the London apothecary James St Amand, a much humbler emissary than was appropriate.[26] More prominent English jacobites were apparently unable or unwilling to take on the task.

[22] Szechi, 'Image of the Court', 49–51; McLynn, *Charles Edward Stuart*, 9, 10, 12, 24, 31.

[23] *Correspondence of Colonel N. Hooke*, ed. Macray, i, 195: Hooke to Torcy, St Germain, 10 June 1705 ns; i, 236: Perth to the countess of Erroll, 7 July 1705 ns.

[24] Jones, *Mainstream of Jacobitism*, 54–5.

[25] http://www.oxforddnb.com/view/article/28289?docPos=1: Edward Villiers, earl of Jersey, by Stuart Handley (accessed 18 Apr. 2007); Edward Gregg, *Queen Anne* (1980), 335; http://www.oxforddnb.com/view/article/25297?docPos=6: John Sheffield, earl of Mulgrave (later duke of Buckingham and Normanby), by Margaret D. Sankey (accessed 18 Apr. 2007); *Original Papers*, ed. Macpherson, ii, 327–31: Buckingham to Middleton, 1/12 July 1712; http://www.oxforddnb.com/view/article/22983?docPos=2: James Radcliffe, earl of Derwentwater, by Leo Gooch (accessed 18 Apr. 2007).

[26] *Original Papers*, ed. Macpherson, i, 608: extracts of John Caryll, Lord Caryll's, letters to St Amand, 26, 29 Apr. 1702 ns; *The History of Parliament: The House of Commons 1660–1690*, ed. Basil D. Henning (3 vols, 1983), iii, 379–80. It should be noted that Godolphin's latest biographer, Roy Sundstrom, is sceptical concerning the evidence for Godolphin's contacts with the jacobites, for which see http://www.oxforddnb.com/view/article/10882?docPos=9&_fromAuth=1: Godolphin, Sidney, 1st earl of Godolphin (accessed 2 Feb. 2008), and Roy Sundstrome, *Sidney Godolphin, Servant of the State* (Newark, 1992).

Scottish jacobitism was in a similar state of hibernation.[27] The last serious jacobite plot had been suppressed in 1694, and the likeliest prospect as leader, James Hamilton, duke of Hamilton, had fled to England and only returned to Scotland in 1699. On his return he set his sights on winning the leadership of the country opposition to James Douglas, duke of Queensberry's, administration, and since many of the country group were presbyterian in sympathy, he was busily playing down his former jacobite connections at the time of Anne's accession.[28] Other former leaders of the Scottish party gave every appearance of being broken men. Colin Lindsay, earl of Balcarres, for example, acted the part of the subservient courtier to perfection after he was pardoned and allowed to return in 1700, and Sir John Maclean seemed to be interested in nothing more than living quietly at home when he first slipped back into the country.[29] Nor did the general situation in Scotland seem to favour any revival of jacobite activity. The jacobite heartland in the north-eastern lowlands and highlands was particularly hard-hit by the famine of the late 1690s, and because elite jacobites had been long out of office by 1702 and had suffered the most financially during the highland war, they were probably even less well placed to surmount the financial losses elite Scots in general suffered as a consequence of the Darien fiasco.[30]

In Ireland there was, *prima facie*, a great deal more jacobite activity. 'All that nation is as fire smothered under flax', Anne Drummond, countess of Erroll, hopefully observed in 1705.[31] The elite catholics who remained in the country after 1692 quietly favoured cultural jacobitism by disseminating hopeful news (true and false) supplied by the Irish diaspora and patronising harpers and poets who promulgated jacobite and catholic ideology. They also seem to have encouraged continued raparee activity, though the jacobite (as opposed to anti-protestant and anti-settler) motivation therein is not so clear. What is more certain is that as soon as war loomed in 1702 plebeian and elite interest in joining the mobilising Irish brigade produced a quiet surge of departures for the continent, probably, in part at least, motivated by pro-jacobite sympathies.[32] Yet this was not necessarily of direct benefit to the jacobite cause. The army of catholic Ireland overseas was not master of its own fate, and its powerful cultural presence tended to de-energise Irish jacobitism at home. It is easy to see why. The Irish brigade's eagerly reported martial accomplishments meant Irish jacobites actually resident in Ireland could remain emotionally and ideologically committed to the Stuart cause while safely staying on the margins of legality at home. The real leaders of Irish jacobitism became men like Arthur Dillon and other officers in the French service, and they were unavoidably removed from Ireland. Hence, ironically, Irish jacobitism proper was subtly deactivated. Ireland had also suffered worse than any of the other kingdoms in the course of the civil

---

[27] *Original Papers*, ed. Macpherson, i, 605: memorial by Henry Neville Paine [1701].

[28] Paul Hopkins, *Glencoe and the End of the Highland War* (rev. repr., Edinburgh, 1998), 372–3.

[29] Hopkins, *Glencoe*, 496–7; *http://www.oxforddnb.com/view/article/16687?docPos=4*: Colin Lindsay, earl of Balcarres, by Paul Hopkins (accessed 18 Apr. 2007).

[30] Ian D. Whyte, *Scotland Before the Industrial Revolution: An Economic and Social History c. 1050–c. 1750* (1995), 118, 124–5; Hopkins, *Glencoe*, 359, 414, 438–9; Christopher A. Whatley with Derek J. Patrick, *The Scots and the Union* (Edinburgh, 2006), 173.

[31] *Correspondence of Colonel N. Hooke*, ed. Macray, i, 307: countess of Erroll to Perth, 4 Sept. 1705.

[32] Ó Ciardha, *Ireland and the Jacobite Cause*, 89–98, 105–8, 114–15, 120–5, 137–9, 151–63.

© *The Parliamentary History Yearbook Trust 2009*

wars of 1689–91, and though it was soon on the road to economic and demographic recovery, memories of those years must have acted as something of a deterrent to jacobite adventurism.[33]

The court interest, too, was torpid in 1702. Retrenchment in 1695 had obliged James II and VII to cut expenditure at St Germain, and a significant number of courtiers, refugees and hangers-on associated with the jacobite court had found themselves in straitened circumstances as a result. Short-term expedients, such as selling royal jewelry, to which the court resorted after 1697 in an effort to alleviate the distress of demobilised Irish troops and their families, could not resolve the larger financial problem. Those who could took the opportunity vouchsafed by the peace to return to the British Isles, leaving behind a diminished court.[34] The remaining court officers and shadow-government ministers, who because jacobite activity was effectively at a stand in the three kingdoms were denied any other business than exalting the exiled royal family by their presence, effectively turned inward. The court's torpor was only broken by a brief renewal of the factional struggle between Melfort and Middleton. After being exiled from the court in the mid 1690s, Melfort had, by 1701, wheedled his way back close to St Germain. While intriguing there to regain his former eminence he wrote a letter to his brother, Perth, in which he mentioned invasion plans secretly being discussed with notable French courtiers (in particular Louis XIV's morganatic wife, Françoise, marquise de Maintenon), contacts with jacobites in the British Isles and other jacobite business. He then directed the letter to the English court, which a French post office official took to be Whitehall rather than St Germain. William III and II promptly had it published and the irate French government insisted Melfort be banished from the jacobite court forthwith, leaving Middleton once more reigning supreme.[35] Then James II and VII died, and the manner of his passing so moved Middleton that he converted to catholicism, effectively breaking a tacit covenant into which the old king had entered in 1693, that a protestant jacobite would be the exiled Stuarts' leading minister.[36] It was *de facto* a small political revolution at the jacobite court, and one that would create problems in the future, though not in the period under consideration here.[37]

3

In sum, the jacobite movement was inert at the turn of the century, and thus it is not surprising that it took external events – the onset of the War of Spanish Succession and the death of William III and II – to jolt it back into action. Even so, the court was still fixated on England in 1702 and its initial response to Anne's accession was simply to try

[33] L.M. Cullen, 'Economic Development, 1691–1750', in *A New History of Ireland, Volume IV: Eighteenth-Century Ireland*, ed. T.W. Moody and W.E. Vaughan (Oxford, 1986), 132–41.

[34] Corp *et al.*, *Court in Exile*, 118–19; Jones, *Mainstream of Jacobitism*, 54.

[35] Jones, *Mainstream of Jacobitism*, 59; Corp *et al.*, *Court in Exile*, 56–7.

[36] Jones, *Mainstream of Jacobitism*, 66–7; Szechi, 'Jacobite Revolution Settlement', 626, 628; http://www.oxforddnb.com/view/article/18665?docPos=1: Charles Middleton, earl of Middleton, by Edward Corp (accessed 20 Apr. 2007).

[37] Szechi, *Jacobitism and Tory Politics*, 22–3, 187.

and revive some of its old connections to English politicians now that certain of them – specifically Godolphin and John Churchill, earl, soon to be duke, of Marlborough – were at the pinnacle of power, Godolphin having been promoted to lord treasurer by the incoming queen, and Marlborough to captain-general of the army.[38] St Amand had approached Marlborough some time before William's death, and received, 'all imaginable assurances', that his appointment to office by the king on the eve of the War of Spanish Succession stemmed, 'merely from a view of being able, in the proper time and place, to pay the debt due to Mr Goodall [James II]'.[39] After Anne's accession the hope that Marlborough, Godolphin and Anne were all secretly committed to restoring James, the old pretender, encouraged the court to believe in the duumvirs' previous positive statements of support and yet accept that they could not immediately, 'expect any present dispatch of our domestick affairs'.[40] None the less, St Amand was directed to continue to try and draw Marlborough and Godolphin into tangible action in favour of James, though John Caryll, jacobite Lord Caryll and second secretary of state at St Germain, who was in charge of the negotiations, was reasonably realistic in his expectations of the best that might be achieved by them. As he admitted to St Amand it was not likely that James would recover his throne: 'as long as Young's [Queen Anne's] life is in the copyhold. To have [the succession] well secured, when that life falls, which probably may not be of a long continuance, is, I am afraid, all that can well be hoped for.'[41]

Our ability to discern what Marlborough and Godolphin were up to in their intermittant negotiations with the jacobites over the next eight years is considerably hampered by the fact that most of the correspondence on the subject is no longer extant. All that survives is on the jacobite side, and even there all but a few of the original letters from St Amand, and others from John Tunstal, Captain John Murray and Colonel Edward Sackville, reporting their meetings with the duumvirs, have been lost. Our knowledge of the intrigue thus comes primarily from extracts of Caryll's letters in reply to these agents, published by James Macpherson in the late 18th century, and the originals of these, too, have been lost. None the less, given what we know of the closeness of the relationship between Marlborough, Godolphin and Queen Anne at this time, and their joint involvement in jacobite conspiracy in the early 1690s, it seems highly likely that all three of them knew what was afoot and were collectively pursuing a common agenda. Following Edward Gregg's astute analysis of Queen Anne's role in British politics, we can further surmise with him that they were simply trying to neutralise any potential jacobite threat by supplying the jacobites with as many promises of future action as they wanted, while systematically working to safeguard the Hanoverian succession.[42] The key question from the point of view of an analysis of jacobite politics then becomes: at what point did the court recognize that it was being duped by the duumvirs?

The answer is almost inevitably complex. The contacts between St Amand and Marlborough and Godolphin were kept very secret, apparently at the two ministers'

[38] Gregg, *Queen Anne*, 83–4, 153, 157–8.

[39] *Original Papers*, ed. Macpherson, i, 588: 'Extract of a letter from Berry [St Amand], concerning Gourny [Marlborough]', June 1701.

[40] *Original Papers*, ed. Macpherson, i, 608: extract, Caryll to St Amand, 29 Apr. 1702 ns.

[41] *Original Papers*, ed. Macpherson, i, 610: extract, Caryll to Berry [St Amand], 23 Oct. 1702 ns.

[42] Gregg, *Queen Anne*, 83, 108, 149.

© *The Parliamentary History Yearbook Trust 2009*

request, so that only the most senior servants of the Stuart shadow-state and the French government were aware of them at the time.[43] And the exiled Stuart court was initially very cautious in its estimation of the value of the connection. 'Your cousin Wisely [Queen Mary of Modena] very much desires that you should again join in trade with Mr Young [Queen Anne] as you formerly have done, that a fair correspondence may be preserved with his partners Gurny [Marlborough] and Gilburn [Godolphin]', Caryll directed St Amand in April 1702, but his reasons for this, 'that so they may have no excuse should they not be just in their engagements when time and opportunity serves', hardly evince much trust in any of the parties on the English side.[44] The evidence indicates that Caryll, in fact, was sceptical from the outset, and certainly he was soon dismissive of the whole business,[45] as may be seen from his observation regarding a preposterous claim about the Scottish court party's role in defeating a bill to secure the Hanoverian succession in Scotland made by Marlborough in 1705:

> I confess it is very surprising to me, for very few men will lye only for lyeing's sake, but [only] for some profit or advantage. Now, considering the present flourishing condition of that merchant, and his creditors' want [of] means, more than ever, to go to law with him, it would be very strange if he should make such promises and protestations without any intention of performing them. On the other side, words are but wind when they are not followed by deeds, and when they clash, the one by the other, the man must be judged by his actions.[46]

But circumstances intermittently obliged Caryll, and St Germain as a political institution, to take the negotiations more seriously than he might otherwise have been inclined.

Principal amongst these was the fact that between 1702 and 1706, and 1708 and 1710, the jacobite court had no other prospects. The War of the Spanish Succession went badly for France almost from the very beginning, and the strain on its economy and society — which was hardly, if at all, recovered from the titanic effort marshalled during the War of the League of Augsbury — quickly began to tell.[47] The court party at St Germain tried whistling in the dark on the subject, for example, directing Simon Fraser, Lord Lovat, to tell the Scots jacobites in 1703 that they were sure Louis XIV would provide them with a suitable invasion force, 'when the conjuncture is favourable', but they well understood that there was little prospect of serious French support for an uprising.[48] As Caryll frankly admitted in 1706, the court had to continue negotiating with Marlborough and Godolphin because:

---

[43] *Original Papers*, ed. Macpherson, i, 609: extract, Caryll to Berry [St Amand, 6 May 1702 ns].

[44] *Original Papers*, ed. Macpherson, i, 608: extract, Caryll to St Amand, 26 Apr. 1702 ns.

[45] *Original Papers*, ed. Macpherson, i, 606, 610, 628–9: Caryll to St Amand, 20 Jan., 23 Oct., 4 Dec. 1702 and 9 Mar., 7 May 1703 ns.

[46] *Original Papers*, ed. Macpherson, i, 699: extract, Caryll to [St Amand?], 25 Apr. [1705 ns].

[47] John A. Lynn, *Giant of the Grand Siècle: The French Army, 1610–1715* (Cambridge, 1997), 8, 21, 25, 47, 55, 262, 350; François Bluche, *Louis XIV*, transl. Mark Greengrass (New York, 1990), 456–8, 526–32; Pierre Goubert, *Louis XIV and Twenty Million Frenchmen*, transl. Anne Carter (New York, 1970), 205–31, 247–60.

[48] *Original Papers*, ed. Macpherson, i, 631: instructions for Lovat, 5 May 1703 ns, but falsely dated 25 Feb. 1703; *Correspondence of Colonel N. Hooke*, ed. Macray, i, 68: 'Suitte du Memoir Concernant d'Ecosse' by M. Leviston [Feb. 1704].

Mr Manning's [Louis XIV's] affairs have gone so much backward of late that there is little hope of his being able to lay down the sum necessary to redeem the mortgage [provide an invasion force], so that we must necessarily make the best of the promises given, by those other merchants, which you know have been such as no honest man could make and not perform when able to do so.[49]

France's military crisis, moreover, steadily worsened, to the point that in April 1709 the jacobite court had to tell its adherents that, 'in the present conjuncture', Louis XIV considered, 'that it was absolutely impossible for him, at this time, to furnish all that was necessary for such an expedition.'[50] For most of the period 1702–10 the court party was accordingly left with nothing more to do than communicate hopefully with the English, Scots and Irish jacobites and continue its empty negotiations with the duumvirs, who duly squeezed the last drop of political advantage out of their duplicitous game. The absolute prize in this area has to go to Marlborough, who shamelessly continued to assure jacobite and French emissaries (including Louis XIV's secretary of state Jean-Baptiste Colbert de Croissy, marquis de Torcy) of how he had been willing to shed, 'the last drop of his blood', for James II and VII, and of his, 'strong desire of being in a capacity to serve' James clear through to the end of the Gertruydenburg peace conference in the summer of 1709.[51] As we have seen, though, Caryll evinced a great deal of scepticism regarding such manifest claptrap from early on in the 'negotiations', and the jacobite court decisively indicated it had no confidence at all in the duumvirs' *bona fides* in mid 1704. Up until then, Middleton had been exuding caution with respect to a military initiative designed to exploit Scotland's political crisis, and though this may, in part, have been owing to his distaste for, and distrust of, the key proponent of such an initiative, Lovat, it may also have stemmed from lingering hopes of the duumvirs.[52] In June 1704, however, St Germain formally requested that France consider an invasion of Scotland, adding its weight to appeals by the Scots jacobites and the arguments advanced on the military side by Colonel Nathaniel Hooke, a French-naturalised Irishman.[53]

Unfortunately for the jacobite court, correctly gauging the emptiness of Marlborough and Godolphin's promises did little to advance the cause of the exiled Stuarts. Indeed, the only positive political achievement during these bleak years was the re-establishment of more regular contact, and better relations, with jacobites operating within conventional politics. After having been a major focus of the court party's efforts in the mid 1690s, attempts to negotiate a parliamentary restoration through the good offices of English jacobite MPs and peers had effectively lapsed after the assassination plot and the

---

[49] *Original Papers*, ed. Macpherson, ii, 4: extract, Caryll to [St Amand?], 28 June [1706 ns].

[50] *Original Papers*, ed. Macpherson, ii, 121: draught answer to the Scots jacobites, Apr. 1709.

[51] *Original Papers*, ed. Macpherson, ii, 126 n: Macpherson's extracts from Torcy's memoirs; see also, *Original Papers*, ed. Macpherson, i, 672, 674: extract, Caryll to ?, 26 Apr., 12 May [1704 ns]; ii, 129: extract, Caryll to ?, 13 June [1709 ns].

[52] *Correspondence of Colonel N. Hooke*, ed. Macray, i, 20, 38, 39, 59.

[53] Bodl., Carte 180, f. 103r–7v: memorandum to Torcy advocating an invasion, St Germain, 22 June 1704 ns; *Correspondence of Colonel N. Hooke*, ed. Macray, i, 21–39: [memorandum on Scotland by Hooke] read to Louis XIV's royal council 10 Dec. 1703 ns; i, 48–59: 'Memoire Sommaire sur les Affaires d'Ecosse', 2 Feb. 1704 ns.

peace of Ryswick.[54] At the prompting of the English nonjurors, James renewed his father's promises of protection for the Church of England and his guarantees of submission to the will of a free parliament, and even added fresh concessions with regard to the appointment of bishops. This was, however, effectively singing to an empty theatre.[55] As is well known, the English tories, within whose ranks the great majority of English jacobites had their home, were beginning to experience some unease at the prospect of the Hanoverian succession, but it was very muted at this time. The queen was in no worse health than she had been since the 1690s, and the Electress Sophia's pro-tory inclinations more than compensated for her son George's less approachable, military *mien*.[56] Correspondingly, in England the best the court could do was vaguely to encourage its agents to, 'act in conjunction with his friend Mr Kensy [tories] towards bringing about Wheatly [Queen Anne] and Mathews [James] trading together in the common stock'.[57] More promising by far was the revitalisation of the court party's connections to Scots jacobite politicians.

These had greatly increased in number since the general election of 1702. Though still a minority in parliament, most of the 'cavaliers', as they were known, were associated with the country coalition that effectively destroyed what little prospect of English-oriented managerial stability remained in Scottish politics between 1703 and 1705.[58] In the process, Hamilton both pushed himself to the fore of Scottish politics, and specifically sought to construct a strong connection with St Germain. He was probably looking to consolidate his hold on the jacobite wing of the Scots country coalition, and, if he could, coax some funds out of the exiled court or its French patron to relieve his straitened finances (he was always refreshingly open about what he intended to do with any money they sent him).[59] In any event, regardless of his motives, Hamilton's encouragement of St Germain's involvement in Scottish politics had a considerable long-term impact. The court, which had neglected Scottish affairs for some time, now began to send agents and emissaries to Scotland on an irregular, but much more frequent, basis.[60] The Scots jacobites also sent over several emissaries of their own.[61] Most of this exchange occurred

[54] *Original Papers*, ed. Macpherson, ii, 572, 578.

[55] *Original Papers*, ed. Macpherson, i, 606–7: 'Copy of his Majesty's Instructions sent into England', 3 Mar. 1702 ns.

[56] Holmes, *British Politics*, 87–8, 90, 95, 188, 194; Ragnhild Hatton, *George I: Elector and King* (1978), 170–3; Gregg, *Queen Anne*, 83, 209–10.

[57] *Original Papers*, ed. Macpherson, i, 683: extract, Caryll to [St Amand?], 1 July [1704 ns].

[58] P.W.J. Riley, *The Union of England and Scotland: A Study in Anglo-Scottish Politics in the Eighteenth Century* (Manchester, 1978), 52–150; Szechi, *Lockhart of Carnwath*, 49–60.

[59] *Original Papers*, ed. Macpherson, i, 667: Captain James Murray's report to Queen Mary as passed on to Torcy, 22 Feb. 1704 ns; Scots Catholic Archives, Blairs Letters 2/83/4, 7: Father James Carnegy to [Father Lewis Innes?], 15 June, 15 July 1703.

[60] *Original Papers*, ed. Macpherson, i, 605: memorial by Henry Neville Paine [1701]; *Original Papers*, ed. Macpherson, i, 626–7: draught instructions and further instructions for Captain James Murray, 1703; *Original Papers*, ed. Macpherson, i, 630: instructions for Captain John Murray, 5 May 1703 ns; *Original Papers*, ed. Macpherson, i, 673–4: memorandum on Carron, a jacobite courier to Scotland, for the French government, St Germain, 6 May 1704 ns; Blairs Letters 2/93/16: Carnegy to [Lewis Innes?], 8 July 1704; *Original Papers*, ed. Macpherson, i, 697–9: letter from Scots jacobites, brought by Carron, 23 Mar. 1705.

[61] *Correspondence of Colonel N. Hooke*, ed. Macray, ii, 31–9: memorandum by Charles Fleming for Queen Mary, Feb. 1706; ii, 88: Memoire sur l'etat present de l'Ecosse donné à M. de Torcy et à M. le Mareschal de Noailles, 7 Dec. 1706 ns; ii, 302: list of suitable jacobite commanders by James Ogilvy of Boyne jr, 21 May/2 June 1707.

in the context of negotiations for a Franco-jacobite invasion, yet the fact that the court party communicated with the Scots jacobites so diligently was of great long-term significance. Though there was something of a hiatus between 1708 and 1710, the Scots jacobites' importance within the movement more and more transcended the success or failure of the military projects.[62] The fact that there were enough of them within licit politics to have a political impact in the Scottish and then British parliament gave the court an option it had not had for some time: manoeuvring within conventional Scottish and British politics. And though the court party ultimately never made effective use of this option (indeed, this was to become a major source of friction between the Scots jacobites and St Germain), the fact that it existed at all enhanced the status of the Scots who were at the core of the parliamentary group between 1708 and 1714.[63] It is no coincidence that the first salaried jacobite agent whose remit specifically covered liaising with MPs and peers in the British parliament, the Scotsman John Menzies, was appointed in December 1709.[64]

More frequent contacts with, and renewed interest in, the Scots jacobites in the years 1702–8 were also bound to lead to a revival of the exiled court's hopes of a military option. As the succession issue progressively polarised political opinion in Scotland, and the Scots court party began to push towards an incorporating union with England as a means of resolving the crisis, the likelihood of violent resistance to the government in Scotland steadily grew.[65] And in the event that there was an anti-union uprising, the Scots jacobites and St Germain hoped they could steer events to the exiled dynasty's advantage. The court, none the less, took a pragmatic, dual track approach, urging its Scots friends in 1703, 'to use all their credit in opposing abjuration, Hannover and union', while at the same time assuring them, 'our friends on this side are resolved to give us what assistance shall be demanded for our immediate restoration', though they also admitted that the French, 'are not willing to venture in matters that are not decisive, and, at best, can but procure delays'.[66] The key problem with a Scots jacobite uprising was that the jacobite court and many of the Scots jacobites themselves were not optimistic about Scotland's prospects of defeating the military forces available to Queen Anne's government in England.[67] It was clearly, however, something the court needed to explore (to maintain its own credibility if nothing else) and one of its emissaries sent to sound out the Scots jacobites on the matter, Captain James Murray, was instructed to persuade them to come up with a concrete proposal for a rising.[68] At the same time, though, the court party made one of its most egregious missteps of the period: it extended its trust to Lovat and made him one of the emissaries sent to sound out the Scots.

[62] Szechi, *Lockhart of Carnwath*, 76–9.

[63] Szechi, *Jacobitism and Tory Politics*, 75–7, 81–2, 93–4, 102–3, 124–6, 157–61.

[64] *Original Papers*, ed. Macpherson, ii, 134: David Nairne to Menzies, 26 Dec. 1709 ns.

[65] Whatley, *Scots and the Union*, 209–14, 225–32; *Correspondence of Colonel N. Hooke*, ed. Macray, i, 39–40: Sir Alexander Maclean to Hooke, 2 Dec. 1703 ns.

[66] *Original Papers*, ed. Macpherson, i, 626: draught instructions and further instructions for Captain James Murray, 1703.

[67] *Original Papers*, ed. Macpherson, i, 626: draught instructions and further instructions for Captain James Murray, 1703; *Correspondence of Colonel N. Hooke*, ed. Macray, i, 292–3: Alexander Rose, bishop of Edinburgh, to Queen Mary, 23 Aug. 1705.

[68] *Original Papers*, ed. Macpherson, i, 626: draught instructions and further instructions for Captain James Murray, 1703.

© *The Parliamentary History Yearbook Trust 2009*

By 1703 Lovat had a well-founded reputation for vaulting ambition and complete unscrupulousness in pursuit of his goals.[69] And, true to form, as soon as he was back in Scotland he began plotting with his old friend Archibald Campbell, duke of Argyll, and, through him, with James Douglas, duke of Queensberry and head of the beleaguered administration in Scotland. The exact content of Lovat's negotiations are obscure, but the indications are that he essentially promised to deliver evidence of Hamilton and Atholl's involvement in jacobite plotting, plus, doubtless, as many lesser actors as he could entrap, to the government, who would in return secure him a pardon for his various crimes and provide other, probably pecuniary, rewards.[70] Lovat was so convinced of his own cleverness, however, that he barely bothered to conceal his double-dealing, and wrote a vainglorious report for the jacobite court and its French ally that reeked of duplicity.[71] Denunciations of him as a traitor to the cause were also streaming in from Scotland, and Middleton seized the opportunity and delated him as a double agent to Torcy.[72] Torcy was convinced, and the protesting Lovat was duly imprisoned, first in the Bastille and later, more comfortably, at Saumur.

What is truly amazing about the whole sordid episode is not that it occurred – all secret and underground organisations are vulnerable to infiltration by charming, plausible villains – but that it did not put the Scots jacobites off further conspiracy with the jacobite court party for some considerable time. Indeed, the fact that their continued efforts to negotiate a military option for themselves in the event the union passed into law scarcely missed a beat may be taken as a token of their determination to resist/ exploit the potential demise of the Scottish polity.[73] They were not about to rush into anything, as can been seen from their insistence that: 'nothing should be undertaken but upon good foundation and after matters were properly concerted and all the necessary measures taken for procuring success', and their inclination to, 'put it off until they saw what turn affairs would take in Parliament'.[74] None the less, encouraged by assurances from Scottish politicians like William Keith, Earl Marischal, that, 'the king's friends augment in number daily, and desire, with impatience, to have an opportunity to give proofs of their loyalty', the court felt confident enough in June 1704 formally to ask the French government to consider an invasion attempt.[75]

It is a measure of how ingrained the assumption that England was the only worth-while target for an invasion had become, even in jacobite politics, that both the Scots and

---

[69] *http://www.oxforddnb.com/view/article/10122?docPos=3*: Simon Fraser, Lord Lovat, by Edward M. Furgol (accessed 21 Apr. 2007).

[70] Hopkins, *Glencoe*, 474; *'Scotland's Ruine': Lockhart of Carnwath's Memoirs of the Union*, ed. Daniel Szechi (Aberdeen, 1995), 49–54.

[71] *Original Papers*, ed. Macpherson, i, 641–50: Lovat's account of his visit to Scotland, Jan. 1704.

[72] *Original Papers*, ed. Macpherson, i, 652–3: Middleton to Torcy, Paris, 16 Jan. 1704 ns; i, 656–62: remarks on Lovat's answers to questions concerning his account [Feb. 1704]; i, 662–5: Captain James Murray's account of Lovat's dealings, 15 Feb. 1704 ns; i, 669–70: extract of letter, Ailesbury to Father Francis, Sanders, Liege, 25 Feb. 1704 ns; i. 671–2: Father Lawrence Farrel to James Fitzjames, duke of Berwick, Apr. 1704.

[73] *Original Papers*, ed. Macpherson, i, 679: account of Captain John Murray, 30 May 1704 ns.

[74] *Original Papers*, ed. Macpherson, i, 668: Captain James Murray's report to Queen Mary as passed on to Torcy, 22 Feb. 1704 ns; *Original Papers*, ed. Macpherson, i, 678: account of Captain John Murray, 30 May 1704 ns.

[75] *Original Papers*, ed. Macpherson, i, 681: Marischal to Queen Mary, 8 Mar. 1704; Carte 180, f. 103r–7v: memorandum to Torcy advocating an invasion, St Germain, 22 June 1704 ns.

© *The Parliamentary History Yearbook Trust 2009*

the court party were still drawn to making it a centrepiece of their thinking on the subject. The Scots jacobites, for example, specifically asked that any rising by them be, 'well concerted with the friends of his Britannic Majesty in England'.[76] In the same vein, the court party's invasion proposal begins by stressing that a small investment of force by France (5,000 men) could set Scotland ablaze, but then immediately advocates a commitment of 20,000 men to an invasion of England. Only there, argues Middleton, would an invasion be, 'speedy and decisive'. In addition, success in England, he contends, will, 'soon draw the other two kingdoms after it'.[77] This despite the manifest unwillingness of the English jacobites to act against Queen Anne. In any event, the beleaguered French state was not in a condition to whip up an invasion (especially a very large one such as St Germain was suggesting), and the disastrous defeat at Blenheim in August 1704 further limited France's military options in the short term. In the long term, though, the course of military events was steadily putting Louis XIV and his ministers in a position where they would be obliged to try desperate measures. The break came almost a year later in the summer of 1705 as Marlborough drove back France's armies in Flanders preparatory to forcing the lines of Brabant.[78] Rightly apprehensive that matters were not likely to go well in the main theatre of the war, the decision was taken to explore other options. Yet the French ministers were still very cautious and were not prepared to take the jacobites at their word. Instead, Hooke was despatched to the British Isles to assess the situation in June 1705 and finally reached Scotland in mid July.[79]

Hooke returned to France within three months and in October presented his report to the French king and his council. From the point of view of internal jacobite politics, the key aspect of his account of the situation in the British Isles is the clear movement of Scottish jacobite opinion since 1702. By late 1705 the Scots were both so confident of their support at home and so alarmed at the gathering prospect of an incorporating union that they were, for the first time, willing to contemplate rising without English concurrence or support.[80] They still insisted on their reinforcement by a body of French troops, who were to bring with them a substantial quantity of money, arms and equipment, but by this willingness to go it alone within the British Isles they changed the dynamics of the jacobite political scene in two critical respects. The first of these related to the movement as a whole: the Scots now became the dominant party in terms of the movement's outlook and orientation. For the next decade the court party would look on the Scots as the principal grouping within the movement. Indeed, as Middleton observed, Scotland was from 1705, '*l'unique ressource qui reste pour le Roy d'Angleterre*'.[81] This is not to say they neglected or abandoned the English jacobites, simply that the

---

[76] *Original Papers*, ed. Macpherson, i, 668: Captain James Murray's report to Queen Mary as passed on to Torcy, 22 Feb. 1704 ns.

[77] *Original Papers*, ed. Macpherson, i, 682: Macpherson's summary and extracts of the jacobite proposal for an invasion [22 June 1704 ns].

[78] David Chandler, *Marlborough as Military Commander* (2nd edn, 1979), 153–62.

[79] John Sibbald Gibson, *Playing the Jacobite Card: The Franco-Jacobite Invasion of 1708* (Edinburgh, 1988), 11–18, 35–65.

[80] *Correspondence of Colonel N. Hooke*, ed. Macray, i, 419, 421, 427–8: Hooke's account of his negotiations, 17 Oct. 1705 ns.

[81] *Correspondence of Colonel N. Hooke*, ed. Macray, i, 197: Hooke to Torcy, St Germain, 10 June 1705 ns; *Diary of Mary Countess Cowper, Lady of the Bedchamber to the Princess of Wales 1714–1720* (1864), 83.

English stepped down in the hierarchy of influence and consideration.[82] The second flowed from the first in that the Scots' willingness to contemplate a solo rebellion meant the court party now had something concrete and practical (rather than airy promises of a grand jacobite rising across the entire British Isles) to offer the French.

St Germain worked its new tool with due diligence over the next two years despite the ebb and flow of official French interest. The basic problem for the jacobite court was that when France was in really serious military trouble, as after the battles of Ramillies and Turin in 1706, Louis and his ministers had no resources to spare for jacobite adventures, and when they were not in such a dire predicament, as in 1707, they tended to be cautious about daring initiatives.[83] Certain French institutions, in particular the navy, were also fundamentally opposed to an invasion of the British Isles because it was bound to commit their overstretched and under-resourced arm of the military to delivering a French force to Scotland, and then supplying it and its Scots jacobite allies in the teeth of the greatly superior naval forces that would be deployed by the maritime powers.[84] The jacobite court, therefore, had to build up a convincing case for a French intervention that would turn the balance of opinion in Louis XIV's councils at a suitably propitious moment. The Scots supported this effort by periodically sending over emissaries who delivered positive accounts of the situation in the country, such as that brought over by Captain Harry Straton in 1706, which concluded in characteristically upbeat fashion:

> I am fully persuaded that the greatest part of the nation is well affected to your Majesty's interest. And I know none that are ill affected but that pernicious, rebellious crew, the presbyterian ministers, and such as are entirely under their direction and influence, which are, for the most part, the common people. For in the western and most Whiggish shires a great many of the chief gentry are well affected, and (as I am informed by the Viscount of Kenmure) those in Galloway, commonly called Cameronians, are generally for your Majesty, and every body knows that all the northern shires, nobility, gentry, and commons, are well affected.[85]

And this finally bore fruit early in 1707, when Michel Chamillart, first secretary to Louis XIV with responsibility for war, was directed to reassess the situation in Scotland with a view to an invasion attempt that would make, 'a diversion in Scotland which will embarrass the English and oblige them to bring back a considerable body of troops to England'.[86] Typically, Chamillart, who like many of Louis's ministers was contemptuous

---

[82] *Correspondence of Colonel N. Hooke*, ed. Macray, i, 190–2: Hooke to Torcy, St Germain, 5 June 1705 ns; Szechi, *1715*, 79–97.

[83] Gibson, *Jacobite Card*, 65, 87.

[84] *Correspondence of Colonel N. Hooke*, ed. Macray, i, 199: Carron to Perth, Dunkirk, 12 June 1705 ns; Claude de Forbin, Comte de Forbin, *Memoirs of the Count de Forbin, Commodore in the Navy of France: and Knight of the Order of St Louis* (2 vols, 1731), ii, 258–62, 265, 267, 269, 272, 281–6.

[85] *Original Papers*, ed. Macpherson, ii, 20: Scot's [Straton's] account of the state of Scot[lan]d, c. July 1706.

[86] *Original Papers*, ed. Macpherson, ii, 80: Hooke's instructions from Chamillart, Feb. 1707. France's military predicament had made the possibility of a Scots revolt diverting English military assets and weakening the Grand Alliance strategically attractive since at least 1704, hence the prominence given to such arguments in memoranda arguing for French support for such an uprising: *Correspondence of Colonel N. Hooke*, ed. Macray, i, 58: 'Memoire Sommaire sur les Affaires d'Ecosse', 2 Feb. 1704 ns.

of the jacobites,[87] insisted on Hooke returning to Scotland to provide independent verification of the readiness of the Scots to rise, which St Germain found irksome after all the information they had carefully fed Louis XIV and his council over the previous three years. None the less, the court swallowed its pride and when Chamillart tried to procrastinate on the grounds that the jacobite court was being obstructive, Middleton outmanoeuvred him by writing an open letter to Hooke, in French so it could be shown to Torcy, assuring him that Queen Mary only, 'imagined it would be sufficient to show the inutility of your journey, without opposing it formally lest they should accuse her of breaking of the project, and of chusing to conceal the state of that country, which is very far from being her intentions'.[88] Even so, St Germain made it very clear that it would not be party to setting off a rising the French had no intention of supporting with regular troops, and insisted that the French make explicit commitments to back the Scots jacobites.[89]

Hooke dutifully went to Scotland in early 1707 and on his return that summer basically confirmed everything the Scots jacobites had been telling Louis and his ministers.[90] Middleton promptly seized on this to pitch a Scots jacobite rising as a strategic golden opportunity for France, one certain to dislocate the English war effort as badly as the Hungarian uprising had the Habsburgs and the Camisards Louis's own plans. 'If a small part of the money and of the troops which are employed here would finish the business there', he argued, 'it would be wrong to hesitate, and what would be formerly prudent and glorious becomes now absolutely necessary.'[91] A couple of French military successes in Spain and Germany, however, had by then removed some of the urgency behind the Hooke mission, and the invasion proposal might once again have languished, but for an appeal by Queen Mary to Louis's wife, Madame de Maintenon, who herself then intervened to wring a commitment to the venture out of Louis.[92]

The actual fate of the abortive 1708 invasion attempt is not relevant to this article except insofar as it affected the contours of jacobite politics, and what is striking about it in that context is that its failure made no difference at all. The Scots jacobites maintained their ascendancy within the jacobite movement, as may be seen from their continuing to be the focus of jacobite planning and negotiations with the French government. Shrinking at nothing to get what the jacobite court party so desperately wanted, Middleton forthrightly told Louis and his ministers in April 1708 that, 'it is evident that it is the interest of his Majesty, as well as of the King of England [James], to do every thing that is possible for fomenting a civil war in Scotland'.[93] Only in April 1709 did the jacobite court finally admit to the Scots that there was no immediate prospect of another attempt, and directed them to, 'take their measures to preserve themselves to a more favourable time'.[94]

---

[87] Corp *et al.*, *Court in Exile*, 11–75.

[88] *Original Papers*, ed. Macpherson, ii, 78: Middleton to Hooke, 13 Feb. 1707 ns.

[89] *Original Papers*, ed. Macpherson, ii, 77, 78: Middleton to Chamillart, 11, 13 Feb. 1707 ns.

[90] *Correspondence of Colonel N. Hooke*, ed. Macray, ii, 347–410, *passim*.

[91] *Original Papers*, ed. Macpherson, ii, 87: Middleton to Chamillart, 27 July 1707 ns.

[92] Gibson, *Jacobite Card*, 19, 104.

[93] *Original Papers*, ed. Macpherson, ii, 102: memorandum for the French government re. Charles Farquharson's instructions for his mission to Scotland, Apr. 1708.

[94] *Original Papers*, ed. Macpherson, ii, 121: draught answer to the Scots jacobites, Apr. 1709.

© *The Parliamentary History Yearbook Trust 2009*

4

The period 1702–14 was a formative one for the jacobite movement. In essence, the anglocentric strategy which had dominated the court's thinking since 1691 was eclipsed by the possibilities arising in Scotland, and the turn to the Scots jacobites which followed transformed its politics. Tired, empty promises of eventual action by senior English politicians (quite possibly acting with the full knowledge and encouragement of Queen Anne) simply could not compete with the actual political clout and potential military opportunity offered by the Scots. As a result, a Scots-driven agenda increasingly took hold within the movement. Despite the fact that most English politicians, including the jacobites among them, soon saw the union as something to England's advantage, the court became explicitly, publicly committed to its termination.[95] Despite the manifest unwillingness of the English jacobites to act against Queen Anne, the court abetted the Scots jacobites' efforts to bring on a fully-fledged rebellion against her. This Scots ascendancy within the movement was to last until the '15, and because of the influx of Scottish jacobite refugees into the administrative structures of the jacobite court as a direct result of that disaster the Scots agenda continued to be in the forefront of jacobite planning thereafter. This is not to say that the Scots jacobites' objectives always trumped those of the English jacobites, which they certainly did not during the Atterbury plot or the tory conspiracy of 1743–4, but rather that henceforth the Scots got far more equal consideration than they had during the 1690s. They became partners rather than subordinates in the jacobite enterprise. It was a bitter irony that the Scots thereby set themselves up to be the perennial losers by their commitment. In every rising that was to follow, the English were supposed to come out alongside their Scots peers, and on each occasion the English flinched and the Scots delivered. All the reward they received was to have the jacobite cause almost wholly identified with Scotland by posterity. Which, for all its value in terms of the heritage industry, was a very poor return on their investment.

[95] Szechi, *Jacobitism and Tory Politics*, 18, 24, 125, 129–31; *The Lockhart Papers*, ed. Anthony Aufrere (2 vols, 1817), i, 426–7; Szechi, *1715*, 81.

Uncovering a Jacobite Whig? The Commonwealth Principles of Henry Booth, 1st Earl of Warrington

MARK KNIGHTS

This article offers new evidence about Henry Booth, 2nd Lord Delamere and then 1st earl of Warrington. It focuses on (and reproduces) a manuscript in which an archetypal true whig, who was publicly hostile to James II in and after 1688, suggests how the whigs and James might be reconciled and how James might return to England. The article places the piece in the context of Warrington's other writings, his sense of betrayal and lost opportunity, the extent to which he agreed with 'whig jacobites' and Warrington's commonwealth principles. It finishes by linking this to the legacy left by Geoffrey Holmes and relating it to some recent research on the state and officeholding.

Keywords: jacobite; whig; revolution of 1689; commonwealth; the earl of Warrington; Geoffrey Holmes; James II; William III; declaration

This article offers new evidence that prompts a re-evaluation of one rather intriguing individual, Henry Booth, 2nd Lord Delamere and then 1st earl of Warrington. It is perhaps the type of material that would have intrigued Geoffrey Holmes who, from all accounts, would have derived pleasure from a quirky and surprising source that adds another small piece to our jigsaw of knowledge about the period. Having unveiled a jacobite text by this fiercest of whigs, I want then to use the case-study to sketch a few ways in which it might be possible to build on the important legacy left to us by the work of Geoffrey Holmes.

Geoffrey Holmes described Henry Booth, Lord Delamere and 1st earl of Warrington, as a 'puritan' and as a 'fiery' and 'radical' whig.[1] On the face of it there seems very little reason to disagree with this assessment. Warrington's credentials as a true whig, and even as a hero of the revolution, seem impeccable. As an MP from 1678 he had shown himself an ardent critic of popery and arbitrary government, and had supported the exclusion of James, duke of York. He had been arrested in 1683, on the discovery of the Rye House Plot, and again in 1685, for suspected complicity in Monmouth's rebellion. Early in 1686 his show trial had become a *cause célèbre* and, sharpened in his hostility to James, he had been one of the most active peers at the revolution in 1688, arming his tenants and marching them south from Cheshire to meet William's troops. He had been vigorous in his support for the transfer of the crown to the prince and, as Clarendon recorded in his diary for 31 January 1689, said: 'it was long since he thought himself absolved from his

---

[1] Geoffrey Holmes, *The Making of a Great Power: Late Stuart and Early Georgian Britain 1660–1722* (1993), 150, 184, 216.

© *The Parliamentary History Yearbook Trust 2009*

allegiance to King James; that he owed him none and never would pay him any; and if King James came again, he was resolved to fight against him, and would die single, with his sword in his hand, rather than pay him any obedience'.[2] Temporarily rewarded with membership of the privy council and the post of chancellor of the exchequer, his firebrand style of whig politics had nevertheless sat uneasily with William's attempt to construct a mixed ministry and in 1690 he had been removed from the exchequer, compensated only with an earldom. He continued to articulate true whig principles in the charges he gave to grand juries (many of which were published) and in 1691 he served as mayor of Chester, using his position to lambast those who had complied with the later Stuart subversion of the corporation's liberties. Although he abandoned the presbyterianism of his father for full conformity with the Church of England, Warrington voiced puritan concerns throughout his career – about vice and immorality and about the persecution of dissenters by high church 'ceremony-mongers'.[3] And his image as a puritan, old whig seemed confirmed and immortalised by his collected writings which were posthumously published in 1694. The printed *Works* reveal a man of piety and principle, of unswerving opposition to James both before and after he acceded to the throne, and of adherence to commonwealth principles.

So in what sense is Warrington a surprising or even significant figure?

The picture of Warrington as the puritan and steadfast whig that I have just outlined is largely the result of our dependence on the printed record he left behind, and on his collected *Works* in particular.[4] This is not surprising, since his personal papers do not appear to have survived in any great number, perhaps because of his rather cavalier approach to record-keeping: at his death he left 'in a corner of his closet a large old Deal Box . . . full of old useless dusty papers confusedly tumbled together, it being his common practice, when he found no further use for a paper, to throw it carelessly away, without further thought of it, or considering whether needfull to destroy it'.[5] Very little of that box's contents is among the family papers in the John Rylands Library in

---

[2] *The Correspondence of Henry Hyde, Earl of Clarendon, and of his Brother Lawrence Hyde, Earl of Rochester,* ed. S.W. Singer (2 vols, 1828), ii, 257.

[3] *The Works of the Right Honourable Henry, Late L. Delamer and Earl of Warrington Containing His Lordships Advice to his Children, Several Speeches in Parliament, &c* (1694), 462. In 1682 Booth told the grand jury that protestant dissenters were 'in a direct way to heaven, though they do not use the ceremonies commanded by the Church . . . It's the heart God regards.' He urged moderation and suggested that the law of 35 Elizabeth should not be enforced: *Works,* 412; C[alendar of] S[tate] P[apers] D[omestic] *1682,* 456–7, 457–8. The church hierarchy, Booth believed, contended so much for ceremonies in order to safeguard their own position, for if they allowed pious men into the church 'their sloath and neglect of their cures would be layed open': *Works,* 461. Yet Warrington 'kept constant' to the Church of England after the Toleration Act; 'religiously observed' every 14 January, the day of his acquittal in 1686, but had 'love and charity for all protestants'; and was zealous against popery: Richard Wroe, *A Sermon at the Funeral of the Right Honourable Henry, Earl of Warrington* (1694), 20–1, 25.

[4] See also, *The Speech of the Honourable Henry Booth, Esq* (1681); *The Late Lord Russel's Case with Observations upon it* (1689); *The Speech of the Right Honourable Henry Earl of Warrington, Lord Delamere, to the Grand Jury at Chester, April 13, 1692* (1692); *An Impartial Enquiry into the Causes of the Present Fears and Dangers of the Government* (1692); *The Charge of the Right Honourable Henry Earl of Warrington to the Grand Jury at the Quarter Sessions held for the County of Chester on the 11th of October, 1692* (1693); *The Charge of the Right Honourable Henry Earl of Warrington to the Grand Jury at the Quarter Sessions held for the County of Chester on the 25th day of April, 1693* (1693); *A Collection of Speeches of the Right Honourable Henry, Late Earl of Warrington* (1694).

[5] Manchester University, John Rylands Library, EGR3/6/2/1/11: George Booth's thoughts concerning his father's will. I am very grateful to the archivist there for providing me with a copy of the catalogue.

Manchester. Perhaps the editor of *Works* had been given the unenviable task of sorting them and never returned them. Certainly *Works* claimed on its title page to be from 'Original Manuscripts Written with His Lordships own Hand'. The dedication was written by John de la Heuze, the French Huguenot exile whom Booth appointed as tutor to his son and who thus probably selected the pieces for publication.[6] He chose pieces out of Warrington's 'Golden Remains' for their instructional value: 'I have fitted you with the Master I look't for and whom you wanted', he told the young 2nd earl. Clearly the intention of the publication was to offer a model not only for his pupil, but also for other readers in need of education in the principles of virtuous politics who had perhaps been disorientated by the rise of new whigs at court, men who appeared able to ditch principles in order to do the king's bidding. In other words, the contents of *Works* were selected for a polemical purpose; not so much self-fashioning as a self fashioned by an editor. This was also clearly the case with a *Collection of Speeches* that had been delivered by Warrington in Chester in the early 1690s. The volume was published in the same year as *Works* by the whig publisher Richard Baldwin, who shaped its reception by inserting an advertisement opposite the title page for James Tyrrell's *Bibliotheca Politica*, as well as a tract supporting the oath of abjuration and Mathew Tindal's *Essay* which asserted revolution principles.

Yet at least two significant manuscripts, anonymous but demonstrably written by Warrington, do survive and both raise doubts about omissions from the published *Works* and *Collection of Speeches* and hence about how we 'read' him. One is a manuscript diary in the British Library of his speeches made in the house of commons between 1677 and 1681 which does not tally with those published in *Works*.[7] The manuscript speeches seem to have been more idealised, and in one case even invented, versions of what he might like to have said, confirming the suspicion that *Works* carefully constructs an image of Booth for public consumption.[8] I want here, however, to focus on the second manuscript, a 20-page piece to be found in the Beinecke Library at Yale and now reproduced in an appendix to this article.[9] Endorsed 'Late Lord Warrington's Papers', the distinctive handwriting and orthography exactly matches letters written and signed by him in the state papers.[10] This document places Warrington among the ranks of the whig jacobites; or at least amongst those capable of envisioning a reconciliation between the whigs and the jacobites, for there is little evidence that Warrington took any action to further his jottings.[11] In them, he not

---

[6] John Simon de la Heuze was appointed rector of Ashton-under-Lyne, by the 2nd earl of Warrington, on 3 May 1700, dying there in 1727: 'The Parish of Ashton-under-Lyne: Church and Charities', in *A History of the County of Lancaster: Volume 4* (1911), 347–52. Available at *http://www.british-history.ac.uk/report.aspx?compid= 41439* (accessed 9 Apr. 2008).

[7] BL, Hargrave MS 149: 'Speeches 1675–1682'. Francis Hargrave owned both the manuscript diary and the British Library's copy of Booth's *Works*.

[8] For a discussion of this see Mark Knights, *Representation and Misrepresentation in Later Stuart Britain: Partisanship and Political Culture* (2005), 93–4.

[9] Yale University, Beinecke Library, Osborn MSS, File W, Folder15756. See appendix below 71–87. It is unclear how it became part of the Osborn Collection and hence from where it came. I am grateful to the Beinecke Library for permission to use the document.

[10] See, e.g., The National Archives (TNA), SP 8/6/47 or SP 8/2/2. As we shall see, there are also striking similarities both of tone and content with pieces published in *Works*.

[11] For discussions of their beliefs see Mark Goldie and Clare Jackson, 'Williamite Tyranny and the Whig Jacobites', in *Redefining William III: The Impact of the King-Stadtholder in International Context*, ed. Esther Mijers and David Onnekink (Aldershot, 2007); Paul Monod, 'Jacobitism and Country Principles in the Reign of

only pours out his frustration and disillusionment with the Williamite regime but goes further to envisage a restoration of James II. Warrington's public statements were critical enough of William's betrayal of the whigs; but in private, this document suggests, Warrington imagined reversing his steadfast opposition to James in order to secure commonwealth principles and, as importantly, to oust the set of advisers who, Warrington believed, had denied him and other supporters of William their just deserts. The man who in 1689 said he would die with his sword in his hand rather than recognize any allegiance to James was now prepared to imagine his restoration.

The Beinecke manuscript begins with an analysis of why the whigs were disaffected and hence why, in Warrington's words, 'tho I will not positively affirme yt ye breach can be intirely made up betwixt K. J[ames] & ye Whigs, yet I may adventure to say That is much nearer than ever it was then, or beleived it could ever have bin'. There follows a close analysis of William's declarations of 10 and 24 October 1688 to show that William had failed to remedy the things that he had found amiss. A blow-by-blow analysis of William's declaration is also the formula for 'Some Observations', published in *Works*, which also clearly sees the revolution as having failed to achieve all its objectives, attacks William's employment of tories and contains veiled references to William as a bad prince.[12] But in that printed text, and presumably in the charge to a grand jury from which it came, Warrington argued that 'I think King James was justly deposed', with no hint of wanting his return; indeed, he argues that although 'we have not everything as well as we could wish, yet that does not proceed from any error in placing the Crown where it is'.[13] The analysis of the Beinecke manuscript, by contrast, uses the analysis of the declaration to argue for replacing the crown on James's head. Key to that *volte-face* was the notion that 'K. Wm & ye P. of O don't act upon ye same principle' and that the new king had broken his word. This he claimed was the 'harshest thing yt one man can do to another' because a man's word was 'ye only ligam[en]t of society, for if it be not inviolably observed, there's an end of all conversation, & dealings betwixt man & man, & ye whole Course of Nature is dissolved'. The prince of Orange had explicitly promised in his declarations that he came 'w[i]th no other designe, than to procure a setlem[en]t of ye religion & of ye libertys & propertyes of ye subjects upon so sure a foundation yt they may be no more in danger of the Nations relapsing into ye like miseries at any time hereafter'. These words were 'not capable of a double sence; & therefore it thence follows, yt ye P of O is under ye greatest obligation in ye world, to suppress yt wch may be a means to bring our religion or liberty into danger'.

Warrington highlighted the inconsistencies in William's actions. In his declaration William had attacked James for appointing judges during the king's pleasure rather than for life; yet his own appointments followed the old formula. William as prince had criticized the appointment of catholic officers; but William as king retained catholic

---

[11] *(continued)* William III', *Historical Journal*, xxx (1987), 290–310; Paul Hopkins, 'Aspects of Jacobite Conspiracy in the Reign of William III', University of Cambridge PhD, 1981.

[12] *Works*, 374, talks of a situation in which a prince is deposed for tyranny 'and the next proves as bad as he'. For a veiled critique of William and his declaration see also, *Works*, 490–1. For the importance of William's declarations see Tony Claydon, 'William III's "Declaration of Reasons" and the Glorious Revolution', *Historical Journal*, xxxix (1996), 87–108.

[13] *Works*, 375.

officers in his army. The declaration had promised to send the Dutch troops back home as soon as possible; yet, in fact, more had been brought over and English forces disbanded. Orange promised to restore the constitution of Scotland; but the king had done so only reluctantly and when forced to do so. In the declaration William had bemoaned the fate of Ireland; yet many of the men who introduced arbitrary power there were still in place, and the relief of Ireland had been delayed and 'purposely spun out'. The prince had complained that the ecclesiastical commission had been illegal; yet as king he brought no one to justice for it, and the mastermind behind it, the earl of Sunderland – the 'evil councillor' of the declaration – had been allowed to kiss William's hand.[14] Indeed, Warrington lamented, Sunderland informally exercised the power he had once exercised formally as secretary of state. As prince, William had attacked James's attempt to pack and overawe parliament and had promised a free parliament. Yet as king, Booth asserted, he had soon dissolved the very parliament which had given him the crown.

Warrington's indictment of William was extensive. When a new parliament was called in 1690, he said, the efforts to influence elections were 'never more barefaced & open . . . never was more foule play in ye returns made by ye officers, scarcely one half of ye house of Comons yt were return'd had a right to sit'. Booth also alleged that in order to influence voters 'those yt in both houses were most zealouse for ye Engl[ish] libertys were turn'd ut of their profitable places & men of another character put in their roomes, so yt thoe there was no closeting as was in K. J his time' it was clear to all 'upon wt termes prefermt was to be had'. Indeed, the failure to punish 'evil councillors' and to reward the whigs who had supported William at the revolution becomes one of the main themes of the text.[15] Warrington could not believe that a revolution grounded on whig principles should result in members of the party being sidelined and castigated as being 'for a Comon Wealth'.[16] Perhaps with his own expenditure in mind, he lamented that 'many of the whigs are ye worse for ys revolution, having layd out a great pt of their substance to help it forward & yet now are as much suspected by ys Governmt as they were in K. J his time'.[17] William had backtracked on his promises, 'even bare faced to lick up his own vomitt'. He had attacked James's evil councillors 20 times in the declaration; '& yet ye storme is pass'd over their heads, & they now sit under their vines & fig trees cheerfully enjoying wt they had gott; & some are in a better condition than ever'. James had let his interest – and the language of interest permeates the text – follow his religion, but William had changed his religion and principles 'to serve his ends' and was thus impossible to trust.

Warrington's revolutionary conclusion was that William's breach of his word was worse than James's, removed any obligation to him, and justified restoring the Stuart

[14] J.P. Kenyon, 'The Earl of Sunderland and the King's Administration 1693–5', *English Historical Review*, lxxi (1956), 578.

[15] The essay in *Works* on 'The Interest of Whigg and Tory' also echoes part of the document's lament about William's employment of tories. See also, *Works*, 82–6.

[16] Cf., *An Impartial Enquiry*, 5, 13.

[17] Warrington estimated that he had spent £1,000 on elections to parliament, £2,000 for his committal and trial in 1686: John Rylands Library, EGR3/6/2/1/1: schedule of debts. His son saw him 'several times the year before the Revolution fall aweeping at the greatness of his debts; and they were increased at the Revolution': John Rylands Library, EGR3/6/2/2/1. In 1688 the estate revenue amounted to £2,100 but outgoings totalled £2,947, and all parts of the estate had been mortgaged: John Rylands Library, EGR3/6/2/1/14.

© *The Parliamentary History Yearbook Trust 2009*

king: '*does it not then become ye Intrest of ye Nation, at least of ye whigs to recall K.J. rather than to support K. Wm[?]*' he asked. Warrington feared that William had become a protestant rather than a catholic tyrant and the more dangerous for it. 'Many hold it as a Maxime That if Eng[lan]d be ever inslaved it will be by a Protest[an]t K; this seems to be founded on good reason, & to be very much supported by experience . . . if a Protest[an]t K yt aims at arbitrary power is more dangerous than a Popish K; is not K.J. rather to be desired at ys time than K.Wm.'[18]

Warrington's text suggested that James should return to England without a force and publish a declaration, a draft of which Booth himself provided at the end of his document. In this James was to disown the bad advice he had received during his own reign, point to the reforms initiated on the eve of the revolution and claim that he had deliberately withdrawn from both England and Ireland, despite superior forces, in order to avoid bloodshed. He was to highlight William's propensity to 'despotick power' and to outline the disparities between what William had promised before being crowned and what he had done since. The wording of William's declaration was to be thrown back in his face, for it was he, not James, who wanted 'to be cloathed wth an arbitrary despotick power, & to have ye lives, libertys, honors & estates of his subjects to depend wholly on his good will & pleasure & be intirely subject to him'. James, by contrast, would 'disclaim any arbitrary power & all pretences to it'. James, in Warrington's formula, should 'declare yt as ye law ought to be ye measure of ye K[ing]s prerogative, so it shall be ye rule by wch we intend to govern our people; & yt ys may be more freely confirm'd & establisht we will give our assent to any bill yt shall be presented to us by our 2 houses of Parl; either to pair off any pt of the prerogative yt is or may be dangerous to ye liberty of our people or other wise for ye reviving & strengthening any of our peoples propertyes so as yt it may not be in ye power of any succeeding K[ing] to bring their laws & libertys into danger'. Here, then, was the conception of a radical reform of the framework of power. Nothing, he made clear, that had been achieved at the revolution was to be lost; but a truly revolutionary settlement was to be advanced.

Fearful of a despotic king ruling with an army, Warrington provided that the king was to renounce his power to raise troops or even a guard without consent of parliament 'because we are sensible yt ye good will of our people is a surer defence & security to our person' and because 'if we should attempt to govern otherwise than according to law we have put a power into their hands to compel us'. James was also to 'restore to our people ye choosing of their sheriffs, in ye sev[er]all Countys of our Kdome of Eng[lan]d as also the electing of ye officers of ye Militia, as it was anciently practis'd & of right did belong'. James would also 'take care yt Parl[iament]s be duely called & held yt ye just

---

[18] Warrington had already worked out a conditional sense of allegiance prior to the revolution and he rehearsed this afterwards, ironically airing it to justify the revolution. In a charge to a grand jury in1692 Booth defended a right of resistance, in terms that owed something to Locke. He attacked 'asserters of arbitrary power', protesting that 'the standing body of our laws is a clear proof that the power of our king is limited', and 'when the king forsakes the law, he ceases to be king'. Every king governed 'upon condition' and when a king had 'set his will above the laws, what other means has the people left, but their arms: for nothing can oppose force but force. Prayers and tears are our proper applications to God almighty, but signifie little with an arbitrary prince', who therefore needed to be opposed by arms, though this was 'not justifiable for every wrong step or miscarriage of the prince, save only in cases of extremity'. Thus 'when the throne is vacant, it naturally comes into the hands of the people, because the original dispose and gift of the Crown was from them'. Men entered society, and thus existed as a people, before they chose their king: *Works*, 388–90, 392–3, 431, 569.

© *The Parliamentary History Yearbook Trust 2009*

Complaints & grievances of ye Nation & of every particular person may be heard & redressd'. Finally there was to be a fundamental purge of officeholders, employing only 'Those of ye best Intrest & reputation in their Countrys & we will not put into office any person yt is not well liked by our people'. But, perhaps with a view to the security of Booth's own elevation and how James would treat his earlier treasonous part in rebellion, the returning king would 'confirme to Every of our subjects ye titles & dignitys to wch they have bin raised by ye P. of O. & do hereby pardon to every one of our subjects all maner of Crimes & offences wtsoever'.

What then are we to make of this document? We could perhaps ascribe it to personal pique, sour grapes, idle musings or what even his admirers called his 'proneness to passion'.[19] The first of these was sharp, for the family's finances were in a shambles and service for the public good had only created debts that forced Warrington's son to live in relative retreat and poverty.[20] Warrington's sense of having been personally slighted was very strong. It permeates both his published and his unpublished output. For example, amongst the state papers is a letter, undated, but probably written after a debate in council in January 1690 about the wisdom (or folly as Warrington saw it) of William going to Ireland to suppress the jacobites there, in which he makes similar complaints that he was distrusted by the king and 'regarded as if I were a knave or a foole, & by him wth whom voluntarily and unaskt I ventured all yt I had in ye world'.[21] His sense of dismay at being sidelined and then dismissed from office recurs in the published *Works*. But both there and in the letter just quoted, Warrington's loyalty to William seems never to have been in question.[22] Indeed, in the letter Warrington said that everybody 'must applaud ye Kings generous inclinations & too much cannot be said in praise of it'. Indeed, he feared that whilst William was away in Ireland James might 'step into ye throne'. There were many, he warned, 'yt it will be for him [i.e., James], yt will make them ye best bargain & do you not imagine he will not bid them fair & offer to submit to ye termes & conditions yt ye Nation will prescribe to him'. Warrington warned that there were too many 'waiting to shutt ye doore upon King Wm'. Yet, the Beinecke text suggests, sometime after writing this, Warrington revised his opinion of William's 'generous inclinations' and became one of those apparently prepared to try to make 'the best bargain' with James.

There were others, who shared Warrington's beliefs, who did not make this move. John Hampden, for example, came from a similarly presbyterian background, had also supported exclusion and suffered imprisonment, and had become an active Williamite. Hampden, too, sought revenge on the tories who had been instrumental in the earlier Stuart 'tyranny', and also published scathing attacks on the Williamite regime including one, in early 1693, that, like Warrington's manuscript, quoted William's declaration against him in its fulminations against the king's opposition to frequent parliaments.[23] Hampden remained hostile to James; indeed, his tract of 1693 warned against those 'who

---

[19] Wroe, *Sermon*, 21.

[20] George Booth, 2nd earl, showed his brother that the family 'could not live in such a popular expensive way as my father and grandfather had done in their time': John Rylands Library, EGR3/6/2/2/1.

[21] TNA, SP8/6/47.

[22] There are nevertheless veiled references to William as a bad prince in *Works*, 374–5, 490–1.

[23] *An Enquiry; or a Discourse between a Yeoman of Kent and a Knight of the Shire, upon the Prorogation of the Parliament to the Second of May, 1693* (1693), 2.

© *The Parliamentary History Yearbook Trust 2009*

would perswade you and the People, to think, that our Religion and Liberties might be secured by a Treaty for bringing back King James'.[24] There are also similarities between Warrington and Hampden's parliamentary colleague in Buckinghamshire, Thomas Wharton. Wharton, too, was a presbyterian turned churchman, exclusionist and revolutionary. And he was the author of a letter to the king on 25 December 1689 that could easily have been penned by Warrington both for content and style. The people, it claimed:

> stand amazed to see that your Majesty, who came in upon one principle, should for the most part employ men who have ever professed another; that the glorious Prince of Orange, who had rendered himself so renowned in the world, for his steadiness to truth, justice, the laws and liberty of his country, and the Protestant religion, should, when he became a King, think himself less obliged to pursue those great and noble ends.[25]

Yet Wharton, too, remained steadfast to William. Even so, his son, Philip, turned to jacobitism and there were other commonwealth whigs who made similar steps. These included John Wildman and Sir James Montgomerie, who turned to, or at least flirted with, jacobitism. These men had a common sense of personal disillusionment and frustrated ambitions as well as agreement that the agents of the former regimes, now favoured by William, were bound to assist a shift towards tyranny.[26] They believed that the revolution had been a missed opportunity to alter structures. In the light of the Beinecke document we might want to add Warrington to the miscellaneous and often rather diverse and loose group of whig jacobites.

Precisely dating the shift of attitude and degree of commitment to it is nevertheless problematic. In 1692 Warrington published a tract, *An Impartial Enquiry into the Causes of the Present Fears and Dangers* – significantly not republished in his *Works* – that offered a sustained critique of William's government, rehearsing many of the points made in the manuscript about the king's error in employing old ministers. It attacks the traitorous advisers who 'sought to subvert all the principles of the Legal English Government by defaming and blackening for commonwealths-men all that durst assert . . . that K. James had broken his Original contract and oath with the kingdom'.[27] But there was no hint in it of support for the exiled king; quite the reverse, the tract imagined preparing militarily against the jacobites. Similarly Warrington's 'Perswasive to Union, Upon King James's Design to Invade England, in the Year 1692' – which is in *Works* – shows that he was openly opposed to James's return then.[28] The most likely dating of the manuscript therefore appears to be early 1693. This was not only when

---

[24] *An Enquiry; or a Discourse between a Yeoman of Kent and a Knight of the Shire*, 7.

[25] 25 Dec. 1689, printed in Sir John Dalrymple, *Memoirs of Great Britain and Ireland* (3 vols, 1771), ii, appendix to part ii, book iv, 84–95, quotation at 87.

[26] Warrington does not, however, display all of the characteristics of a jacobite whig as identified by Goldie and Jackson. He was not hostile to the Dutch; he seemed relatively unconcerned about the economic dimension of the war; he does not seem to have been deeply influenced by Harrington or classical republicanism; he did not minimise the threat from catholicism; and he has very little to say about the treason law or the place bill.

[27] *An Impartial Enquiry*, 5.

[28] *Works*, 401–11.

Sunderland's informal power over William was growing, as noted in the text, but on 17 April 1693, James issued a much more moderate declaration which was the product of negotiations since the previous year with the discontented in England and represented the high point of commonwealth influence on the exiled king. As early as July 1692 James's secretary of state, the earl of Melfort, was assuring whig jacobite Charlwood Lawton that the exiled king was 'resolved to governe by the knowen lawes of ye Kingdome, to consult wth his Parliament in all things relating to the establishment of peace and quiet in his Kingdomes, to maintain ye liberties and properties of all his subjects, to protect ye protestant religion, and to obtain a liberty of conscience for dissenters'.[29] Over the following months Melfort and Lawton corresponded to inform and refine the content of any new declaration by James. Thus it duly promised that the people could 'depend upon every thing their own representatives shall offer to make our Kingdoms happy'; a free pardon; reward for all who supported him 'according to their respective degrees and merits'; the protection of the Church of England; liberty of conscience; the retention of the Test Acts; assent to bills 'to secure the frequent calling and houlding of Parliaments, the free elections and fair returns of members, and provide for impartial tryals'; the ratification of legislation passed since 1689; and 'to relieve our people from oppression and Slavery . . . we come to vindicate our own right and to establish the liberties of our people'.[30] Whether Warrington was consulted during the declaration's drafting, or whether the declaration might have inspired his thoughts is unclear. Nothing in Melfort's correspondence indicates direct contact with Warrington, but it is quite possible that Warrington picked up what was afoot or that Lawton actually told him.[31] Yet, one imagines that if Warrington's work had ever reached the jacobite policy makers it would not have been received sympathetically. Warrington was clearly still intolerant of any tory and bent on revenge; his commonwealth principles were partisan. It is also worth noting that whereas Lawton published material to generate public sympathy – he penned about half of the 40 or so jacobite whig pamphlets and broadsides published in the 1690s – Warrington's thoughts remained in manuscript and were possibly, probably, not even circulated.

How, then, might we think about Warrington's document and the programme it puts forward? Geoffrey Holmes did as much as, if not more than, anyone to put ideological division back at the heart of our understanding of the later Stuart period. Alongside Bill Speck, he convincingly showed that politics was not simply one of personal connections and that the ideological rifts were present throughout a divided society and permeated local as well as national debates. He was also a historian who tended to disregard the sub-disciplinary boundaries, moving easily from discussions of politics at Westminster to local electioneering, from debates about social policy to analysis of the middling sort's professionalisation. Yet developments in the historical profession meant that the impact

---

[29] BL, Add. MS 37,661, f. 4: Melfort to 'Laty', 4 July 1692. For the identification of Lawton and other correspondents see Hopkins, 'Jacobite Conspiracy', ch. 6.

[30] Hopkins, 'Jacobite Conspiracy', 502–5.

[31] Melfort was worried that Lawton might be 'imposed on by some individuals who make their case that of ye whole', but this could be a reference to any number of people: BL, Add. MS 37,661, f. 87: Melfort to [Lawton], 17 Oct. 1692. In Dec. 1692 Melfort told Lawton that he knew 'ye need ye King has of the State Whig and therefore I would willingly correspond with some of them', but we don't know if Warrington was one of them: BL, Add. MS 37,661, f. 148, 1 Dec. 1692.

© *The Parliamentary History Yearbook Trust 2009*

of some of Holmes's work was perhaps more muted than it might have been. Revisionism moved attention away from the later to the early Stuart period; political history, in the hands of Elton, became strident in its insularity; and increasing specialisation and the development of social history as a distinct sub-discipline, often explicitly rejecting concerns with high politics, meant that conversation between social history and political or religious history tended to be muted. Fortunately that situation no longer prevails. Social historians have become far more interested in the conjunction between politics from above and politics from below; whilst political historians have, in turn, become more interested in how affairs at Westminster played out to a wider public and how power was socially and culturally constructed. One area on which both fields converge is that of the state. In the light of this I therefore want to consider how our changing model of the state might be useful for understanding Booth.

Geoffrey Holmes did much to illuminate the forms of local governance to show how they shaped the electoral processes and he often described the functions of the state. His studies of electioneering necessarily meant that he broke down the distinction between the 'centre' and the 'locality'. In recent years, though, this approach has been more fully developed, in ways that Holmes would surely have applauded, by social historians, who have stressed that the state was present not just in 'central' institutions but also in the parishes and in the boroughs, through the variety of institutions and officeholders there. Work by Keith Wrightson, Patrick Collinson, Mike Braddick, Steve Hindle, John Walter and Phil Withington in particular has explored what Mark Goldie has called the 'unacknowledged republic' within the monarchical state and the negotiations that occurred within it.[32] This decentred concept of the state is tremendously useful in a number of ways.

First, it focuses our attention on the importance of officeholding. For sure, Booth's concerns about officeholding were motivated by personal pique; but there is a larger structural point behind them. For much of the 17th century there was a series of crises generated by the conflict between the fiscal, military and administrative demands of the state and the nature of the officeholders who peopled that state. Mostly unpaid, they were motivated by a strong sense of conscience and duty – two qualities that clearly shine through most of Booth's public and private expressions. A fundamental question facing the early modern state, posed more strongly in the 1690s than perhaps at any time since the civil wars, was how far the model of voluntary and public-spirited officeholders could hold against the demands of a country at war, an emerging fiscal-military state in the hands of a king who put the war effort above all else. Though he denied commonwealth principles if that meant government without a monarchy, Warrington was very

---

[32] Patrick Collinson, *De Republica Anglorum; Or, History with the Politics Put Back* (Cambridge, 1990); Keith Wrightson, 'The Politics of the Parish in Early Modern England', in *The Experience of Authority in Early Modern England*, ed. Paul Griffiths, Adam Fox and Steve Hindle (1996); Steve Hindle, *The State and Social Change* (2000); Mark Goldie, 'The Unacknowledged Republic: Office-holding in Early Modern England c. 1640–1740', in *The Politics of the Excluded c.1500–1850*, ed. Tim Harris (Basingstoke, 2001); Joan Kent, 'The Centre and the Localities: State Formation and Parish Government in England c.1640–1740', *Historical Journal*, xxxviii (1995), 363–404; *Negotiating Power in Early Modern Society: Order, Hierarchy, and Subordination in Britain and Ireland*, ed. Michael J. Braddick and John Walter (Cambridge, 2001); Michael J. Braddick, *State Formation in Early Modern England c. 1550–1700* (Cambridge, 2000); John Walter, *Understanding Popular Violence in the English Revolution: The Colchester Plunderers* (Cambridge, 1999); Phil Withington, *The Politics of Commonwealth: Citizens and Freemen in Early Modern England* (Cambridge, 2005); Alex Shepard and Phil Withington, *Communities in Early Modern England: Networks, Place and Rhetoric* (Manchester, 2000).

much a believer in the commonwealth of officeholders.[33] As he put it in his draft declaration, local officeholding should be in the hands of those with the 'best interest and reputation in their countries'. Warrington was an officeholder in his locality as well as in London. His roles as lord lieutenant, *custos rotulorum*, jp, royal forester, commissioner of assessment, but also as alderman and then mayor of Chester, shows him not only as an active citizen but also as a broker of power in his locality. He was nicknamed the 'king of hearts' because of his populist stance and certainly he saw himself as a cultural broker with the 'common people'.[34]

Second, the decentred state of officeholders was a self-governing community or rather a series of self-governing communities. The importance of self-governance emerges clearly in Warrington's draft for a declaration – in the demands for elected sheriffs and militia officers. Warrington's outlook can be summarized in Goldie and Jackson's comment that 'the Whig Jacobites embraced a populist programme for the devolution of executive power and the restoration of what they perceived to be England's tradition of local self-government'. An important context for understanding Warrington's views is thus his role within the Chester corporation. He was mayor in 1691, and his acceptance speech lamented how the corporation's liberties had been 'ravish'd' from them by a party of men who complied in the 'wicked' demands of the court.[35] Local and national perspectives were thus but two sides of the same coin. Warrington remained very active in support of Roger Whitley, whose mayoralty temporarily secured whig dominance in Chester. Nor is it coincidental that so many of his charges to local grand juries were published – he clearly saw these as highly important platforms for his rhetoric, epitomising as they did the self-governing community. Indeed such charges are an important source for students of political discourse interested in how ideas and languages were disseminated.

Third, self-governance required certain virtues. In his excellent study of citizenship in early modern England, Phil Withington shows that the politics of commonwealth required a society of free men united by a common accord and covenants among themselves. A good citizen should eschew his own will, lust and private interest for the public good and public wealth.[36] He should exhibit virtues of honour, honesty, reason, discretion, sobriety, fitness, civility and wisdom. Here, then, in the language of the corporations, was precisely the same set of ideals and virtues prized by Booth. We noted earlier that Warrington saw breach of word and trust as fundamentally important issues – these were the things that broke or made those communities.[37] And throughout Warrington's writing we can find the stress on the common good and active citizenship. He believed that the 'publick concern is to be preferr'd before a p[ar]ticular interest' and advised his children, next after honouring God, to seek 'the common good; it is to be preferred to your life, estate or family'.[38] He also wrote, at the time of the succession

---

[33] See, e.g., the essay 'Monarchy the Best Government', in *Works*, 645–80.

[34] For the epithet see Arthur Mainwaring's hostile *The King of Hearts* [1690], endorsed on the Harvard University copy as 'on the earl of Warrington'.

[35] *A Collection of Speeches of the Right Honourable Henry, Late Earl of Warrington* (1694), 2–3.

[36] Withington, *Politics of Commonwealth*.

[37] See also, C. Muldrew, *The Economy of Obligation: The Culture of Credit and Social Relations in Early Modern England* (1998).

[38] BL, Hargrave MS 149, ff. 54–5; *Works*, 1, 4–5.

© *The Parliamentary History Yearbook Trust 2009*

crisis, that 'for my own part, I will obey the king but I think my obedience is obliged no further than what he commands is for the common good'.[39] In this sense we can break down the distinction between public and private, since private virtues were ones sought after for good public governance. Booth's private sphere, his godly household, was also a commonwealth and his private virtues were also ones fitted for the commonwealth. Indeed his own religiosity merely reinforced his commitment to commonwealth values, for the christian virtues were also the ones necessary for civil life. He had culled the scriptures for 'such directions as might be useful upon all occasions and applicable to the several emergencies of his actions. To which end he had drawn up several heads (above an hundred in number) in a large book for that purpose, and under them had noted in his own hand, such places of scripture as were properly reducible to them.'[40]

Fourth, the decentred state was one in which authority and ideology were negotiated and contested through a process of dialogue.[41] At one level this was about the different forms in which such conversation could take place. Warrington used speeches in parliament, speeches to grand juries, speeches to tenants and speeches in privy council – until he found himself so disregarded there that he refused to speak there.[42] Silenced orally in one sphere, he instead penned his discontent, first as a letter and subsequently in the memorandum and draft jacobite or commonwealth declaration. Print offered him yet another form, throughout his career, in which the dialogue could take place. But it was also a dialogue in which a public was involved as participant: Warrington's speeches, his publications, his actions all courted popularity – sometimes excessively so, in the eyes of some of his contemporaries.[43] Certainly he sought to connect across the social scale.

The dialogue within the state is also metaphorical.[44] If we accept that power was, in part, brokered by local officeholders acting with discretion, and that the state had institutions that were in the parish and borough as much as at Whitehall or Westminster, then we necessarily have a series of dialogues or conversations taking place within the state. This dialogue could take a number of forms. It could, as we have just seen, share a common terminology of vices and virtues, of commonwealth and its principles; but equally, as Warrrington's own case again demonstrates, that language could be contested and challenged as part of a wide public debate. His many speeches were published, in part, to try to imprint his language both on his locality and more widely; but at every stage, that language was challenged and contested by critics who put forward another (to

---

[39] *Works*, 560.

[40] Wroe, *Sermon*, 23. But he also sought to separate church and state. He thought it injurious to religion 'when the discipline and government of the church interferes with the state, breaking into the methods and foundations of it, and to advance the power and greatness of the clergy', so that 'in all well regulated constitutions, the government of the church is moulded according to the principle upon which the civil government stands': *Works*, 495–6.

[41] I am drawing here on ideas discussed in a British Academy funded project investigating the concept and language of commonwealth, the fruits of which will be published in due course, and I would like to acknowledge the suggestions of its participants.

[42] This is the claim made in TNA, SP8/6/47 (part published in Dalrymple, *Memoirs*, appendix to book iv, 100). He believed, even before the revolution, that a major cause of differences between king and people arose when the privy council was 'turned into a cabinet, the former being only kept up for a shew': *Works*, 39.

[43] *The Lord Delamere's Letter . . . Answered* [1688] and *King of Hearts*, though for a sympathetic view see *An Account of the Lord Delamere his Reception and Wellcome in Cheshire and at the City of Chester* [1689].

[44] Here I wish to acknowledge the stimulating conversations of colleagues involved in a British Academy funded collaborative exploration of 'commonwealth'. The output of this group is forthcoming.

him, corrupted) vision of the commonwealth and who sought to de-legitimise his discourse, as he himself noted, by calling him a commonwealthsman. Warrington thought a commonwealth the inevitable outcome of a bad king succeeding a tyrant, yet he did not seek a republic. He was aware that he had been 'accused to be a commonwealths man, but were I permitted to speak for myself, I would say that I like this constitution under king, lords and commons better than any other . . . I say withal, that if through the administration of those who are trusted with the executive power or by any other means, my liberty shall become precarious, I will then be for any other form of government under which my liberty and property may be more secure, and till then I don't desire to change'.[45] In 1693 he was still apparently sufficiently wedded to monarchy to contemplate a return of James II in order to secure commonwealth principles.

Appendix

Yale University, Beinecke Library, Osborn MSS, File W, folder 15756
Endorsed 'Late Lord Warrington's Papers'
Note on editing:
The manuscript is written in Warrington's hand on numbered, folded sheets, giving four sides of writing per sheet. The first sheet has been separated into two separate, double-sided sheets.
I have used wavy brackets to indicate where the ms has been damaged, torn or is obscured by ink blotches and guesses about possible readings for missing or obscured words have been prefixed by a question mark. Deletions have been placed in footnotes, and insertions in italics after the symbol ^.
Contractions have been expanded in square brackets, but original spelling, capitalisation and punctuation has been retained, as have the short forms of those [yos], this [ys], that [yt], which [wch], with [wth], without the original's use of superscript. The abbreviation of K or Kg for King has been retained, as has C for Charles, P for Prince, O for Orange, J for James, and Wm for William.

'There is not any thing in ye last age yt has bin so remarkable as the reign of K. Wm of wch ye most unaccountable pt of it, has bin his treatm[en]t of the Whigs, & particularly yos yt are eminent, or had suffer'd under either of ye late reigns; for thoe K. J his Maleadministration was ye ground of ye P. of O his declaration,[46] & yos yt gave him ye Crown acted by whigish principle, yt Kg Wm does now so much endeavour to depress ye reputation of all [47]men, yt are of yt principle, & to baffle ye doctrine yt Kings hold their Crowns upon Condition; That it looks more like a fault than merrit, to have bin a sufferer in ye late times, whilest at ye same time he cheifly imploys men of a Contrary opinion, even till it comes to yos evel Councellors of whom he complain'd in his declaration.[48] Some thing of ys sort was practis'd by C.2d,

---

[45] *Works*, 374–5.

[46] William issued two declarations. The first, on 10 Oct. 1688, the second, on 24 Oct. Both are printed in Robert Beddard, *A Kingdom Without a King* (Oxford, 1988), 124–8, 145–50.

[47] Deletion of 'yos'.

[48] The key target appears to have been the earl of Sunderland who had been James's secretary of state. He returned to England, after fleeing at the revolution, in Apr. 1690 but remained in disgrace until Apr. 1691 when he was admitted to the king's presence. His advice was increasingly sought in an informal capacity by William

© *The Parliamentary History Yearbook Trust 2009*

Hyde[49] giving it as the advice of Achitophell to reward his enemys, & his freinds would be freinds still because hereby he would make ye whole Nation sure to him: & fro[m] ye like pollicy & gratitude, ye Whigs are thus treated at this day, Because it is taken for granted, That a Reconciliation betwixt K. J & ye Whigs is Impracticable; Now thoe this were never so certain, wch yet is a question wth very many, yet the indeavoring to explode yt principle upon wch ye Crown was given to K. Wm. & ye discountinancing yos yt were most Zealous to get him into ye throne; has too great a resemblance wth ye Gratitude of Lewis ye 14th to ye Hugenots, who having [w]th ye exspence of their blood fixt[50] him on ye throne of his Kdome, were afterwards indeavord to be extirpated by him for no other reason, but because they yt could set up a K, could also upon occation pull him down again.[51] A sort of Pollicy never heard of before, at least its ye first instance yt it was put in practise, as this is ye second.

It is not deny'd but yt ye enmity of ye Whigs ag[ain]st[52] K.J. is as great as ever any people had to the P., & so long as things remain'd in ye same Circumstances as when ye P. of O. landed at Torbay, there was no [p]rospect of an accommodation; but since sev[er]all things have happen'd {?wch wer}e neither foreseen or thought on (except by a very few) wch have in

[verso] some measure alter'd ye Case, thoe I will not possitively affirme yt ye breach can be intirely made up betwixt K. J & ye Whigs, yet I may adventure to say That is much nearer than ever it was then, or beleived it could ever have bin.

K.J his religion was ye Originall of ye disklike yt was taken to him yet not barely because it was yt religion, but because of ye ill effect it would have not only upon ye Protestant religion, but also upon our Civile libertys, That is, yt arbitrary power would be set up by ye self same means, whereby Popery would be establisht, or rather yt we must first be bereaved of our Civil rights before yt Popery can prevaile in Eng[lan]d, as is seen by all examples, where ye protest[an]t religion has bin extirpated, ye loss of liberty has led ye way; For Nothing but force can impose popery upon a Protest[an]t people, & therefore there must be such a power as can compell ye disobedient & refusers, unless any man can be so vain as to imagine, yt any thing can be effected without means, espetially a thing so large & Comprehensive as yt will be found to be, I mean ye establishing of popery in Eng[lan]d: And certainly ye apprehension of being thereby made slaves, is yt wch creates such an aversion in ye people of Eng[lan]d to popery, for can it be imagin'd yt so many Millions of people in Eng[lan]d who know nothing beyond their plow & Cart, can be distasted at Popery for any other reason than upon ye score of their property: The religion in Eng[land]d was popery for sev[er]all hundreds of years & yet in ye most superstitious times, ye people look'd closely to their civile rights, it were to be wisht yt ye people were now as Carefull to preserve ye antient land Markes,

---

[48] *(continued)* from the spring of 1692, ironically urging the king to embrace the whigs. Although some whigs were employed in 1693 they were suspected by country whigs and in 1694–5 Sunderland was attacked in parliament through his long-term ally Henry Guy, who was accused of bribery.

[49] Laurence Hyde, 1st earl of Rochester, who became a royal minister in 1679. In 1681 Dryden praised him in *Absolom and Achitophel* as 'the friend of David in distress' because of his financial competence. He became lord treasurer on James's accession but was dismissed in Apr. 1687.

[50] Deletion.

[51] In 1685 Louis XIV had revoked the edict of Nantes, which had given the Huguenots a measure of religious toleration.

[52] Deletion of 'to'.

© *The Parliamentary History Yearbook Trust 2009*

for they were then so Zealous, yt they seem'd inclined rather [to] abandon [53]ye Pope, than to quitt their libertys, if they must be put {?to} ye Necessity of parting wth one of ym: if a people are secure in their propertyes they can hold every thing else, but it has always bin found, yt when people have lost their libertys, they could keep their religion no longer than it pleases their P, it being wholly in his choice wt religion shall p[re]vaile in yt Country & the P. of O. in his additionall declarat{ion} lays it down, yt an arbitrary & despotick power, was the root of [ms torn at end of page, perhaps one or two words missing]

[start of loose sheet] oppression & of ye totall subversion of ye Governm[en]t. Upon ye foregoing reason was it yt C.2d was to corrupt ye Nation by his example [54]by reason, yt if ye people once come to loose their vertue they will then have so much ye less sence & regard of their liberty[55] & when ever a K. is Master of yt he may bring in full speed Popery or wt else he likes best because there remains Nothing to hinder his purpose;

The Making of lawes for ye better support of religion, has some times bin used as an artifice to destroy yt very religion, as was seen by C.2d, when ever he was Nibbling at ye peoples rights he coverd his intentions not only with a speech to ye Parl top full of care for the Protest[an]t religion but even gave his assent to some law, yt tended to ye support of it; knowing yt it signified Nothing, if ever he could get ye law into his power, for thoe it would make him so much ye more infamous for ingratitude & p[er]jury yet yos things we see are little regarded by Ps yt are so unjust & wicked, as to invade the rights of their people; & assume to ymselves a power above ye law.

The next thing yt prejudiced ye people ag[ain]st K.J. & was also an effect of his religion was this. The distrust they had to all his promises & ingag[e]ments, knowing how difficult a thing it is for a P. of yt religion to keep {h}is word, thoe never so solemnly given, further than his Ghostly father {?sh}all approve of it, & thoe he be otherwise never so well disposed & inclined

This objection was indeavord to be palliated by calling him James the {?jus}t, he having in a great measure gott a pretence to yt character by {?all ye} good turns he had done to sev[er]all, for whilest he has D. of Y. he {?mu}st be allow'd to have bin a very good Master & friend. but those who were not blinded by such p[ar]ticular obligations, & were not interrupted fro[m] looking as far as their sight might carry them, saw plainly yt ys at best hand served only to gaine him credit, & yt if ever he came to ye Crown he must not regard either his word or gratitude further {th}an either of them served to advance ye Catholick Cause.

{?w}hen he came to ye Crown, his promise to maintain ye religion establisht [verso] & our Just rights, was as great & full as words could make it.[56] This afforded fresh occasion to his depend[en]ts & all others yt had any expectation fro[m] him to speak lowder in his praise, & to extoll him as a most sacred observer of his word, A great many were satisfied therew[i]th & the mouths of most were stopt, either because they

---

[53] Deletion.

[54] 'That ye Nation' deleted.

[55] Deletion.

[56] His speech to privy council was published as *An Account of What his Majesty Said at his First Coming to Council* (1684).

© *The Parliamentary History Yearbook Trust 2009*

were content or durst not speak; till yt his Zeale for ye Catholick faith overcame at once both his gratitude & reason, so far as to p[re]vaile w[i]th him to lay [57]his old freinds aside & imbrace others, who were Notorious for Corrupt principles[58] & to break his word publickly & solemnly given in ye most Matteriall & import[an]t p[ar]ts of it. These were ye things yt overthrew him, & will be no less fatall to any other K. yt shall do ye like:

Had ye K.J bin content wth ye exercise of his religion, for himself & yos of his opinion, so as to have left others secure in ye injoymt of theirs, & of their libertys few they were yt would have grudg'd at it & happyly he might have lived & gone to his grave in peace; but he proved so bigotted & Preist-ridden,[59] as to abandon his word & friends, & thereby made it plain to every body wt was his purpose; & it is no less evid[en]t yt ye consciousness of his own guilt more than any other force drove him out of Eng[lan]d.

Upon yes 2 things was it, yt ye P. of O. grounded his confidence, yt ye Nation would approve & assist him in his undertaking, for ye more Notorious & palpable were K. J. his crimes, so much ye more was ye P. of O. Justifyed in wt he did, & under so much ye greater obligation to [60]remedy wt should {?be} found amiss, & p[re]venting ye like for ye future; And ys brings it to be consider'd how far it may come to ye Intrest of ye whigs to see K. J again upon ye throne

Should any man have s[ai]d w[he]n ye P. of O. landed yt there was a thought in {? his} heart tending to wt we now see; yt man would have bin call'd a Maliciou{s} traducer of ye P. of O; & an enemy to Eng[lan]d because Nothing else was expec{ted} fro[m] him, than a New heaven & a New Earth, even so clean a reformation of state, yt none of ye old rust should have remained. This was it, wch made ye nation so universally [61]& heartely wish ye P.s success; for otherwise his troopes would have bin lookt upon but as an addition to K. J his forces, & instead of so hearty a welcome would have met wth ye reception of an Invader & have turn'd upon himself a great p[ar]t of yt indignation wch ye Nation had to K.J.

This being so, then so far ye Nation falls short in its acc[oun]t fro[m] ys r{?esolution}by so much will ye odium be taken off fro[m] K. J & layd some where {ms blotted at end, obscuring last word or 2 words}

[new sheet] 2. if it arise from things, yt have nay resemblance wth wt K.J. did & consequently brings it so much ye nearer to a reconsiliation betwixt him & ye whigs.

There is no one passion, of wch all men do more equally participate, than yt of revenge, none being more violent & lasting than it is, & therefore it is probable; That where it is s[ai]d in holy writ, Vengeance is Mine:[62] That yt declaration was rather to keep yt passion w[i]thin reasonable limitts, than wholly & absolutly to restrain man kind in ye point, for ^by yos examples of ye distruction of ye 2. Ks of ye amorits, of Moab & Amalak, thoe G[o]d did fro[m] thence take an occasion to accomplish his eternall

---

[57] Deletion of 'aside'.

[58] James had parted with many of his tory ministers. The earl of Sunderland may be one of the 'corrupt' ministers, since he converted to catholicism in 1687 and his readmission to favour by William disconcerted Warrrington.

[59] 14.

[60] Deletion.

[61] Deletion of 'unanimously'.

[62] Romans 12 v.19.

purpose upon ym for their Idolatry & wickedness yet ye im[m]ediate & visible cause of their extirpation was in reveng for wt they did ag[ain]st ye Israelites w[he]n they came out of Egypt.[63] but we must leave ys point, it not being design'd to be disputed much here, nor any where else. Yet however so long as we have passions & infirmityes, & are capable of being injured, we shall shew our resentm[en]ts w[he]n such occasions happen, thoe it were forbid under much greater penaltys than are yet expresst, till we come to a more p[er]fect state than we are capable of in ys life.

Of all injurys none make so deed [sic] an impression as yos yt come without any p[re]vious provocation fro[m] ye injured p[ar]ty & espetially if there be any spice [sic] or mixture of Ingratitude in ye Case.

The Whigs & yos yt sufferd for yt Principle under ye 2 late reigns have Nothing to boast of fro[m] ys revolution, but yt they are so much ye poorer, for ye expence {th}ey were at in Contributing to it, & yt ye more they suffer'd then, renders ym so {m}uch ye more unfit to be now made use of; for as they were not many yt were {brough}t into imploymt when ys K came to ye Crown, so very few of ym held their {pl}aces so long as to be ye better for ym,[64] & now receive no greater benefit by {this} governm[en]t than wt ye Papists equally enjoy as well as they; & seem to be {y}e last sort of people yt ys governm[en]t intends to make use of, the Papists not {ex}cepted, because at ys day in ye Dutch troopes, sev[er]all have very good Posts.[65] Why ys is so, is not so plain as yt it ought to be otherwise; For ye P. of O. his declaration was grounded upon wt the whigs had professt & practised, during ye 2 late reigns, the argum[en]ts for ye abdication were all fetch'd fro[m] their principles{.} It was ye Whigs yt principally appear'd to Joyne wth ye P. of O. & others yt did so first renounced their former principles & confess't their Mistake, the Whigs were ye most Zealouse for ye abdication & giving ye Crown to K. Wm. & yos yt argued for it, did own yt ye whigs were in ye right whilest others were in the wrong during ye 2 late reigns, Whereas on ye other side The Torys & High [verso] Church p[ar]ty pulled as hard as they could ye Contrary way; & yet K. Wm. Courts ym before they sought to him & even yos yt will not allow him to be lawfull & rightfully K. of Eng[lan]d. This seems to be w[i]thout p[re]cedent & to exceed any thing in story. But yt wch makes it ye more extraordinary is ye reason assign'd for it, viz. Because ye whigs are for a Com[m]on wealth, this surely is far fetcht, & made use of because a better can't be found. For their Trying so hard to get him into ye throne, is no less than demonstration yt they p[re]fer'd ys form of governm[en]t to yt of a Com[m]on wealth, because a regency at best hand was an express alteration of ye Governm[en]t & wt could more directly lead ye way to a Com[m]on wealth? For so long as ye Regency lasted, as wel ye Regent as K.J. were upon their good behaviour; & if any dispute arose betwixt them, ye appeale must be to ye 2 houses of Parl: and consequently ye whole guidance of affairs would rest in ye people: & then wt could have hindred ye Com[m]on wealth p[ar]ty fro[m] effecting their purpose, since ye longer yt ye regency lasted ye more ye

---

[63] In 1 Samuel 15 v.3 God ordered the destruction of the Amalekites 'for what they did to Israel when they waylaid them as they came up from Egypt'. In Numbers 25 vv.1–6 God ordered the destruction of those who had been lured into fornication and idolatry by the Moabites.

[64] Warrington had been appointed chancellor of the exchequer on 28 Mar. 1689 but lost the post in the spring of 1690. For his critique of the return of tory ministers see *An Impartial Enquiry.*

[65] John Miller, 'Catholic Officers in the Later Stuart Army', *English Historical Review*, lxxxiii (1973), 53 n 1 gives references in state papers to their employment, but found their number very difficult to quantify.

© *The Parliamentary History Yearbook Trust 2009*

people would grow in love wth it, & quickly rellish ye sweet & advantage of it, having so lately had their necks gaul'd wth K. J his Yoak. so yt finding so much ease under this change they would not easely be p[er]swaded to change again. But if ye whigs are more inclin'd to a Com[m]onwealth than a K[in]gly governmt, then surely K. Wms obligation to them is so much ye greater, in yt they did at once forgoe both their intrest & inclinations to serve him in so import[an]t an affair & consequently his treatm[en]t of ym must grate so much ye harder.

It is certain yt K. J. did look upon ye whigs wth a very evill eye & [66]it was so, because he beleived yt they would obstruct him in ye carrying on {word illegible} yt work, wch he took to be not only his Intrest, but duty to promote, & fo{r} ye Contrary reason he cast so pleasing an aspect upon ye Torys & High Church party. He was not known to do an ill Natur'd thing to any, save such of ym as had bin active in carrying on ye Bill of Exclusion, wch was an attaque so directly ag[ain]st his p[er]son, & all yt he had, yt it's no wonder he sate as heavy as he could upon their skirts, & was nothing more than wt they might reasonably expect, how ever he had {?n}ot bin thereto so provoked, yet one lash fro[m] K. Wm must make ye whigs smart, much more than ten fro[m] K.J. For wt have ye whigs done, but to serve him wth all their might, upon yt principle, wch gave him a p[re]tence to come into Eng[lan]d &

[second side of large folio]

upon wch he took ye Crown, & according to yt principle in wch he had bin educated, & wch he had practised till he came into Eng[lan]d & by wch only he can be sure to keep ye Crown on his head, if he be guided by ye same politicks yt others have practised, who held their Crowns by like title. But if he had other intentions than wt appear'd till he had ye Crown, or else after he had it, chang'd his principle, That he only is to answere, the whigs gave no occasion for it, nor are any way in fault, so yt this proceeding is of so dark a complexion, as to take off a great deale of[67] odium fro[m] K.J. For when a man has done an infamous thing & another afterwards does ye like, or worse, its a Com[m]on saying & no less true, That such a man is beholding to such a one, for he has helpt to save his credit.

To sum up then ys point, Considering yt all ys is fallen upon ye whigs, yt evil is return'd them for the good they have done, Not for any infaithfulness or chang[e] yt is found in them, or any deceit yt is discover'd in ye Principle yt brought ye P. of O. into Eng[lan]d & afterwards gave him ye Crown; but because K. Wm & ye P. of O don't act upon ye same principle: Many of the whigs are ye worse for ys revolution, having layd out a great p[ar]t of their substance to help it forward & yet now are as much suspected by ys Governmt as they were in K. J his time; & may not ys kind of treatm[en]t take off much of the scandale yt lay upon K.J for his ingratitude to his old freinds, & fro[m] a Just resentm[en]t & indignation make ye whigs to have as good an opinion of K. J as of K. Wm, especially if it be observed, yt he now makes use of yos very men {o}f whom he complained in his declaration, & ye rest are such as were ye [m]ost scandalous in C.2ds time: If then it was a crime in K. J to imploy {yo}s men, is it less a fault in K. Wm to use ym, or rather is not he ye less excusable {?of} the two, in so doing, in as much as he yt reproves a thing in another

---

[66] Deletion of 'yet'.
[67] Deletion of 'ye'.

© *The Parliamentary History Yearbook Trust 2009*

& afterwards {c}omits ye like himself, is so much ye more to blame, because he sins knowingly & [68]p[er]haps ye other either did not know or beleive it to be a fault. If ye imploying men of Corrupt principles was an indication of K. J his wicked purpose, Is it an argum[en]t of K. Wms Juster intentions, when he makes use of yos very men, even to having an aversion for his old friends & their principles. Or rather is it not so much ye nearer to demonstration ypon wt he has set his heart, when in ye face of ye [69]sun, his actions contradict his declaration; even bare faced to lick up his own vomitt, & so directly to excuse if not justify wt K.J did in yt particular.

The harshest thing yt one man can do to another is to break his word, its the hardest to be forgiven of any thing, because its more difficult to find out a reparation [verso] for that than any other injury; For a word or promise is ye surest tye yt one man has upon another, Its ye only ligam[en]t of society, for if it be not inviolably observed, there's an end of all conversation, & dealings betwixt man & man, & ye whole Course of Nature is dissolved; Its ye most contemptable character yt any man can ly under to say of him, yt he does not regard his word, the religious keeping of it is a duty incumb[en]t on all degrees & conditions of men; only ye more publick & emin[en]t character they bear, ye more they are obliged to an exact p[er]formance of it, by reason, yt ye higher station they are in, so many more they are yt are intrested in it; & ye greater ye number is yt are injured by any man falsefying his word, by so much is ye offence the greater & less pardonable.

All promises are either expresst or implyd, yt is, They are so declared, in plain & direct words, or else they are so circumstanc'ed yt ye thing can honesty & fairly bear no other construction, or meaning: Both of yes are equally obligatory & a breach in either case is equally dishonest & grievous.

If ye P. of O. had not expressly tould ye world in his declaration yt he came into Eng[lan]d to cut up Popery & arbitrary power by ye roots yet wt could his complaining of K.J his exorbitances amount to less than a promise [70]yt he would not only releive us, for ye p[re]sent, but also p[re]vent ye like oppression for ye future. But in his additionall declaration, he says, That his undertaking was wth no other designe, than to procure a setlem[en]t of ye religion & of ye libertys & prop[er]tyes of ye subjects upon so sure a foundation yt they may be no more ^*in* danger of the Nations relapsing into ye like miseries at any time hereafter.

The words are as plain as ye matter is of import & sacred to wch they relate, & as they need no explication, so they are not capable of a double sence; & therefore it thence follows, yt ye P. of O. is under ye greatest obligation in ye world, to suppress yt wch may be a means to bring our religion or liberty into danger as well things yt were not named, as yos yt are menion'd in his declaration & he is equally obliged in both Cases; but if one Case be more obligatory than ye other, Then it is yt he take care, yt K. Wm.'s actions do not thwart or go Counter to ye P. of O his declaration, where Paragraph 5t & 11 he complains That they examined secretly ye opinion of ye Judges concerning ye dispensing power, & yos yt would not comply were turn'd out: This was very mischievous & all yt evell arose fro[m] ye Judges Pat[en]ts being only during pleasure, whereas had they ran

---

[68] Deletion.
[69] Deletion.
[70] Deletion.

© *The Parliamentary History Yearbook Trust 2009*

quam diu se bene gesserit[71] they would have stood more in aw of their consciences then of ye Court, & no such opinion could have bin obtaind if it

[sheet] 3. had not really bin their Judgm[en]t & therefore it's strange yt ye Pat[en]ts of the first Judges made by K. Wm should be during pleasure, & ye rest had bin so, if the house of Lords had not taken Notice of it, & upon yt ye stile was chang'd to good behaviour, but however all other places yt in ye 2 late reigns were usually given for life, are now held during pleasure.[72]

Parag. 6 he complains yt sev[er]all not qualified by law, in not having taken ye oaths [73]& Test were put into imploym[en]ts: If this was a crime, how then does K. Wm reform it by keeping up in his dutch troopes sev[er]all papists. Nay how comes it ab[ou]t yt sev[er]all (wth p[re]ference to other more deserving who stood candidates) were by his express com[m]and put into yos very imploymts wch they had forfeited for want of qualifying themselves according to law: & could not hold ym but by virtue of a New patent.

Parag. 7 He complains of ye Ecclesiasticall Com[m]ission, for being set up wthout any Colour of law, & ag[ain]st express laws to ye Contrary, & yt it was executed contrary to all law: This was indeed a Crying sin, yet how comes it ab[ou]t yt no body is called to acc[oun]t & punisht for it, so far fro[m] yt That many of those Com[m]issioners, hold ye same advantageous places as they did in K.J his time yt Com[m]ission only eccepted, & are in ye same plight & condition to all intents & purposes; saving yt one or two of ym are eccepted out of ye act of grace, to be reserved for no further punishm[en]t than only to be worse frightend than hurt, as is pritty plain by yt Minister of state, whom he no less than names in his declaration, yet now is received to kiss his hand & in so gracious a Man[n]er yt he seems not to stand very remote fro[m] his former place of secretary of state.[74] But ys surely is a New way of reformation, & is so far fro[m] p[re]venting ye like to ye future yt it looks rather like an approbation & incouragm[en]t of it.

Parag. 11 He again complains of turning out such Judges, as gave more regard to their Consciences then ye directions wch they rec[eive]d fro[m] others, & that thereby a great deale of blood has bin shed w[i]thout so much as suffering ye persons yt were accused to plead their own defence. This was true: But how is ys yet p[re]vented for ye future, where is yt p[er]son yt has yet bin punisht, either for prosecuting or giving sentence in yos Cases, wt mark of respect is set upon ye familys of yos yt so suffer'd,[75] Nay are not some of their posterity ready to perish, thoe they have petitioned for some small charity.

Parag. 13. He complains of ye Condition of Ire[lan]d for yt the whole governm[en]t being put into ye hands of papists, & yt ye Protest[an]t inhabitants are under the dayly fears of wt may be justly apprehended fro[m] ye arbitrary power wch is set up [verso] there. How much ye Matter is mended is rather to be wisht for, than yt it can be boasted of yt it is so in regard yt many of yos very men, & others yt are men of ye same complexion, do

---

[71] For as long as he shall behave well.

[72] A bill passed both houses in 1692 to ascertain commissions of judges but it failed the royal assent. It was not until the 1701 Act of Settlement that appointments were laid down as *quam diu se bene gesserint*.

[73] Deletion.

[74] Another reference to Sunderland.

[75] Warrington may have had his own financial difficulties in mind here.

now fill all ye places of profit & trust in yt K[ing]dome who p[re]paired ye way for popery, having first establisht & exercised yt arbitrary power of wch he complains.

Parag. 18 He complains what artifices were used to obstruct ye calling of a free & legall Parl[iamen]t least ye evill concellors yt he mentiond should be called to acc[oun]t; & in order to ys there were [76]indeavors to sow divisions between [77]yos of ye Church of Eng[lan]d & ye dissenters, & next yt yos in imploymt, or yt were in any considerable esteem in ye sev[er]all Counties of Eng[lan]d were required to declare beforehand yt they would concur in ye repeale of ye Test & penal lawes, or give their votes for such as would do so; & yt by reason of these & other foule practices, ye people of Eng[lan]d cannot expect a remedy fro[m] a free Parl[iament] legally called & chosen; but they may p[er]haps see one called in wch all elections will be carried by fraud or force, & wch will be composed of such p[er]sons of whom yos evil Councellors held ymselves well assured, in wch all things will be carryd on according to their direction & Intrest wthout any regard to ye Good or happiness of ye Nation:

This indeed was a bould stroke of yos yt then sate at ye helme; yet [78]might it not be more ^*probably* be expected than to see yt Parl[iament] so soon dissolved yt gave K. Wm ye Crown & next to see ye Methods yt were used to have one of another complexion & after all to continue so long wthout any prospect of another to be called. For ye first Parl[iament] were upon ye right scent, by doing yt wch could have brought yos evel councellors & other Criminalls to Justice & wt else was Necessary to support yt power wch they had set up.[79] They were forward to supply wt was necessary to carry on ye War, but not inclined to give too great a revenue for life, knowing how fatall to ys Governm[en]t a revenue for life is, yt it will do more than pay off ye Civile list: Wt more could have bin expected fro[m] ym or wherein did they faile of wt might be required fro[m] ym & wt could yos evil councellors more at yt time than to see yt Parl[iament] dissolved, yet it was sent away before it had finisht its work & thereby ye Nation was frustrated in much of its expectations, & ye K. lost [£]600000 yt ye Parl[iament] had ingaged to supply him wth & had found out means to raise ye money speedily. The reason ye K. gave out for ys untimely dissolution was ye he might be more at leasure to p[re]pare for his Irish expedition, wch is

[next side of large sheet]

no less remarkable than all ye rest if it be but remember'd yt he called another Parl[iament] before he went into Ire[lan]d, wch has made ^*it* not difficult to guess whether it was a true reason, or else a p[re]tence to have a Parl[iament] of another complexion. Considering besides yt indeavors to influence ye election of members for Parl[iament] was never more bare faced & open than was for yt.[80] A reverend Prelate sent his circular letter to ye clergy of his dioceses & some body whose word carryed authority wth it, spoke to Sir R.H. yt he would take care to choose right church of Eng[lan]d

---

[76] Deletion of 'as a means'.

[77] Deletion of 'amongst'.

[78] Deletion of 'but'.

[79] The dissolution of the Convention Parliament in January 1690 had frustrated whig attempts to be revenged on the tories.

[80] Henry Horwitz, 'The General Election of 1690', *Journal of British Studies*, xi (1971), 77–91.

© *The Parliamentary History Yearbook Trust 2009*

men, for they were for ye Crown.[81] To second it those [82]yt in both houses were most
Zealous for ye Engl[ish] libertys were turn'd ut of their profitable places & men of
another character put in their roomes, so yt thoe there was no closetting as was in K. J
his time, nor p[er]sons were not required beforehand to promise to raise ye p[re]rogative,
& give all ye revenue for life; yet wt could more plainly give people to understand upon
wt termes p[re]ferm[en]t was to be had, & as ye p[re]liminarys were as effectuall as any
other yt could be used to influence elections, so never was more foule play in ye returns
made by ye officers, scarcely one half of ye house of Com[m]ons yt were return'd had
a right to sit: What Parl[iament] can take less notice of yos evel Councellors, wt worse
practise as to influence [83]elections, would have bin made use of by K.J wt more undue
returns, wt Parl[iament] can be guided more by directions & less regard ye good &
happyness of ye Nation than ys & yet it is continued & like to do so: Notwithstanding
Parag. 21 He says yt his expedition is intended for no other design, but to have a free
& lawfull Parl[iament] assembled, yt indeed is ye proper & Naturall remedy for a diseas'd
governm[en]t, but if he thinks ys to be such a Parl[iament] then where is ye difference
betwixt ys Parl[iament] & such a one as ^*perhaps* K.J might have called

Parag. 23d He promises to send back all his foreign forces, as soon as ye state of ye
Nation will admit of it: What ever occation there may be for ye keeping of these foreign
forces here; yet wheres ye p[re]tence for the bringing over of so very many more
foreigners, & at ye same time to discourage & disband his Engl[ish] troopes, & espetially
yos yt were rais'd to assist him at his landing, or serve [84]him now upon an Engl[ish]
principle.

Parag. 25 He invites & requires all p[er]sons of wt rank or quality soever to come
to assist ^*him* in order to ye executing of his design; wt can ye meaning of ys be, but
yt he would esteem of Every man according to ye readiness yt he should ^*shew* in
obeying his summons & yt Every man should be [85]placed in his favour according to
ye Zeale & assistance yt he gave to ye Cause, & yt every man should reap ye fruits of
his labours. Not yt they should hazard their lives, the ruine of their posteritys & familys
& be at a certain great expence & after all not to be thanked for wt they have done,
but the more they have done to be ye worse look't on: yet it proved in ye Issue yt yos
who came into ye P. are never ye better for it, & yos yt stay'd at home are never ye
worse; Nay ye more early & considerably yt any man appear'd in yt business, ye more
its indeavor'd to depress his credit, & a worse argum[en]t for ye obtaining of anything
cant be used, than to say yt he appeared early & eminently upon ye P. his landing, &
every man is so much a worser subject, by how much he is Zealous to assert ye liberty
of ye subject.[86]

Parag. 26 He promises to restore ye ancient constitution of ye K[ing]dome of
Scot[lan]d. Surely he took yt constitution to be differ[en]t fro[m] wt it is, or else why did

---

[81] Bishop Compton of London appeared at both the Middlesex and Essex polls, and sent out a series of
circular lettes to the clergy reminding them 'how highly the Church of England is concerned to send good
members to the next Parliament': Horwitz, 'General Election', 84.

[82] Deletion of 'the most'.

[83] Deletion of 'elect'.

[84] Deletion of 'served'.

[85] Deletion of 'have'.

[86] Warrington's own case seems uppermost here.

he delay & even seem resolved not to grant sev[er]all things wch were part of ye Conditions upon wch he took ye Crown,[87] till a necessity afterwards compelled him to it, & yet as soon as he found himself more at ease, again to obstruct it all he Could, & openly to oppose wt had bin setled by himself.

Parag. 27 He promises yt ye British intrest shall be secured in Ire[lan]d. When he will do yt or wt intrest he means is not yet well understood; for otherwise wherefore were the succour for yt K[ing]dome so notoriously delay'd & thereby give occation to believe yt a Conquest was rather intended, than a timely relief, & happyness of yt Nation; since ye war is purposely spun out, wthout paying his army there, yt they must subsist [88]on free quarter or starve.[89]

Thus religiously he has observ'd his declaration & ye Nation is to be establisht upon such a principle & such Justice.

When K. J saw yt ye P. of O. was resolved to come, he then indeavoured to retract sev[er]all things yt he had done;[90] the deceit of wch ye P. did indeavor to discover in his additionall declaration, where amongst other things he says, That they lay down Nothing wch they may not take up at pleasure; & they reserve entire & not so much as mention their claims & Pretences to an arbitrary & despotick power; wch has bin ye root of their oppression; & of ye totall subversion of ye governm[en]t. This indeed was a true saying; but did ye P. mend ye matter when he made so great a difficulty to take ye Crown upon Conditions, only because

[sheet] 4. he p[re]tended <u>That it would touch his honor</u> to take ye Crown upon terms. Now wt words can more plainly express a desire to be cloathed wth a despotick & arbitrary power, & yt ye lives, libertys, honors & estates of ye subjects should depend wholly on his good will & pleasure; for yes are his own words in the 4th Parag. of his declaration; Wt can make a K more absolute than yt wt the subject enjoys, is a concession of ye Crown; but when he found yt this expression gave distast then it was given out, yt if the Crown were given wtout any conditions yt he would of his own accord grant more than they had ask't But is any good quarter to be expected fro[m] him, yt wthout any reason or Colour grasps at that wch is ye unquestionable right of another, & wt his Concessions would have bin may be guesst at by ye exact observation of his declaration: Besides all yt has bin s[ai]d, it is no less observable how he has turn'd ye tables betwixt K.J & his evell Councellors; on whom he loads all ye blame of K. J his Maleadminis-tration, but charges K.J wth nothing; in his declaration he calls them Evell Councellors no less than 20 times, & yet ye storme is pass'd over their heads, & they now sit under their vines & fig trees cheerfully enjoying wt they had gott; & some are in a better condition than ever, whilst K.J is gone away wth ye loss of 3 K[ing]domes & like ye scape Goat sent into ye wilderness of exile to bear ye iniquitys of his evell Councellors, & thereby has appeas'd ye Wrath of K. Wm as if ye Crown was wt he ment by his declaration.

---

[87] The declaration of the Scottish Convention, 11 Apr. 1689.

[88] Deletion of 'live'.

[89] The relief of Ireland was the occasion of an outspoken letter of criticism by Warrington in 1690, although ironically his fear then was that William's absence would let James return to his throne: TNA, SP8/6/47. For a critique of William's Irish policy see *An Impartial Enquiry*, 10–12, which names many officers there who should have been purged from William's force.

[90] Detailed in *The Life of James the Second*, ed. J.S. Clarke (1816), 185–91.

© *The Parliamentary History Yearbook Trust 2009*

But had K.J ye courage to have stay'd, wt could there have bin done; there would have bin a great cry & no wooll;[91] A great deale of Mischeif & no body yt did it. For Nothing was layd to K. J his charge, nor would a hair of his head have bin toucht, & if it had then bin just to have fallen upon yos evell ministers, is it not as unjust yt they are now in so good a Case: for K.J his staying or going, does not make them less or more guilty or innocent, nor does it, more or less oblige, or aquitt K. Wm strictly to pursue ye P. of O. his declaration. And since K.J his Maleadministration is so easyly passed over, its no wonder yt ye reign of C. 2d must be thought so very regular.[92] Were there a disposition to make us a happy people & yt it should be a lasting felicity, we should ^go as far back as to ye beginning of C. 2ds time, for can he be altogether blameless & K.J be in fault[,] wt did he do more than take up things where K. C left them, & had it bin possible for K.J to have gone so far as he did, if C. 2d had not made way for him, & therefore if ye root be not cut up it will in time bring forth ye like fruit again, & no man ever designedly leaves ye root, but in hopes & expectation yt it will spring again.[93]

Upon ys whole Matter then, if K.J disobliged ye Nation so very much by {?breaking his} [verso] word, how far has K.Wm mended ye Matter by ye better observation of his promise. If ye breach of a Princes word can disintrest ye people fro[m] him, How far has K.Wm obliged ye Nation to be in his Intrest, by a more sacred regard to his ingagm[en]ts.

KJ indeed broke his promise [94]very Notoriously, yet did he do anything yt did not directly tend to promote yt wch he had always professt & practised, or did he do any thing yt was not consist[en]t wth ye principles of his religion, & wt unp[re]judiced people foresaw & expected, because his Intrest & religion naturally led him to it, & would not be p[re]vented or delayd longer than there wanted opertunity & power to effect it: But on ye other hand can it be s[ai]d yt ye wors[hi]p wch K.Wm now professes & seems Zealous in was yt ^in wch he was educated, & has ever since professt & practised[?][95]. Was ye ground of his declaration & quarrel to K.J founded upon ys Tory & High Church principle, was it men of yt principle yt helpt him to ye Crown; & was ye argum[en]ts for placing him on ye throne derived fro[m] yt principle. Did any foresee or expect yt he would govern by yt principle wch now he does; or at least yt he would discard all his old [96]& best freinds, upon ye score yt he has parted wth ym: If therefore ye breach of promise is more scandalous in ye one case then in ye other, <u>if he is more reprovable yt finds fault wth another, yt he may first suppl[an]t him & then do ye like himself, does it not then become ye Intrest of ye Nation, at least of ye whigs to recall</u>

---

[91] A proverbial saying expressive of contempt or derision for one who promises great things but never fulfils the promises.

[92] Like other whigs, Warrington thought the origins of the revolution lay at least as far back as Charles II's reign, if not earlier. 'Some Observations' began its account of the revolution with Charles II's reign. Tories, however, charted the revolution from James's reign. So the implication is that William has an inadequate sense of the causes of the revolution.

[93] Warrington is arguing for a more fundamental revolution, that would remodel the government as restored in 1660 in order to prevent any possibility of the return of tyranny.

[94] Deletion of 'word'.

[95] William had been raised a calvinist but conformed to the Church of England.

[96] Deletion of 'friends'.

K.J. rather than to support K.Wm for may they ^not say, as ye ten tribs to Rehoboam,[97] wt portion have we in K.Wm wn we have none inheritance in ye house of Nassau; & may not they well repeat yos words when they see ye Governm[en]t wholly put into their hands who in ye 2 late reigns were ye instrum[en]ts of their oppression; are not ye same things to be expected when you have ye same men again? Wt signe is there yt they have chang'd their principle or in wt have they discover'd yt they have a better inclination to ye publick Intrest, & then if a mans throat is to be cut, is it any thing ye better by wt hand, or at whose command it is done.

The people of Eng[lan]d dislike a Popish K. only because they can have no dependence on his word, when it comes to interfere wth ye Catholick Cause: & for ye same reason can he be better esteemed who has actually broke his word, & seems resolved to p[er]sist in a Course yt in Every step must thwart his ingagm[en]ts to ye Nation: Is not he less dangerous yt makes his Intrest follow his religion, & if he break his word it is to promote his religion, than he yt makes his religion follow his Intrest, nay yt can change his religion & principle to serve his ends. And is not he much more[98] to be trusted yt is firm in his religion thoe a false wors[hi]p, than he yt either had no religion or else can shift it as a seaman does his sailes to serve his Turne; for ye first you may know where to have him, but for ye other his ways are past finding out.[99]

[next side of double sheet] Many hold it as a Maxime, That if Eng[lan]d be ever inslaved it will be by a Protest[an]t K; this seems to be founded on good reason, & to be very much supported by experience; for ye Jealousy yt ye people have of a Popish K. makes ym ever so wary & Circumspect yt they will hardly be imposed on wtever he may propose, in relation to ye pubick, thoe honestly & bona fide intended as proposed yet they suspect yt it is only a disguise to cover some thing yt is design'd agt ym: His Oaths & Ingagm[en]ts they reckon as no sort of security & put ye worst construction upon every thing he does, thoe it will naturally bear a better meaning, & all ys is so, because they know his Intrest & religion draws him another way: But as to a Protest[an]t P. ye people are too apt to have an implicite confidence in him; because they think there can be no danger if he is either a wise or an honest man, & its hard to find so wretched a Creature yt is neither wise nor honest: For if he be an honest man & religiously observe his word, Oaths & other ingagm[en]ts wch he enters into, before ye Crown can be set on his head, they are safe enough: Or if he be so wise as to pursue his true Intrest, then yt way also they are safe; because no K. of Eng[lan]d can be so great as he yt has ye hearts of his people; & he yt will have ye hearts of his people, must make ye law ye measure of his power, & ye Com[m]on good ye end of his Governm[en]t;[100] fro[m] hence it is yt ye people grow careless & negleg[en]t of ye publick & put [101]soe favourable

---

[97] 1 Kings vv.1–24 relates how Rehoboam became king of Israel on the death of his tyrannous father and was asked to lighten their yoke; when he refused, the people asked 'what portion have we in David?' and 'departed to their tents' in rebellion.

[98] Deletion of 'reliable'.

[99] This reverses the argument of his 'Persuasive to Union' of 1692 which asks 'though a reconciliation with King James were practicable, could there be any Moral assurance that he would sacredly keep his Word, and that he had more just and right intentions than heretofore?'. He argued that James's declaration of 1692 should be 'abhorred by every man, that values himself upon the title of a honest Man or English Man': *Works*, 404.

[100] This had been Warrington's own reasoning in his previous public statements.

[101] Deletion of 'such'.

a construction upon all his actions, yt they believe every thing to be well done because he does it, & if they find him out of ye way, they look upon it as a Casuall Mistake, & no ill designed thing; & thus they suffer their eyes to be blinded, yt they cannot see ye things yt belong to their peace, & will hardly be convinc'd yt they are in danger till ye yoak is ready to be put upon their Necks. Therefore if a Protest[an]t K yt aims at arbitrary power is more dangerous than a Popish K; is not K.J. rather to be desired at ys time than K.Wm seeing that upon no better a foundation to begin wth he has adventured further than ever any K. of Eng[lan]d did in so short a time & has provided himself wth better means to effect his purpose than ever any K. of Eng[lan]d had, his army being far greater, & made up of foreigners, or such as he thinks are best consern'd for their loyalty; He holding it as a Maxime yt none ought to serve in his troopes, yt have a principle for ye good of their Country, & accordingly he has broke & disbanded all such as he beleives are so inclind; And Therefore if K.J had ye Courage to come into Eng[lan]d wthout bringing a force along wth him & put out a proclamation to ye effect wch follows wh{?at} opposition would he meet wth.

[verso]

James 2d &c. Every man must believe yt a greater affliction can[n]ot befall a Prince than to be driven out of his K[ing]domes, of wch burden we have bin no less sensible during this our exile, yet nothing afflicted us so much as to see our people seduced by ye malicious insinuations of ye P. of O. who at ye same time intended nothing less than to assume yt despotick power, wch he charged us to have designed. We do not deny yt some things were done in our reign, wch were not warranted by law, yet it was not so much our own inclination, as ye ill advice of others yt prevailed wth us wch may appear in yt as soon as we perceived our error, we did immediately give wt redress was possible in so short a time; & had done all things else yt might have given our people satisfaction, if we had not bin prevented by yt fondness wch our people had taken to ye P. of O. whereby they would not suffer themselves to see wt we would further have done, or wt he intended to do. & therefore finding ye nation in so great a ferm[en]t; we wthdrew ourselves to save ye efusion of our subjects blood, for had not we more regarded their good than our own, its very well known yt we had a force more than sufficient to have driven ye P. of O. out of Eng[lan]d,[102] & out of ye like tenderness to our people we also wthdrew ourselves from our K[ing]dome of Ireland for its plain by yt little progress yt ye P. of O. has made there, yt it would have bin yet less; had we stayd wth our Troops, by reason that [103]our p[re]sence amongst them would have animated them very much; yet we wthdrew ourselves hoping by a quiet retreat to bring our people to a better temper, & now do most confidently believe, That they are sensible yt Matters are very little better than they were, & yt as we never burden'd our people wth Taxes, not desired any aid, so yt ye vast sums wch they have since given, are disposed of to their disadvantage. For wherein does he accuse us [104]whereof he is not guilty himself. Parag. 5t & 11th of his declaration he complains, That ye opinion of ye Judges were examined secretly concerning ye dispensing power; & yos yt would not comply were turn'd out,

---

[102] A different analysis of James's forces and the reasons for his flight are given in 'Reasons why King James ran away from Salisbury', in *Works*, 56–69.

[103] Deletion.

[104] Deletion of 'me'.

© *The Parliamentary History Yearbook Trust 2009*

in order to set up arbitrary power. If ye P. of O was such an enemy to arbitrary power wherefore did he desire to have ye Crown wtout conditions, & why did he say, it toucht his honor to take ye Crown upon terms: does any man intend ye more honestly because he desires more than comes to his share, & yt is ye undoubted right of another? does any man desire all only yt he may give it again? & can a K. be more absolute than to have all in his power: And wt could he intend less than to have ye Judges at his beck when he made ye Judges patents during pleasure, & its plain the rest had run in yt style if ye house of Lds {?had} not interposed.

[sheet] 5. Wherefore does he complain Parag. 6 That sev[er]all not qualified by law in not having taken ye Oaths & Test were put into imploymets Seing yt in yos very Troopes wth wch he invaded Eng[lan]d there were severall papists & are still continued in their posts? & how comes it ab[ou]t That by his express Com[m]and sev[er]all were put into yos very imploymts wch they were uncapable to hold, but by virtue of a New Grant, by reason yt they had faild to qualify themselves according to law? And wherefore is he so angry wth ye p[ers]ons yt were imployd by us, calling ym no less than 20 times, evel Councellors, seing he now makes use of them himself, even till it comes to yt Minister of state whom he loads wth so heavy a Character Parag. 7th for changing his religion & being in ye ecclesiasticall Com[m]ission, for he received him in so gracious a Man[n]er to kiss his hand, yt he seems to stand fair[105] to be in statu quo: Wherefore Parag. 13th does he complain of Arbitrary power being set up in Ire[lan]d seing he has put yt Governm[en]t wholly into ye hands of men of Arbitrary & Corrupt principles. And Parag. 18 he speaks of wt artifices were made use of to obstruct ye calling of a free & legall Parl[iament]. And were[106] ye indeavers ever greater to have a Parl[iament] chosen to serve a particular end, then has bin used to compass ys? was any thing omitted yt might influence ye elections, to have such a sort of men chosen? did not he & others solicit ye Matter both in publick & private as much as they could? & was not there a generall remove out of all imploym[en]ts men of one Complexion to make roome for yos of another Principle; & wt was ye great partiality wch he shewd to ye high church p[ar]ty but to sow division betwixt yos of ye church of Eng[lan]d & others[107] yt were more moderate & plainly to tell ye world upon wt terms p[re]ferm[en]t is to be had & kept? was ever so may false returns in any Parl[iament] as is in ys? & was ever any Parl[iament] more guided by private directions, or yt did less regard ye good & happyness of ye nation; why then has he suffer'd it to sit so long[108] & yet no prospect of its dissolution. If this be such a free ^& *legall* Parl[iament] as he means, then where's the difference betwixt ys & ye Parl[iament] wch he says might p[er]haps have bin called by us. Its only thus. That wt he maliciously did suggest ag[ain]st us[109] he has actually done yt very thing so yt were there nothing else, ys alone does make it plain, yt he raised[110] the greater Noise & Cry ag[ain]st us, yt he might be less observed whilest he did ye same things where he accused us.

---

[105] Darker ink, suggesting a revision.

[106] This word is in a darker ink and corrects 'was'.

[107] Deletion of 'dissenters'.

[108] Presumably in comparison with the Convention Parliament.

[109] Deletion of 'to have intended'.

[110] Deletion.

© *The Parliamentary History Yearbook Trust 2009*

Parag. 23d He promises to send back all his foreign forces, as soon as ye state of ye nation will admit of it; but wt prospect is there yt he either designs to govern wthout an army or to send yos troops away whilest dayly he sends for more, & at ye same time disbands all such of his troops as were raised to assist him at his landing or yt now serve him upon an honourable principle. Wherefore did he [verso] p[re]fer such of our troops as basely & treacherously deserted us, to yose yt rose to assist him upon a principle, but yt he beleived ye one would serve his will & pleasure without asking a question, where as ye other would scorne to do any thing ag[ain]t ye Intrest of their Country. And is it not very plain yt all ye vast sums wch have bin given him to put a speedy end to ye war, have bin lay'd out to prolong ye war; & wt can ys mean, but to bring it to a necessity yt he may govern by an army.

Prerog. 25 He invites & requires all persons of wt rank or quality soever to come to assist him in order to ye executing of his design; now wt design could he mean but yt of arbitrary power? Considering yt althoe great Crowds came into him & may of ym of great quality, & I beleive most of ym fro[m] a p[er]swasion yt their libertys were in danger; & beleiving yt it was their dutys at all times to rescue their Country; yet all such are now not only lay'd aside, but they & all of yt principle for ye publick good are discountenanced, as people suspected [111]by ye governmt, whilest all imploym[en]ts are put into ye hands of men Notorious for arbitrary & Corrupt Principles.

Can it be beleived yt he intended to setle things in Scotland as he promised. Parag. 26 seing he delay'd to grant sev[er]all things upon wch he accepted ye Crown till by a Necessity he was afterwards compelled to it, & then again when he thought [112]he had a more favourable opportunity, he indeavor'd to obstruct wt had bin setled by himself & as ys Method is impossible to work a setlem[en]t, so wt can he mean by promoting of divisions, than to make a necessity of having a standing army. And there he promises Parag. 27 to secure ye British Intrest in Ire[lan]d: Wt else could he mean, than a conquest of yt Country, for else whereof did he delay ye sending of succors thither, & now does manifestly spin out ye war, & leaves his army unp[ai]d, yt they may susbsist on free quarter or starve.

Upon ye whole matter, wt other construction can all ys naturally bear but yt althoe he p[re]tended yt setlemt of Eng[lan]d Scot[lan]d & Ire[lan]d yet yt he intended nothing less than, as his own words are Parag. 4 of his declaration, to be cloathed wth an arbitrary despotick power, & to have ye lives, libertys, honors & estates of his subjects to depend wholly on his good will & pleasure, & be intirely subject to him; for can ye Method in wch he proceeds by ye proper way to setle ye K[ing]domes upon so sure a foundation yt there may be no danger of ye Nation's relapsing into Slavery?

We for our parts do disclaim any arbitrary power & all pretences to it, & do declare, yt as ye law ought to be ye measure of ye K.s prerogative, so it shall be ye rule by wch we intend to govern our people; & yt ys may be more [next side of sheet] freely confirm'd & establisht; we will give our assent to any bill yt shall be presented to us by our 2 houses of Parl[iament] either to pair off any p[ar]t of the p[re]rogative yt is or may be dangerous to ye liberty of our people, or other wise for ye reviving & strengthening any of our peoples propertyes, so as yt it may not be in ye power of any succeeding K

[111] Deletion.
[112] Deletion of 'had'.

© *The Parliamentary History Yearbook Trust 2009*

to bring their laws & libertys into danger. And since we do Intend nothing more than yt our people may live happyly & securely under us in a full & perfect enjoym[en]t of their lawes & liberties, & yt our intention therein may ye more clearly appear, We do hereby declare That as we have brought no troopes wth us, so we will never attempt to raise any wthout ye Consent of our 2 houses of Parl[iament]: Neither do we desire any Guards for our p[er]son either horse or foot further than wt our 2 houses of Parl[iament] shall like of for decency, but not to ye Terror of our subjects; because we are sensible yt ye good will of our people, is a surer defence & security to our p[er]son than Guards, or any other force: And we do hereby restore to our people ye choosing of their sheriffs, in ye sev[er]all Countys of our K[ing]dome of Eng[lan]d as also the electing of ye officers of ye Militia, as it was anciently practis'd & of right did belong &[113] will give our assent to any bill whensoever p[re]sented to us for yt purpose: And yt it may ye better appear yt we will pursue no other Intrest but yt of our peoples happyness, We do hereby declare & promise, yt we will put into all places of honor Trust & profit, Those of ye best Intrest & reputation in their Countrys & we will not put into office, any person yt is not well lik'd by our people, & we will take care yt Parl[iament]s be duely called & held, yt ye Just Complaints & grievances of ye Nation, & of very particular p[er]son may be heard & redress'd: And yt ys our return into Eng[lan]d may not be an occation of disordering any thing yt has bin setled during ys our absence, nor yt any man may [114]be under any app[re]hension by reason of any thing ^*done during* ye administration of ye P. of O: We do hereby confirme to Every of our subjects ye titles & dignitys to wch they have bin raised by ye P. of O. & do hereby pardon to Every one of our subjects all man[n]er of [115]Crimes & offences wtsoever, & because theyr may have bin some things don wch are not in ye power of ye Crown to pardon, we will therefore give our assent to a Bill for ye Confirming to all persons their titles & dignityes & for a generall oblivion & amnesty.

And after all we can[n]ot but believe, yt our people are clearly convinc'd how grossly they have bin abused & imposed on by ye P. of O. & yt. they are no less satisfied of our better intentions, Considering yt if we should attempt to govern otherwise than according to law, we have put a power into their hands to [116]compell us to do ym right: Therefore being confident yt our people do see it is as their intrest as well as duty to receive us, & return to their duty, we are come in a most peacable Man[n]er wthout troopes or force to let our people see ye good opinion we have of them.

---

[113] Deletion of 'will'.
[114] Deletion of 'think'.
[115] Deletion of 'offences'.
[116] Deletion of 'pull'.

© *The Parliamentary History Yearbook Trust 2009*

'Rendering the Union more Complete': The *Squadrone Volante* and the Abolition of the Scottish Privy Council*

GRAHAM TOWNEND

The 22nd article of the Treaty of Union had settled the Scottish representation in the parliament of Great Britain. Although both the old and the new parties had readily agreed to modify its terms before the union came into effect most Scots blamed the new party for this unpopular amendment. As well as evading this censure the old party was also able to use the union to consolidate its grip on the government of Scotland. Intensely annoyed at this the new party retaliated by arguing that Scottish institutions should be remodelled along English lines. The first step was the abolition of the Scottish privy council. When it failed to persuade Lord Treasurer Godolphin to assist, the new party, or the *Squadrone* as it was now more commonly known, turned to the whig junto. It was eager to oblige and a bill to abolish the council was introduced during the first session of the British parliament. Godolphin's hesitant response to the *Squadrone* and the junto was criticised by the northern secretary of state, Robert Harley. He appealed to the duke of Marlborough for help, but this merely intensified the differences with Godolphin. Harley also turned to the queen and with her approval took the unprecedented, and unusual, step of supporting abolition in the house of commons. Although this brought the disagreement with Godolphin to a head, the lord treasurer responded with a vigorous, but unsuccessful, attempt to amend the bill in the Lords. The court's failure was quickly forgotten, however, as most Scots damned the *Squadrone* for once more betraying its country.

Keywords: old party; new party; *Squadrone Volante*; Scottish privy council; Harley; Godolphin; Scottish parliament; British parliament; Treaty of Union; Queen Anne; whig junto

Forty years ago Geoffrey Holmes's magisterial *British Politics in the Age of Anne* was first published. As a scholarly analysis of the workings of politics between roughly 1702 and 1714 it is still unsurpassed. One of the most impressive of its many outstanding qualities was its willingness to study British rather than just English politics and particularly in its use of the family papers of James Graham, first duke of Montrose. Montrose's correspondence allowed Holmes to trace the activities of the *Squadrone Volante* in his chapter on the structure of the whig party. He noted that whilst there had been informal contacts between the leaders of the *Squadrone* and the whig junto prior to 1707 it was only after the meeting of the first British parliament that the close links 'between the two groups

* I should like to thank Sir Robert Clerk of Penicuik for permission to quote from the manuscript in his possession. I am grateful to Clyve Jones for his comments on an earlier draft of this article. I would also like to thank Aileen Lightbody for proof-reading, David Pettigrew for IT backup, and Dominic Bere, Mary Ross and Tina Wood for discussions on this subject. Original spelling and punctuation have been retained in quotations.

were forged in the session of 1707–08 as a mainly tactical arrangement, initially developing out of Junto support for the abolition of the Edinburgh privy council, a body dominated by the *Squadrone*'s bitter rivals, the Queensberryites'.[1] Although Holmes then went on to examine in some detail the oft-troubled partnership between the *Squadrone* and the Junto during the last four years of Queen Anne's reign, the Montrose Papers were unable to help him clarify the *Squadrone*'s entry into British politics. Now, however, to mark the 40th anniversary of the publication of his work, it is worth extending his analysis back to 1707 to examine the *Squadrone*'s involvement in the development of British politics after the conclusion of the Treaty of Union.

The last meeting of Scotland's parliament, which began at Edinburgh in the autumn of 1706, had seen the court party, led by the duke of Queensberry and the earls of Seafield and Mar, co-operating closely with the *Squadrone*, led by the earl of Marchmont, in ratifying the Treaty of Union. At this time both groups still made use of their respective titles of the old and new parties, labels which were used interchangeably with the court and the *Squadrone*, and which were only finally abandoned during the first sitting of the British parliament. Their unanimity was evident on 7 January 1707 when the 22nd article of the Treaty of Union was considered in the parliament house. This article concerned the Scottish representatives who were to sit at Westminster after the union. The two parties ensured that parliament approved the clause in the article, which set the number of Scots representatives in the British parliament at 61, 16 representative peers in the Lords and 45 members in the Commons, by 114 votes to 73.

They then conjured up a controversial proposal to amend the article so that the choice of the Scots representatives would be 'in such manner as by a subsequent Act of this present Session of Parliament of Scotland shall be settled which Act is hereby Declared to be as valid as if it were a part of and engrossed in this Treaty'.[2] Two days later the article was approved and a committee appointed to bring in a separate act about how the Scots who were to attend the British parliament were to be chosen. The remaining articles of the treaty were then approved and on 15 January a draft of an act ratifying the treaty was presented to parliament, but before it could be read it was moved that the House 'should first proceed to the Constitution of the manner of electing the representatives for Scotland to the Parliament of Great Britain'.[3] Debate followed on whether to proceed to ratify the treaty or to consider the constitution, and just before the vote was taken it was agreed that if it was decided to ratify the Treaty of Union first then the constitution would be considered immediately afterwards. The vote went in favour of ratifying. This was done on the next day and five days later the House came to consider the choice of the Scottish representatives in accordance with the amendment to the 22nd article.

The earl of Marchmont gave in a proposal 'that the 61 Members from this Nation to the Parliament of Brittain, be chosen by the House'.[4] Two days were spent discussing this and on 21 January it was objected that this resolve 'was inconsistent with our standing

---

[1] Geoffrey Holmes, *British Politics in the Age of Anne* (1967), 243.

[2] *Acts of the Parliaments of Scotland* [hereafter cited as *APS*], xi, 390.

[3] *APS*, xi, 402.

[4] Sir David Hume of Crossrigg, *A Diary of the Proceedings in the Parliament and Privy Council of Scotland* (Bannatyne Club, Edinburgh, 1828), 19.

© *The Parliamentary History Yearbook Trust 2009*

laws, and the 22d Article as ratified', to which it was answered 'that the seeming inconsistencie was taken off by the clause added to the Article, whereby that matter was left alone, to be determined as the Parliament should think fit'.[5] Marchmont's proposal, however, was not entirely welcome to all members of the old party. Some, like the earl of Leven and John Clerk of Penicuik, opposed it whilst others, like the earl of Rosebery, were absent from the House, but as Marchmont's son-in-law, George Baillie of Jerviswood, observed it was supported by Lord Chancellor Seafield and the senior secretary of state in Scotland, the earl of Mar. Despite this division, Marchmont's resolve seemed likely to be approved. Anticipating that the vote would go against them the country opposition lodged a number of protests, most noticeably that of the duke of Hamilton, who complained that the sitting parliament's choosing Scotland's representatives was inconsistent with the 22nd article where it was expressly stated that once the time and place of the meeting of the parliament of Great Britain had been appointed by the queen, 'a writ shall be immediately Issued under the Great Seal of Great Britain directed to the Privy Council of Scotland for summoning the sixteen Peers and for electing fourty-five members'.[6] When the House divided, Marchmont's resolve carried with a reduced majority of 84 votes to 65.

The reluctance of some members of the old party to support this resolution was a source of considerable unease to the new party. Its anxiety intensified when it was suggested that the choice of the Scots representatives should be postponed until after the election of a new parliament. The old party then arranged a meeting with Marchmont and his colleagues where it tried to persuade them to agree to an election after the union had come into effect. If the new party agreed the old party assured it that in return it would support all its candidates when parliament choose its representatives, whereas if the selection was made during the present session the claims of others, who had recommendations from London, would have to take precedence. This idea was instantly dismissed, the new party insisting that the duke of Queensberry was not bound by agreements made at London because he had the power to choose whoever he pleased. The new party also argued that it was not in the national interest to have an election, which, in the present uncertain circumstances, it claimed was bound to be disorderly and might produce a parliament hostile to the union. Surprisingly, the old party suddenly gave in to these objections and agreed that the Scots representatives would be selected by the sitting parliament. Parliament then approved the Act of Constitution on 5 February, but Jerviswood remained suspicious of the old party, writing to James Johnston 'their secret reasons I know not'.[7]

He would have been even more troubled if he had seen the letter which the earl of Mar wrote to the Scottish under secretary of state at London, Sir David Nairne, on the same day that the Act of Constitution was passed. Although the old party appeared to have conceded all the new party's demands about the selection of the Scots representatives Mar was more than happy with the Act of Constitution. 'I hope it will please', he wrote, 'for Friends to the Union here think it very right adjusted, wch was pretty difficult to get done. Our election will I believe be made some day next Week, & we

---

[5] *Correspondence of George Baillie of Jerviswood* (Bannatyne Club, Edinburgh, 1842), 182.

[6] *APS*, xi, 415.

[7] *Baillie Corr.*, 186.

have little fear but those chosen will all be those who have been for the Union.' He was confident, once the representatives had been chosen and other minor business finished, that it would be judged to have been 'a glorious session of Parl: and in a little time I hope you will be able to tell me the same thing of that of England'.[8] The difficulty Mar identified in finishing the Act of Constitution was getting the new party to oppose any suggestion that there should be an election in Scotland. Once it took this stand the old party immediately abandoned this idea knowing that it could claim that it had been forced to accept this unpopular arrangement by the intransigence of the new party.

Speculation about the motives of the new party had been current from the day that parliament had first considered the 22nd article of the Treaty of Union. There were rumours circulating that there was a design 'to make a comonwealth for wch yrs a great pairty in England & our Squadroni in Scotland'.[9] The new party was also closely scrutinised on 21 January when Robert Wodrow sent his father an account of the proceedings in parliament the previous day. He noted that Marchmont's resolve 'was violently opposed by the other side as qt was a very early incroachment upon the articles of union nou Touched and ane odd specimen that they would turn ym to a nose of wax'. He continued that this article of the treaty expressly stated that a writ should be issued 'to ye Shires and Bourroughs to choice ym but these will be no further binding yn they see Convenient. you may easily see ye drift. they knou ye nations inclinations and doe think feu that voted for ye union will be chosen in the shires, and burroughs'.[10] Flouting the Treaty of Union in this manner set the new party on a course that would make it the most reviled party of politicians in Scotland to the obvious benefit of the old party.

Once the Act of Constitution had passed not only did the disagreements between the old and new parties increase, but the outcome of the disputes clearly highlighted that the new party was becoming increasingly unpopular in parliament. The old party carried its proposal for a sum of money to be paid to the Scottish commissioners, who had negotiated the Treaty of Union at London in 1706, when the duke of Hamilton and his followers stood aside rather than join the new party in the debate. The old party then inflicted a heavy defeat on the new party in the election of the 16 Scottish representative peers. Accusations of bad faith were heard on both sides, but the harsh fact for the new party was that only two of its number, Tweeddale and Roxburgh, were chosen by parliament, the remaining 14 nominees belonging to the old party. The new party had better success in the election of the Scots members who were to sit in the house of commons, but even this was heavily qualified by the fact that in Scotland they were 'like to reap no other advantage by the union for the small government that will be here is to be in ye hands of Queensburry and Seafeild'.[11] Not surprisingly, once the Scottish parliament rose on 25 March Marchmont hurried south to make sure he reached London before any of the old party.

[8] National Archives of Scotland [hereafter cited as NAS], GD124/15/487/7: earl of Mar to Sir David Nairne, 5 Feb. 1707.

[9] Scottish Catholic Archives [hereafter cited as SCA], Blairs Letters, BL 2/140/6: James Carnegy to Thomas Bayards, 7 Jan. 1707.

[10] National Library of Scotland [hereafter cited as NLS], Wodrow Papers, Wod. Lett. Qu. iv, f. 150: Robert Wodrow to his father, 21 Jan. 1707.

[11] SCA, BL 2/140/15: James Carnegy to Thomas Bayards, 15 Mar. 1707.

© The Parliamentary History Yearbook Trust 2009

During April it was noted that 'the Squadrone behaves very discretly for they never make a complaint',[12] but at the same time it had raised the idea of fundamental changes in the government of Scotland with Lord Treasurer Godolphin. It was only some weeks later that a slight hint of the *Squadrone*'s dealings came to light in a letter written on 13 May by John Clerk to his father. He mentioned that 'the English are thinking of sinking all our great offices at once, this you may easily belive disquiets not a feu . . . 'Tis found nou that the Squadrone have a littel hand in thise things.' As Clerk observed, however, 'the affair [MS torn] come to no conclusion, nor indeed are they come to [MS torn] conclusion about any thing'.[13] Godolphin's reluctance to listen to their advice prompted a growing chorus of discontent in the letters sent back to Scotland by leading members of the *Squadrone* at London.

Not surprisingly, although the *Squadrone* was happy to air its grievances, it was reluctant to publicise its unsuccessful flirtation with Godolphin. Jerviswood wrote to the marquess of Tweeddale on 29 April remarking that: 'I know nothing but what I hear from persons as ignorant perhaps as myself for neither Scots Ministry nor English Ministry have thought fit as yet to consult New Party in any thing.'[14] There was little change in the coming weeks and on 22 May it was the duke of Roxburghe's turn to lament to Tweeddale that: 'none of us have been in the least consulted in either what has been done but you Lop- cannot but perceive, that the difference betwixt the new party and the old party was still designed to be kept up'.[15] Worse than this was John Haldane of Gleneagles's report, five days later, that the queen had appointed Queensberry, Mar, Seafield, Loudoun and Montrose as privy councillors and was planning to make 'a full nomination of Councelors for our Countrie it's generaly thought that our Government will continow on the same foot it was att least till the meeting of our British parliament'.[16]

By this time the *Squadrone* was not the only group of politicians expressing unease at Godolphin. Gleneagles had discovered that the leaders of the whig junto claimed to be as ignorant as the *Squadrone* about Scottish politics. He advised Tweeddale: 'Wharton Sumers Halifax . . . ar mightie oblidgeing & generaly say they doe not know what's doeing in Our affairs.'[17] The junto was no wiser at the end of July when Halifax's brother, Sir James Montagu, wrote to the earl of Manchester observing that although he had attended numerous committees of English and Scots lords on Scottish business, since his appointment as solicitor general in April 1707: 'I don't find that many of our friends have been much consulted in the Scotch affairs, since the passing the Act of Parliament for the Union; but all that has been done is by the direction of the Lord Treasurers.'[18] Neither the *Squadrone* nor the junto needed any further encouragement to consider 'abrogating the queen's privy-council in Scotland'.[19]

---

[12] NAS, GD18/3135/12: John Clerk to his father, Sir John Clerk, 24 Apr. 1707.

[13] NAS, GD18/3135/18: John Clerk to his father, Sir John Clerk, 13 May 1707.

[14] NLS, Yester Papers, MS 14413, f. 148: George Baillie of Jerviswood to the marquess of Tweeddale, 29 Apr. 1707.

[15] NLS, MS 14413, f. 154: duke of Roxburgh to the marquess of Tweeddale, 22 May 1707.

[16] NLS, Yester Papers, MS. 14415, f. 150: John Haldane of Gleneagles to the marquess of Tweeddale, 27 May 1707.

[17] NLS, MS 14415, f. 150: John Haldane of Gleneagles to the marquess of Tweeddale, 27 May 1707.

[18] Duke of Manchester, *Court and Society from Elizabeth to Anne* (2 vols, 1864), ii, 233.

[19] Alexander Cunningham, *The History of Great Britain* (2 vols, 1787), ii, 135.

Their intent did not go unnoticed and by the autumn the secretary of state for the northern department, Robert Harley, expressed his concern about this. The lord treasurer reacted angrily and instead of listening to Harley's complaints accused him of disloyalty. Godolphin simply ignored Harley who, as a matter of some urgency, wrote to the duke of Marlborough on 16 September claiming that his actions were being misrepresented. Marlborough tried to reassure Harley, begging him to 'do me the justice to believe I am sincerely yours, and that I am sorry from my heart that you have any reason given you to be uneasy'.[20] Encouraged by this response Harley was ready to develop his argument by reminding Marlborough that because he had anticipated this danger 12 months ago this recent tension between him and Godolphin was no surprise, merely confirming his suspicion that he would 'be misrepresented by those who had no other way of doing me a mischief, and I have not wanted sufficient warning that I was to be torn from Lord Treasurer'.[21]

Prompted by Marlborough, Godolphin wrote to Harley on 23 October, the day that the parliament of Great Britain sat for the first time, to arrange a meeting about foreign affairs. When it came to domestic politics, however, Godolphin remained irritatingly uncommunicative. He told Harley: ' 'tis true, the affairs at home would require a good deal to be said upon them, if talking would mend them; but I find they must go as they will, and I can do no more than I have done'.[22] Harley was furious. Stung by the fact that Marlborough appeared to have done nothing to encourage Godolphin to act more constructively he penned an angry warning. 'As to home affairs' he wrote, 'the little experience I have had inclines me to think that they never succeed so well as when they are directed. The people will follow somebody, and if your lordship will not think fit to explain your own thoughts, others will make use of your authority.' Judging that plain speaking was his only hope, Harley continued: 'it may not be much to your satisfaction whenever your Lordship thinks fit to let me know anything of what you judge proper to be done. I will not be wanting in my duty to tell your Lordship my poor opinion, and to act according to the best of my understanding.'[23]

Harley received a response six days later but the letter came from Marlborough rather than Godolphin. Now that the campaigning season was finished the duke was at The Hague preparing to return to England. He promised that he would take the first favourable opportunity to set sail 'being very desirous of being with you, for I long to have one hour in which I may speak freely to you'.[24] When Marlborough reached London the *Squadrone* and the junto were completing their preparations for the attack on the Scottish privy council.

Marchmont had sought legal advice about abolishing the council and the response was delivered to him in November. He was told 'that it is no way Suiteable to the Intire and Compleat Union to have in Scotland a Privie Council separat and Distinguished from Her Majesties privie Council of Great Britain or any other privie council save that one'. So that the British privy council could maintain peace and order in Scotland there was

[20] HMC, *Bath MSS*, i, 184.
[21] HMC, *Bath MSS*, i, 185.
[22] HMC, *Bath MSS*, i, 186.
[23] HMC, *Bath MSS*, i, 186.
[24] HMC, *Bath MSS*, i, 187.

a very strong recommendation 'that in the Counties of north Britain, justices of the peace be appointed with justices of the Quorum and Custodes Rotularum in the same manner and with the same powers as the like are in south Britain and formerly had been in England'. It was anticipated that objections would be raised to this proposal 'because by the 20th article of the Treaty of Union Heretable jurisdictions for life are reserved to the owners thereof as Rights of property in the same manner as they are now enjoyed by the Lawes of Scotland'. The answer to this argument was that although an heritable jurisdiction could not be taken from the owner by the crown: 'yet the soveraigne and parliament can always make Lawes whereby they are to judge, or Lawes determining rules and methods for them And can alter or repeal such Lawes so as justice may require and for the better administration thereof'.[25] The *Squadrone* was once again ready to tamper with the Treaty of Union.

The question of the Scottish privy council was first raised in the house of commons on 29 November in a committee of the whole House appointed to consider the part of the queen's speech relating to the union. Spencer Compton was chairman of the committee and the dukes of Argyll, Montrose and Roxburghe were in the gallery as William Bromley stood up and asked the Commons to 'contribute all their good offices, so that the business of rendering the union more complete might be dispatched before any other'.[26] This cue was taken up by Jerviswood who concluded his speech with a motion 'that for the future there shall be but one Councell in Great Brittain'.[27] He was seconded by John Cockburn of Ormistion and opposed by John Pringle and Francis Montgomery. The Scots dominated the debate for three hours and though they seemed to be equally divided on Jerviswood's motion 'the Southern Tories, and a great body of the Whigs joyning for the Question, it was carried by an infinite majority without a division'.[28]

The committee sat again on 4 December and with the earl of Mar watching from the gallery, Gleneagles spoke for putting the Scottish militia on the same foot as the English and 'that the justices of peace in Scotland should have the same power as in England'.[29] This produced the first stirrings of unease amongst English MPs concerned that this might constitute an encroachment upon the union. Lord Coningsby voiced this alarm when he 'moved an addition to the question, that the Justices in Scotland should have the same powers, as far as was consistant with the 20th article of the treaty, which is very express for preserving all heritable rights and jurisdictions as they were at the time of framing the treaty'.[30] Some English MPs seemed rather confused at this point so it was explained that heritable jurisdictions reserved all prosecutions to themselves for 15 days and it was only after this that the justices could take up anything that had been neglected or overlooked. Jerviswood tried to reassure the English that giving this power to the justices did not violate the 20th article because other articles, particularly the 19th, allowed the British parliament to alter the jurisdiction of the court of justiciary, the court

---

[25] NAS, GD158/952/1: 'Notes Concerning the wayes for keeping the peace in North Britain'.

[26] Cunningham, *History of Great Britain*, ii, 135.

[27] HMC, *13th Report, Appendix, Part vii*, 117.

[28] HMC, *13th Report, Appendix, Part vii*, 118.

[29] *Letters Illustrative of the Reign of William III*, ed. G.P.R. James (3 vols, 1841), iii, 295.

[30] *Letters Illustrative*, ed. James, iii, 295.

of admiralty and all other inferior courts, but he was unable to stifle the objection that there could be no exceptions from the 20th article.

Although the committee was then adjourned until 9 December, Harley, who had been encouraged to defend the Scottish privy council by hearing Bromley's speech on 29 November opposed by 'the Earl of Godolphin's friends',[31] had now seen enough to convince him that he must speak to Godolphin directly. The next day he wrote seeking 'leave to wait upon your Lordship this evening at your house at eight, having some account to give your Lordship which in duty to your service I ought to acquaint you with; and I should be very glad my Lord Duke of Marlborough would be present'.[32] Godolphin's hostile reply was far from encouraging, but despite his violent objection that, 'I should be extremely sorry if I were capable of giving to anybody living, and much more to you, to write me a letter in so very extraordinary a style as yours seems to me', he was willing to grant Harley's request telling him: 'that if you have any commands for me I will be at home between eight and nine this night to receive them, and send to the Duke of Marlborough to meet you there'.[33]

Whilst Harley, Godolphin and Marlborough met on the evening of 5 December, English unease at the *Squadrone*'s reckless tampering with the Treaty of Union was mounting. When the Commons went into committee again on 9 December it was argued that Scots' justices of the peace having the same powers as their English counterparts was inconsistent with the 20th article of the treaty which stipulated that 'all Heretable Offices, Heretable Jurisdictions, Offices for Life and Jurisdictions for Life be reserved to the Owners thereof as Rights of Property in the same manner as they are now enjoy'd by the Laws of Scotland notwithstanding of this Treaty'.[34] Once more, however, it was insisted that the Scots' justices exercising these powers was consistent with the other articles of the treaty and this claim ensured the proposal to abolish the council was carried 'as nakedly as it was proposed'.[35]

Two days later the committee's resolutions were reported back to the House. The Commons agreed that there should be only one privy council for Great Britain and that the militia in Scotland should be regulated in the same way as the English militia, but when it came to the question of the justices of the peace, Sir David Dalrymple spoke out powerfully proposing amending the committee's recommendation so that they would only exercise powers in Scotland that were 'consistent with the articles of the treaty'.[36] His amendment was rejected by 149 votes to 113, but it was a matter of great concern to the leaders of the junto that it had been supported by the likes of Sir Joseph Jekyll, Sir Thomas Parker, Henry Boyle and Robert Eyre. The committee's last two resolutions, about sending the lords of justiciary on circuit twice a year and for directing election writs to the sheriffs, were then accepted and a bill ordered to be brought in upon these resolutions. It had been expected that it would be presented to the House on 19 December, but because of the uncertainty generated by Dalrymple's speech it was decided to postpone its introduction

---

[31] Cunningham, *History of Great Britain*, ii, 135.

[32] HMC, *Bath MSS*, i, 188.

[33] HMC, *Bath MSS*, i, 188.

[34] *APS*, xi, 204.

[35] *Letters Illustrative*, ed. James, iii, 289.

[36] *Letters Illustrative*, ed. James, iii, 291.

© *The Parliamentary History Yearbook Trust 2009*

until after Christmas. The solicitor general explained this decision to the House the next day insisting that the delay was due to having to make a separate bill for the militia: 'because that being in the nature of a money bill, if it were joined with the rest might raise a dispute, if the Lords make amendments'.[37]

Two days later the earl of Glasgow had an audience with the queen where she expressed her fear that the 'proceedings of ye hous of Coms for takeing away ye privie Councell might alarum the presbyterians in Scotland, but she said she would doe hir outmost to have ye councell continowed or a Comission to some well affected persons to whom they might apply'.[38] Glasgow sent a letter with the queen's sentiments to be laid before the commission of the general assembly of the Church of Scotland, which he hoped would reinforce the appeal, made by some of the Scots representative peers, that the commission should protest against the abolition of the council. Its response was very disappointing. The commission decided that rather than issue a public remonstrance, individual clergymen would be at liberty to make a protest, but only on the understanding that their views were not representative of the commission. Once the decision had been taken the commission adjourned to March 1708.

This refusal to intervene was a consequence of instructions sent from London at the end of 1707 by the old party. These had been instigated by the principal of Edinburgh University, William Carstares, who, on 16 December, had written to the queen's junior secretary of state in Scotland, the earl of Loudoun, to inform him how unpopular the abolition of the privy council was amongst the ministers of the Church of Scotland because they believed it would make it more difficult to remedy presbyterian grievances. Loudoun expressed sympathy for the ministers in his reply on 30 December, but agreed with Carstares 'in thinking that it is not proper for the ensueing Commission of the Assemblie or ani Ecclesiastical Judicatur to interpose in these matters'. The secretary said he had no wish to discourage individual ministers from expressing their concerns but warned that any action by the commission was 'a road so dangerous for the Church Judicaturs that ani probabilitie that there may be of good consequences from ane Adress in the present case is not enuch to answer the hazardous, if not pernicious consequences that the meddling in things of that kinde may in course of time have'.[39] When the bill to abolish the privy council came before parliament in 1708 the general assembly remained silent.

Once the bill came before the Commons on 13 January the queen and Harley began to meet regularly to review its progress. After the second reading on 15 January it was referred to a committee of the whole House a week later and on the evening of 21 January the queen sent a letter to Harley 'to desire you would come to me to morrow morning at eleven o'clock, or next day at the same hour, as is most convenient to yourself'.[40] The next day Sir James Montagu took the chair of the committee and on 23 January reported the amendments made to the bill to the House. The only contentious question was the suggestion that the council should be abolished on 1 May 1708 but

[37] *Letters Illustrative*, ed. James, iii, 300.

[38] NAS, GD220/5/152/3: Adam Cockburn of Ormiston to the duke of Montrose, 24 Jan. 1707.

[39] Edinburgh University Library, Laing MSS, La. II. 577.I: earl of Loudoun to the reverend William Carstares, 30 Dec. 1707.

[40] HMC, *Bath MSS*, i, 189.

upon a division the Commons comfortably favoured this amendment by 179 votes to 118. The third reading of the bill on 27 January was little more than a formality, but during this debate many MPs were shocked when 'Mr. Harley suddenly changed his sentiments, and gave his judgement for the abrogation of the council.'[41] Later that day the queen wrote once more to Harley hoping to 'see you to-morrow in the evening'.[42]

After his second meeting with the queen Harley received a visit from the attorney general, Sir Simon Harcourt, on 29 January, the day that the Lords gave a first reading to the privy council bill. Without giving away any of the details, Harcourt told Harley that Godolphin was angry with him. Next morning Harley visited Marlborough who explained that Godolphin was incensed by Harley's speech in favour of abolishing the Scottish privy council, which he believed was designed to embarrass him and force the court to vigorously oppose the bill in the house of lords as the only way to remove the suspicion, deliberately fostered by Harley, that he secretly supported the bill. Harley wrote to Godolphin protesting against the charge of disloyalty. 'I am confident of my own innocency, and I know no better way to clear myself than to desire your Lordship will let me by my actions demonstrate the uprightness of my intentions, and my zeal and duty for your Lordship's person and service.'[43] When he received the letter Godolphin lost no time in replying. He told Harley that he had received 'your letter, and am very sorry for what has happened to lose the good opinion I had so much inclination to have of you, but I cannot help seeing and hearing, nor believing my senses. I am very far from having deserved it from you. God forgive you.'[44] Instead of sending this terse note to Harley, Godolphin took the unusual step of delivering it in person that night at the secretary's office at the Cockpit. Whatever was said went unrecorded. Harley simply acknowledging his receipt of the letter by endorsing it: 'Delivered me at the Cockpit by the Lord Treasurer, Jan 30, 1707–8.'[45]

Six days later the privy council bill was read for the second time in the Lords where it was immediately ordered to be considered in a committee of the whole House with the bishop of Salisbury in the chair. Though the various reports of the debate are often contradictory, it appears that Godolphin led the defence of the council by arguing that the bill should be amended to delay abolition until October 1708. He was assisted by Lord Chancellor Cowper and Mar, the latter uttering 'with great vehemance all he had to say, in favour of the Council'.[46] More surprising was the fact that the duke of Argyll, who had 'been thought to favour the soonest determination of the council', now expressed 'his dislike of the bill, as not having clearly and sufficiently secured the heritable jurisdictions'.[47] Godolphin was vigorously answered by Lord Somers, who insisted that abolition should be on 1 May as stipulated in the bill, and he was joined in this argument by the earl of Sunderland and Lord Halifax. The *Squadrone* then followed the junto's example with Montrose, who was president of the council, and Roxburgh,

---

[41] Cunningham, *History of Great Britain*, ii, 138.
[42] HMC, *Bath MSS*, i, 189.
[43] HMC, *Bath MSS*, i, 190.
[44] HMC, *Bath MSS*, i, 190.
[45] HMC, *Bath MSS*, i, 190.
[46] Cunningham, *History of Great Britain*, ii, 140.
[47] *Letters Illustrative*, ed. James, iii, 341.

© The Parliamentary History Yearbook Trust 2009

who was also a member, 'declaring that Scotland ought not to be given up in slavery either to them or any other Scotsmen; and that in order to have the government there administered after the English model, they were willing to resign some of their own rights'.[48] They were supported by the marquess of Tweeddale and the earl of Sutherland. The bishop of Salisbury also spoke out strongly against the proposed amendment as did the majority of the bishops. It was left to the duke of Buckingham to soften the rather earnest mood of the discussion with his customary wit. He observed that 'he understood both sides thought the council a nuisance, and there ought to be no question, but a nuisance should be abated immediately'.[49] When the division was called Godolphin's motion was defeated by just five votes.

This debate was something of a revelation. Many observers were surprised at the ferocity of the attempt to preserve the privy council until October. 'The Court appeard wt more warmth for it than any thing I have seen them speak to in the house', a somewhat stunned earl of Mar told his brother the same day.[50] A letter sent to the earl of Manchester on 6 February noted "tis remarkable, though the Court made these efforts for their continuance',[51] whilst James Vernon told the duke of Shrewsbury that on the court side it 'was chiefly argued by my Lord Treasurer'.[52] A notable exception to this, however, was the duke of Marlborough. Unlike Godolphin there is no record of his having spoken out against abolition at any time in the house of lords. The only notice taken of his conduct at this time recorded that during 'all these debates, the duke of Marlborough appeared neutral; declaring in parliament, that it was indifferent to him which way the matter were determined; however, it is believed, that he underhand opposed the bill with all his interest'.[53]

Three days later, on 7 February, the bill was read for the third time. Once again the court rose to the defence of the council arguing that abolishing it was 'directly a breach of the 20 article of the Union',[54] but upon the question the bill was again carried by a narrow majority of seven votes. Twenty-five peers, including 11 Scots' representatives, the duke of Argyll and Godolphin and Marlborough, then signed a protest against its passing. They complained that the bill did not allow enough time to satisfactorily establish the justices of the peace in Scotland before 1 May 1708, and, because it also empowered justices to proceed against offenders in the first 15 days after a crime was committed, it 'might be construed to be an Encroachment upon the Twentieth Article of the Union, and by that Means be the Occasion of raising great jealousies and discontents'.[55] One signature absent from the protest was that of the duke of Queensberry who, as Mar informed his brother on 10 February, 'has been so ill that he has not been able to come abroad . . . so that he cou'd not signe our dissent wch is no small grief to him'.[56]

---

[48] Cunningham, *History of Great Britain*, ii, 139.

[49] *Letters Illustrative*, ed. James, iii, 342.

[50] NAS, GD124/15/754/6: earl of Mar to his brother, James Erskine, 5 Feb. 1708.

[51] Duke of Manchester, *Court and Society*, ii, 276.

[52] *Letters Illustrative*, ed. James, iii, 341.

[53] Cunningham, *History of Great Britain*, ii, 141.

[54] NAS, GD124/15/754/7: earl of Mar to his brother, James Erskine, 10 Feb. 1708.

[55] *LJ*, xviii, 451.

[56] NAS, GD124/15/754/7: earl of Mar to his brother, James Erskine, 10 Feb. 1708.

Strangely, despite having supported the unsuccessful attempt to delay abolition of the council until October, Mar then expressed some regret at taking this step. 'I wish that we may not have laid a foundation for reviveing it again & continowing it longer than any of us had a mind to.'[57] It seems that he and the other members of the old party had no serious regrets at the abolition of the Scottish privy council after all, but like the passing of the Act of Constitution a year previously, they had made sure that their compatriots would not hold them responsible. Once again the blame fell squarely upon the *Squadrone*. Mar had constantly urged his brother to keep him informed of opinion in Scotland and he must have been delighted to learn at the beginning of February how unpopular the *Squadrone* was over the abolition of the council. He was told that people seem 'very dissatisfied with them and always express their joy when any story happens to go of the Squadrone's losing ground; and everybody here speaks of that party as the most selfish interested and spleenatic set that can be'.[58]

[57] NAS, GD124/15/754/6: earl of Mar to his brother, James Erskine, 5 Feb. 1708.
[58] NAS, GD124/15/768/3: James Erskine to his brother, the earl of Mar, 29 Jan. 1708.

© *The Parliamentary History Yearbook Trust 2009*

Tom Wharton and the Whig Junto: Party Leadership in Late Stuart England*

GEOFFREY HOLMES

This previously unpublished lecture by Geoffrey Holmes looks at the parliamentary career of Thomas, 6th Baron Wharton, 1st earl and 1st marquess of Wharton, a leading member of the whig junto in the reigns of William III and Queen Anne. It examines his 'unsavoury' character and how his reputation as a libertine and swordsman may have helped his role as a party leader. It also examines his historical reputation, partly through the works of Jonathan Swift, Richard Steele and Lord Macauly and attempts to restore his position as a much-maligned major figure in Augustan parliamentary and electoral politics.

Keywords: Thomas, 1st earl of Wharton; whig junto; party leadership; electoral politics; house of lords; Lord Macaulay; Jonathan Swift; Richard Steele; Sir John Fenwick; Henry Sacheverell

When that ripe and unrepentant old tory Dr Samuel Johnson was compiling his dictionary in the middle of the 18th century and reached the word 'leader', he wrote as one of his definitions: 'one at the head of any party . . . as the detestable Wharton was *leader* of the the Whigs'. At the time the doctor's famous dictionary was published, in 1755, the whigs no longer constituted a 'party' in any meaningful sense. Forty years of supremacy had seen them split into a variety of factions, often pitted against each other according to whether they were 'ins' or 'outs'. The tories, too, while they had, for some decades after 1714, preserved a fair measure of their integrity as a party in parliament – even though a massively outnumbered one – were now losing even this, and their leadership indeed had long been fragmented. To most of the men of their generation – the age of the Pelhams and the elder Pitt – the name of Thomas, Lord Wharton, was a distant memory. But in Samuel Johnson's earliest boyhood (b.1709), it was a name to conjure with, and for every tory household, like Johnson's in his native Lichfield, a name to fear. At a time, in Queen Anne's reign, when party divisions, in something like our modern sense, had become the essence of politics, Tom Wharton was, as much as anyone of his day, the embodiment of the party spirit.

Late Stuart England was, of course, the apprentice-shop of party, the period when men were learning, for the first time, how to contend with and how to hammer out into

* This lecture, which had been given by Geoffrey Holmes on many occasions, has been edited for publication by Clyve Jones (who was privileged to have heard it delivered to the History Society at the University of Lancaster in 1968 before Professor Holmes joined the staff), with the help of Alasdair Hawkyard. It is based on a typescript with manuscript annotations (some of them illegible), many of which have been incorporated into this version. The original lecture had no footnotes. The editor is grateful to Professor Holmes's widow, Ella, for granting permission to publish this lecture.

© *The Parliamentary History Yearbook Trust 2009*

political action deep differences of political and religious opinion; not by resorting to armed force, as in the recent past, but by exploiting to the full the possibilities of a parliamentary and electoral system, a limited monarchy, and a public opinion increasingly responsive to the printed word. This apprentice period was a relatively short one. The whigs and tories, whatever their antecedents, only emerged as parties during the exclusion crisis late in Charles II's reign, 1679–80. Thereafter for much of the eighties the whigs were in relative eclipse, indeed for a while in serious danger of extermination. The revolution of 1688 was a bipartisan revolution, and although whig-tory divisions reasserted themselves strongly in the early years of William III's reign, for much of the nineties the far older cross-currents of court and country were running as strongly, at times more strongly, than the tide of party. It was only by the very end of William's reign, 1701–2, that the two-party framework of politics had become universally accepted (though even then freely deplored in certain prominent quarters). By 1716 or so it was beginning to disintegrate again.

In these relatively brief and often confused apprentice years – from the late 1670s to the early years of George I – there were many problems for the party politicians to try to solve: problems of parliamentary discipline, for example, of both parliamentary and constituency organisation, and there were many skills which had to be painfully learned and cultivated. Of these, the art of leadership was the most challenging, and the most difficult to acquire. For the early parties were by nature antipathetic to leadership, at least to the leadership of a single man. Both whigs and tories in the house of commons, for instance, rested heavily on a bedrock of independently elected and independent country gentlemen. Such men needed leadership, for effective political action, but they did not readily accept it. The first whigs in Charles II's reign did, in the end, almost all accept the primacy of the 1st earl of Shaftesbury until his exile in 1682; but it was a slow business. The first tories looked not to a peer or a commoner but to the king for direction. And indeed when first James II turned against them, and then William III proved inappropriate as the figure head of a church and prerogative party, the tories never did solve their problem of leadership. In the first half of Anne's reign, for instance, the high tory wing looked either to the 1st earl of Rochester or to the 2nd earl of Nottingham or to Sir Edward Seymour; the moderate wing to Robert Harley or to Godolphin.

The whigs, too, when they re-emerged as a formidable political force in the first two to three years after the Glorious Revolution, were discomforted and almost crippled at times by the lack of an accepted leadership. It was only in the mid 1690s that a small group of whigs emerged which began to make a conscious bid for the allegiance of the parliamentary party, and gradually to extend their influence deep down into the local grass roots through a network of friendships, connections, loyalties and electoral influences. This group came to be called the junto. And in the end, by 1701 or 1702, the primacy of the junto was at last acknowledged, however grudgingly, by at least a majority of whigs, certainly in times of adversity. It could well be argued that this fact was to prove the most important single reason why the whigs, despite being a clear minority in the political nation, survived the furious onslaughts of their opponents in Anne's reign – and were thus in a position to take advantage of the Hanoverian succession to establish an impregnable supremacy.

The junto consisted in William's reign of four men. First, John Somers, lord keeper and later lord chancellor, perhaps the greatest lawyer of his age; second, Edward Russell,

© *The Parliamentary History Yearbook Trust 2009*

earl of Orford, the naval victor of La Hogue, and later the leading figure at the board of admiralty; third, Charles Montagu, later Lord Halifax, the financial genius behind the Bank of England and the system of credit finance by which the country largely paid for the wars against Louis XIV; and fourth, Tom Wharton, who succeeded his father Philip as the 5th Baron Wharton in 1696, and who at the time the junto came together was noted mainly for his robust debating powers in the Commons and his passionate interest in electioneering. In Anne's reign the four lords of the junto, as they were, were joined by a fifth: Charles Spencer, 3rd earl of Sunderland, son of the notorious turncoat minister of Charles II, James II and William III.

Of these five men, Wharton is probably least well known to posterity; mainly because, by one of those freaks which govern the survival of historical manuscripts, no large collection of private papers has survived for the junto lords (with the exception of Sunderland). Wharton in recent years has had to be rescued almost from the lumber room of history by the political historians of the period. And he is still an incredibly neglected figure, in view of the fact that he was not only the most controversial and colourful figure of his age, but arguably, in terms of party development, the most important figure of his age. It is in these terms that I want mainly to deal with him; and to try to illuminate at certain phases of his career at least, especially its final stages, what leadership implied and involved in these apprentice-years of party in late Stuart England.

Before I do this, however, I really must try to sketch some picture of Tom Wharton, the man and the whig; for in both respects he was a character very far indeed from the normal mould. He was the son of a noted puritan peer of the 17th century, who was sometimes known as Saw-Pit Wharton, because he was widely believed to have led his (parliamentary) regiment at Edgehill (if 'led' is the right word) from the discreet level of a neighouring saw-pit: but more often remembered as 'the Good Lord Wharton', since it was his famous charity which provided bibles more or less in perpetuity for the children of the deserving poor. The Good Lord Wharton's eldest son, the Honourable Thomas, was born a few months before the execution of Charles I and died a few months after the accession of George I. From 1673 he was MP for Wendover, and between 1696 and 1715 he became successively Baron Wharton, earl and finally 1st marquess of Wharton; and thus for 42 years of a long life he was actively engaged in politics.

The main problem in trying to portray Wharton is not absence of material – for although most of his private papers have been lost, he was the kind of man people constantly wrote about; the big problem is rather the fact that the material on him is so heavily loaded. There were very few people who had lukewarm feelings about Wharton. He was either idolised or he was loathed, depending, for instance, on whether he had lambasted you in the house of commons, lavished his money on you in one of his parliamentary boroughs, or made a monkey out of you in a duel; whether he made your fortune on the racetrack, or (perhaps the likeliest contingency of all) whether he had just seduced your wife. So, much of the material is malicious; some of it is certainly apocryphal; and one is always in some danger, consequently, of conjuring up the legend rather than the man.

Jonathan Swift and Lord Macaulay, I suppose, are, the chief culprits: Swift because he wrote his scurrilous pamphlet, called *A Short Character of Thomas, Earl of Wharton*, under the goad of what he took to be a personal insult in 1710, when Wharton was viceroy of Ireland; Macaulay, because in one of his most memorable pieces of prose he left us with a dazzling little sketch of Wharton which unfortunately followed Swift far too uncritically.

There is one thing which in the intoxication of his prose Macaulay does not quite bring out, that is that behind this raffish air of the Don Juan, and underneath the borrowed plumes of the cavalier, so to speak, Tom Wharton, even as a young man, and still more as a mature one, always preserved the hard centre of the traditional roundhead. As with the greatest whig of the next generation, Robert Walpole, one has this bluff and genial exterior masking a character that could be as tough and ruthless as any in late-Stuart politics. In 1696 when the jacobite conspirator Sir John Fenwick was arrested, and then tried to save his neck by threatening to accuse a number of whig ministers of a traitorous correspondence with the exiled court of James II, the whigs were at their wits' end to know how to stifle him, for the evidence they had unearthed against him was too thin to guarantee his conviction in an ordinary court of law. It was Wharton who provided the answer. It was he who decided that judicial murder by an act of attainder, the most brutal of all legal processes known in England, was the best way of silencing Fenwick. And to judge from his letters at the time, he lost no sleep over the decision.

Thirteen years after the Fenwick case, in December 1709, Wharton was one of those members of the cabinet who pressed most insistently for the impeachment of Dr Henry Sacheverell, the tub-thumping Oxford divine who had preached a sermon in St Paul's churchyard (appropriately enough on Guy Fawkes Day) questioning the whole basis of the revolution settlement, and railing against the 'false brethren', as he called them, in the whig government, who were betraying the Church of England by their sympathy towards dissent. To choose such an ostentatious method as parliamentary impeachment as a means of silencing a man who could pose as a champion of anglicanism was probably not a very wise thing to do, and as it began to appear that if they pressed on with their attack they would stir up a hornets' nest round their heads, some members of the ministry began to waver in their loyalties. But not so Wharton. When the duke of Marlborough stopped him one day and anxiously asked his advice about what should be done with the doctor in the present climate of public opinion, the gist of Wharton's reply – after he had expressed incredulity at Marlborough's dithering – was confined to five simple words – 'damn 'im and hang 'im'. And I don't doubt that if he could have persuaded the house of lords to sanction it, he would have hanged this noisy, mediocre clergyman without a qualm.

This tough core of Wharton's was appropriately enough matched by a thick hide. This was an age when journalists and pamphleteers revelled in personal invective, and in this sort of world such a thick skin was very necessary for any politician. No one at this period was able to take the gibes and the insults of his opponents with such unflappable good humour as Wharton who expected hard knocks to be taken as well as given. The publication of Swift's *Short Character* of him in 1710, followed by a number of swingeing articles from the same pen in the tory magazine *The Examiner*, left him even more cheerfully unmoved. A few months after they appeared he put Swift to rout with the most disarming display of bonhomie when the two men accidentally met in public. Swift was still feeling a little shamefaced when he wrote the same evening: 'I intended to dine with Mr. Masham today, and called at White's chocolate-house to see if he was there.

Lord Wharton saw me at the door, and I saw him, but took no notice, and was going away, but he came through the crowd, called after me, and asked me how I did, etc.' 'This is pretty', Swift acknowledged, [though] 'I believe he wished every word he spoke was a halter to hang me.'

Wharton was a man of many contrasts and some quite striking contradictions. On the one side of the coin, the man of pleasure; on the other, the hard, uncompromising politician. At one moment, a leading light and noted wit in the most fashionable and the most exclusive social club in Queen Anne's England, the famous Kit-Cat Club; at the next moment, a man of action, a man whose physical toughness and courage were the envy of most professional soldiers.

That Wharton possessed great physical courage as well as political courage, was not irrelevant to his success as focus of party loyalties. He was a great sportsman; a fearless and bruising rider – even when he was 60 years old, it was said he walked like a jockey – and he owned one of the finest racehorse studs not only in England but in Europe, the envy even of Louis XIV. His reputation as a swordsman and a duellist was, if anything, even more enviable than his record on the turf. According to Richard Steele, his friends used to boast that he had never thrown down a challenge, that he had never refused one, that he had never killed an opponent, and yet that he had never fought without having his antagonist's life at his mercy.

Now you will appreciate that Wharton's rare combination of social talents and sporting prowess on the one hand with a pretty comprehensive range of vices could prove over the years quite an asset to the whigs. It made him, for instance, an invaluable recruiting officer for the party among the young-men-about-town, especially among the young nobility. It also helped him as a canvasser, and indeed Wharton was a superb canvasser. During much of Anne's reign he was the party's unofficial chief whip in the house of lords, and unlike the modern 'whip' he did not confine his activities merely to obvious and known supporters. He worked on the principle that no man's vote was predetermined in any division. Swift, in one of his more revealing passages, once said of Wharton: 'he will openly take away your employment today, because you are not of his party',

> tomorrow he will meet or send for you, as if nothing at all had passed, lay his hands with much friendliness on your shoulders, and with the greatest ease and familiarity tell you that the faction [Wharton's invariable name for the tories] are driving at something in the House; that you must be sure to attend, and to speak to all your friends to be there, although he knows at the same time that you and your friends are against him in the very point he mentions; and however absurd . . . this may appear, he has often found it successful; some men having such an awkward bashfulness, they know not how to refuse on a sudden; and every man having something to fear, which often hinders them from driving things to extremes with persons of power, whatever provocations they may have received.

I have said that Wharton was man of paradoxes and contrasts; and surely the most striking contrast of all was between his private standards, or lack of them, and the principles which governed his public life. The 3rd earl of Shaftesbury, moralist and philosopher, and grandson of the man who virtually created the whig party in the 1670s, wrote of Wharton in 1709: 'If ever I expected any public good where private virtue was wholly sunk, 'twas in his character, the most mysterious of any in my account for this reason . . . I have seen many proofs of this monstrous compound in him of the very best and the very worst'. It is impressive to find a man like Shaftesbury, an austere guardian of the old country party tradition who disliked the methods and the power-politics of the junto, conceding that, whatever his private depravities, Wharton, the politician, was always – as Shaftesbury himself put it – 'as true as steel'. Indeed, it was remarkable that the same man who in so many respects was totally without principle, was in politics probably the most principled of all the leaders of either party in the years between the Glorious Revolution and the Hanoverian succession.

Just as he referred to the tories scathingly as 'the faction', so to him the whigs were always 'the honest party', 'the honest interest'. In Wharton's vocabulary you could not say any more of any man than he was 'honest': it meant that he was politically sound, of firm and unimpeachable revolution principles, on a different plane not only from the tories, but also from the monstrous regiment of trimmers, and the renegade whigs like Robert Harley. So, when his friends continued to call him 'Honest Tom Wharton', long after he had inherited his father's peerage in 1696, they were paying him the sort of compliment he himself most appreciated. Whether consciously or unconsciously, he cultivated the image himself by declining to use the normal aristocratic form of autograph, even when he became an earl in 1706, he still signed most of his letters as he always had, 'T. Wharton'.[1]

Wharton's own whiggery, was straightforward and undeviating. He played quite a conscious part in the revolution of 1688. But long before the revolution, in the very early years of his political career in the middle of Charles II's reign, he equipped himself with a few crisp and uncomplicated political maxims; and these same maxims, with relatively little modification, saw him through the rest of his life. For one thing, unlike some of his most eminent contemporaries, he not only accepted the existence of parties in the body politic but welcomed them with relish. What is more, he carried his convictions to their logical conclusion by accepting, the absolute necessity of one–party government. For him this was not primarily a matter of political theory; it was a matter of common sense, almost of political sanity. In Wharton's eyes the only people fit to be trusted to govern the country, under the king, were 'honest' gentlemen like himself and his junto friends – and that was all there was to it. The tories, as he never tired of reiterating, 'could not do business'. So only a matter of months after he had given William of Orange a helping hand on to the British throne, we find him writing to his new sovereign giving him some of the bluntest advice that can ever have been offered to an English king:

Wee have made you king [he told William, with more confidence than accuracy], as the greatest return wee could make for so great a blessing . . . and if you intend to governe like an honest man, what occasion can you have for knaves [i.e., tories] to serve you . . . Can this same man who contrived and brought our ruin be fitt for our salvation? . . . The pretence of their being experienced is very weak. Their

---

[1] Here, Professor Holmes is making too much of this point. It was not uncommon for peers to sign with their title together with an initial for their first name. Many examples can be found in the signatures to protests in the *Journal of the House of Lords* (editor).

© *The Parliamentary History Yearbook Trust 2009*

expectation was only in doing ill. . . . Wee are willing to lay all faults at their doores, if Your majesty will not protect them, and take all upon yourself. this is a rock wee hope you will avoid; [and, he adds with unmistakable menace] for it hath been fatal to several Kings of England.

It will be pretty obvious from the kind of language he used here to William III that Wharton's brand of whiggery embraced not only a firm belief in one-party government but also a view of monarchy in which sentiment or humbug had no place whatever. He was never suspected of downright republicanism, as his junto colleague Sunderland sometimes was, but he never doubted the ultimate sovereignty of parliament, and his attitude to the crown was in consequence realistic and even harsh. During the debates in the house of lords in March 1710 which followed immediately after the trial of Dr Sacheverell, Wharton made the opening speech of the first day's proceedings, and in front of Queen Anne herself he told the House without batting an eyelid that without the revolution the queen's title to the throne was worthless: 'My lords, if the Revolution is not lawful, many in this House, aye and vast numbers without, are guilty of blood, murder, rapine, and injustices; and the queen herself is no lawful queen, since the best title she has to the crown of these realms is her parliamentary title, founded on the Revolution.'

You can well imagine that during the first few years of her reign, when Anne had been utterly resolved to have no truck with the lords of the junto – 'the five tyrannizing lords' as she called them – this straight-laced queen regarded Wharton personally as little better than the devil incarnate. When, after 1705, her prime minister, Godolphin, had to contemplate progressive concessions to the whigs in order to keep his head above water in parliament, the prospect of having Wharton actually sitting with her round the cabinet table at some not-too-distant date was enough to curdle the queen's blood. In fact, it was months before she would even agree to Godolphin's suggestion that Honest Tom should be given an earldom in the hope of keeping him quiet in the meantime. Wharton himself got a good deal of ironic satisfaction out of Anne's discomfiture. While other lords promoted at the same time as he (at the end of 1706) employed Grub Street hacks as usual to concoct the preambles to their patents of nobility, vying with each other in extolling the virtues and services of their families in past generations and tracing their noble origins back to the Conqueror, and so forth, Wharton decided to keep his own preamble as simple as possible. All he would have, as he said, was that he was created earl of Wharton 'by the Queen's gracious will and pleasure'.

A curious sequel to all this is that when Wharton did eventually bulldoze his way into the cabinet in November 1708, Anne found the reality nothing like so fearsome as the prospect. He appears to have behaved with quite unexpected decorum at court; he also had the good sense to accept an office (the lord lieutenancy Ireland) which relieved Anne of his presence for many months of the year, and when he eventually resigned in the whig débâcle of September 1710, the queen parted with him almost on terms of cordiality.

To return to Wharton's whiggery. It was nothing if not essentially practical and relevant; and this realistic attitude was not confined to his views on party and on the monarchy. A third feature, for instance, is that he accepted the principle of religious toleration, and consistently defended the limited toleration granted by the (Toleration)

© *The Parliamentary History Yearbook Trust 2009*

Act of 1689, not primarily because of his dissenting background or connections (as was the case with many whigs), and certainly not because of any burning belief in freedom of conscience and freedom of worship as an inalienable human right, but mainly, one suspects, because he thought it quite monstrous that any country should willingly place serious disabilities on a large, loyal, and, above all, economically important part of its population, the protestant nonconformists. This would seem self-evident now, but remember it was a pretty modern view to take in 1700. The same realism unfettered by preconceptions, coloured his attitude towards foreign policy from the early 1690s, and towards that old whig bugbear, a large standing army. Once Louis XIV had become the protector of the catholic ex-king, James II, and later of his son, it seems axiomatic to Wharton that a good whig should oppose French aggression wherever it raised its head. If this involved maintaining a large army that was that.

However, when Shaftesbury wrote in 1709 that Wharton was as 'true as steel', he was not thinking only, or even perhaps mainly, of fidelity to the principles of whiggery. But where he was invariably 'true as steel', he was thinking also of fidelity to his whig colleagues. Indeed, it was as an example of personal loyalty that he was so remarkable. Even the junto, easily the most disciplined and tightly-knit of all the party groups of the day, had found it hard to accept the full logic of joint responsibility. When forced out of office towards the end of William's reign, for instance, they resigned piecemeal. On more than one occasion, in June 1710, when Robert Harley was known to be scheming their downfall, they once again failed to resign as a body when their colleague Sunderland was made the first victim of Harley's policy and dismissed from the government. They even began to negotiate both jointly and singly with Harley, in the hope of saving themselves at the expense of Godolphin and the Churchills.

Wharton's reaction to this crisis in 1710 is illuminating. When it began, unfortunately for the whigs, he was in Ireland, far removed from the scene of action. But gradually his uncompromising spirit began to make itself felt even by correspondence. The attitude he took was, in an early 18th-century context, startlingly modern. It was quite simply that he and his friends and all the leading whigs in the ministry must stand together, and if necessary, fall together. In the end he brought all his junto colleagues and their allies to their political senses with one devastating philippic. They should have nothing to do with Harley, he told them, not only because he was treacherous, but because he was not worth dealing with:

> He can do no business [he assured them]; he will very soon break his neck, and then all things will be in such confusion as to force the Queen back again into the hands of the Whigs. And this is the situation of power we ought to be in; not to have a motley ministry with such a rat as Harley at the head of it.

Actually, Wharton's prophecies about Harley's administrative incompetence proved not very accurate; but his personal loyalty, his party zeal, his political judgment, and not least his flair for leadership, all told him that there was only one sane path the whigs could take if they were to have any future as a party. And here he was absolutely right.

Back in 1708 he had given a still more striking example of his own exciting personal concept of party ties: when in spite of the most desperate financial plight, he refused point blank an invitation to advance his own prospects of cabinet office at the price of selling his friend Lord Somers down the river. He was asked in a nutshell to drop his support for Somers's claims to the lord presidency of the council in expectation of his own personal advancement. His reply was devastating in its directness. 'I think', he said, 'that making distinctions among men of the same principle and interest is not the way to do the nation's business; and that if I have ever been of any service, it was chiefly owing to the assistance of those friends from whom I will never divide, nor can do so without making myself quite inconsiderable.' One could indeed proliferate examples of this sort about him. But enough has been said to make it crystal clear why it was he always remained 'Honest Tom' to contemporary whigs, and why a later historian, G.M. Trevelyan, once wrote of him: 'His colleagues could trust him with their political, though not with their marital honour.'

The most spectacular way in which Wharton's complete dedication to whiggery was demonstrated was by the sheer selflessness with which he poured out his personal fortune in parliamentary elections. As his party's chief election-organiser and manager, as well as its chief individual electioneering magnate and borough monger, the demands made upon his purse were more or less unceasing. You will remember that in the 20 years from 1695 to 1715, mainly owing to the Triennial Act, there was an extraordinary crop of general elections, an average of one every second year, and in most of these elections Wharton was involved, in some degree, in roughly a score of different constituencies. Heavy spending alone was only a small part of the secret of his success – he was, for instance, a masterly canvasser, as expert at cajoling voters – whether prosperous noblemen or humble shoe-makers – as he was at drumming up support at Westminster. But naturally the strain which the 'nursing' of all these constituencies placed on his purse was massive. Richard Steele, writing a short memoir after Wharton's death in 1715, put his total expenditure on elections since the revolution alone at £80,000. (His income, after his second marriage, was reckoned at £16,000 a year; this should be compared with the annual income of the dukes of Newcastle (£40,000), Bedford (£35,000) and Beaufort (£30,000).)

Wharton was on the verge of bankruptcy by the time Queen Anne at last succumbed and appointed him, along with Somers, to high office in November 1708. As a matter of fact his London house in Dover Street was at one point close to forfeiture, all the furniture having been removed from it, during a momentary lapse in the vigilance of Wharton's doorkeeper, who was normally well-trained for such emergencies. Like the born gambling man he was, he probably calculated that his two years in Ireland as lord lieutenant would see him on the right side of the ledger with plenty in hand before the next general election. In the event a premature dissolution of parliament only allowed him 18 months as viceroy. But, judging by the amount of money he was spending again in the election campaign of 1710, even 18 months in that jobber's paradise across the Irish Sea was more than enough to put him in business again.

It is generally imagined that Wharton's main parliamentary services to his party, at least after he left the Commons in 1696, were performed before parliament ever met, that is to say in the constituencies; and that subsequently his job was mostly confined to backstage management, leaving more gifted orators like Somers or Halifax or Cowper to play the leads on the floor of the house of lords. The failure by historians to appreciate Wharton's parliamentary talents is to some extent understandable. In a way it is a natural consequence of the imperfect reporting of parliamentary debates in the late 17th and early 18th centuries.

© *The Parliamentary History Yearbook Trust 2009*

I have been lucky myself in that the later years of Anne, on which I have done more work than any other period, are years when material on debates, and particularly on Lords' debates, begin to get a little more plentiful. This material has led me to two conclusions about Wharton, which I would say are valid, not just for 1710–14 but for Anne's reign as a whole: first, that although one would not rank him with the greatest of parliamentary orators, he was in his day one of the most effective, and probably the most feared, debater on either side of the house of lords, and this at a time when the upper House was probably at its peak period of influence in the political system; and second, that Wharton's greatest services to his party there, and his most vital contribution to its leadership, were invariably performed in opposition. In years of prosperity, or relative prosperity, for the whigs, he was content to leave the major operations to others. But in the dark days for whiggery, in Anne's first three years, and above all in her last four, when the whole party was under heavy siege, and a destruction at least as complete as that of 1683 threatened it, it was then that Wharton really came into his own.

After the end of 1711, especially, Wharton began to shoulder more and more of the burden of active leadership in parliament as well as behind the parliamentary scene, and in the constituencies. This became absolutely necessary, with Halifax compromised to some extent by a rather dubious relationship with the head of the tory ministry, Harley, and with Somers, who for many years had been the most eminent figure in the junto, by now increasingly immobilised by physical ailments and by the decay of his remarkable intellect. Tom Wharton, at the age of 64 years, showed no sign whatever of declining faculties. Even his appearance was still astonishingly youthful – it must have made many a man of regular habits and moral life feel that there was no justice – and by 1714, when both the great parties faced the biggest political crisis since the revolution, he was as near to being the undisputed leader of the whigs as anyone could be in a period when the structure of parties was still relatively loose.

On the last lap of my lecture, therefore, I should like to touch on a number of incidents from Wharton's 'golden period' as a parliamentarian, between November 1710 and July 1714, incidents which seem to me to illustrate the sheer variety and resource-fulness of his parliamentary techniques in opposition and foreshadow to a remarkable degree the armoury of the successful modern party leader. Bur first a brief reminder that British politics from 1710–14 was dominated by two great issues. One was the question of peace with France, which Harley was determined to conclude, if necessary, by separate negotiations with the enemy. The other especially acute in 1713–14 when it was obvious that Anne had not long to live; and for the whigs both questions were bound up not only with their policies and principles but with their very political survival. From the start the tory right wing made it clear that, given half a chance, they would use their supremacy to proscribe the whig leaders, and force the government into a total purge of every office in church and state.

In this situation the whigs had most of the cards stacked against them – a huge tory majority in the Commons, a public opinion strongly in favour of peace, and a high church queen; but they did hold two good cards: one was their numerical strength and superior talent in the house of lords, and another was that the tories, while recently united on many issues, were divisible on the vital subject of the succession, and that their divisions increased the tension in the ministry between Harley and his ambitious rival, Henry St John, later Lord Bolingbroke. It was in exploiting these two precious, almost

© *The Parliamentary History Yearbook Trust 2009*

solitary, assets, and, above all, in making the succession the focus of the whole opposition campaign in the final year of the queen's life, that Wharton revealed his full political genius.

If we look at various contemporary assessments of Wharton as parliamentary speaker, it is plain that his style was not to everyone's taste. Lord Dartmouth, who was secretary of state under Harley, wrote that he 'had the most provoking, insolent manner of speaking that I ever observed in any man, without regard to civility or truth'. It was not only tory peers, but some whig peers too, who complained that there was too much of the demagogue about Wharton's parliamentary style to make him an adornment to the house of lords. It is certainly true that he loved to shock. In April 1714, for instance, he and the duke of Bolton proposed that the queen should issue a proclamation, offering a reward for the pretender's capture, 'dead or alive'. Surely Wharton did so in the full knowledge that it would make not only every tory hair stand on end, but that it would even make many of his own side, especially the bishops' bench, squirm uncomfortably.

Even when his speeches were not openly provocative, there was usually an astringent quality about them which was disturbing and could be seductively effective. Yet every now and then at these rare moments Wharton suddenly revealed a rhetorical art which, as one admirer said, 'worked like magic on your yielding heart'.

Like many great parliamentarians Wharton possessed a real dramatic flair and a gift for showmanship. He loved suddenly to produce newspapers or books out of his capacious pockets, as though he had just spirited them out of thin air, and to read some damning passage or other on which he would then try to get a snap debate. Usually, of course, the whole gambit was carefully planned beforehand. Occasionally it backfired, as it did when Wharton planned to lead the first whig sally of the 1714 session by demanding the discovery and prosecution of the writer of a new political tract called *The Public Spirit of the Whigs*. This move was to be his tit-for-tat with his old foe Jonathan Swift, whom he well knew to have written this pamphlet, though he could not prove it. 'But Lord Wharton was out in his intended introduction of the matter', wrote Peter Wentworth:

> for he begun by telling the house, [that] as he passed through the Court of Requests [just now] the Book was put into his hands, and lighting accidentally upon the 20th and 21st pages [he found this] reflection upon the whole Scottish nation. But when he came to read the words he [found he] had bought a second edition, where those pages were left out, so he was forced to call to some lords that had the first edition in their pockets.

Occasionally this flair for the dramatic could be really devastating. One such occasion is well known. It was on the first day of the session of 1711–12, on 7 December 1711, when the opposition brought to a climax almost two months of careful preparation for a major assault on the government's peace policy. For the first time since their fall in 1710 the whigs appeared to have a real chance of victory in the Lords and a prospect of destroying the government. The feeling of the House seemed to be with the opposition from the start of the debate, and towards the end of this extremely intense evening, each time a minister rose to speak, Wharton, leaning back in his seat and wearing his sardonic smile, drew his finger slowly and so suggestively across his throat. 'Everyone of either party', Swift wrote, 'understood the thing as intended directly against my lord treasurer's head.' And when, at the evening's end, the whigs triumphed on the division by a tiny majority, only Wharton could have had the panache to walk across to Harley, the minister, to clap his hand on his shoulder, and say in everyone's hearing: 'By God, my lord, if you can bear this you are the strongest man in England.'

One of the things his opponents most resented about his tactics – no doubt because it was one of the very things that made him so able a debater – was that he had brought house of commons' methods with him to the Lords in 1696 and never really tried to adapt himself thereafter to the more staid procedure of the upper House. In the Commons he had been recognised as a master of the shrewd debating point, and especially of the art of interjection. But such techniques were pretty new even in the Commons, and quite unknown in the Lords where they had a most unsettling effect on the more stick-in-the-mud peers, accustomed as they were to highly formal proceedings, with long set speeches (sometimes an hour long; see, for example, the speeches of Haversham and Nottingham) and great attention to the courtesies and proprieties of debate.

The greatest weapon in Wharton's parliamentary armoury, however, was his command of irony. He had a caustic wit that could wither anyone. When Harley found himself faced with the imminent ruin of his peace policy after that crucial vote in December 1711, and the whole cabinet was in despair, he rescued himself and his colleagues by the desperate, and unprecedented expedient of persuading the queen to create at one swoop 12 new peers. When the house of lords reassembled after the Christmas recess, the premier forced a division on an adjournment motion to demonstrate his new strength. As the tellers were preparing to count the heads, Wharton, who had noted that there were just enough of the newcomers in the chamber to constitute a jury, turned to one of them and enquired with deadly politeness: 'Tell me, my lord; do you vote singly, or by your foreman?' There were many peers, even on the tory side, who felt Harley had acted unconstitutionally, and Wharton stored up these doubts and resentments as ammunition for the future. His chance to use it came two-and-a-half years later, on 5 April 1714, when Harley's government survived that critical division on the motion that the succession was in danger by exactly 12 votes. This would in any case have been regarded as a moral defeat, but Wharton made it doubly so when he called mockingly across the floor to where the lord treasurer was sitting: 'Lord Treasurer, you are saved by your dozen.'

The chief target of Wharton's irony was always Harley himself. Instinctively he realised that the prime minister's political position was basically an incongruous one – after all here was an ex-whig and ex-dissenter and an apostle of non-party government who found himself the leader or, perhaps, it would be better to say half the leader, half the prisoner – of tories and rabid high churchmen. From the time Harley entered the house of lords as earl of Oxford in the summer of 1711 Wharton made him the special object of his attentions. He harried him and baited him unmercifully. He interrupted him whenever he could. And as soon as Harley had taken his seat after one of his characteristically tortuous and evasive speeches Wharton would rise almost automatically to give battle. Sometime it would just be to raise a point of procedure. When Harley was new to the house of lords Wharton delighted in reminding him of his ignorance of remote points of the House's procedure – all the more so because in the Commons Harley, ever since the 1690s, had been the authority on procedure. More often, however, it was to fire heavier broadsides that Wharton intervened. In March 1714 the whigs were attacking the ministry for deserting the inhabitants of Catalonia, who had been the one part of Spain to support the Grand Alliance in the War of the Spanish Succession; but which had been left to its fate at the peace. On the afternoon of Friday, 19 March, the opposition was so hot on the trail that when the adjournment was proposed the whigs suggested it should be for the weekend only. Harley, by this time desperately anxious to relieve the pressure, then got up, put on his gravest and most devout look, and asked the House to adjourn for 12 days, for, as he said, 'with the solemnity of the Easter festival approaching, the next week ought . . . to be set aside for works and exercises of piety'.

'God forbid', an equally solemn voice rang out, and there was old Tom Wharton, getting to his feet and assuming an austere puritan cast of countenance so like Harley's, and yet so unlike his own, that few peers even on the tory benches could keep their faces straight:

> God forbid I should oppose the noble lord who has made so pious and so religious a motion. But I appeal to this venerable bench [pointing to the bishops – Wharton loved appealing to the bishops, and wherever possible quoting scripture at them], whether humanity, and Christian charity, do not require it at their hands, not to lose one moment of time in addressing Her Majesty on behalf of the Catalans, who are reduced to such extremity that the least delay in procuring them relief may prove their . . . irretrievable ruin.

He got his address.

Most of all did Wharton delight in baiting Harley, 'Robin the Trickster', about his dissenting past, especially when it gave him an opportunity to cast an ironical eye back over his own. (The irony was heightened by the fact that Harley had been appointed an executor of old Lord Wharton's will.) There is a delicious entry in Lady Cowper's diary for 22 June 1713:

> I was told the Ld Treasurer having occasion in a speech in the House of Lords to mention the dissenters called 'em Fanaticks. To which the Ld. Wharton reply'd, 'my Ld, why should you and I reflect upon our forefathers? I know your father and mine were dissenters, & you and I have been often at Pinner's Hall together, and if God had given us Grace we might have gone thither still.'
>
> To which the lord treasurer, in acute embarrassment, answer'd, 'My Ld, you are mistaken, I suppose you mean my brother Ned'. 'No my Lord', reply'd my lord Wharton, 'I mean Ned's brother, Robin.'

Perhaps the greatest of all his parliamentary performances came during the debate on the first reading of the Schism Bill in June 1714 – this was Bolingbroke's bill aimed ostensibly at destroying the dissenting academies, but also designed to present his leader Harley with a fatal dilemma; as Daniel Defoe later told the world, it was 'a mine to blow up the White Staff'. Here was a straight issue of party principle, toleration versus persecution, given peculiar piquancy by the dissenting backgrounds of both Harley and Bolingbroke, and also by the bitter rivalry between them; and it stimulated Wharton to heights of virtuosity. The barbs of his wit flew thick and fast in all directions, at

Bolingbroke most of all, but also at Harley, whose discomfiture he could not resist increasing though official whig policy at this time in June was to shore Harley up as a last line of defence against Bolingbroke and the jacobites:

> I am agreeably surprized, my Lords, to see that some men of pleasure are on a sudden become so religious as to set up for patrons of the church [this aimed at Bolingbroke, a notorious rake]. But I cannot but wonder that persons who have been educated in dissenting Academies, persons to whom I could point at, and whose tutors I could name, should appear the most forward in suppressing them. This is but an indifferent return for the benefits the public has received from these schools, which have bred these Great Men, who have made so glorious a peace, and treaties that execute themselves; who have obtained such great advantages for our commerce and who have paid the publick debts without further charge for the nation. Indeed I can see no reason for suppressing these academies, unless it arises from an apprehension that they might produce still greater geniuses, who may drown even the merits and abilities of these Great Men.

And then, the sudden change of mood at which Wharton was so adept:

> My Lords, to be serious. 'Tis no less melancholy than surprizing, that at a time when the Courts of France prosecute the design they have long since laid to extirpate our holy religion; and when not only secret practices are used to impose a Popish Pretender on these realms, but men publickly enlisted [here] for his service; it is melancholy and surprizing. I say, that at this very time a Bill should be brought in which cannot but tend to divide Protestants, and consequently to weaken their interests and hasten their ruin. But then the wonder will cease if we consider what madmen were the contrivers and promoters of this Bill.

One could go on for a long time illustrating Wharton's mastery of the parliamentary techniques of opposition. In any case, in the final reckoning I really believe Wharton's greatest service to his party's cause in opposition, and his more distinctive contribution to the canons of party leadership, was probably made, not by anything he said in the Lords, nor even by anything he did organising electoral or parliamentary campaigns, but simply what he was. That the whigs succeeded in keeping up their morale at a time when both the influence of the crown and a powerful tide of popular opinion was generally against them, and when political extinction was never far round the corner, was due in a very large measure to the true steel of Honest Tom Wharton. There was an indestructible quality about him which continually put heart into his friends, just as it infuriated his opponents. And in the end it was this quality as much as anything which kept his party together.

Wharton died in April 1715. He wasn't granted much time to enjoy the fruits of his 40 years of labour in the Old Cause: but it was time enough to be tolerably certain that the cause had finally triumphed. Actually the last few months of his life were rather sad ones, mainly for personal reasons. But one thing at least would have given him rich satisfaction could he have read his own obituaries. They were all intensely partisan. From the 'honest' side, eulogies by the score, a memoir of his life specially written by Richard Steele, and great significance attached to the fact that as Wharton's body was being

© *The Parliamentary History Yearbook Trust 2009*

brought in procession from his town house in Dover Street to his Buckinghamshire mansion there was a total eclipse of the sun. From the tory side the sighs of relief were almost audible through the pages of their letters. Pillars of high church politics (and this would have pleased Wharton perhaps most of all) gave vent to the most unchristian expressions of satisfaction, and few of them had any private doubts, as to the destination of Wharton's immortal soul. 'Tommy is gone', one of them wrote, 'like Judas, *ad locum proprium suum.*'

© *The Parliamentary History Yearbook Trust 2009*

The Clash of Interests: Commerce and the Politics of Trade in the Age of Anne

PERRY GAUCI

This article celebrates the contribution which Professor Holmes made to the field of British politics and society by the study of an important collection of political tracts. The compiler of the collection is identified as Sir Charles Cooke, one of the most significant commercial politicians of his day. The organisation of the collection illuminates the ways in which City politicians used various channels of information, both printed and personal, to support their political platforms. It also demonstrates how Cooke contributed to the defeat of the tories over the French Commerce Bill of 1713, by supplying key sources to combat the ministry's position. On a wider plane, although it suggests that partisan politics tainted all information advanced in the public sphere, this did not relieve political rivals of the need to establish the superior authority of their sources, and political success only saw Cooke redouble his efforts to gain as wide a base of information as possible. Statistical precision remained elusive, but his archive stands testament to a growing need for authority of source in a political world of party and vested interests.

Keywords: political tracts; City of London; Sir Charles Cooke; whig and tory (party divisions); French Commerce Bill; Levant trade; political arithmetic

In common with so many other students of the Augustan age, my first and abiding impression of early 18th-century politics came from reading *British Politics in the Age of Anne*. Its sheer authority immediately impressed, its judgments delivered with an elegance rarely matched by any work I have encountered. It is a regret that I never met the author, but my appreciation of his achievement only grew when working with his research materials at the History of Parliament Trust. I had frequent recourse to work with the notes donated by Ella Holmes to the project, and came to marvel even more at his mastery of source. This article aims to celebrate that consummate professional skill by analysing a collection of political papers which speak directly to some of the core themes of his great work. More particularly, it will seek to build on our understanding of the relationship between commercial and political development in Anne's reign, one of the themes to which Professor Holmes contributed enormously in a famous chapter on the 'Clash of Interests' between the forces of land and money.[1]

At its publication, the 'Clash of Interests' represented a pioneering study of the relationship between economic change and political conflict in the Augustan age. On the basis of a wide trawl of manuscript and printed matter, Professor Holmes identified a strong socio-economic context for the partisanship of the time, as a new, whiggish

---

[1] G.S. Holmes, *British Politics in the Age of Anne* (1967), 148–82.

© *The Parliamentary History Yearbook Trust 2009*

monied interest squared up to a tory landed elite suffering from the effects of high taxation and low rents. Twenty years later, he conceded that some reassessment was necessary, confessing that the chapter had 'weathered the intervening years less well than the rest'. Subsequent work had shown that the monied interest was a more complex entity than contemporary partisans might have suggested, and Gary De Krey's in-depth study of the City had shown than other social dynamics were at work, most obviously the tensions between London's commercial-financial plutocracy and its lesser traders.[2] Even so, few in 1987 would have doubted his original claim that the political character of the reign was 'moulded by social prejudices and economic pressures as well as by the forces of principle and power', and more recent work has continued to focus on the relationship between political activity and socio-economic change. This article takes its lead from this exciting work, and focuses on a contemporary collection of commercial tracts to highlight the strategies adopted by City politicians as they endeavoured to achieve significant commercial advantage in a party-riven age.[3]

The collection in question centres on two volumes of political tracts, deposited at the Bodleian Library.[4] It has been rarely used by historians, for its printed contents are available elsewhere, and the anonymous annotations and marginalia appear fairly random in character. My interest in the papers was sparked by their overwhelmingly commercial character, but it was only with closer inspection that I realized that its owner was one of the most significant commercial politicians of his day, Charles Cooke. The two volumes, in fact, represent one of Cooke's key political resources, and reveal much about the ways in which the trading classes struggled to adapt and direct the fluid political world of the age of Anne. Many historians have regretted the lack of surviving merchant papers as a bar to understanding their political strategies and outlook, and thus the Cooke collection will permit a more thorough review of their political methods and attitudes, which goes beyond the evidence of officeholding or voting patterns.[5]

Charles Cooke was not a prominent political figure for most of the reign of Anne, and could never be ranked alongside the great City magnates such as Sir Gilbert Heathcote or Samuel Shepheard, who mixed with ministers and dominated the boards of the great monied companies. The son of a modestly successful Hackney merchant, he had only reached his 30th birthday at the accession of the queen, and had no obvious claim to a

---

[2] G.S. Holmes, *British Politics in the Age of Anne* (rev. edn, 1987), pp. xliv–lxi; G.S. De Krey, *A Fractured Society: The Politics of London 1689–1715* (Oxford, 1985).

[3] Holmes, *British Politics*, 182. For subsequent modifications of his argument, see G.S. Holmes, *The Making of a Great Power: Late Stuart and Early Georgian Britain 1660–1722* (1993), 287–91. For the interesting directions in which the interaction of economic and political change has been pursued since 1987, see S. Pincus, 'Neither Machiavellian Moment Nor Possessive Individualism: Commercial Society and the Defenders of the English Commonwealth', *American Historical Review*, ciii (1998), 705–36; B.G. Carruthers, *City of Capital: Politics and Markets in the English Financial Revolution* (Princeton, 1992); W. Pettigrew, 'Free to Enslave: Politics and the Escalation of Britain's Transatlantic Slave Trade 1688–1714', *William and Mary Quarterly*, lxiv (2007), 3–38.

[4] Folio Theta 665 and 666. The provenance of the volumes is unclear, although it appears that they were catalogued in the 1860s. I am very grateful to Professor Henry Horwitz, who first drew my attention to the first of these volumes.

[5] Note, for instance, Natasha Glaisyer's recent observation on economic literature that 'evidence for how readers engaged with their texts is sparse': Natasha Glaisyer, *The Culture of Commerce in England 1660–1720* (Woodbridge, 2006), 185. Richard Grassby offers a stimulating interpretation of the various political and personal stimuli behind merchant officeholding in *The English Gentleman in Trade: The Life and Works of Sir Dudley North 1641–91* (Oxford, 1994), 151–76.

natural interest in the City hierarchy. However, his political services in the last years of Anne laid the foundations for his public career, in particular his support for the whig campaign against the French Commerce Bill in 1713–14. As an ally later revealed, Cooke was one of the key members of the team which ran a concerted press campaign to sink the measure, one of the most stunning ministerial reverses of this age. At the accession of George I his political skills were duly recognized, with appointment to the board of trade in 1714, election to a parliamentary seat at Grampound in 1715, and elevation to the aldermanic bench in 1717. A knighthood in January 1717 further underlined his favour at the whig court, although he was only to enjoy these honours until his death in 1721. While his political star might seem to have shone brightest under George, it is especially fortunate that Cooke's working collection of commercial tracts for the reign of Anne survives, for it throws light on his activity outside of office, and at a time of significant development for the politics of trade. The first section of this article will discuss the provenance and organisation of these volumes, thereby shining light on the political habits of leading City politicians. It will then discuss Cooke's more specific role in the debate over the French Commerce Bill, and assess how his response to that controversy reflected the wider impact of the public sphere on commercial politics.[6]

Although Bodleian records give little clue as to the origins of this collection, it can be confidently identified as Cooke's working archive from internal evidence. The printed papers all date from his lifetime, and while their content, and that of the annotations, ranges enormously, one of its major themes regards the export of cloth, a key interest for Levant merchants. As we shall see, the annotations suggest an insider's familiarity with the workings of the Levant Company, and a particular interest in the debate on the French Commerce Bill. More particularly, one annotation dated 1716 records a coach journey from the Cockpit (the location of the board of trade's offices) to Devonshire Square (Cooke's City domicile), which also took in the Mercers' Hall (Cooke's livery company). Little has survived of Cooke's papers, but the handwriting of a letter he penned in May 1710 also matches that used in both volumes. More conclusively still, a tract in the second volume of papers is addressed to 'Charles Cooke, Member of Parliament, Westminster'.[7]

The organisation of the volumes, especially the first tome, is far from straightforward, but its complexities reflect Cooke's political working practices, and the uncertain history of the collection after his death. In the first instance, this disorder stems from Cooke's possession of a very sophisticated range of sources for his political activities, which he was prepared to rearrange during his lifetime according to his particular needs. The contours of the archive have been further obscured by substantial re-editing since Cooke's death, and it is clear that many papers were additions to Cooke's original collection. It also appears that a subsequent owner tried to follow Cooke's own

---

[6] For the only short biography, see *The History of Parliament: The House of Commons 1715–54*, ed. R. Sedgwick (2 vols, 1970), i. 573–4. His partisan convictions are best represented by his prominence in the whig club which co-ordinated party activity in the capital in 1714–17: 'Minutes of a Whig Club', ed. H. Horwitz (London Record Society, xvii, 1981).

[7] The only signed Cooke letter traced can be found at the BL, Add. MS 61535, f. 68. Another suggestive familial reference comes with the inclusion of a printed order to Cooke's father, Thomas, in 1694: Folio Theta 665, f. 141. Its survival may well have great personal significance, for Thomas Cooke died shortly afterwards while Charles was in the Levant.

© *The Parliamentary History Yearbook Trust 2009*

numerical ordering scheme without recognizing the logic behind it, ensuring that materials were taken from a range of his papers without distinction. Nevertheless, sufficient internal evidence survives to permit a reconstruction of his working archive, and to gauge how he compiled and used it.[8]

The two volumes cover very distinct periods of Cooke's career, the first broadly spanning the reign of Anne, the second his more public life under George I. The first is the smaller, although including no less than 105 printed titles, while the second a hefty 210. The inclusion of an index in Cooke's hand in the first volume suggests that his collecting habits were of no mere antiquarian interest, and that he regarded it as a set of working papers. The index, in fact, only covers 62 titles, but there is a thematic logic behind the organisation of the titles, and Cooke added his own brackets to signify titles embracing a clear theme, such as tracts concerning new taxes, or duties on silks. Given this index, it suggests that Cooke had created a bound version of these papers for his own use, which he, or a later editor, decided to supplement with other printed and manuscript matter. The second volume has no index at all, although Cooke's numerical annotations run straight through until number 202, and thus can be very much viewed as his collection. Its superiority in terms of both quantity and order also reflect Cooke's enhanced status as a lord of trade, from which office he had both the need and opportunity to enhance his collection.

Internal evidence gives no clear sign as to the date when Cooke started to build up this collection, although a recognizable core of commercial tracts begins in 1705, which date accords with our knowledge of his career.[9] Born in 1671, he was apprenticed to Sir John Morden, and sailed to Smyrna in 1693. His father died in the following year, but he probably remained in the eastern Mediterranean, for the Levant Company granted him liberty to trade at Smyrna in June 1698. The first certain proof of his return to England came in May 1705, when he took his freedom of the company.[10] Once back in the capital, he was able to partake freely of the burgeoning London press, for he established bases in both Devonshire Square, on the northern fringe of the working City, and at Hackney, the family home and one of the most popular suburban sites for active merchants. Having been absent from Britain since the lapsing of the Licensing Act in 1695, the politically active Cooke was doubtless impressed by the liberal distribution of newspapers on his return, but his collection suggests that the appetite for printed tracts could be just as strong among City consumers. More interestingly still, Cooke's collection is noticeably limited to short papers on economic matters, the profusion of which reflects the increasing business of parliament during the reigns of William and Anne. These volumes suggest that their brevity and obvious self-interest did not preclude them

---

[8] The binding of these volumes only dates from the mid 19th century, shortly before their deposit in the Bodleian Library.

[9] The first volume does include papers dating back to the Popish Plot, but the vast majority pertain to Anne's reign.

[10] The National Archives (TNA), SP 105/155, f. 221; SP 105/156, p. 192; Folio Theta 665, f. 46v. He had probably been back in the country for some time before his admission to the freedom, for a list of the English Factory at Smyrna of January 1704 does not include him: Folio Theta 665, f. 192v. He was later to become a trustee of Morden College, founded by his former master: *The Survey of London Monographs 10: Morden College, Blackheath*, ed. T.F. Green (1916), 47.

from more serious study, and that contemporaries did not necessarily regard them as mere political ephemera to be forgotten at the end of each session.[11]

The collecting bug appears to have bitten Cooke particularly hard from 1708, when a variety of interests took an evident personal appeal. In a commercial vein, parliamentary proposals to levy new duties on imports and exports account for some 15 tracts, with predictable interest shown in the silk trade. However, other issues can be less obviously tied to his personal interests, most notably imprisonment for debt and the legal status of quakers. Of a more directly political interest, there was also a small collection of election papers, which show an early sign of the political ambition which led to a place on the common council by the end of Anne's reign.

As proof of the political habits and interests of leading citizens, the collection of printed tracts is significant, but the extensive annotations on these tracts, and the public use to which they were put, render them of particular importance. The annotations demonstrate that Cooke was not merely content to collect printed works, but that he used them as a primary working tool, alongside several other collections. While their selectivity suggests that Cooke had very particular priorities in assembling the collection, the tracts must be seen as a basis for a more general reference work for use in commercial and political affairs. The tracts clearly held an intrinsic interest for him, but he was also ready to use them as a convenient repository for adding materials from elsewhere.[12] Internal evidence suggests that he had probably arranged the order of the tracts by the time of the great French commerce treaty debate of 1713, for even some of the earliest tracts contain annotations of especial pertinence to that controversy. Indeed, it is plausible to suggest that Cooke ordered his papers, and supplied the index, in preparation for that contest, or for the publications which appeared in its wake.[13]

The ordering and content of these manuscript entries indicate that Cooke used the political tracts in tandem with other kinds of political papers, both printed and unpublished. The profusion of cross-references to different alphabetical series of sources suggests a very mercantile approach to the organisation of his political sources, replicating the recommended book-keeping practices for running a business.[14] Most interestingly, he was not content to rest on the public sphere to provide political ammunition, and was evidently very resourceful in sourcing materials. It is clear, for instance, that he possessed a separate collection of manuscript items relating to economic and political affairs. Copies of petitions to parliament, and of the minutes of executive boards, feature prominently in this category, and Cooke numbered them in a different sequence from

---

[11] For the rise of parliamentary business, see J. Hoppit, *Failed Legislation 1660–1800* (1997); P. Gauci, *The Politics of Trade: The Overseas Merchant in State and Society* (Oxford, 2001), 195–233.

[12] The annotations usually have very little relevance to the tract itself, and thus up until the time when he systematised the ordering of the tracts, Cooke must have only regarded the tracts as a general storehouse of information.

[13] This would accord with the claim of Charles King that the key sources for his later work were 'the originals of Sir Theodore Janssen, bt., Sir Charles Cooke, Henry Martin esq., etc.': Charles King, *The British Merchant* (3 vols, 1721), i, title page.

[14] For the paramount need for order in the layout of merchant businesses, see D. Hancock, *Citizens of the World: London Merchants and the Integration of the British Atlantic Community, 1735–1785* (Cambridge, 1995), esp. 99–102. References within the Cooke volumes suggest that he may have had as many as five classes of records, of which class A dealt with statistical data, class D covered laws and customs, and class E focused on Levant Company affairs.

© *The Parliamentary History Yearbook Trust 2009*

the tracts.[15] Most of these copies were not written by Cooke himself, which suggests that they came via political connections. Significantly, he rarely included transcripts of short political tracts, presumably because he could obtain them fairly easily through City channels.[16]

Beyond this series of manuscript sources, other annotated number sequences suggest that he was also attempting to create a more systematic review of global commerce, a practice in keeping with the general intellectual tendencies of the Augustan age.[17] At several points in the first volume the names of specific countries appear as headings to notes on their trade and customs, and this trend becomes even more defined in the second volume. Indeed, at several points a heading appears without any information supplied, as if Cooke was planning to fill in gaps in his commercial knowledge. This more ambitious project can be plausibly linked to his elevation to the board of trade in late 1714, especially given the extensive interest shown in these entries to the Atlantic trades, with which he had little personal connection.[18]

The annotations also indicate that Cooke had his own library of commercial authorities, which he used alongside the series of tracts and notes already mentioned. Significantly, his choices mirrored those normally referenced by commercial authors, and confirm that active traders did recognize a canon of superior economic literature. His favourite sources thus include Sir William Temple's *Observations upon the United Provinces of the Netherlands* (7th edn, 1705); John Pollexfen's *Discourse of Trade, Coin and Paper Credit* (1697), Lewes Roberts's *Merchant's Map of Commerce* (2nd edn, 1677), and various works by Charles Davenant. These works were predictably combed for information and arguments to support the dearest of Cooke's political causes, but they were not solely employed for polemical purposes. Often they simply filled gaps in Cooke's commercial knowledge, for instance the works of the great Elizabethan geographer Richard Hakluyt to supply details of customs in Russia and the Far East. Moreover, when using more controversial works, he was keen to note their strengths and weaknesses. For instance, he evidently found the work of the early 17th-century merchant, Thomas Mun, useful to warn of the danger of increasing imports, but he was concerned to date the work more precisely, for 'as appears by his preface [it] was written some time before'. This suggests that even such an avid collector and reader as Cooke was not cavalier in the use of printed sources, and in general he was scrupulous in comparing their findings with those derived from a range of other channels.[19]

---

[15] Cooke's post-mortem editor evidently conflated the printed and manuscript numbering when creating this volume, even though there appears to be little direct correspondence between the two classes.

[16] The earliest evidence of Cooke's close involvement in national politics comes with the inclusion of manuscript copies of City and Levant Company petitions concerning the Garbling Act of 1708: Folio Theta 665, ff. 23, 29.

[17] For commentary on how an increasing level of information on commerce reflected wider trends in intellectual thought and didactic literature, see Glaisyer, *Culture of Commerce in England*, esp. 100–42; W.E. Houghton, 'The History of Trades: Its Relation to Seventeenth-Century Thought', *Journal of the History of Ideas*, ii (1941), 33–60.

[18] The second volume has no less than 16 geographical headings in Cooke's hand, as well as many pages devoted to information concerning specific commodities: Folio Theta 666.

[19] Folio Theta 665, f. 122. Cooke cites the use of Mun by the well-known tract, *Britannia Languens* (1680). This work does reference Mun's preface, but Cooke's care in recording this remains significant. A new edition of Mun appeared in 1713, probably sponsored by the whigs: *England's Treasure by Foreign Trade* (1713).

Cooke's readiness to compile such a diverse and wide-ranging set of working papers must be linked to his political goals, both personal and party-linked. Although it is tempting to see the primary significance of the collection as its utility for the French commerce debates of 1713, the annotations to the first volume provide wider insights into the kinds of intelligence deemed politically useful for an active City merchant. A great deal of the information supplied centred on the affairs of the Levant Company, and was evidently generated by Cooke's experiences in the Mediterranean. Thus, there are many references to the costs of shipping in the region, and to the expenses of the company's officials in their Ottoman bases.[20] More interestingly, there is great interest in the identity of the admirals stationed in the Mediterranean since the Glorious Revolution, and in the membership of the English factories from Cadiz to Constantinople. On the domestic front, there is even a remarkable attempt by Cooke to list all the members of the Levant Company in order of the date of their admission to the freedom, probably attempted at the outset of Anne's reign. Marginalia entered by many of the names indicates that this paper was used by him as a working list of the current membership.[21]

Thus, it is important to see that this personal archive served a general set of working political practices and goals. It is also clear, however, that the great debate on the French commerce treaty of 1713 galvanised Cooke in a manner which no other political endeavour had, and that the contest proved the greatest test of the political utility of his collections. In particular, a further probing of the detailed evidence shows how Cooke endeavoured to use his commercial knowledge and expertise to clear political advantage, both within his own trading circles and before a wider public audience. In tandem with other politicians seeking to gain partisan advantage, the battle to present the 'truth' of the matter was a conflict which Cooke was determined to win, and spared no source to achieve that goal.[22]

No citizen could ignore the battle over the proposed commercial treaty with the French, which conflict raged from the spring of 1713 onwards.[23] Intended by the tory administration as a sweetener to garner an additional peace dividend ahead of the ensuing general election, the measure went disastrously wrong, sparking widespread controversy. The most vociferous opposition came from sectors most likely to be affected by a mutual lowering of tolls across the Channel, led by cloth producers and exporters, who feared that increased French wine competition would threaten the lucrative trade

---

[20] These records can be linked to his appointment as the Levant Company's husband in October 1706: TNA, SP 105/156, p. 248.

[21] Folio Theta 665, f. 97. The list begins with the admission of Sir Samuel Barnardiston in 1652, and runs through to 1699. There follows a list of omissions dating from 1672–98, and then further entries up to 1701. Crosses are applied next to many names, most of whom died after 1700, thus suggesting that Cooke kept this list as a working copy for organising company affairs. For instance, the earliest entrant, Barnardiston, died in 1707.

[22] M. Knights, *Representation and Misrepresentation in Later Stuart Britain: Partisanship and Political Culture* (Oxford, 2005).

[23] For accounts of this key contest, see D. Coleman, 'Politics and Economics in the Age of Anne: The Case of the Anglo-French Trade Treaty of 1713', in *Trade, Government and Economy in Pre-Industrial England*, ed. D. Coleman and A.H. John (1976), 187–211; G. Holmes and C. Jones, 'Trade, the Scots and the Parliamentary Crisis of 1713', *Parliamentary History*, i (1981), 47–77; Gauci, *Politics of Trade*, 234–70; D.A.E. Harkness, 'The Opposition to the Eighth and Ninth Articles of the Commercial Treaty of Utrecht', *Scottish History Review*, xxi (1924), 219–26.

© *The Parliamentary History Yearbook Trust 2009*

to Portugal, secured by Britain's favoured status to port wine. Amongst those groups alarmed by the changing *status quo*, the Levant merchants appeared especially vulnerable, their woollen exports placed in jeopardy and their silk imports facing the prospect of stiff Gallic rivalry. Indeed, one of the first groups attempting to influence a possible Anglo-French accord was the Levant Company in 1709–10, but a resurgent war effort had put paid to their overtures. When peace finally materialised in 1713, Turkey traders were once more to the fore, especially after the administration introduced a bill in May of that year to confirm the 8th and 9th articles of the commercial treaty. This measure was to give Cooke a taste of the political spotlight for the first time, when, as an 'eminent' merchant, he testified on 4 June at the bar of the house of lords. However, his collected papers suggest that he had already made sterling efforts on behalf of the bill's opponents.[24]

Cooke's first political attempts against the bill centred on the production of a Levant Company petition to protect domestic silk manufacturers, and to return French tariffs on British exports and re-exports to their 1664 level. On 28 May the company's general court had met to decide their position on the treaty, and voted overwhelmingly by 35 votes to 11 (with eight abstentions) to back a petition against it. The company was clearly divided along partisan lines on this measure, for only two of these 54 members deviated from these established party lines at the subsequent City of London election. Cooke could obviously take great pleasure in this victory, but such was the contentiousness of this battle that he felt constrained to take further steps to confirm the advantage of his party. In particular, he took seriously the rumours spread abroad that the whig victory had been achieved at the expense of the more established traders, and that the lesser merchants had simply outnumbered the more prestigious magnates. Evidently concerned that these allegations might harm whig aspirations to present themselves as the more knowledgeable party in trade, Cooke therefore endeavoured to provide statistical proof that the anti-treaty group included the principal merchants in the trade. The pains he took in this regard support recent arguments that the 18th century was no lacuna in the development of political arithmetic, and again suggest a mercantile commitment to transparency and exactness of dealing.[25]

His principal winning strategy was to calculate how many cloths had been exported to the Levant in 1712 by the rival factions. He concentrated first of all on members present at the vote of 28 May, and produced the satisfactory majority of 15,858 cloths for the whigs against 9,059 for the tories and abstentions. These figures demonstrated that the whigs had failed to win over two of the greatest exporting merchants (John Williams and Thomas Vernon), and their prominence probably lay behind tory claims that their support was superior in quality, if not numerically. Significantly, Cooke did not rest there, and made further calculations to cover members who were not present at the key vote, but who had expressed support for or against petitioning at other times. This produced overall totals of 17,203 cloths exported by pro-petitioners, and 11,639 exported by those 'against petitioning'. More problematically for him, he also felt

---

[24] A. Boyer, *The Political State of Great Britain* (60 vols, 1718–40), v, 358. Boyer does not make it clear whether Cooke testified on the 2nd or 4th of that month, but the Levant merchants were heard on the latter date, after they had petitioned on the 2nd: *LJ*, ix, 557, 562.

[25] Folio Theta 665, f. 190; J. Hoppit, 'Political Arithmetic in Eighteenth-Century England', *Economic History Review*, xlix (1996), 516–40.

© *The Parliamentary History Yearbook Trust 2009*

constrained to list the cloths exported by those absent at the key meeting: another 29 names, who had exported 8,536 cloths; a significant figure given the difference between the two sides.[26] It is plausible to suggest that these absentees frustrated Cooke's plans to publish his findings, for it would only fuel divisions still further, and allow the tories to point to the wavering of other key company figures.[27]

Even though Cooke's calculations did not surface in print, he had the satisfaction of seeing the French Commerce Bill fall to an ignominious defeat in the house of commons on 18 June, its fate sealed by a sizeable group of tory rebels. This tory disaster only further stirred up contention on the fate of British trade, and saw notable clashes at the subsequent general election and beyond. Stung by tory success at the polls, and by reports of a new French commerce treaty, Cooke then became part of the whig team backing the tri-weekly *The British Merchant*, a direct contender against the government-backed *Mercator*. The contest gave Cooke's collection continued value as a political tool, as the battle raged over the commercial 'authority' of the ministry and its opponents.[28]

The principal protagonists in this debate were the *Mercator*'s Daniel Defoe, and *The British Merchant*'s Henry Martin. Although the former had some claims to a commercial education, neither were active traders, and thus both sides delighted in rubbishing each others credentials as economic commentators. For instance, in November 1713, the *Mercator* claimed that its rival had 'two attorneys set up for the champions of merchants, who understood railing better than trade'. Martin could not deny this, but his enlistment of Cooke and other merchants emboldened him, declaring ''tis sufficient for me that I have been assisted by gentlemen of as great skill and experience as are to be found in this kingdom'. Unable to deny the commercial expertise behind *The British Merchant*, Defoe thereafter contented himself with questioning the patriotism of his mercantile opponents, saving particular criticism for Sir Theodore Janssen. Cooke was spared direct attack, but closer inspection of *The British Merchant*'s arguments demonstrates that he was a key part of the anti-government team.[29]

The pages of *The British Merchant* indicate that Cooke's collection was put to very direct use in the contest, and that it compensated for a serious deficiency in the anti-ministry platform. As Martin conceded, Defoe had better access to customs records because 'his interest is better', and he argued that 'every office in the kingdom has been

---

[26] Significantly, a scrupulous Cooke refused to include the figure of Sir Randolph Knipe, 'who was at the last court, but [I] cannot tell how he gave his vote'. A leading cloth exporter, Knipe later sided with the whigs at the City election of 1713: Folio Theta 665, f. 190.

[27] Note the observations of Cooke's ally Henry Martin with regard to the limitations of statistical records: Hoppit, 'Political Arithmetic', *Economic History Review*, 532. A fair copy of his calculations by another hand is included in the same volume of *Economic History Review* (xlix (1996)), and thus his table might have circulated in manuscript. Cooke's jottings include a calculation of the costs for publishing 1,000 half-sheets (at 66s. 8d.), which may refer to this table: Folio Theta 665, f. 106v.

[28] In King's later work, Cooke was the first-named of the merchants who helped *The British Merchant* to fruition, the others being Sir Theodore Janssen, James Milner, Nathaniel Toriano, Joshua Gee, Christopher Haynes and David Martin. 'Several other very able and worthy merchants' were also said to have helped: King, *British Merchant*, i, pp. ix–x.

[29] *Mercator*, no. 81, 26–8 Nov. 1713; *The British Merchant*, no. 20, 9–13 Oct. 1713. A possible reference to Cooke comes in *Mercator* no. 153 [13–15 May 1714] with mention of 'the foreign knight [Janssen], the ignorant lawyer [Martin] and their yet more ignorant abettor', although this may refer to another member of the whig team.

© *The Parliamentary History Yearbook Trust 2009*

rummaged to equip him'.[30] Cooke certainly helped the whig team to overcome that disadvantage, and *The British Merchant* is littered with references from annotations in the first volume of Cooke's papers. For instance, issue 63 cites Samuel Puffendorf's *Introduction to the History of the Principal Kingdoms and States of Europe* (1711) for information on French exports, which accords directly with Cooke's own 7th edition. Sir William Temple's respect for Dutch frugality and religious tolerance, echoed in issues 82 and 84, directly matched the pagination listed in notes from Cooke's collection. More generally, the paper also supplied informed commentary on the Levant trade, and was clearly abetted by Cooke's calculations on the price and volume of English imports and exports. Cooke's first volume suggests that as early as issue fourteen he was taking private soundings over the real value of goods to perfect the whig claim over the serious imbalance of trade with France in 1685–6. Cooke was merely one of a team, but there can be no doubt that his knowledge and records were a significant boon to the whig platform.[31]

Ultimately, Cooke and his allies emerged victorious from the protracted contest, for the Oxford ministry never attempted to re-introduce the French Commerce Bill, and the death of Anne spelt disaster for the tory cause in general. It is easy to dismiss the significance of the City battle in this whig triumph, and to suggest that *The British Merchant* had little more than an immediate importance, but Cooke's collection suggests that the commercial battles of Anne's reign represented an important stage for economic debate in the public sphere. Cooke himself appears to have re-doubled his efforts after 1714 to gain as wide a knowledge of global trade as possible, and to keep his working archive up-to-date and well-ordered. His new responsibilities as a lord of trade were doubtless behind this diligence, but the collection also suggests that he had learnt important lessons from the battles of 1713–14. In particular, he appears to have taken additional pains to garner good statistical evidence of trade flows, and to learn a great deal more about global commercial practices. In this vein, he was perhaps conscious of Defoe's claim that 'such is the misfortune of the times that if an untruth will but stand uncontradicted one half an hour, it is of use'. This universal, systematic approach was certainly reflected in the most concrete legacy of the commercial controversy, Charles King's three-volume digest of *The British Merchant*. Not only did it directly acknowledge Cooke's contribution to the commercial politics of its era, but its format imitated his political working habits, for it provided a 'very copious' index to ensure its 'constant use' when commercial matters came before the state.[32]

As ever, one must be wary of ascribing general practice from the jottings of one individual, and few could have matched Cooke's industry in amassing such a formidable collection of papers, particularly in the field of commerce. None the less, his remaining archive faithfully reflects an array of responses to a fast-changing political landscape. For all its limitations as a coherent collection, it provides access to the more mundane workings of the political minds of the age, and permits us to see beyond the finished

---

[30] *The British Merchant*, no. 28, 6–10 Nov. 1713; no. 80, 7–11 May 1714.

[31] *The British Merchant*, no. 14, 18–22 Sept. 1713; no. 82, 14–18 May 1714; no. 84, 20–5 May 1714; Folio Theta 665, ff. 110–111v, 123. Humphrey Willet, a merchant-turned-broker, provided Cooke with the prices of Levant goods sold to France in 1685–8: Folio Theta 665, f. 96v.

[32] *Mercator*, no. 68, 27–9 Oct. 1713; King, *British Merchant*, i, p. ix. Commerce clearly benefited from a wider publishing trend to provide universal guides, such as Malachy Postlethwayt's monumental, *The Universal Dictionary of Trade and Commerce, Translated from the French of the Celebrated Monsieur Savary* (1751).

© *The Parliamentary History Yearbook Trust 2009*

product, and to assess how various kinds of resources were used to build a political case. In this vein, it commemorates both Geoff Holmes's mastery of source, and his famed ability to recreate political personality. Moreover, these volumes validate his commitment to constructing a social history of politics, and would doubtless have further convinced him of the importance of Anne's reign for the development of the economy as an issue of fundamental national concern.

© *The Parliamentary History Yearbook Trust 2009*

Geoffrey Holmes and the Urban World of Augustan England

PETER BORSAY

Urban history as a sub-discipline within history began to emerge in Britain in the 1960s and early 1970s. Attention initially focused heavily on the 19th century, but the Tudor and early Stuart town also soon attracted attention. Academic interest in the post-restoration and 18th-century urban world emerged a little more slowly, but the closing decades of the 20th century produced a mounting volume of research on the subject. Geoffrey Holmes was one of a group of post-war historians rewriting the history of Augustan Britain and re-establishing its significance in the longer-term development of the country. Though not a specialist urban historian, Holmes saw towns playing a vital part in shaping the character of the period. His research anticipated and inspired many of the facets of the rapidly-emerging historiography on the 18th-century town, intersecting with it in three particular areas. First, in demonstrating the important role played by towns, in particular as the home of four-fifths of the seats in the house of commons, in the broader political system; second, in highlighting the position of London at the hub of the Augustan world; and third in revealing the part played by towns, and especially those who inhabited them, in promoting social change at the same time as securing long-term political stability.

Keywords: Augustan; borough; England; 18th century; electorate; Geoffrey Holmes; London; professions; social structure; town; urban history; urbanisation

Had Geoffrey Holmes, by some miracle, been able to transport himself to live in Augustan England, I have never been entirely sure whether he would have chosen to do so as a *countryman* or a *townsman*. For the country gentleman the rural world offered the pleasures of leisured living without the hustle and bustle of the city, country sports (including the first stirrings, at least in the south east of England, of the modern form of cricket, a sport close to Geoff's heart),[1] space for a commodious library and study, plenty of time for scholarly investigation, intimate engagement with nature through gardening and walking, and patronage of the local anglican church. But would it have all been just a little too tedious? In 1715 Alexander Pope may well have been driven to distraction to issue his famous cry: 'Dear, damn'd, distracting Town, farewell!', but his reason for flight: 'Why should I stay? Both parties rage', would be more inclined to attract than repel a committed political historian.[2] Compared with the energy and dynamism of the town, and its thrusting inhabitants, would the country have simply been too boring, and even boorish? As Joseph Addison reminded the readers of that most urbane publication, *The*

---

[1] D. Underdown, *Start of Play: Cricket and Culture in Eighteenth-Century England* (Harmondsworth, 2000).

[2] 'A Farewell to London: In the Year 1715', in *The Poems of Alexander Pope*, ed. J. Butt (1965), 245.

Spectator – appearing on a daily basis between March 1711 and December 1712, and feeding the conversation and gossip of London's hundreds of coffee houses – 'If . . . we look on the People of Mode in the Country, we find in them the Manners of the last Age. They have no sooner fetched themselves up to the fashion of the Polite World, but the Town has dropped them.'[3] Though at one level Geoffrey Holmes's research may be seen as an anatomy of the lifestyle and political machinations of a rural-based landed ruling order, at another level it constantly turned to the town and its inhabitants to explain both the workings of that order and the changing character of Augustan society.

I think that was why the first few weeks of Geoffrey Holmes's celebrated under-graduate special subject on Augustan England – which I was privileged to take in the class 1971–2 – began not with a run down of the great families of England, but a tour round the regions of England in the company of the diarist and gentlewoman Celia Fiennes and the journalist, novelist and guidebook writer Daniel Defoe, both of whom were much more interested in towns than the countryside.[4] At the beginning of the 1970s, systematic research into the English town in the century or so after the Resto-ration was still very limited. There were pioneering studies like Dorothy George's *London Life in the Eighteenth Century*, first published in 1925, W.G. Hoskins's *Industry, Trade and People in Exeter, 1688–1800* (1935), and John Summerson's *Georgian London* (1945), but these were all over a quarter of a century old and, significantly, were studies of individual towns. There was no serious treatment of towns as a generic phenomenon in the period, and no real sense of an urban historiography. On a broader chronological front this was changing with the emergence in Britain of urban history as a sub- (but, decidedly not, separate) discipline,[5] under the influence of figures like Jim Dyos and his brainchildren, the Urban History Group (established c.1966) and *The Urban History Newsletter*, first published in 1963, which transmuted into the *Urban History Yearbook* in 1974.[6] However, at this stage the focus of urban history was almost entirely on the modern period and the era of the industrial revolution. Scanning the proceedings of the first conference (held at Leicester in 1966) of British urban historians, published in 1968 as *The Study of Urban History*, and edited by Dyos, what is striking is how few contributions there were on the pre-modern era and the 18th century in particular.[7] For this reason I can still remember the frisson I felt in 1972 when Peter Clark and Paul Slack published their edited volume entitled *Crisis and Order in English Towns, 1500–1700*.[8] The essays revealed a new wave of research underway – emanating from Oxford and London in the 1960s, and yet to reach monographic level – that paralleled in its range and innovation that on the modern era. But if *Crisis and Order* raised expectations in one respect, in another it dashed them. This was a volume which stopped at 1700 – a date which, if Geoffrey

---

[3] *The Spectator*, 17 July 1711, in *Selections from the Tatler and the Spectator*, ed. A. Ross (Harmondsworth, 1982), 277.

[4] *The Journeys of Celia Fiennes*, ed. C. Morris (1947); D. Defoe, *A Tour through the Whole Island of Great Britain*, ed. G.D.H. Cole and D.C. Browning (2 vols, 1962).

[5] 'Introduction', in *The Pursuit of Urban History*, ed. D. Fraser and A. Sutcliffe (1983), p. xi.

[6] J. Dyos, 'Editorial', *Urban History Yearbook* (1974), 2.

[7] *The Study of Urban History*, ed. J. Dyos (1968).

[8] *Crisis and Order in English Towns 1500–1700: Essays in Urban History*, ed. P. Clark and P. Slack (1972). The impressive introduction later formed the basis of P. Clark and P. Slack, *English Towns in Transition 1500–1700* (Oxford, 1976), published, in part, to service the new Open University course A322 on the early modern town.

© *The Parliamentary History Yearbook Trust 2009*

Holmes's work revealed anything, meant absolutely nothing. Here was a classic example of the tyranny of chronology and periodisation. In truth, the principal focus of the volume was the Tudor and early Stuart era, the 'take off' to, and period of, the civil wars, the event which dominated and defined early modern English historiography at the time. So much was this the case that the century or so after the Restoration had become relatively speaking a historiographic backwater, squeezed between the 'English revolution' and that other iconic phenomenon, the 'industrial revolution'. However, frustration was not simply borne of chronological angst. The underlying theme of the volume, 'crisis', was quite at odds with what I was learning as I took my journey around England with Fiennes and Defoe. Whatever the position before 1660, it was perfectly clear that after 1660, though individual towns may have been experiencing problems at particular moments in time, the general picture was of growth and prosperity not crisis.

Over the next three to four decades this air of neglect (and negativity) was to be transformed. As Jeremy Gregory and John Stevenson have commented: 'the days are long gone when "keeping up with the reading" was easier for historians of the eighteenth century than for most of their colleagues'.[9] Geoffrey Holmes was one of a group of historians who were challenging the bipolar – English revolution/industrial revolution – model of British historiography, reasserting the significance of the Glorious Revolution, revealing the continuing strength of political/party fissures, affirming the dynamism of the period and in general re-energising post-Restoration and 18th-century studies. It was a project that for Geoffrey Holmes culminated in a magisterial two-volume text book, which he completed with Daniel Szechi, surveying the years 1660–1783.[10] The long 18th century is now one of the most hotly researched and debated, and as historical best sellers and raunchy television programmes are demonstrating, one of the most popular areas of British history. Research into towns has followed, and in some respects led this trend, with a proliferation of theses, articles, monographs and particularly significantly, given the previous paucity of systematic analysis, general surveys of the subject.[11] It is unlikely that Geoffrey Holmes would ever have defined himself as an urban historian. He would probably have resisted vehemently any form of categorisation other than 'historian'. But he did have an intuitive understanding, which he transmitted to his students, of the importance of towns as one of the primary motors of change in Augustan Britain. His interest in the urban dimension stemmed from three particular points of contact between his research and the town: politics, the metropolis and social change.

In one sense control of the political system rested in towns. It was a point recognized by James II when he implemented his dramatic campaign in the 1680s to remodel urban corporations. Moreover, it is significant that much of Defoe's material for his *Tour* was

---

[9] J. Gregory and J. Stevenson, *The Longman Companion to Britain in the Eighteenth Century, 1688–1820* (2000), 480.

[10] G.S. Holmes, *The Making of a Great Power: Late Stuart and Early Georgian Britain, 1660–1722* (1993); G.S. Holmes and D. Szechi, *The Age of Oligarchy: Pre-Industrial Britain, 1722–1783* (1993).

[11] The most important overall survey is provided in *The Cambridge Urban History of Britain, Volume II, 1540–1840*, ed. P. Clark (Cambridge, 2000), but there have also been a number of texts dedicated to the 18th century: P. Corfield, *The Impact of English Towns, 1700–1800* (Oxford, 1982); *The Eighteenth-Century Town: A Reader in English Urban History, 1688–1820*, ed. P. Borsay (1990); R. Sweet, *The English Town 1680–1840: Government, Society and Culture* (Harlow, 1999); C. Chalklin, *The Rise of the English Town, 1650–1850* (Cambridge, 2001); J.M. Ellis, *The Georgian Town, 1680–1840* (Basingstoke, 2001).

gathered not as he claimed during a disinterested fact-finding tour in the 1720s (there must be serious doubts over whether such a comprehensive tour ever took place), but when, travelling from town to town in the early 1700s, he carried out secret political research primarily on the state of the borough constituencies for Robert Harley.[12] Urban political leverage stemmed from the fact that though only a minority of the population were town dwellers – at the most generous estimate about a third of the inhabitants of England and Wales in 1700[13] – four-fifths of parliamentary seats in the house of commons were located in boroughs; before 1707 it was 81%, after the union with Scotland it dropped slightly to 77%.[14] Many of these boroughs were very small. However, there is little reason to doubt that the vast majority would have been considered by contemporaries to be towns. Though at one stage there was a tendency among historians of the early modern period to dismiss places of below 2,500 and even 5,000 people as not truly urban, research on small towns has not only confirmed the urban character of such places – some as small as 400–500 people (in the late 17th century over 90% of the 1,000 or so towns in mainland Britain had populations of under 2,500) – but also the resilience and vitality of the sector throughout the 18th century.[15] It is, of course, true that voters could be drafted into urban constituencies from outside the town, that the rural elite heavily influenced the outcome of borough elections and that landed gentlemen supplied the majority of MPs. However, towns were not a pushover. There was invariably some degree of mutual give and take in the relationship between town and country. In offering the key to the control of the house of commons, urban electorates, though the nature of these varied a good deal, possessed a powerful bargaining chip. Landed patrons and MPs had to earn electors' support, both at the time of the contest, but also, and in some respects just as importantly, in between contests. That meant representing and protecting the town's vital interests in parliament and government, assisting in moments of crisis, and regularly grooming the town with gifts. Many an addition to the urban infrastructure – such as a new town hall, market hall, grammar school, church, landscaped walk, set of oil-fired street lights and fire engine – in this period owed its origin to the need to gratify urban voters.[16] Though it is tempting to see this in crude terms of buying support, the high-minded nature of the gifts – their emphasis upon the town as a whole rather than the individual citizen, and upon the morally elevating goal of 'improvement' – suggests something more subtle, what may be termed the politics of altruism.

[12] Defoe, *Tour*, i, 5; J.H. Andrews, 'Defoe and the Sources of His Tour', *Geographical Review*, cxxvi (1960), 268–77; F. Bastian, 'Defoe's Tour and the Historian', *History Today*, xvii (1967), 845–51; M.E. Novak, *Daniel Defoe: Master of Fictions* (Oxford, 2003), 242–6, 267–72, 631–2.

[13] Corfield, *Impact of English Towns*, 9; P. Clark, 'Small Towns 1700–1840', in *Cambridge Urban History*, ed. Clark, ii, 736.

[14] Calculated from Gregory and Stevenson, *Longman Companion*, 82.

[15] Clark, 'Small Towns', in *Cambridge Urban History*, ed. Clark, ii, 733–73; *Small Towns in Early Modern Europe*, ed. P. Clark (Cambridge, 1995); A. Dyer, 'Small Towns in England, 1600–1800', in *Provincial Towns in Early Modern England and Ireland: Change, Convergence and Divergence*, ed. P. Borsay and L. Proudfoot (Oxford, 2002), 53–67; J. Langton, 'Urban Growth and Economic Change: From the Late Seventeenth Century to 1841', in *Cambridge Urban History*, ed. Clark, ii, 463.

[16] P. Borsay, 'The Landed Elite and Provincial Towns in Britain, 1660–1800', *The Georgian Group Journal*, xiii (2003), 285–7.

British Politics in the Age of Anne made no secret of the fact that it concentrated 'very largely . . . on the centre of politics'.[17] However, the decision was, as the preface makes clear, a pragmatic one – not one that implied the relative unimportance of provincial politics – driven by the need to keep the size of the study under control and a knowledge that Bill Speck was working on the constituencies. Tory and Whig, which appeared three years after British Politics, contained a chapter on 'Party organization in the boroughs' and noted the distinctive qualities of town politics: 'the boroughs were not mere microcosms of the counties . . . Thus although the actual mounting of campaigns bore many resemblances to those in the counties, the careful cultivation of an interest between elections was a feature of party organization which did not concern county agents to anything like the same extent.'[18] It is arguable that the boroughs demanded more regular attention because their electorates were in a stronger position to exploit their position. Geoffrey Holmes turned his attention to the boroughs in his brilliant analysis of The Electorate and the National Will, his inaugural lecture at Lancaster University (where he moved from Glasgow University in 1969). In this he came to the, perhaps surprising, conclusion that in the early 18th century the towns, if not the regions, of Augustan England were fairly represented by the distribution of seats, unlike the position later in the century, and that was one of the reasons there was so little pressure for electoral reform. This went some way to counter the hoary historical image that parliamentary boroughs were generally miniscule and decayed – Holmes argues that 'it was very hard in 1700 to point to more than a handful of towns with a clear-cut case to replace them'[19] – and it suggested that most towns were capable of sustaining a credible political culture.

The pioneering work of Holmes and Speck pointed to the importance of towns in, and distinctive contribution to, the Augustan political system. The challenge they posed has subsequently been taken up in a number of important studies of provincial urban politics. John Triffit's examination of parliamentary boroughs in the south-west of England in the early 18th century emphasizes the relative independence of towns – stressing that deference and government patronage did not determine electoral outcomes – and contends that 'eighteenth-century politics has become an urban problem'.[20] In his investigation of Yarmouth between 1660 and 1722, Perry Gauci explicitly acknowledged his debt to Plumb, Holmes and Speck for identifying 'the borough as a key arena of party conflict', exploring the complex and vital role played by the corporation in managing the town's internal and external political relations.[21] Corporations are also key institutions in Paul Halliday's and John Miller's overviews of English provincial urban politics between the mid 17th and early 18th centuries.[22] Town councils were at the heart of a good deal of the conflict over the period, but ultimately they were also a force for

[17] G.S. Holmes, British Politics in the Age of Anne (1967), p. ix.

[18] W.A. Speck, Tory and Whig: The Struggle in the Constituencies (1970), 47.

[19] G.S. Holmes, The Electorate and the National Will in the First Age of Party (an inaugural lecture delivered on 26 Nov. 1975), (Lancaster, 1976), 26.

[20] J.M. Triffit, 'Politics and the Urban Community: Parliamentary Boroughs in the South West of England 1710–1730', University of Oxford DPhil, 1985, pp. 12, 36–7.

[21] P. Gauci, Politics and Society in Great Yarmouth, 1660–1722 (Oxford, 1996), 255.

[22] P.D. Halliday, Dismembering the Body Politic: Partisan Politics in England's Towns, 1650–1730 (Cambridge, 1998); J. Miller, Cities Divided: Politics and Religion in English Provincial Towns, 1660–1722 (Oxford, 2007).

internal and external stability, critical to creating a viable political system that linked local and national states. Gauci's, Halliday's and Miller's volumes finish in the 1720s. The implication would seem to be that a certain watershed had been reached, and that the ideological fires that had been lit in the 1640s, and had continued to burn so fiercely in the decades after the Restoration, had finally begun to abate. The heavy hand of the whig settlement, combined with a measure of exhaustion, the emergence of new mechanisms to resolve conflict, and a deep pragmatic reflex among town authorities to get on with the business of government, introduced a measure of equipoise. Geoffrey Holmes himself suggested that a combination of economic, social and cultural forces focused on the town, including ' "the new urban society" and "the urban renaissance" ', worked 'in the long term, down to the mid 18th century, towards fusion rather than towards fission in the social order . . . contributing to the ultimate achievement of greater political stability'.[23] Towns may have been influential in introducing a more stable form of politics, but, paradoxically, greater stability would appear to reduce towns' leverage on the political system. Less elections and contested seats deprived towns of the capacity to play their electoral aces, and seemingly lessened their significance in the political process. The traditional images of the corrupt and moribund 18th-century corporation, and of towns firmly under the control of the landed gentry, reinforced this post-Augustan picture of urban torpor and impotence.

Yet such a picture is inherently implausible. Urbanisation was increasing the proportion of townspeople in the population and the contribution of the urban sector to the economy as a whole. In these circumstances it was unlikely that the internal structures of urban governance were ossifying – an impression David Clemis argues of Ipswich 'bequeathed to historians by the 1835 municipal commission via the Webbs'[24] – or that townspeople were ceding their influence over wider political developments. Research during the last few decades has revealed both the flexibility and inventiveness of towns in adapting and adding to existing modes of government to cope with rapid change – the introduction of the improvement commission and the proliferation of civic-minded voluntary societies are cases in point[25] – and the existence of a vibrant urban political culture, much of it extra-parliamentary, well able to exert an influence on the course of local and national politics. The town remained a theatre of conflict. How much this went for the smaller parliamentary boroughs, and particularly the mass of unincorporated towns may be a matter for debate, but it was certainly the case for the larger provincial cities and London as the work of Kathleen Wilson and Nicholas Rogers has shown.[26]

Geoffrey Holmes's focus on the political centre meant that one town above all others coloured his vision of Augustan England: London. Much of the political business

[23] G.S. Holmes, *British Politics in the Age of Anne* (rev. edn 1987), p. xvi.

[24] J.D. Clemis, 'Government in an English Provincial Town: The Corporation of Ipswich, 1720–1795', University of Leicester PhD, 1999, p. 291.

[25] E.L. Jones and M.E. Falkus, 'Urban Improvement and the English Economy in the Seventeenth and Eighteenth Centuries', in *Eighteenth-Century Town*, ed. Borsay, 137–41; J. Innes and N. Rogers, 'Politics and Government, 1700–1840', in *Cambridge Urban History*, ed. Clark, ii, 529–74; Sweet, *English Town*, 27–161; P. Langford, *Public Life and the Propertied Englishman, 1689–1798* (Oxford, 1994), 207–32.

[26] N. Rogers, *Whigs and Cities: Popular Politics in the Age of Walpole and Pitt* (Oxford, 1989); N. Rogers, *Crowds, Culture and Politics in Georgian Britain* (Oxford, 1998); K. Wilson, *The Sense of the People: Politics, Culture and Imperialism in England, 1715–1785* (Cambridge, 1995).

© *The Parliamentary History Yearbook Trust 2009*

described in *British Politics* was transacted in the metropolis, and not only in the more obvious seats of government. He describes with some relish – anticipating later interest among historians in the growth of the public sphere – how the clubs, coffee houses, theatres and recently-established newspaper press of early 18th-century London reflected and fertilised party conflict.[27] Moreover, his forensic account of the trial of Henry Sacheverell in 1710 and the disturbances that accompanied it, particularly the movements of the rioters during 'the night of fire', is an exposition of the political (and because the mob turned their fury on the nonconformist meeting-houses, the religious) topography of the capital.[28]

Location mattered and it is undeniable that London exerted a huge influence over the political world. It could hardly be otherwise, given the capital's extraordinary early modern growth (from about 75,000 people in 1550 to 575,000 by 1700, from under 3% to over 10% of the English population); its size compared with other provincial towns (its nearest provincial rival in 1700, Norwich, contained a mere 30,000 inhabitants); its wealth and economic power; its role in the financial revolution; and its monopoly of all the key organs of state.[29] The consequence of the capital's powerful position was that for an aristocrat or country gentleman with economic, social or political aspirations, a visit to, and stay in, London – and when in the country intimate and continuous connection with the metropolis – was *de rigueur*.[30] Cutting a political figure among the national elite made a long stay in the capital essential, particularly during parliamentary sessions, and for many that would mean the occupation and preferably acquisition of a London residence, in proximity to St James's, Westminster and Whitehall, from which to conduct affairs. It was this that led to the remarkable post-Restoration expansion of the ever-expanding and mutating West End, with its fashionable squares and aristocratic residences that have attracted a good deal of attention from urban and architectural historians.[31] Indeed, it has been claimed that for some of the aristocracy their spectacular London houses constituted their primary residences, rather than their country estates and homes.[32]

One reason that the landed elite came to London was to take advantage of its proliferating financial services. This included not only the facilities provided by the metropolis for raising capital through mortgaging property, but also the need, in a pre-electronic communications age, to be close to the burgeoning securities market. As Defoe argued: 'many thousands of families are so deeply concerned in those stocks, and

[27] Holmes, *British Politics*, 21–4, 30–3.

[28] G.S. Holmes, *The Trial of Dr Sacheverell* (1973), 156–78.

[29] J. Boulton, 'London, 1540–1700', in *Cambridge Urban History*, ed. Clark, ii, 316; E.A. Wrigley and R.S. Schofield, *The Population History of England 1541–1871* (1981), 208–9; R. Porter, *London: A Social History* (1994), 93–159.

[30] J.M. Rosenheim, *The Emergence of a Ruling Order: English Landed Society, 1650–1750* (Harlow, 1998), 215–58.

[31] John Summerson, *Georgian London* (first published 1945); L. Stone, 'The Residential Development of the West End of London in the Seventeenth Century', in *After the Reformation*, ed. B.C. Malament (Manchester, 1980), 167–212; D.J. Olsen, *Town Planning in London: The Eighteenth and Nineteenth Centuries* (2nd edn, New Haven, 1982); E. McKellar, *The Birth of Modern London: The Development and Design of the City, 1660–1720* (Manchester, 1999).

[32] M.H. Port, 'West End Palaces: The Aristocratic Town House in London, 1730–1830', *London Journal*, xx (1995), 37–40.

find it so absolutely necessary to be at hand to take the advantage of buying and selling, as the sudden rise or fall of the price directs, and the loss they often sustain by their ignorance of things when absent, and the knavery of brokers and others, whom, in their absence, they are bound to trust, that they find themselves obliged to come up and live constantly here, or at least, most part of the year'.[33] The financial revolution of the late 17th century enhanced the already powerful position of the City of London allowing its leaders to exert considerable influence over national politics. Much of this clout derived from the unprecedented sums of money that the government was required to raise to finance the wars against Louis XIV. The City in large measure bank rolled the war. Those involved in supplying the government's monetary requirements, directly or indirectly through the purchase of stocks in institutions like the East India Company, the Bank of England and the South Sea Company could make huge profits. In chapter five of *British Politics* Geoff identified the so-called monied men, those holding their wealth in predominantly non-landed assets, as among the super rich of the age, and as one of the prime targets of tory propaganda. The land tax, introduced in the 1690s to fund the war effort and service government debt, was seen to be penalising country gentlemen, dependent on their landed estates, at the same time as lining the pockets of the monied men. Portrayed in these terms, as a confrontation between landed wealth and monied capital, chapter five, 'The Clash of Interests', seemed to point to party divisions being underpinned by ones of social class. Perhaps the struggle between tory and whig constituted a proto-class conflict, a forerunner of the greater battles ahead, as Britain underwent its first engagement with economic modernisation. This may all seem rather odd now, but it must be remembered that *British Politics* was published only four years after the appearance of Edward Thompson's *Making of the English Working Class* (1963), and just two years before Harold Perkin's *Origins of Modern English Society* (1969), and at a time when every serious student carried around the campuses of Britain their copies of *The Communist Manifesto, Grundrisse* and *Das Kapital*, even if they did not read them. It is hard, in today's climate of centrist politics, in which the word 'class' scarcely passes the lips of politicians and pundits, to remember how influential were economic and social explanations of political change – social class was in the academic ether – and it seems unlikely that Geoffrey Holmes was not influenced by these.[34] Later, in the introduction to the 1987 edition of *British Politics*, he retreated somewhat from the social analysis contained in chapter five, arguing that the chapter 'has weathered the intervening years less well than the rest. A high tide of new research into the economy, finance and society has left its timbers somewhat battered.'[35] Research revealed that

---

[33] Defoe, *Tour*, i, 336; P.G.M. Dickson, *The Financial Revolution in England: A Study in the Development of Public Credit, 1688–1756* (1967).

[34] His analysis of the Sacheverell riots, published in *Past and Present*, reflects a willingness to engage with the 'history from below' strand of 18th-century historiography particularly associated with Edward Thompson. However, Holmes's conclusions that the riots 'were no protest of the miserably poor and inarticulate', that the mob displayed a 'patent lack of economic motivation', and the 'incontrovertible evidence of incitement' and manipulation from above, perhaps also demonstrates the limits of how far he was willing to travel along the Thompsonian road. See G.S. Holmes, 'The Sacheverell Riots: The Crowd and the Church in Early Eighteenth-Century London', *Past and Present*, no. 72 (1976), 73, 84; see also, R. Shoemaker, *The London Mob: Violence and Disorder in Eighteenth-Century England* (2004).

[35] Holmes, *British Politics* (rev. edn), p. xliv.

© *The Parliamentary History Yearbook Trust 2009*

the relationship between economic interests, social categories and political affiliations was more complex, and less deterministic, than originally appeared. It should also be added that by this time Marxism and class as historical meta-narratives were rapidly being discredited, and that either traditional modes of historical analysis were making a comeback, or economic and social explanatory models of change were being replaced by cultural ones.

However, it would be wrong to imply that Geoffrey Holmes simply abandoned social interpretations, or retreated into the comfortingly self-sustaining world of high political analysis, something that he could easily have done. Whatever the reality or otherwise of the monied men, there was no doubt that London, and towns in general, were home to well-off (in some cases extremely well-off) individuals, who earned their income primarily from sources other than land, and who chose to live for the most part in an urban rather than a rural world. It was a social group, or more accurately groups since they were very diverse in wealth and status, that Holmes demonstrated was seriously under-represented in Gregory King's celebrated table of the social structure of England in 1688, a document that had guided, and misled, generations of historians. King's profoundly conservative social and political instincts led him to ignore or conceal the considerable, and in terms of the future, highly significant changes taking place in the social structure. Critical here was the dynamic growth of the upper middling and middling ranks of society; the urban or so-called pseudo-gentry,[36] the professions, and the bewilderingly varied middling sort (merchants, manufacturers, wholesalers, shopkeepers, tradesmen, innkeepers, and such like).[37] All these shared the characteristic of being predominantly urban-orientated; and not just because that was where they happened to live or make their money, but because they were attached to the ambience and spirit of the town.

Among these middling groups Geoffrey Holmes was most fascinated by the professions, to whom he dedicated his British Academy Raleigh Lecture in 1979, a taster for the monograph, *Augustan England*, that followed in 1982.[38] That he should have devoted so much attention to the subject suggests the prominent position that social history, in the broadest sense – the sub-title of his book, 'professions, state and society', demonstrates that for him social and political history were not mutually exclusive categories – had come to occupy in his personal agenda, and perhaps reflected the influence of his colleagues at Lancaster. His interest in the subject arose in particular because he was keen to identify the degree of social change underway in Augustan England, and the professions' key role in stimulating this; 'it is only in the context of a society decade by decade becoming more broadly based, in both economic and social structural terms, that we can fully appreciate the extent of the mobility which remained possible within it and the vital importance of the professions as vehicles of this mobility'.[39] Holmes's work

---

[36] A. Everitt, 'Social Mobility in Early Modern England', *Past and Present*, no. 33 (1966), 70–2.

[37] G.S. Holmes, 'Gregory King and the Social Structure of Pre-Industrial England', *Transactions of the Royal Historical Society*, 5th ser., xxvii (1977), 41–65; Holmes, *Making of a Great Power*, 70–9; T. Arkell, 'Illuminations and Distortions: Gregory King's Scheme Calculated for the Year 1688 and the Social Structure of Later Stuart England', *Economic History Review*, lix (2006), 32–69.

[38] G.S. Holmes, 'The Professions and Social Change in England, 1680–1730', *Proceedings of the British Academy*, xlv (1979), 313–54; G.S. Holmes, *Augustan England: Professions, State and Society, 1680–1730* (1982).

[39] Holmes, *Augustan England*, 15–16.

anticipated and inspired growing interest in the history of the professions,[40] and more broadly the middling sort in the long 18th century.[41] Professionalisation owed much to war and the growth of the state;[42] but it was also tied closely, in Holmes's view, to the manner in which 'the urbanization of England's pre-industrial society was going steadily but significantly forward'.[43] Subsequent research has more than confirmed the extent of early modern urbanisation. In theory rapid urbanisation has the potential for creating a class society and class conflict. But though Holmes recognized the way economic and social change was generating serious tensions in Augustan society in the form of 'the clash of interests', urbanisation and professionalisation were for him forces which in the final analysis knitted together the social and political fabric rather than tearing it apart; 'by a curious paradox that same transformation of the professions which was so vital a force for social change in England became, almost by the same token, a powerful tranquilizing and stabilizing agent as well'.[44] This was primarily because the ideological forces which divided 17th-century society were not *between* town and country but *within* urban and rural society alike. I think that Geoffrey Holmes would argue that urbanisation, as long as this was 'steady' and not over-heated, created an environment and culture, together with urban-based social groups, which helped to transcend rather than exacerbate the ideological divisions that separated tory and whig. This was to be very different a century later, as rapid industrialisation and urbanisation opened the gap between town and country, and energised divisions of social class latent in early modern society.

Geoffrey Holmes, the consummate professional by nature and practice, would, I think, have inclined towards the town. But even if, having alighted from his time machine, he had plumped for the life of a country gentleman, I suspect that the conundrum posed at the beginning of this piece was a misguided one. For those with sufficient wealth it was not a matter of choosing either one location or the other. The Augustan landed elite, at least among its upper echelons, was an amphibious class, as Susan Whyman's

---

[40] *The Professions in Early Modern England*, ed. W.R. Prest (Beckenham, 1987); D. Lemmings, *Gentlemen and Barristers: The Inns of Court and the English Bar, 1680–1730* (Oxford, 1990); P.J. Corfield, *Power and the Professions in Britain, 1700–1850* (1995); R. O'Day, *The Professions in Early Modern England, 1450–1800* (Harlow, 2000); D. Lemmings, *Professors of the Law: Barristers and English Legal Culture in the Eighteenth Century* (Oxford, 2000); W.M. Jacob, *The Clerical Profession in the Long Eighteenth Century, 1680–1840* (Oxford, 2007).

[41] *The Middling Sort of People: Culture, Society and Politics in England, 1550–1800*, ed. J. Barry and C. Brooks (Basingtsoke, 1994); J. Barry, 'Review and Commentary: The State of the Middle Classes in Eighteenth-Century England', *Journal of Historical Sociology*, iv (1991), 75–86; P.J. Corfield, 'Class by Name and Number in Eighteenth-Century Britain', *History*, lxxii (1987), 38–61; P. Earle, *The Making of the English Middle Class: Business, Family Life and Society in London 1660–1730* (1989); H.R. French, 'Social Status, Localism and the "Middle Sort of People" in England 1620–1750', *Past and Present*, no. 166 (2000), 66–99; H.R. French, *The Middle Sort of People in Provincial England 1600–1750* (Oxford, 2007); H. Horwitz, ' "The Mess of the Middle Class" Revisited: The Case of the "Big Bourgeoisie" of London Reconsidered', *Continuity and Change*, xx (1987), 275–83; M.R. Hunt, *The Middling Sort: Commerce, Gender and the Family 1680–1780* (Berkeley, 1996); P. Langford, *A Polite and Commercial People: England 1727–1783* (Oxford, 1989); N. Rogers, 'The Middling Orders', in *A Companion to Eighteenth-Century Britain*, ed. H.T. Dickinson (2002), 172–82; J. Smail, *The Origins of Middle-Class Culture: Halifax, Yorkshire, 1660–1780* (1995); D. Wahrman, *Imagining the Middle Class: The Political Representation of Class in Britain, c. 1780–1840* (Cambridge, 1995).

[42] Holmes, *Augustan England*, 239–87; see also, J. Brewer, *The Sinews of Power: War, Money and the English State, 1688–1783* (1989), 59–60.

[43] Holmes, *Augustan England*, 11.

[44] Holmes, *Augustan England*, 18.

© *The Parliamentary History Yearbook Trust 2009*

revealing study of the Verneys suggests,[45] neither exclusively rural nor urban, but moving seamlessly between the two environments. This was a state of affairs encouraged by the expanding professions, as they absorbed so many of the younger offspring of the gentry, and sought to create a commodious urban environment in which the better-off from town and country could meet and mix, and in which the character of the social elite could be subtly remodelled.

[45] S. Whyman, *Sociability and Power in Late Stuart England: The Cultural World of the Verneys, 1660–1720* (Oxford, 1999).

© *The Parliamentary History Yearbook Trust 2009*

'Last of all the Heavenly Birth': Queen Anne and Sacral Queenship*

HANNAH SMITH

This article considers Queen Anne in her capacity as a royal politician. In particular, it examines how she attempted to represent her political authority and how this intersected with prevailing perceptions of female rule and ideas about the sacred basis to monarchy. It analyses the iconographical meanings embedded in Antonio Verrio's decorative scheme of 1703–5 for the queen's drawing room at Hampton Court and suggests ideas behind Anne's revival of the ceremony of touching for the king's evil. The article argues that Anne used both initiatives to emphasize the sacral quality of her queenship and it goes on to explore her reasons for doing so in the context of pre- and post-revolutionary projections and understandings of kingly – and queenly – authority.

Keywords: Queen Anne; monarchy; divine right; revolution of 1688–9; Antonio Verrio; Hampton Court; scrofula; Charles II; William III; George I; Britannia; Astraea

In *British Politics in the Age of Anne*, Geoffrey Holmes broke with the traditional presentation of Queen Anne as an unintelligent woman dominated by her favourites. Instead, he presented her as a serious political figure who fought fiercely in her attempts to protect the prerogatives of the crown and her own personal royal authority, an interpretation which has set the prevailing tone of scholarship on Anne for the last four decades.[1] While research on the crown has shifted away from Holmes's focus on its dealings with ministers and parliaments, his characterisation of Anne as a determined politician remains central to each new approach. R.O. Bucholz has shown how Anne engaged with older and more modern ways of representing the monarchy and tried, with a limited degree of success, to promote her political authority by attempting to make her court the focus of aristocratic life. Bucholz has also underscored how Anne and her husband, George of Denmark, adopted a frugal, respectable, and pious style which was a precursor of the approach endorsed by the crown in the late 18th century.[2] Similarly, research into the rhetorical fashioning of Anne's queenship has explored how her supporters used longstanding frames of historical and biblical reference to contextualise

* I wish to thank Katherine Clarke, Julie Farguson, Gabriel Glickman, and participants of the symposium 'British Politics in the Age of Anne – 40 Years On', London, Dec. 2007, for their assistance in the preparation of this article.

[1] Geoffrey Holmes, *British Politics in the Age of Anne* (1967, rev. edn 1987), 194–216; see also, Edward Gregg, *Queen Anne* (New Haven, 2001), 401–5.

[2] R.O. Bucholz, *The Augustan Court: Queen Anne and the Decline of Court Culture* (Stanford, 1993), 246–7, 251.

© *The Parliamentary History Yearbook Trust 2009*

her monarchy. They depicted her as the new Elizabeth I; as the bountiful 'nursing mother' of the Church of England; and as a war-leader like the Old Testament prophetess Deborah.[3] But they also drew on the more modern and increasing influential view that marriage was foremost a companionate union to present Anne as a dutiful wife and describe her relationship with George of Denmark as one based on mutual affection and fidelity that gave 'so good an example to all Her Majesties Subjects, and to all other Princes and their Subjects'.[4] However, there remains one aspect of Anne's monarchy that has received comparatively little scholarly analysis – its sacral dimensions.

In the years after 1689, divine right monarchy, and the ideas associated with it, evolved and adapted in response to the revolution of 1688–9 and the progress of the French war. The principles of passive obedience, strict hereditary succession, and royal absolutism continued to find their defenders. However, a growing number of writers began to shear divine right theorising from its increasingly unattractive absolutist elements. Indeed, from the mid 1690s, some jacobites were starting to distinguish between the constitutionally prescribed function of the royal office itself and the divine right principles that governed the succession.[5] From the opposite end of the spectrum, supporters of the post-revolutionary monarchs manoeuvred to provide parliamentary monarchy with some type of divine approbation. They drew on long-established providential beliefs to put forward the idea that William III, Mary II, and Queen Anne had a divine mandate since God had favoured them and their godly mission.[6] As a loyal address to Anne after the battle of Blenheim declared: 'Heaven designed the Glory of these Victories wholy to Your Majesty as a Reward of Your Majesty's Royal Virtues.'[7]

Queen Anne's own attitude towards divine right theorising reflected these manifold approaches to the issue of royal divinity. She was dismissive of divine right claims on a number of occasions (especially when they critiqued the revolution in which she had actively participated).[8] Indeed, in the aftermath of the Sacheverell affair, she was reported as taking exception 'to the expression that "her right was Divine" ', and 'having thought often of it, she could by no means like it, and thought it so unfit to be given to anybody that she wished it might be left out'.[9] Nevertheless, despite these protests, Anne's vision of monarchy still contained a strongly sacral element; so much so that she ordered the printing of Ofspring Blackall's controversial sermon, *The Divine Institution of Magistracy* (1709) which argued that 'the Authority exercis'd by the Magistrate is a Ray or Portion

---

[3] Carol Barash, *English Women's Poetry, 1649–1714: Politics, Community, and Linguistic Authority* (Oxford, 1996), 216–58; Rachel Weil, *Political Passions: Gender, the Family and Political Argument in England, 1680–1714* (Manchester, 1999), 162–8.

[4] John Tribbeko, *A Funeral Sermon on the Death of His Royal Highness Prince George of Denmark* (1709), 15; see also, Toni Bowers, 'Queen Anne Makes Provision', in *Refiguring Revolutions: Aesthetics and Politics from the English Revolution to the Romantic Revolution*, ed. Kevin Sharpe and Steven N. Zwicker (Berkeley, 1998), 57–8; Charles Beem, *The Lioness Roared: The Problems of Female Rule in English History* (Basingstoke, 2006), 128–39.

[5] Gabriel Glickman, *The English Catholic Community, 1688–1745: Politics, Culture, and Ideology* (forthcoming), ch. 3.

[6] Tony Claydon, *William III and the Godly Revolution* (Cambridge, 1996).

[7] *London Gazette*, 4–7 Sept. 1704.

[8] J.P. Kenyon, *Revolution Principles: The Politics of Party, 1689–1720* (Cambridge, 1990), 6–7, 81–2, 90–1, 96–101, 148.

[9] Cited in Holmes, *British Politics*, 187.

© *The Parliamentary History Yearbook Trust 2009*

of the Divine Authority, communicated to him, and entrusted with him by God'.[10] Anne seems to have been receptive at some level to the suggestion that hers was a 'godly' monarchy favoured by providence, and she took an active role in the thanksgiving services that regularly punctuated her reign, reviewing the prayers to be used and, on one occasion, choosing the text of an anthem.[11] She appears to have retained, perhaps quite naturally, some sort of belief in strict hereditary succession, and she side-stepped around the issue of her half-brother's claim by holding fast to the warming-pan myth of his origins (a myth that Anne had been prominent in spreading since his conception).[12] She also believed that the monarch possessed divinely endowed healing powers.

This article will explore such ideas further and consider how Anne's political ambitions intersected with prevailing perceptions of female rule and beliefs about the sacred basis to monarchy. Focusing on the queen's own strategies, it will examine two initiatives relating to the projection of her authority. First, it will analyse the iconographical meanings embedded in Antonio Verrio's decorative scheme of 1703–5 for the queen's drawing room at Hampton Court; and, second, it will investigate the motives behind Anne's revival of the ceremony of touching for the king's evil or scrofula (a tubercular disease of the lymph glands). Highlighting how Anne drew on aspects of Charles II's monarchical culture, it will argue that Anne, like many of her subjects, still viewed the monarchy as having at least some sort of a sacral element and that she had particular reason, as a female ruler in the post-revolutionary period, for wishing to emphasise her sacral queenship.

1

The most striking iconographical depiction of Queen Anne can be found in the queen's drawing room, Hampton Court (see Figure 1). The room had originally been part of Sir Christopher Wren's apartments for William III and Mary II. However, Mary's death had halted plans to decorate the apartments and by the time that work had began on the queen's drawing room, Anne had not only succeeded to the throne but had dismissed most of the team who had managed the project in William's reign.[13] The decorative artist, Antonio Verrio, was a key exception. Verrio was now in his sixties, pre-eminent in his field, and with three decades' worth of experience of decorating English royal palaces. He was probably responsible for the design scheme for the room which drew substantially on his work elsewhere for the Restoration crown. Verrio was at this stage suffering from deteriorating eyesight and his assistants, who possibly included the young James Thornhill, may have played a large role in implementing the scheme.[14] Anne herself was no connoisseur and, like her artist, suffered from poor eyesight. Nevertheless,

---

[10] Ofspring Blackall, *The Divine Institution of Magistracy and the Gracious Design of its Institution* (1709), 2; Kenyon, *Revolution Principles*, 120; Andrew Starkie, 'Ofspring Blackall', *Oxford Dictionary of National Biography*.

[11] *Memoirs of Sarah, Duchess of Marlborough*, ed. William King (1930), 232–3; Gregg, *Anne*, 165; Donald Burrows, *Handel and the English Chapel Royal* (Oxford, 2005), 36–7.

[12] Rachel J. Weil, 'The Politics of Legitimacy: Women and the Warming-Pan Scandal', in *The Revolution of 1688–1689*, ed. Lois G. Schwoerer (Cambridge 1992), 67–72.

[13] H.M. Colvin, *The History of the King's Works* (6 vols, 1976), v, 34–5, 162–75.

[14] Simon Thurley, *Hampton Court: A Social and Architectural History* (New Haven, 2003), 213.

© *The Parliamentary History Yearbook Trust 2009*

Fig. 1. Verrio's wall and ceiling paintings in the queen's drawing room, Hampton Court.
(Crown copyright: Historic Royal Palaces. Reproduced by permission of Historic Royal Palaces under licence from the Controller of Her Majesty's Stationery Office.)

© *The Parliamentary History Yearbook Trust 2009*

she seems to have had a longstanding interest in portraiture and in her own visual image. Prior to her succession, she had visited studios, compared and tested the merits of different 'picturedrawers' in producing 'flesh and bloud' likenesses, and patronised a range of portraitists. There is also some suggestion that she reviewed the royal mint's design for the coinage.[15] It is likely that Anne took an alert interest in Verrio's final scheme for the room.

The ceiling of the queen's drawing room depicts Anne in *apotheosis* as Astraea-Virgo, goddess of justice. She wears Garter regalia and wields the scales and sword of justice. As such, she bears a strong resemblance to the figure of 'Justice inviolable' as described in a 1698 translation of Caesar Ripa's celebrated *Iconologia*, the crown indicating that justice is the queen of virtues, the bare sword demonstrating that she will always be swift in punishing vice, and the scales alluding to her role as judge.[16] Justice was one of the four cardinal virtues and Verrio elaborates on this theme by depicting the three others, prudence, temperance, and fortitude, alongside Anne, who is crowned by Neptune and Britannia, and is also accompanied by the attributes and deities traditionally allied with good government, including Jove, Apollo, Diana, Mercury (who was associated with Virgo), vigilance, fame, and time unveiling truth. Anne rests on a cornucopia of gold since Astraea symbolised peace and plenty, and a golden age of imperial prosperity.

An allegory of Anne as Britannia decorates the central wall. While this figure – unlike that of Astraea – bears no physical resemblance to Anne, Britannia's regal status is indicated by the orb she holds, the royal arms above her head, and the motto, *Semper Eadem*, which Anne had adopted from Elizabeth I.[17] Britannia holds a spear in one hand and is flanked by religion and reformation. The four continents kneel at her feet in homage. To the right, Mars and Victory defeat the nation's enemies, while to the left Minerva and Hercules ('heroic virtue') crush heresy. The two remaining walls are devoted to depictions – with varying degrees of allegory – of Anne's consort, George of Denmark, as lord high admiral; naval victory and imperial sway proceeding hand-in-hand.[18]

Astraea represented an obvious choice of allegory to depict a queen regnant. Astraea was the goddess of justice who had fled the earth in the age of iron to become the constellation Virgo but whose return would bring about a new age of gold. The myth was widely known through Ovid's *Metamorphoses* and Virgil's *Fourth Eclogue*. Elizabeth I's admirers had deployed it, and it flourished more generally as a staple of early modern monarchist discourse.[19] Depicting Anne as Britannia was an equally obvious choice, particularly since the image of Britannia, which was still evolving in this era and of which Anne-Britannia is a modified version, bore iconographical similarities to traditional allegories of government.[20] But the figures of Astraea and Britannia have further

---

[15] Margaret Toynbee, 'Princess (afterwards Queen) Anne as a Patroness of Painters', *Burlington Magazine*, cxii (1970), 149–53; John Craig, *Newton at the Mint* (Cambridge, 1946), 51.

[16] Caesar Ripa, *Iconologie ou la Sciences des Emblemes* (2 vols, Amsterdam, 1698), ii, fig. 38.

[17] John Watkins, *Representing Elizabeth in Stuart England: Literature, History, Sovereignty* (Cambridge, 2002), 206–8.

[18] It may have been Anne's intention that George should occupy the queen's apartments (Thurley, *Hampton Court*, 213).

[19] Frances A. Yates, *Astraea: The Imperial Theme in the Sixteenth Century* (1975), 29–34, 50–87.

[20] Caesar Ripa, *Iconologia: Or Moral Emblems* (1709), 80, fig. 321; Herbert M. Atherton, *Political Prints in the Age of Hogarth* (Oxford, 1974), 91–2.

© The Parliamentary History Yearbook Trust 2009

strata of historical significance. Both were associated with Charles II, as indeed was the artist himself since Verrio had made his career working for Charles II at Windsor from c.1675.

The idea of the return of the Golden Age had been a dominant rhetoric in Charles's reign. It found artistic expression in John Michael Wright's decorative scheme for Charles's bedchamber at Whitehall. This depicted Astraea pointing to Charles's portrait.[21] The figure of Astraea was also present in the lower third of Verrio's *apotheosis* of Charles for the ceiling of St George's Hall, Windsor.[22] Catherine of Braganza featured as Britannia on Verrio's ceilings at Windsor, and Verrio seems to have reused something of the scenario from the queen's guard chamber, Windsor, where Britannia is paid homage by the four continents, for Anne at Hampton Court.[23] Verrio also drew directly upon his work for Charles II in three other ways. The designs for the walls of the queen's drawing room depicting George of Denmark echo Verrio's painting *The Sea Triumph of Charles II* of c.1674.[24] The apotheosis of Anne in the queen's drawing room resembles Charles's in St George's Hall, both of which depict the monarch being crowned by two allegorical figures. Lastly, although the figure of Hercules was closely associated with William III, especially at Hampton Court, it was part of Charles II's cultural apparatus too. The king's withdrawing room, Windsor prominently depicted Hercules, and aspects from Hercules's life formed the centrepiece of De Wet's work at Holyroodhouse for Charles.[25]

The similarity in iconographical content between the decorative work for Charles II and Anne is conspicuous. But so, too, is its divine impetus, Verrio's representation of the monarch as a god. Verrio had depicted Charles II as Apollo, the sun god, aboard his chariot in the king's withdrawing room at Windsor, while the ceiling of St George's Hall showed Charles II's *apotheosis*, the act of deification whereby a mortal was received into heaven by the gods.[26] By contrast, Verrio's work for William III at Hampton Court had treated the idea of royal divinity in a more subtle fashion. Verrio's mythological themes are present in his work for William but there is, nevertheless, a more restrained tone in evidence. Verrio depicted deities such as Mars and Venus on the ceiling of the king's little bedchamber, and one wall of the king's staircase depicts the Saturnian plenty brought by Williamite rule.[27] However, Verrio also drew upon classical history as much as he did myth. It has been suggested that Verrio took Julian the Apostate's *The Caesars* as his urtext for the king's staircase and depicted the supremacy of Alexander the Great (William III) over the Caesars (the Stuarts), including the figure of Hercules introducing Alexander to the gods in a variant of *apotheosis*.[28] This identification has been queried.[29]

[21] Edward Croft-Murray, *Decorative Painting in England, 1537–1837* (2 vols, 1962), i, 228–9.

[22] Katharine Gibson, 'The Decoration of St. George's Hall, Windsor, for Charles II', *Apollo*, cxlvii (1998), 33, 35.

[23] Croft-Murray, *Decorative Painting*, 241.

[24] Thurley, *Hampton Court*, 419 n. 15.

[25] Gibson, 'Decoration of St. George's Hall', fig. 6; Ian Gow, *The Palace of Holyroodhouse* (2002), 41–3.

[26] Gibson, 'Decoration of St. George's Hall', 34.

[27] Croft-Murray, *Decorative Painting*, 237; Thurley, *Hampton Court*, 203–4.

[28] Edgar Wind, 'Julian the Apostate at Hampton Court', *Journal of the Warburg and Courtauld Institutes*, iii (1939–40), 127–37.

[29] T.R. Langley, *Image Government: Monarchical Metamorphoses in English Literature and Art, 1649–1702* (Cambridge, 2001), 152, 158. Nicholas Tyacke is currently working on a study of the Williamite iconography at Hampton Court.

Certainly William's hang of Mantegna's *The Triumphs of Caesar* elsewhere in the palace suggests that he also held more positive Caesarian associations.[30] But however we interpret the king's staircase, crucially William himself was not directly depicted. Verrio's design for Anne, with its depiction of the queen in *apotheosis* is striking in this context, as is his association of Anne with a mythological goddess. And not only was Astraea a goddess, she was the 'last of all the heavenly birth', as George Sandys phrased it in his often-republished translation of the *Metamorphoses*.[31] Astraea was a remarkably apt choice for the last of the Stuart monarchs.

Why might Verrio's decorative schemes for the queen's drawing room place so much emphasis on divinity? One explanation centres on Anne's fellow princes. By adopting this visual language, Anne was attempting to state the sacred underpinnings to her own rule to other crowned heads who themselves used this form of representation.[32] Another reason might lie with Anne's own subjects. Neither Verrio nor his art were exclusive to the crown and he utilised the same type of design schemes for both his private clients and his royal patrons. For instance, Verrio used the Banquet of the Gods, which adorned the ceilings of both the king's eating room, Windsor and the king's staircase, Hampton Court, at Lowther Castle for Viscount Lonsdale, and at Teddington for Sir Charles Duncombe.[33] Further research is needed into the relationship between the iconography of privately-commissioned work and royal decorative schemes, and the extent to which the former operated as a tribute to the reigning monarch rather than a direct panegyric to the patron. But it could be argued that while no private client appears to have committed such *lese-majeste* as to be depicted openly in *apotheosis* amidst deities, when the monarch declined to be directly depicted in this way, then the iconographical differences in decorative commissions between the crown and the elites became more blurred. From these perspectives, Verrio's depiction of Anne as Astraea can be viewed as an effort to re-appropriate the grand mythological style for the crown and emphasise the sacral nature of Anne's monarchy. In practice, though, the strategy had a decidedly limited impact. After finishing the queen's drawing room, Anne concluded that she could not afford to complete the remaining rooms on the queen's side, and instead used the apartments on the king's side.[34]

2

If Anne's attempt to communicate the sacred nature of her authority via Verrio's decorative art was unsuccessful, the same could not be said about her revival of the royal touch, which advertised sacral monarchy to a much wider audience than did the iconography of the queen's drawing room.[35] Although William III and Mary II had

---

[30] Susan Jenkins, 'The Artistic Taste of William III', *Apollo*, cxl (1994), 5.

[31] George Sandys, *Ovid's Metamorphosis Englished* (1626), 4.

[32] Peter Burke, *The Fabrication of Louis XIV* (New Haven, 1992), figs 9, 11, 78.

[33] Croft-Murray, *Decorative Painting*, 236–41.

[34] Thurley, *Hampton Court*, 213–16.

[35] For visitors' comments see *London in 1710 from the Travels of Zacharias Conrad von Uffenbach*, ed. W.H. Quarrell and Margaret Mare (1934), 155; *The Journeys of Celia Fiennes*, ed. Christopher Morris (1949), 356. Sir John Clerk may have had the queen's drawing room in mind when he advocated in 1726–7 the construction

abandoned touching for scrofula in 1689 (William appears not to have credited the practice with any efficacy), Anne resumed it in the first year of her reign and practised it until her death, sessions being announced in the *London Gazette*.[36] It is impossible to establish the precise numbers of participants at these sessions but the queen was reported to be touching 40 per session in the spring of 1703 and was hoping to increase numbers to '2 or 300 at a time' since there were 'now in London several thousands of people . . . come out of the country waiting for Her Healing'. As she herself wrote in April 1703:'I intend (an it please God) . . . to touch as many poor people as I can before hott wheather coms.' She may have touched around 1,800 people in 1706–7.[37] Anne was catering to undoubted popular demand by reviving the touch. However, it can be speculated that she also revived it because it so very clearly emphasized the sacred nature of the royal office.

The royal touch had long formed part of the monarch's duties as the governor of the Church of England. 'Kings and Queens . . . as Nursing Fathers and Mothers, have been always thus qualified with this Sanative Virtue', John Browne remarked in his account of the royal touch in 1684, and he went on to cite cases of dissenters converting to the church after being cured by the monarch.[38] The ceremony was included in the Book of Common Prayer and Anne, rather typically, saw her role in a devotional light; she was reported as fasting and abstaining before touching.[39] The French crown was a rival, active (and catholic) practitioner of the touch and it is also conceivable that Anne adopted the practice for reasons of foreign policy, as a pious anti-French act of patriotism that likewise affirmed her sacral status to her princely allies and enemies.[40] 'All the World may admire our English Isle, and have the most Venerable and Sacred Thoughts of her Mighty Monarchs, who thus can banish Diseases by their Touch' wrote Browne back in Charles II's reign, and Browne claimed that not only were the English kings the first to practise the touch but that they had been given 'this Miraculous Gift' first because the English had converted to christianity earlier than the French.[41]

Using the royal touch as a way of stressing royal sacrality (and English christian piety), however, was not necessarily without ideological complications by the early 18th century. The royal touch was closely associated with the later Stuarts: Charles II may

[35] *(continued)* of a royal palace containing murals of British history, including one of 'Brittannia's self/ In every shape and Feature like Queen Anne' (Stuart Piggott, 'Sir John Clerk and "The Country Seat" ', in *The Country Seat*, ed. Howard Colvin and John Harris (1970), 113).

[36] Narcissus Luttrell, *A Brief Historical Relation of State Affairs from September 1678 to April 1714* (6 vols, Oxford, 1857), v, 223; *The Flying Post*, 26 Nov. 1702; *London Gazette*, 24–8 May 1705, 29 Apr.–2 May 1706, 28 Feb.–1 Mar. 1712, 17–19 Apr. 1712, 28 Feb.–3 Mar. 1713, 16–20 Feb. 1714, 23–7 Mar. 1714; Bucholz, *Augustan Court*, 210–11. For medical discussion of scrofula in Anne's reign see Harold Weber, *Paper Bullets: Print and Kingship under Charles II* (Lexington, 1996), 81–4.

[37] B.C. Browne, 'A Letter of John Sharp, Archbishop of York', *English Historical Review*, v (1890), 122; Gregg, *Anne*, 148.

[38] John Browne, *Charisma Basilicon, or the Royal Gift of Healing Strumaes or the King's Evil* (1684), 'To the Reader', 173, 188–9.

[39] *Verney Letters of the Eighteenth Century from the MSS. at Claydon House*, ed. Margaret Maria Verney (2 vols, 1930), i, 356–7. Even if Anne did not believe she could literally heal by her touch, it is possible that she saw the ceremony as operating as an extended prayer for the sufferers (for an early 17th-century manifestation of this idea see Marc Bloch, *The Royal Touch: Sacred Monarchy and Scrofula in England and France* (1973), 191).

[40] Bloch, *Royal Touch*, 204.

[41] Browne, *Charisma Basilicon*, 'To the Reader', 64–6.

have touched around 100,000 people in his reign; James II possibly touched around 4,400 in the first year of his reign, and he continued to practise it in exile (as did his son).[42] Reviving the royal touch undoubtedly allowed Anne to underline her Stuart inheritance in a very effective and positive way. But, on another level, it also associated her with what some saw as the more negative aspects of the late Stuart monarchy – its absolutist ambitions. The royal touch was particularly linked to controversies over royal absolutism via the longstanding debate as to whether the monarch's miraculous healing powers began at the very moment of his or her accession or whether they were conferred by the act of anointing during the coronation service.[43] Both Charles II and James II had touched for scrofula prior to their coronation thereby emphasizing that their status derived directly from God and not through human agency.[44]

The royal touch had the potential to be an unsettling problem for supporters of the revolution (of which Anne was one). That it did not become an issue may have been down to two factors. Firstly, absolutism and the royal touch were not necessarily analogous. Theorists did not use 'miraculous' practices, such as the royal touch, to justify royal absolutism, and a monarch's willingness to touch might well depend more upon his or her thoughts concerning the efficacy of the practice than his or her position regarding the divine rights of kings *per se*: James I was happy to theorise on the latter, while at the same time being deeply unconvinced about the former.[45] Secondly, Anne – so it seems – did not practise the touch before her coronation, perhaps because she felt that she was not fully vested with the gift until she had been anointed. If it was indeed the case that Anne did not touch before her coronation, it meant that she could still use the royal touch to emphasize the sacred nature of her monarchy without appearing to repudiate her parliamentary title to the crown.

The image, then, that Anne projected via the iconography of the queen's drawing room and by her revival of the royal touch was one that stressed continuity with certain aspects of Charles II's monarchy. By taking her cues from her uncle, Anne not only emphasized her dynastic claims; she also recreated a monarchical style that had explicitly sacral elements but that was still relatively harmonious with the spirit of the revolutionary settlement. This sacral dimension vested her with an authority that her subjects lacked and which put her on a recognizable par with – or indeed elevated her above – her fellow monarchs, Louis XIV included. But arguably, her adoption of such a strategy was not just a response *per se* to post-revolutionary redefinitions of the origins of royal authority. Rather, because the authority of the post-revolutionary crown came to be justified in markedly more militarised (and thus masculine) terms than it had been prior to 1689, the full political ramifications of the revolutionary settlement were felt more by queens than kings.

---

[42] Bloch, *Royal Touch*, 212, 219; Edward Gregg, 'The Exiled Stuarts: Martyrs for the Faith?', in *Monarchy and Religion: The Transformation of Royal Culture in Eighteenth-Century Europe*, ed. Michael Schaich (Oxford, 2007), 205.

[43] Bloch, *Royal Touch*, 128.

[44] Bloch, *Royal Touch*, 128, 211, 219.

[45] Mark Goldie, 'Restoration Political Thought', in *The Reigns of Charles II and James VII and II*, ed. Lionel K.J. Glassey (Basingstoke, 1997), 16; Bloch, *Royal Touch*, 191.

© *The Parliamentary History Yearbook Trust 2009*

3

The succession of a female monarch did not in itself cause difficulties in 1702. 'Crowns know no Sexes', Daniel Defoe declared.[46] Indeed, a female monarch – what Matthew Prior termed a 'softer King' – was seen by some as the ideal parliamentary monarch.[47] As Thomas Sherlock put it: 'the *Majesty* of the Crown is displayed in the *Softness* of Her Sex who wears it, and seems rather to invite than to command Obedience'.[48] But while such a perception of female rule might reassure those who feared royal despotism, its corollary, the traditional concern that the female monarch, by virtue of her sex, would be a weak ruler, easily influenced by those around her, remained an underlying worry. This was particularly so when Anne's closest servants were viewed by their opponents as party intriguers.[49] Shortly after Anne's death, Defoe described how Anne had been imposed upon by her favourites and explained it in explicitly gendered terms: 'she was but a Woman'.[50] Anne's generous friendship with the Marlboroughs did nothing to dispel this prejudice, and the duchess of Marlborough herself was party to it when she attacked Anne's friendship with Abigail Masham. Such a perception angered Anne, who complained that 'every thing I say is imputed ether to partialety, or being imposed upon . . . all I say proceeds purely from my own poor Judgment, which tho it may not be soe good as other people, I'me sure is a very honest one'.[51] Mary II's willing surrender of her hereditary claims to sovereignty to William on the grounds that as a man and as her husband, he was fitter to exercise them, may have also enhanced a fundamental sense that a queen lacked both natural ability and authority in governance.[52] It was a view which the tory writer Mary Astell challenged when she wrote, in 1706, that if all women were naturally inferior to all men then 'the greatest Queen ought not to command but to obey her Footman'.[53]

The post-revolutionary queen regnant was ideologically exposed on another front too. Although the revolutionary settlement had insisted upon William III's parliamentary title to the crown, his supporters had bolstered William's sovereign authority by stressing his ability to perform the long-established kingly role of the nation's military leader, a role which his Stuart predecessors had been unwilling to take on.[54] While military kingship played to the strengths of William III and George I – and was much flaunted by their advocates – it was not one that a queen regnant could draw upon, and even Anne's advocates, such as Defoe in 1702, were troubled by the fact that she could not actively

---

[46] Cited in Manuel Schonhorn, *Defoe's Politics: Parliament, Power, Kingship, and Robinson Crusoe* (Cambridge, 1991), 92.

[47] Matthew Prior, *Poems on Several Occasions* (1709), 292.

[48] Thomas Sherlock, *A Sermon Preach'd Before the Honourable House of Commons at St. Margaret's Westminster on Monday March 8 1713/4 Being the Day of Her Majesty's Happy Accession to the Throne* (1714), 19.

[49] Weil, *Political Passions*, 164–6.

[50] Cited in Schonhorn, *Defoe's Politics*, 91.

[51] Cited in Gregg, *Anne*, 193.

[52] Barash, *English Women's Poetry*, 210–16. It has been argued that a stronger image of Mary's monarchical authority was projected by 1695: Lois G. Schwoerer, 'Images of Queen Mary II, 1689–95', *Renaissance Quarterly*, xlii (1989), 748.

[53] [Mary Astell], *Reflections upon Marriage* (1706), preface; Weil, *Political Passions*, 156.

[54] Abigail Williams, *Poetry and the Creation of a Whig Literary Culture, 1681–1714* (Oxford, 2005), 105–9.

fulfil a military role.[55] The female monarch could, of course, present herself in other ways. She might win acclaim for her personal morality and through promoting the piety of the nation, as Mary II and Anne both did, or for her learning and wisdom, as did Anne's heir, the Electress Sophia.[56] Verrio alluded to these types of fashioning in his design for the central wall of the queen's drawing room when he depicted the figures of religion and reformation alongside Anne-Britannia. But this was, in effect, an extension of the traditional and complementary role of the queen consort. It gave the female monarch a moral vigour, but did not invest her with the type of authority that military kingship, or even the potential ability to fight, brought to a male ruler. And therein lay the difficulty for the queen regnant, like Anne, who wanted to rule as well as reign.

The married female monarch could try to negotiate this particular difficulty by entrusting military command to her husband so as not to separate civil and military government, a strategy that seemed to work reasonably well for Mary I and Philip of Spain.[57] But Anne's invalid husband was unable to move into the military role vacated by William III. Consequently, it was one of the queen's subjects who took William's (and George of Denmark's) place and led the British army to a series of spectacular victories. And Marlborough not only took this place on the battlefield. He was praised in a poetic register that was more frequently used for kings than their subjects.[58] He was even depicted as almost equal to Anne herself. William Congreve, for instance, enthused that 'Again *Astraea* Reigns!/ Anna Her equal Scale maintains/ and Marlbro wields Her sure deciding Sword.'[59] The visual arts depicted Marlborough in a like manner. Kneller planned an equestrian portrait of him in c.1706 (which included the figures of Hercules and Astraea) that was similar to Kneller's earlier one of William III, and Marlborough also appeared on the same commemorative medals as the queen.[60] Anne colluded in the creation of Marlborough as a quasi-royal. Indeed, since Marlborough was openly acknowledged as her favourite, he can be viewed as operating as an appendage to her monarchy in the early years of her reign. Hence she permitted him to be elevated to the status of an imperial prince and her gift of the royal manor of Woodstock as the site of Blenheim Palace also underscored such princely associations. It was only when her relationship with the Marlboroughs was deteriorating that the duke became a rival, particularly after he asked for the office of captain-general for life in 1709.[61]

Nevertheless, from early on, Anne's officials and supporters also attempted to construct her queenship in a manner that engaged with the post-revolutionary military

[55] Hannah Smith, *Georgian Monarchy: Politics and Culture, 1714–60* (Cambridge, 2006), 21–32; Schonhorn, *Defoe's Politics*, 92.

[56] For Sophia see Justin Champion, *Republican Learning: John Toland and the Crisis of Christian Culture, 1696–1722* (Manchester, 2003), 131–3.

[57] Glyn Redworth, ' "Matters Impertinent to Women": Male and Female Monarchy under Philip and Mary', *English Historical Review*, cxii (1997), 611–12.

[58] Williams, *Poetry*, 139.

[59] William Congreve, *A Pindarique Ode Humbly Offer'd to the Queen on the Victorious Progress of Her Majesty's Arms Under the Conduct of the Duke of Marlborough* (1706), 6.

[60] J. Douglas Stewart, *Sir Godfrey Kneller* (1971), 15, 68; Edward Hawkins, *Medallic Illustrations of the History of Great Britain and Ireland to the Death of George II* (2 vols, 1885), ii, 246.

[61] Gregg, *Anne*, 286–7; Peter Barber, 'Marlborough as Imperial Prince, 1704–1717', *The British Library Journal*, viii (1982), 46–8.

© *The Parliamentary History Yearbook Trust 2009*

justification of kingship. Although Anne could not physically lead her armies into battle, she was portrayed as a martial figure, a leader of Amazons, a Deborah to Marlborough's Barak, personally clipping the wings of France.[62] Her coronation medal emphasized her militarised (and divine) persona by portraying her as Pallas – 'vice-regent of the Thunderer' – hurling a thunderbolt against the Hydra.[63] Anne herself attempted to bolster the warlike representation of her queenship by giving her husband a military title, as lord high admiral and generalissimo, and a corresponding persona. George of Denmark had arrived in England in 1683 with a reputation for military bravery and his portraits consistently suggested his martial metier, in particular Dahl's 1704 equestrian portrait, which echoed Kneller's of William III.[64] Verrio also emphasized George of Denmark's naval role in his decorative scheme for the queen's drawing room, the prince taking up almost as much square footage as the queen. Yet for all this fashioning, the fact remained that neither Anne nor her husband could take on Louis XIV's armies on the battlefield. Ultimately, military queenship was of limited use since it had no practical military application.

Anne and her supporters used a range of images in their attempts to legitimate her position, and her undoubted personal popularity may well have lain in the fact that she projected not just one sympathetic image but several. But Anne possibly sensed that although these images were compelling, she had to embody an older form of legitimisation if she, as a post-revolutionary female ruler, were to be anything more than a popular figurehead, a feeling assisted by her own inclinations about the sacred character of the monarchy. Hence, Verrio's decorative scheme for the queen's drawing room not only attempted to prop up Anne's personal authority by portraying her as the ultimate judge on earth. By depicting her as a goddess, in *apotheosis*, the last of a divine race, and in a manner that echoed his work for her uncle, Charles II, Verrio presented her as embodying a form of sacrality. Touching for scrofula was another way in which she could assert her sacral queenship, as well as her Stuart lineage. While Anne's reign can be seen as heralding newer ways of conceptualising and legitimising the English monarchy, in recognizing this we must also acknowledge that it contained a strongly sacral element, one which links it to Charles II's and James II's monarchy – and severs it from George I's.

This severance was not immediate, despite George I's apparent dislike of sacral kingship and its uses (as a warrior king, George, like William III, had less need of it to augment his authority). Although George I declined to touch for scrofula, some of his new subjects still believed that he had the ability to do so.[65] Verrio's mantle was taken on by his one-time assistant, Sir James Thornhill, who decorated the Painted Hall at the Royal Hospital, Greenwich with a series of designs that were heavily imbued with classical mythology. It was here in Anne's reign that William III and Mary II were posthumously commemorated, in triumph, surrounded by deities, in a noticeably different manner to the king's staircase at Hampton Court. Thornhill went on to depict

[62] Barash, *English Women's Poetry*, 229–31.

[63] Hawkins, *Medallic Illustrations*, ii, 228–9; Carolyn A. Edie, 'The Public Face of Royal Ritual: Sermons, Medals and Civic Ceremony in Later Stuart Coronations', *Huntington Library Quarterly*, liii (1990), 326–8.

[64] Oliver Millar, *The Tudor, Stuart and Early Georgian Pictures in the Collection of Her Majesty the Queen* (2 vols, 1963), i, 140, 151.

[65] Smith, *Georgian Monarchy*, 95–6.

George I and his family at Greenwich in a composition redolent with golden age symbolism and Olympian majesty, and suggestions of this style were also present in his decorative ceiling for the queen's bedchamber, Hampton Court, which he undertook early in George I's reign when the queen's side was finally completed.[66] But it was a decorative style that George I did not favour, and when he appointed William Kent, rather than Thornhill, to decorate the state apartments at Kensington palace, the result – with its emphasis on 'grotesque' patterning – was removed from the explicitly allegorical schemes at Windsor, Hampton Court, and Greenwich.[67] Thus Queen Anne's death brought an end to sacral monarchy in England as practised by its rulers and in this respect she was, indeed, the 'last of all the heavenly birth'.

[66] John Bold, Greenwich: An Architectural History of the Royal Hospital for Seamen and the Queen's House (New Haven, 2000), 149–52; Colvin, King's Works, v, 176.

[67] Smith, Georgian Monarchy, 197.

© The Parliamentary History Yearbook Trust 2009

'Ladies are often very good scaffoldings': Women and Politics in the Age of Anne

ELAINE CHALUS

The age of Anne saw unprecedented politicisation of society, the expansion of patronage and the election of ten parliaments between 1695 and 1715. If, as has been argued for the second half of the 18th century, such factors facilitated women's political participation, then the prerequisites for women's political involvement, at least at the level of the political elite, existed in the age of Anne. Yet we still know surprisingly little about the shape and extent of women's political participation beyond the dynamics of the Augustan court. This article encourages historians of women and politics to return to the age of Anne and consider women's political participation writ large. Was this period, which has often been seen as a political watershed, also a watershed for women's political involvement? Through an examination of Elizabeth Coke's involvement in the Derbyshire election of 1710, where she served as her brother's political agent, this article calls historians' attention to the activities of one group of politically-active Augustan women – those who served as intermediaries and agents. It argues that politics could be one aspect of a broader familial agency, one which saw women step in and out of family, household, estate and political management, as necessary. Nor, it argues, should these women be seen as mere Swiftian 'scaffoldings' – as means to an end for politically-ambitious men. As agents and intermediaries, women as well as men played recognized political roles, in similar ways, in campaigns across the country; their involvement requires closer examination.

Keywords: Queen Anne; Elizabeth Coke; Derbyshire; election; 1710; political; agents; intermediaries; familial

As to yourself, madam, I most heartily congratulate with you for being delivered from the toil, the envy, the slavery, and vexation, of a favourite; where you could not always answer the good intentions that I hope you had. You will now be less teazed with solicitations, one of the greatest evils in life . . . Mr. Pope has always been an advocate for your sincerity; and even I, in the character I gave you of yourself, allowed you as much of that virtue as could be expected in a lady, a courtier, and a favourite . . . I could have been a better prophet in the character I gave you of yourself, if it had been good manners, in the height of your credit, to put you in mind of its mortality: for, you are not the first, by at least three ladies, whom I have known to undergo the same turn of fortune. It is allowed, that ladies are often very good scaffoldings; and I need not tell you the use that scaffoldings are put to by all builders, as well political as mechanical.[1]

---

[1] *The Works of the Rev. Jonathan Swift, D.D., Dean of St. Patrick's, Dublin*, corr. and rev. by John Nichols (24 vols, New York, 1813), xviii, 27: Jonathan Swift to John Gay and the duchess of Queensberry, Dublin, 19 Nov. 1730.

© *The Parliamentary History Yearbook Trust 2009*

So wrote Jonathan Swift to Kitty, duchess of Queensberry, when she fell out of favour with George II in 1730. In reflecting upon the transience of favour, Swift's double-edged congratulations speak tellingly, both of his deep-seated misogyny and of his carefully nurtured bitterness towards courtiers and court politics. Despite fawning attendance on Abigail Masham and Robert Harley in particular, in the later years of Queen Anne's reign, he had failed to secure the patronage and recognition he felt he deserved. Subsequent approaches to the princess of Wales (later Queen Caroline) and the countess of Suffolk had been equally futile, leaving him with an abiding belief that he had been ill-treated, used and discarded, by those in power. His dismissive comments about women at the centre of politics – as little more than the means to men's political ends – must, therefore, be read carefully. While at first glance they serve as one interpretation of the rise and fall of the court favourites he knew best, Sarah, duchess of Marlborough, and Abigail Masham, they also reflect his own manipulative and self-interested approach to women, political or otherwise. More importantly, they need to be placed in the larger context of his constitutional cynicism and his overarching belief that he, too, had served only as 'scaffolding' for others.

Swift's assumptions provide a useful starting point for a consideration of women's involvement in Augustan political life on this, the 40th anniversary of the publication of Geoffrey Holmes's *British Politics in the Age of Anne*. They reflect an enduring theme in the history of early-modern women and politics, and, to some extent, an enduring reality. The participation of even the most politically active and aware women of the 18th century was, after all, constrained by the gendering of the polity. At a time when it was a commonplace that women 'did not pretend to meddle in public matters',[2] as Lady Harpur assured Elizabeth Coke in 1710, before going on to add the almost inevitable caveat, 'yet . . .', the fact that the female members of the political elite could and did 'meddle', for any number of personal, familial, factional or ideological reasons, underlines the powerful contradictions which permeated both early-modern women's political involvement and their reception by contemporaries. By custom, women did not vote in parliamentary elections; nor did they sit in the Commons or the Lords, hold cabinet appointments (or the accompanying patronage), or take an official part in the creation and passage of legislation or diplomacy. In these formal political arenas, they operated at one remove and may, at times, have been little more than Swiftian 'scaffoldings' for ambitious men. Recent research, however, primarily on the political involvement of elite women in the second half of the century, has revealed that there was substantially more scope for them to participate in 18th-century political life than had previously been assumed.[3] Not only were there some elite women who were political actors in their own rights, but there were also others who served as agents, brokers and facilitators in social politics, patronage and/or electoral politics, and their activities need to be taken seriously as well. While gendered constraints on women's political involvement certainly existed, so too did their ability to work within and around limitations, and to justify their political participation with arguments of family, duty or expediency.

[2] HMC, *12th Report, Appendix, Part iii*, 97: Elizabeth Coke to Thomas Coke, [Melbourne], 11 Sept. 1710.
[3] See, e.g., Elaine Chalus, *Elite Women in English Political Life, c.1754–1790* (Oxford, 2005); Judith S. Lewis, *Sacred to Female Patriotism: Gender, Class, and Politics in late Georgian Britain* (2003); Ingrid Tague, *Women of Quality: Accepting and Contesting Ideals of Femininity in England, 1690–1760* (Woodbridge, 2002).

To date, significantly less is known about the detail and extent of elite women's involvement in political life in the age of Anne. While the combination of a ruling female monarch and a highly politicised court riven by intense female rivalries has long proved seductive to political historians, few have focused on women and politics beyond the court.[4] Consequently, our knowledge of elite women's overall engagement in Augustan political life remains patchy and uneven. Yet it bears serious consideration, not only because added knowledge will help to recover women as historical actors and enhance our understanding of women's place in Augustan political culture, but also because it engages with larger questions about the impact of political instability and change on women's historical experience.

Some compelling research has begun to emerge from historians whose interests intersect with political history. For example, Paula McDowell's *The Women of Grub Street: Press, Politics and Gender in the London Literary Marketplace, 1678–1730*, which looks below the elite to focus on the women who worked as producers and distributors of print culture, makes a good case for their politicisation and challenges their exclusion from the Habermasian public sphere.[5] Rachel Weil, in *Political Passions: Gender, the Family and Political Argument in England, 1680–1714*, uses gender as a category of analysis in her

---

[4] For Queen Anne, see Edward Gregg, *Queen Anne* (New Haven, 1980) and, more recently, his short but valuable contribution: Edward Gregg, 'Anne (1665–1714)', *Oxford Dictionary of National Biography* at http://www.oxforddnb.com/view/article/560 (accessed 10 Aug. 2008). For a persuasive picture of Anne as a moderate queen and a detailed examination of the personnel who made up the court, see R.O. Bucholz, *The Augustan Court: Queen Anne and the Decline of Court Culture* (Stanford, 1993). While Bucholz makes a good case for Anne's not being dominated by her female favourites, his interest in the court as an institution in decline, in the face of the expansion of English political culture, leaves a number of unanswered questions about the social politics of the court and particularly about the part(s) played by the women of the court. Sarah, duchess of Marlborough, has attracted several recent biographers; however, the most sophisticated and insightful account remains Frances Harris's, *A Passion for Government: The Life of Sarah, Duchess of Marlborough* (Oxford, 1991).

[5] Paula McDowell, *The Women of Grub Street: Press, Politics and Gender in the London Literary Marketplace, 1678–1730* (Oxford, 1998). Jürgen Habermas's highly influential and controversial work on the public sphere, first published in German in 1962, was translated into English in 1989 as *The Structural Transformation of the Public Sphere: An Inquiry into a Category of Bourgeois Society*, trans. Thomas Burger, assisted by Frederick Lawrence (Cambridge, 1989). In it, Habermas posited the emergence of a bourgeois public sphere, c.1700, which provided (male) individuals with a variety of politicised public arenas – most notably, such homosocial venues as inns, coffee houses and clubs – which, in turn, facilitated socio-political conversation and debate, both in person and via the rapid expansion of print culture that marked the period, and resulted in the development of public opinion as a political force. This public sphere, which Habermas sees flourishing in the 18th century, was an idealised, intermediary space, interposed between the private lives and interests of individuals and the dominion and concerns of the state. From the 19th century onwards, it was in decline, eroded by the expansion of the state, which increasingly encroached on private life and undermined the differences between the public and private spheres, and by the rise of powerful media corporations which structured, controlled and constrained public discourse. The active citizen-participant of the 18th century had become the passive citizen-spectator of the second half of the 20th century. Habermas's work has spawned intense debate, particularly for its idealisaton of the 18th-century public sphere and for the way that it privileges the male, bourgeois public sphere above all others. As feminist critics like Mary Ryan have argued, this monolithic view not only ignores women's public spheres, but also dates the decay of the public sphere to the period when women were becoming an undeniable political force. For feminist responses, see, for instance, Mary P. Ryan, 'Gender and Public Access: Women's Politics in Nineteenth-Century America', in *Habermas and the Public Sphere*, ed. Craig Calhoun (Cambridge, 1992), 259–88; *Women, Writing, and the Public Sphere, 1700–1830*, ed. Elizabeth Eger, Charlotte Grant, Cliona O'Gallchoir and Penny Warburton (Cambridge, 2001); Joan B. Landes, *Women and the Public Sphere in the Age of the French Revolution* (Ithaca, 1988); Joan B. Landes, 'The Public and the Private Sphere: A Feminist Reconsideration', in *Feminists Read Habermas: Gendering the Subject of Discourse*, ed. Johanna Meehan (New York, 1995), 91–116.

© *The Parliamentary History Yearbook Trust 2009*

examination of the relationship between gender and politics in the period. Her subtle reading of the images of Queen Anne and the political experiences of Sarah, duchess of Marlborough, contribute to her overall conclusion that whigs and tories alike appropriated gendered arguments for their own purposes and that the 'boundaries between and meaning of, virtue and corruption, public and private, family and state, and ruler and subject – all of which were integral to the construction of gender – were continually re-invented in the heat of political debate'.[6] Similarly, Susan Whyman's elegant reconstruction, *Sociability and Power in Late-Stuart England: The Cultural World of the Verneys, 1660–1720*, throws new light on the political value of familial and social networks, and the participation of women in provincial as well as metropolitan political culture at the beginning of the 18th century.[7] The most exciting glimpse in to elite women's wider involvement in politics beyond the court, can be found in Ingrid Tague's *Women of Quality: Accepting and Contesting Ideals of Femininity in England, 1690–1760*.[8] Her all-too-brief dip in to the 'politics of politeness'[9] and her examination of women's involvement in public life, influence and politics[10] is scattered with examples and makes a strong claim for women as participants 'in the huge network of influence that characterized political life during the eighteenth century'.[11] The part that the age of Anne played in facilitating what Tague identifies as elite women's 'open participation in the political realm' needs further explanation.[12]

It is with this in mind that historians of women and politics should consider how the circumstances that resulted in unprecedented politicisation of society, expansion of patronage and the election of ten new parliaments between 1695 and 1715 affected women (and vice versa). Queen Anne's reign is generally seen as an important transitional period, even a 'watershed', in British political history, but the degree to which this watershed involved and affected women is uncertain.[13] To what extent, for instance, did women share in the 'fears and jealousies'[14] of Holmes's 'volatile, intimately-involved political nation'?[15] What contribution, if any, did they make to the way that these were played out? How were women's political activities received by contemporaries? What part did the rage of party play in providing elite women with the modes, means and motivations for political involvement? And, perhaps most importantly, to what extent were the political circumstances of Anne's reign formative for 18th-century elite women? Was the age of Anne also a watershed in the history of women and politics?

If, as has been argued for the second half of the century, the very nature of 18th-century politics facilitated women's engagement – by its emphasis on personality,

---

[6] Rachel Weil, *Political Passions: Gender, the Family and Political Argument in England, 1680–1714* (Manchester, 1999), 236.

[7] Susan E. Whyman, *Sociability and Power in Late-Stuart England: The Cultural World of the Verneys, 1660–1720* (Oxford, 1999).

[8] Tague, *Women of Quality*.

[9] Tague, *Women of Quality*, 182–9.

[10] Tague, *Women of Quality*, 194–217.

[11] Tague, *Women of Quality*, 217.

[12] Tague, *Women of Quality*.

[13] Geoffrey Holmes, *British Politics in the Age of Anne* (rev. edn 1987), p. xiii.

[14] Holmes, *British Politics*, 405.

[15] Holmes, *British Politics*, 406.

© *The Parliamentary History Yearbook Trust 2009*

family, connection, interest and influence; by the importance of patronage as a primary means of personal and familial advancement; and by the interweaving of society and politics – then the prerequisites for women's political involvement existed in the age of Anne. Furthermore, if women were more likely to be politically active as the political temperature rose, then the febrile atmosphere of Anne's reign should have served as an ideal breeding ground for political women. Dynastic instability, sharp ideological differences, incessant and acrimonious electioneering, unsettling ecclesiastical politics, attempted invasion, and assorted intrigues, rivalries and cabals should have all been spurs to politicisation.[16] Indeed, it might well have been difficult for elite women to avoid politicisation, for the Augustans, as Holmes remarked in *British Politics in the Age of Anne*, lived their politics 'whole-heartedly':[17] 'party coloured the social life of the upper and middle classes to a remarkable degree . . . the clubs and the fashionable dinner tables all reflected the political schism within the nation';[18] '[e]ven an evening spent at Drury Lane or the Haymarket would often stir party blood as much as a morning at the St. James's or the Cocoa Tree'.[19] In fact, as Holmes and W.A. Speck pointed out in *The Divided Society*, elite women were participants in the party conflict of the period:

In the divided society of the years 1694–1716, and especially after 1701 when the issues between Whig and Tory became sharply delineated, many upper-class women took an eager interest in politics and were strongly partisan. Some were far more passionately involved than thousands of men who had the vote . . . .[20]

In order to explore what this meant and begin to answer the questions it poses, historians need to know substantially more. We must delve in to personal and family correspondences to gain a clearer understanding of women's place in, and use of, the social arena for political ends, both in London and the provinces; we need to mine politicians' correspondences to recover women's participation in patronage; and we must examine the surviving papers of women, as well as men, from politically active families in order to determine what part(s) if any women played – and when – in electoral politics. To what extent, for instance, were women ideologically aware? How did identification with party affect the way that they participated in politics? We also need to pay more attention to the everyday responses of everyday people to politically active women in order to determine how their participation was viewed on the ground and what factors were important in establishing the limits of acceptable female behaviour. Ironically, given that Holmes wrote *British Politics in the Age of Anne* to counter the wholesale application of the Namierite political model to the period,[21] accumulating this sort of evidence will necessarily be painstakingly prosopographical.

---

[16] See, e.g., Holmes, *British Politics*.

[17] Holmes, *British Politics*, 23.

[18] Holmes, *British Politics*, 21.

[19] Holmes, *British Politics*, 23.

[20] Geoffrey Holmes and W.A. Speck, *The Divided Society: Party Conflict in England, 1694–1716* (1967), 82.

[21] Robert Walcott, *English Politics in the Early Eighteenth Century* (Oxford, 1956).

© *The Parliamentary History Yearbook Trust 2009*

1. *Women in* British Politics in the Age of Anne

Before moving on to consider the political activities of one provincial woman – Elizabeth Coke, the sister of and political agent of Thomas Coke, vice-chamberlain to Queen Anne – in the lead-up to the hotly contested general election of 1710, it is salutary to recall just how recently the subject of early-modern women and politics has emerged as an area of study. In 1967, when Holmes published *British Politics in the Age of Anne*, second-wave feminism had only begun to spill over into women's history and, when it subsequently did, historians of women and politics were primarily concerned with the 19th century.[22] Eighteenth-century political historians generally had other preoccupations. For many, including Holmes, it was party, and the 'men, the mentality and the measures' which perpetuated it.[23] While Holmes's awareness of politicised women and their sources is reflected in occasional quotations from women like the 'firebrand', Ann Clavering, or her sister, Lady Cowper, he, like Sir Lewis Namier and J.H. Plumb before him, drew upon women's sources primarily to provide colour or bolster an argument.[24]

Where women do feature most prominently in *British Politics* is, unsurprisingly, in the discussion of the court and the influence of the 'backstairs'. Given the 'Sarah factor' in Augustan politics, it could hardly be otherwise. Few women have occupied as potentially powerful an official position as Sarah, duchess of Marlborough, and no other early-modern woman was as vociferous and determined to use her pen and the power of the press to justify her actions and ensure her place in history. Holmes treats the dysfunctional Anne–Sarah–Abigail triangle, and its political implications, cursorily. He acknowledges the strength of the whigs' belief in the duchess of Marlborough's power (and the tories' fear of it), even well after her fall from favour, but he downplays her influence, measuring it in terms of her limited success in securing appointments in her own right.[25] Less attention is paid to her less-easily-quantifiable value as a political weather-cock, a conduit to the queen or a patronage broker. He is similarly bemused by the 'almost pathological' fear that ministers had of Abigail Masham's influence, especially during the crisis over the Essex regiment.[26] On the one hand, he takes at face value her calculated self-deprecation and obsequiousness, and her protestations to Harley of lack of influence; on the other, he acknowledges her importance as Harley's primary avenue to the queen at the beginning and end of his administration. In his essay 'Harley, St John and the Death of the Tory Party', he goes further, laying at Masham's feet two of the three immediate causes for the swift downturn in Harley/Oxford's fortunes in the summer of 1713.[27] Both speak tellingly of Masham's influence and of the way she

[22] E.g., Constance Rover, *Women's Suffrage and Party Politics in Britain, 1866-1914* (1967); Martin Pugh, 'Politicians and the Woman's Vote, 1914–18', *History*, lix (1974), 358–74; Maeve Denby, 'Women in Parliament and Government', in *Women in the Labour Movement: The British Experience*, ed. J. Middleton (1977), 175–90.

[23] Holmes, *British Politics* (rev. edn), p. xxviii.

[24] Holmes, *British Politics*, 106, 332. There is a long tradition of doing this. See, similarly, J.H. Plumb, *Sir Robert Walpole* (2 vols, 1956–61); Sir Lewis Namier, *The Structure of Politics at the Accession of George III* (2nd edn, 1957).

[25] Holmes, *British Politics*, 210–11.

[26] Holmes, *British Politics*, 213.

[27] Geoffrey Holmes, 'Harley, St John and the Death of the Tory Party', in *Politics, Religion and Society, 1679–1742* (1986), 149.

© *The Parliamentary History Yearbook Trust 2009*

operated. She abandoned Oxford for Bolingbroke while Oxford was away from court for his son's marriage to Lady Henrietta Cavendish Holles. Then, when Oxford later requested the dukedom of Newcastle for his son in an effort to placate his son's formidable mother-in-law, she astutely leaked this information to Bolingbroke, who used it successfully to accuse Oxford of putting personal (that is, family) aggrandisement before party politics.[28]

It is the more shadowy figure of Elizabeth, duchess of Somerset – tactful, gracious and canny, a woman steeped in intrigue from childhood – who captures Holmes's fancy and emerges as the most interesting political woman at the court. He sees her as 'securing a measure of dominance' over the queen's thinking in the first year-and-a-half of Harley's ministry.[29] Rumours of her desire to replace the duchess of Marlborough as groom of the stole were already circulating by early autumn 1709[30] and, by the time that the duchess was forced out of place in 1711, her appointment surprised no one. Sought out by the whigs thereafter, and courted by both Bolingbroke and Oxford, especially as they jockeyed for position in 1714, her power lay in withholding as well as exercising influence. Oxford, when struggling for his political life in June 1714, paid more than lip service to her perceived power when he noted, prior to his meeting with the queen: 'Send for the Dchss of Somerset – no body else can save us.'[31]

2. The Current State of Play

One of the reasons why our knowledge of Augustan women and politics remains uneven is because Augustan political history as a whole has not attracted a good deal of attention recently. Additionally, those political historians who are interested in women have tended to concentrate their attention prior to 1700 or after 1750. There is, for instance, no corresponding volume of wide-ranging essays to fill the gap between James Daybell's *Women and Politics in Early Modern England, 1450–1700*[32] and Kathryn Gleadle and Sarah Richardson's *Women in British Politics, 1760–1860: The Power of the Petticoat.*[33]

This is not to say that the Augustan period is a desert: far from it; some excellent work has been done by political historians. Sarah, duchess of Marlborough, has attracted several recent biographers;[34] however, the most sophisticated and insightful account remains Frances Harris's *A Passion for Government: The Life of Sarah, Duchess of Marlborough.*[35] Harris subjects the political activities of the duchess – and, to a lesser degree, those of Abigail Masham – to scholarly scrutiny. Taken together with her other publications, she

---

[28] Holmes, 'Harley, St John and the Death of the Tory Party', 149.

[29] Holmes, *British Politics*, 215.

[30] Harris, *A Passion for Government*, 159.

[31] Holmes, *British Politics*, 215, 216.

[32] *Women and Politics in Early Modern England, 1450–1700*, ed. James Daybell (Aldershot, 2004).

[33] *Women in British Politics, 1760–1860: The Power of the Petticoat*, ed. Kathryn Gleadle and Sarah Richardson (Basingstoke, 2000).

[34] Ophelia Field, *The Favourite: Sarah, Duchess of Marlborough* (2003); Christopher Hibbert, *The Marlboroughs: John and Sarah Churchill, 1650–1744* (2002).

[35] Harris, *A Passion for Government*.

presents the most comprehensive and balanced view of the duchess's political conduct and influence to date.[36]

Harris and Robert Bucholz suggest that there is room for more research on the social politics of the court and female courtiers' involvement therein. Bucholz has made a strong revisionist case for Queen Anne as a conscientious and moderate, if limited, monarch, neither dominated by her female favourites nor the dull nonentity of the duchess of Marlborough's outpourings. His interest in the court as an institution in decline – as a result of the queen's increasing isolation, bad health, and the rising importance of the three Cs of club, coffee house and country house – leaves a number of unanswered questions, particularly about the extent and meaning of women's socio-political activities at the court and about the part(s) women played in linking together court and parliament.[37]

The politicisation of Augustan society itself also demands additional research. Women may have had little part in 18th-century club and coffee house culture (although, as Holmes pointed out, some coffee houses, such as the *Old Man's* in the Tilt Yard, had politically-minded proprietresses),[38] but at a time when, 'party coloured the social life of the upper and middle classes to a remarkable degree . . . the clubs and the fashionable dinner tables all reflected the political schism within the nation',[39] the politicisation of the social arena, and women's part in it, calls for closer examination. Augustan London lived its politics 'whole-heartedly'[40] and, for elite women in town, there may have been, at times, little chance of escape. Party politics permeated culture and women, as well as men, were producers and consumers of culture. Whether it was by securing a ticket to the political theatre that was Sacheverell's trial, as many women did,[41] or by attending such plays as Addison's *Cato: A Tragedy* in 1713,[42] or one of Handel's early operas,[43] or by familiarising themselves with any of the newspapers, pamphlets, handbills, broadsheets, squibs, ballads, satires and prints that were being printed in ever larger numbers, women were integrated in to political culture. How they reacted to this, and to what ends, bears analysis. *The Spectator*'s famous encounter at the Haymarket theatre with ladies who wore their patches on different sides of their faces to declare their party allegiance during the parliamentary season of 1710–11 is often cited, yet seldom taken seriously. It should be. Women's contribution to the creation and maintenance of politicised society invites

---

[36] See Frances Harris, 'Accounts of the Conduct of Sarah, Duchess of Marlborough, 1704–42', *British Library Journal*, viii (1982), 7–35; 'The Electioneering of Sarah, Duchess of Marlborough', *Parliamentary History*, ii (1983), 71–92; 'Parliament and Blenheim Palace: The House of Lords Appeal of 1721', *Parliamentary History*, viii (1989), 43–62; Clyve Jones and Frances Harris, ' "A Question . . . Carried by Bishops, Pensioners, Place-Men, Idiots": Sarah, Duchess of Marlborough and the Lords' Division over the Spanish Convention, 1 March 1739', *Parliamentary History*, xi (1992), 254–77.

[37] See Bucholz, *Augustan Court*; also, R.O. Bucholz, 'Queen Anne: Victim of her Virtues?', in *Queenship in Britain, 1660–1837: Royal Patronage, Court, Culture, and Dynastic Politics*, ed. Clarissa Campbell Orr (Manchester, 2002), 94–129.

[38] Holmes, *British Politics*, 23.

[39] Holmes, *British Politics*, 21.

[40] Holmes, *British Politics*, 23.

[41] Holmes and Speck, *Divided Society*, 86.

[42] Joseph Addison, *Cato, A Tragedy* (Dublin, 1713).

[43] The link between opera and politics is best made by Paul Monod in 'The Politics of Handel's Early London Operas, 1711–18', *Journal of Interdisciplinary History*, xxxvi (2006), 445–72.

© *The Parliamentary History Yearbook Trust 2009*

study, be it through their use of clothing and accessories, such as patches and fans, or by means of their social networking, visiting, dining and socialising, in London or the provinces. What we can learn about the culture of politics will augment our understanding, not just of women's use of ritual and display, but it will also provide us with a more comprehensive picture of Augustan political culture and a better understanding of women's place in society.

3. *Elizabeth Coke and the Derbyshire Election of 1710*

Women from politically active families who lived outside London may not have been as consistently politicised as those who regularly frequented the court, but it would have been difficult for them to be oblivious to politics given the political circumstances of the period. Political publications travelled the country, as did political gossip, rumour and news, disseminated through networks of correspondents, male and female alike. Moreover, as the frequency of elections fed local intrigue and party animus, candidates and grandees played out personal and political rivalries in the electoral arena. The resultant campaigns were often heated and divisive. The country was no sanctuary for the politically disinterested: 'the upper strata of county society were as thoroughly permeated as any sector of the nation's life by the strife of Tory and Whig'.[44] As Jonathan Swift commented, upon arriving in Leicester during an election caused by the death of a sitting member, elections had a remarkable way of politicising society: 'not a chambermaid, prentice, or schoolboy . . . but what is warmly engaged on one side or the other'.[45]

While some women were political actors in their own rights, by dint of birth and/or inheritance, others became political actors, at least temporarily, as representatives of their families. Familial and ideological allegiances tended to be tightly interwoven. Establishing and sustaining a political interest was a mark of status for a man and his family, but the rage of party made it ever more costly and labour-intensive. It required attention to detail, good knowledge of local people and their concerns, excellent social skills and sufficient access to patronage to satisfy at least the most pressing demands. MPs who were away from their power bases for extended periods while fighting overseas, attending parliament or serving at court, needed trusted agents in the country who could keep them abreast of local issues and developments, and maintain a political presence in the locality. In at least some families, mothers, wives, sisters and daughters filled this role.[46] They gathered information about people and events, reported conversations, separated rumour from fact (often annotating the resulting 'news' with their own opinions based on personal knowledge and experience) and sifted through patronage requests before forwarding them. Operating with varying degrees of autonomy, they can be found consulting, proffering advice, implementing decisions and, at times, taking decisions on their own accord. They drew upon their kin, their friends and their networks of

---

[44] Holmes, *British Politics*, 25.

[45] *The Correspondence of Jonathan Swift, D.D.*, ed. Francis Elrington Ball and John Henry Bernard (6 vols, 1910–14), i, 62: Jonathan Swift to Archbishop King, Leicester, 6 Dec. 1707.

[46] For the second half of the century, see Elaine Chalus, ' "My Minerva at My Elbow": The Political Roles of Women in Eighteenth-Century England', in *Hanoverian Britain and Empire: Essays in Memory of Philip Lawson*, ed. Stephen Taylor, Richard Connors and Clyve Jones (Woodbridge, 1998), 210–28.

acquaintances, and put their social skills to political use. While their activities were shaped by contemporary notions of polite sociability and feminine respectability, and the best of efforts of any agent could not guarantee success if the electorate was determined to oust a candidate, their contributions were no less real than those of their male counterparts.

For some women, political involvement for absent menfolk was only one aspect of a broader agency. Serving as *de facto* heads of family in the locality, they stepped in and out of the management of family, household and estate business as necessary. Their stewardship of estates, which was recognized and commonly accepted by contemporaries, has begun to be recovered by historians,[47] but our knowledge of their political agency, which needs to be seen in the same context, is still limited. Moreover, uncovering their activities can be difficult, given the way that women's sources have often been hidden by the cataloguing of family papers.

Elizabeth Coke (c.1676–1739), who served as her brother's political agent in the lead-up to the 1710 Derbyshire election, provides a case in point. Her letters to her brother, primarily on estate and political affairs, were edited and included – fortuitously – in HMC, *Cowper, 12th Report, Appendix, Parts i–iii*, published in 1888.[48] Beyond this, Elizabeth remains a shadowy figure and it would be easy to overlook her. Searches for her via Access to Archives (A2A) and the National Register of Archives (NRA) are unrevealing. Moreover, the Coke family papers (Coke of Melbourne, Derbyshire), from which the HMC report was compiled, are part of the Kerr family papers (NRA 30228 Kerr), which are still in private hands and lack a readily accessible catalogue. Even the British Library, which holds some of her brother's political correspondence, does not hold any of hers. Without the benefit of HMC, *Cowper*, therefore, information about Elizabeth and her political activities would have to be gleaned from snippets in the surviving papers of her more distant relations, friends, neighbours, tenants and clients. This might be possible, but it would be painfully slow and the result would be fragmentary. The circularity of it is also worth emphasizing for what it says about the difficulties inherent in this sort of research: without already knowing about Elizabeth, it would be tricky to know what to look for, or feasible to pursue her social and political networks.

When the newly widowed Thomas Coke (1674–1727), knight of the shire for Derbyshire, returned to London and a life of court politics and being a rake in 1704, he left his unmarried sister, Elizabeth, in charge of his house, estate, political interest and the upbringing of his daughters.[49] The family was close and Thomas trusted his sister. He had chosen well. Elizabeth and her sister, Alice, spent most of their time in the country, so they knew the area around Melbourne Hall and its people well. Intelligent, conscientious and quietly capable, Elizabeth was both a good listener and someone who could speak her mind without upsetting others – particularly valuable traits for a woman dealing with estate and political business. Moreover, her opinions and advice were valued. It is a mark of the esteem in which she was held that, when their old neighbour and political

---

[47] Tague, *Women of Quality*, 123.

[48] See, for instance, Bucholz who mentions estate and political activities: R.O. Bucholz, 'Coke, Thomas (bap. 1674, d.1727)', *Oxford Dictionary of National Biography* at *http://www.oxforddnb.com/view/article/63012* (accessed 12 Aug. 2008).

[49] Bucholz, 'Coke, Thomas'.

© *The Parliamentary History Yearbook Trust 2009*

supporter, Robert Hardinge, was dying, he told his son and daughters that, 'both he and they are to be advised by me in all they did'.[50]

Elizabeth's correspondence reveals that she took her new responsibilities in her stride. Just how much her quick sensitivity to social and political nuance owed to her upbringing in a politically-active family, or developed in response to rising political tensions in the county after 1704, is difficult to determine; however, it is clear that her role as her brother's agent became more openly political between 1704 and 1710, at the same time that her brother was becoming progressively more London-based and court-orientated. Coke, who was first appointed a teller of the exchequer in May 1704, became vice-chamberlain of the household in 1706, a post he held until his death in 1727.[51] A tory by name and a Harleyite by inclination, Coke became, increasingly, a courtier.[52] Initially elected as knight of the shire for Derbyshire in 1698, he was defeated in 1700/1 and then re-elected in 1701, 1702, 1705 and 1708.[53] Despite the best efforts of Elizabeth and his friends in the county – and the whigs' decisive national defeat – he was one of the 145 MPs (out of 271) whose vote against Sacheverell's impeachment in February cost him his seat in the October 1710 election.[54] The fact that he was unwilling throughout the 1710 campaign to make an effort to justify his stance and win over those who were wavering only compounded the problem.[55] Most importantly, he committed a cardinal political sin: he neglected his electorate. Notwithstanding Elizabeth's repeated pleas, he remained firmly fixed in London, unable and/or unwilling to travel to Derbyshire and campaign in person. Bucholz puts this down to the queen's reliance upon him and the demands of his court position.[56] Coke's second wife was also due to give birth, which may have contributed to his reluctance to leave London;[57] however, Elizabeth's need to chide him about the importance of staying in touch with those in the country suggests either an inability to juggle the competing demands of town and country, or a lack of concern about what happened in the latter. Elizabeth was all too aware of the potential consequences of neglecting the electorate:

> if any new aggravation should arise by your seeming neglect of them (which is a particular they are very jealous in that are your friends, and are willing to aggravate and make use of that are not) I fear it would then be much more difficult to procure a right understanding and settlement of affairs than at this time.[58]

Elizabeth's interest in political affairs had begun well before the 1710 election. As early as 1703/4, when she was in London and her brother was at Hampton Court, she was already

---

[50] HMC, *12th Report, Appendix, Part iii*, 82: Elizabeth Coke to Thomas Coke, Melbourne, [17 Oct. 1709].

[51] Bucholz, 'Coke, Thomas'.

[52] Holmes, rather uncharitably, labelled Coke and James Brydges 'Leech-like placemen': Holmes, *British Politics*, 50.

[53] Bucholz, 'Coke, Thomas'.

[54] John Oldmixon, *The History of England during the Reigns of William and Mary, Anne, George I* (1735), 439–42.

[55] HMC, *12th Report, Appendix, Part iii*, 84: Elizabeth Coke to Thomas Coke, Chilcote, 3 June 1710.

[56] Bucholz, 'Coke, Thomas'; HMC, *12th Report, Appendix, Part iii*, 87: Elizabeth Coke to Thomas Coke, [Melbourne], 8 July 1710.

[57] HMC, *12th Report, Appendix, Part iii*, 87: Elizabeth Coke to Thomas Coke, [Melbourne], 26 July 1710.

[58] HMC, *12th Report, Appendix, Part iii*, 87: Elizabeth Coke to Thomas Coke, [Melbourne], 8 July 1710.

performing one of the key functions of a political woman and sending him political news, gossip and anecdotes that she had gathered from her network of acquaintances: 'I can't forbear telling you of a disaster that happened yesterday in the House of Lords to my Lord Ferrers, which my Lady Carnarvon sent us word of. . . .'[59] Similarly, when she was in London again in April 1705, she reported rumours which were making the rounds: 'The town takes care of you in your absence in providing you variety of good places, which perhaps may be as great news to you as it is to us: though since they are good, I should be glad of the certainty of it.'[60] During the lull between elections, politics might take a back seat to news about his children, the progress on his house at Melbourne, or the superabundance of fruit in his garden,[61] but they did not entirely vanish. Whether it was in paying a congratulatory visit to the wife of Coke's close friend and political ally, Henry St John, after his appointment as Prince George's secretary in 1705 – 'I have not been to wait of Mrs. St. Johns since his place. I find there is some little ceremony paid to her upon it, which I hope to do on Thursday'[62] – or commenting somewhat acidly on having received a ceremonial visit from the father of her brother's fellow MP, John Curzon – 'how highly we have been favoured by the Curzon family, Sir Nathaniel himself, lady, sons and daughters all came about a fortnight since and dined with us: and since we all met again one day to dinner at Newton'[63] – her correspondence makes clear that she understood the importance of using the social arena to maintain good political relations. She kept her brother informed of visits and dinners accordingly. In the months before the 1710 election, with no hint of when or whether Coke would be returned for the country, and with opposition to him rising, she made a point of paying visits in the neighbourhood:

I am sure I find the particular of visits so necessary to maintain a good correspondence amongst us, that without giving you the trouble of asking your leave, at the beginning of the year I set your chaise upon the four wheels again, . . . With it I have with great ease compassed all your neighbours, except the Vernons, who my cousin Fitzherberts (that have been sometime at Newton lately) tell me are very full of resentment at my sister Alice and I upon that account.[64]

As the election loomed, her visiting, and visits to her, tended to be dominated by politics. Visits to the extended Coke family at Trusley, Twyford and Dunisturp in June 1710, for instance, placed her at the centre of a group of men who saw her as a direct link to her brother and dealt with her as his agent. Thus, they took the opportunity to update her: they pledged their support to Coke, made patronage requests, filled her in on the latest rumours about potential candidates, informed her about who did and did not support Coke on the other side of the county, reported on the recent meetings at Swarkeston and Kedleston and, in the case of John Harpur, complained that he was withholding his support until Coke himself had demonstrated that it was not his fault that Harpur had been retained as Sheriff another year. Harpur also warned Elizabeth that disaffection was

---

[59] HMC, *12th Report, Appendix, Part iii*, 32: Elizabeth Coke to Thomas Coke, London, [1703/4].

[60] HMC, *12th Report, Appendix, Part iii*, 59: Elizabeth Coke to Thomas Coke, London, 8 Apr. [1705].

[61] HMC, *12th Report, Appendix, Part iii*, 73–4: Elizabeth Coke to Thomas Coke, Melbourne, 26 Aug. [1706].

[62] HMC, *12th Report, Appendix, Part iii*, 60: Elizabeth Coke to Thomas Coke, London, 18 Apr. [1705].

[63] HMC, *12th Report, Appendix, Part iii*, 77–8: Elizabeth Coke to Thomas Coke, Melbourne, 2 Aug. [1707].

[64] HMC, *12th Report, Appendix, Part iii*, 87: Elizabeth Coke to Thomas Coke, Melbourne, 8 July 1710.

© *The Parliamentary History Yearbook Trust 2009*

running high and that support for Sacheverell would be a telling issue in the upcoming county election; Coke's actions against Sacheverell would count against him.[65] This prompted Elizabeth to speak out in turn. Despite prefacing her response with the mandatory caveat, the point she made about honour in politics was unmistakable:

> I said politics was not belonging to me to judge in, but that I thought if the gentlemen you served was dissatisfied in anything you did for them, they might find a friendly and honourable way of letting you know their dislike, without taking the advantage of your absence (which they knew your service to the Queen obliged you to) by any underhand proceedings. He said I was right. . . .[66]

Although she was sorry, she said, that circumstances were such that she felt 'obliged' to relate these conversations in detail, she was careful to tell her brother all that was said: 'I could not tell but it might be some service you should know how they stand affected.'[67]

Elizabeth's knowledge of people and situations was also put to political use. As the country gentlemen began to meet around the county, rumours flew as to who had attended what meetings and what had been discussed. Obtaining this kind of information was vital to any campaign and Elizabeth collected it and passed it on in detail to her brother. That Coke's neighbour, young John Hardinge, the heir of one of his closest political allies, had attended the first Swarkeston meeting was certain; whether he had come out against Coke was not. Hardinge himself hastened to explain the situation to Elizabeth: he had attended the meeting socially, but, torn between his personal ties to Coke and Sir Nathaniel Curzon, he had chosen to be neuter.[68] Elizabeth reassured her brother that he should accept Hardinge's account. She believed that he could be relied upon: 'as far as I can understand [he] has not made one false step in regard to you, though he has not only been pressed, but near insulted by some'. She drew on her knowledge of his family to explain his actions: Sir Nathaniel's friendship with Hardinge's father had led him to show particular kindness towards the young man's children, so his desire to stay neutral in a contest that involved the Curzon and Coke families was understandable, particularly as his political interest was small. Elizabeth advised her brother that it would be useful if Coke could take the time to write to Hardinge, because 'he suffers so much at present in your service'.[69] Later, when the Derbyshire tories revived the Swarkeston Club in late July 1710, Elizabeth's trust in young Hardinge was vindicated. The club made a point at their first meeting of expressing their disapproval for Thomas Coke's stance on Sacheverell by refusing to readopt him. They adopted Coke's brother-in-law, Godfrey Clarke, instead.[70] Hardinge, who did not support the proposal, acted as Elizabeth's eyes and ears at the meeting, reporting the proceedings to her so that she could pass them on.[71]

[65] HMC, *12th Report, Appendix, Part iii*, 84: Elizabeth Coke to Thomas Coke, Chilcote, 3 June 1710.

[66] HMC, *12th Report, Appendix, Part iii*, 84: Elizabeth Coke to Thomas Coke, Chilcote, 3 June 1710.

[67] HMC, *12th Report, Appendix, Part iii*, 85: Elizabeth Coke to Thomas Coke, Chilcote, 3 June 1710.

[68] HMC, *12th Report, Appendix, Part iii*, 85: John Hardinge to Elizabeth Coke, [King's] Newton, 5 June 1710.

[69] HMC, *12th Report, Appendix, Part iii*, 86: Elizabeth Coke to Thomas Coke, Melbourne, 26 June 1710.

[70] Holmes, *British Politics*, 333.

[71] HMC, *12th Report, Appendix, Part iii*, 88–9: Elizabeth Coke to Thomas Coke, [Melbourne], 5 Aug. 1710; Holmes, *British Politics*, 315.

As electioneering commenced in earnest, Elizabeth's letters to her brother indicate that she took on an increasingly managerial role. From the outset, her Coke, Harpur and Burdett cousins, and others who were canvassing for Coke, regularly brought or sent her news of their success, or lack thereof. She also took some steps to secure her brother's interest herself. On the advice of her cousin, John Burdett, who had declared that he would not meddle in the election, she sent notes to several voters in his town, seeking their votes. Then, having heard that her cousins Fitzherbert and Boothby were canvassing for Clarke, she wrote to them to find out if this was actually the case.[72] She also continued to pay attention to the niceties of social politics. As she informed her brother, she had invited Mrs Turner of Derby, who was 'in a great heat for you', over for dinner.[73]

Ever more involved in the minutiae of securing votes as the campaign progressed, she also grew progressively more frustrated with her brother. As late as 12 August, she was still unsure whether he was actually going to stand.[74] When he finally did decide that he would, she sent him a letter brimming with frustration over his shilly-shallying and lack of planning. She was annoyed and blunt: the campaign lacked direction; no one was in overall control; as far as she knew, he had given Fisher no orders; and, to make it worse, while she knew the various people who were campaigning for him, they did not know of each other's proceedings.[75] And then, to top it all off, she was still uncertain when, or if, he was going to come to Derbyshire to campaign:

What your particular reasons have been to prevent your coming and now deter you, to be sure you best and only know: but whilst you are absent things, I believe, go backward every day. And yet one may find that votes are to be had wherever I could try, and in places where they say with great assurance all are engaged; but as nothing to the purpose, nor in a regular way, can have been done here, so 'tis not possible to make any judgement of the matter.[76]

This seems to have marked the turning point in her involvement. Her subsequent letters suggest that thereafter she stepped decisively in to the breach and took on the role as his primary political agent. She certainly did her best to co-ordinate the campaign and give it direction. She sent for the records of previous polls, examined and amended them and then divided the areas up, assigning them to men she knew and trusted 'to be on the constant move' in seeking out votes. One of these was her brother's butler. Although she noted that his 'headpiece is not great', he made up for it by having a good knowledge of people and places, and being well-spoken and good-mannered. She then assembled a small group of four local men to regulate the list of the poll. Having decided that she had some reservations about the loyalty of one of the four, Mr Fisher, who would not canvass for Coke anywhere that Lord Chesterfield also had an interest, she contemplated removing him, but decided that it was better to keep him involved for form's sake. She would ensure, however, that any information he provided would be double-checked by

---

[72] HMC, *12th Report, Appendix, Part iii*, 90: Elizabeth Coke to Thomas Coke, [Melbourne], 7 Aug. 1710.

[73] HMC, *12th Report, Appendix, Part iii*, 90: Elizabeth Coke to Thomas Coke, [Melbourne], 7 Aug. 1710.

[74] HMC, *12th Report, Appendix, Part iii*, 91: Elizabeth Coke to Thomas Coke, [Melbourne], 12 Aug. 1710.

[75] HMC, *12th Report, Appendix, Part iii*, 91: Elizabeth Coke to Thomas Coke, [Melbourne], 16 Aug. 1710.

[76] HMC, *12th Report, Appendix, Part iii*, 92: Elizabeth Coke to Thomas Coke, [Melbourne], 16 Aug. 1710.

© *The Parliamentary History Yearbook Trust 2009*

others she believed more trustworthy.[77] She also appears to have spurred her brother into at least some action. By the end of August, she had secured from him letters to the clergy, in an attempt to mollify them, and was reporting that they had met with unexpected civility in response.[78] Having canvassed the surrounding area, she began to send her agents further afield to seek out votes in areas that had not yet been canvassed. The results were mixed, but votes were consistently there to be made. Still insistent that Coke travel to Derbyshire to join the campaign, she made a point of including references in her letters to people like Mrs Cavendish at Nottingham, who refused to assign her interest to him until 'she finds you come down'.[79] When she was particularly frustrated, she went even further: 'There is none of your friends will make a step further till they see you, and are free in saying your success is an impossibility, which is one great help towards it, for the freeholders are not willing to disoblige to no purpose, and therefore every day will lose ground.'[80] Despite her growing pessimism, her last letters before the polls opened reflect the fruits of her activity and the constant canvassing she had set in motion. They are crammed with the names of supporters and with Elizabeth's own evaluations of the state of the county and the reliability of individual voters.

Coke would go on to lose the election to his brother-in-law and it seems likely that there is little that Elizabeth could have done to prevent this without her brother's presence in the county and a good deal of grovelling from him over his parliamentary conduct regarding Sacheverell. This should not detract from her emergence as his political agent, though, or from the efficiency that she showed in managing the campaign. For a woman like Elizabeth, who was already used to standing in for her brother in personal and estate affairs, and was well-known as his representative in the area, taking up a managerial role in the election was not that large a step. She was well-versed in the people and politics of the area, and used to working with and directing groups of men. While she was, of course, constrained by gender in some ways (a man, for instance would have been able to attend the meetings of local gentlemen that she could not), her letters indicate that she found ways to work around these limitations. The records of the campaign reveal a number of women who had political interest in the county and suggest that this was the norm; similarly, the fact that Elizabeth was a woman running an election campaign also appears to have been accepted without a fuss or a press campaign – unlike that of some female-dominated campaigns later in the century.[81] Motivated as she was by personal pride, which did not allow her to sit by and see her brother's campaign become shambolic, and a strong sense of duty to family, she identified with the tories, but was not driven by ideology. Most importantly, as a respectable and respected woman in the locality, fulfilling a recognized familial role, she was able to step in and out of the role of political agent as circumstances required.

[77] HMC, *12th Report, Appendix, Part iii*, 92: Elizabeth Coke to Thomas Coke, [Melbourne], 19 Aug. 1710. See also her subsequent letters, 93–9.

[78] HMC, *12th Report, Appendix, Part iii*, 94: Elizabeth Coke to Thomas Coke, [Melbourne], 27 Aug. 1710.

[79] HMC, *12th Report, Appendix, Part iii*, 95: Elizabeth Coke to Thomas Coke, [Melbourne], 30 Aug. 1710.

[80] HMC, *12th Report, Appendix, Part iii*, 96: Elizabeth Coke to Thomas Coke, [Melbourne], 2 Sept. 1710.

[81] See, for instance, Lady Susan Keck's involvement in the Oxfordshire election of 1754 or Georgiana, duchess of Devonshire's notorious participation in the Westminster election of 1784: E.H. Chalus, 'Keck, Lady Susanna (bap. 1706, d.1755)', *Oxford Dictionary of National Biography* at *http://www.oxforddnb.com/view/article/68355* (accessed 19 Aug. 2008); Amanda Foreman, *Georgiana, Duchess of Devonshire* (1998).

After the 1710 election defeat in Derbyshire, Coke was provided with the safe Cornish seat of Grampound and had no further need for a political agent in Derby-shire.[82] Elizabeth, accordingly, was able to step back. Was her involvement unique? It seems highly unlikely, but only more research will be able to put her activities in their larger Augustan context. Was she one of Swift's 'scaffoldings' – a means to an end for a politically ambitious man? No more so than any of the other men or women who served in similar ways, as agents and intermediaries, in campaigns across the country – and, as such, her involvement and that of other women who played a part in Augustan politics, requires closer examination. Was the age of Anne a watershed in the history of women and politics in England? That still remains to be determined.

---

[82] Coke owed this seat to George Granville. Holmes, *British Politics*, 264; Bucholz, 'Coke, Thomas'.

© *The Parliamentary History Yearbook Trust 2009*

Geoffrey Holmes and the Public Sphere: Augustan Historiography from Post-Namierite to the Post-Habermasian

BRIAN COWAN

This article attributes the relative lack of attention to the 'public sphere' in Geoffrey Holmes's work to the pervasive influence of Lewis Namier and the Namierite conception of political history. Holmes's *British Politics* can be understood as a product of what might be called the revisionist's dilemma. Because the main thrust of the argument of this work was to challenge the Namierite interpretation of the structure of politics in Anne's reign, Holmes could not fail but to replicate the structures of the original Namierite paradigm. Nevertheless, Holmes's demolition of the Namierite view of Augustan politics also opened up new possibilities for further research; it ultimately widened our understanding of the 'political' and it prepared the ground for the remarkable interdisciplinary dialogue between literary historians, intellectual historians, and political historians. The article concludes with a discussion of how Holmes's successors began to build on his work in ways that can help explain why the Habermasian public sphere paradigm emerged to the foreground of current scholarship in a field where it had been ignored for three decades. Historians are now beginning to build a detailed post-Habermasian understanding of the ways in which the public sphere affected the structures of politics in later Stuart Britain. Work along these lines may well finally help explain the transformation of British politics from an age of Stuart revolutions to the age of Hanoverian oligarchy.

Keywords: Geoffrey Holmes; Lewis Namier; Jürgen Habermas; public sphere; historiography; Queen Anne; revisionism; Namierism

There is a certain perversity to the title of this article: Geoffrey Holmes wrote in an age when the concept of a 'public sphere' was not part of the Augustan historian's lexicon and he never used or referred to the concept.[1] Although Holmes and Jürgen Habermas were born within a year of one another in 1928 and 1929 respectively, their scholarly labours did not coincide. One might presume that there is nothing to say about the topic. It would be absurd to expect a historian to be capable of such profound powers of prolepsis as to be able to anticipate the concerns of a future generation of scholars.

[1] For discussions of this argument in its formative stages, thanks are due to Alex Barber, Alan Downie, Mark Knights, Steve Pincus and Stephen Taylor; various audiences at the Eighteenth-Century Studies Centre at the University of Warwick, a symposium on 'Rethinking the Public Sphere' at McGill University, and *Parliamentary History*'s Dec. 2007 symposium, '*British Politics in the Age of Anne* – 40 Years On', organised by Clyve Jones and Alan Marshall.

© *The Parliamentary History Yearbook Trust 2009*

Geoffrey Holmes did not write about the public sphere, nor indeed did he even use the term, because the terminology and concerns of a German philosopher trained in a continental tradition of critical social theory were not part of the scholarly agenda of the historian of Augustan Britain when Holmes was writing from the 1960s through to the early 1990s. The belated translation of Habermas's 1962 *Habilitationsschrift, Strukturwandel der Öffentlichkeit* into English as *The Structural Transformation of the Public Sphere* in 1989 did not have an immediate effect on historical studies of later Stuart and early Hanoverian Britain.[2] The first sign that it would do so began with the 1992 publication of a collection of essays edited by Craig Calhoun entitled *Habermas and the Public Sphere*, which featured contributions by historians of Germany and France and an essay on 17th-century England by the historical sociologist David Zaret.[3] Soon thereafter, the 'public sphere' gained increasing prominence in the British historian's lexicon, particularly after the publication of influential books and articles by David Solkin, John Brewer and Lawrence Klein on the 18th century, as well as Steven Pincus and Joad Raymond on the 17th century.[4] Given Professor Holmes's untimely death in 1993, he was not able to see the development of this new narrative theme and research agenda in the field which he dominated for three decades.

Yet there is a sense in which one can speak of studies of the Augustan 'public sphere' long before its emergence as an influential catchphrase in historical scholarship. Most historians who have used the term have not felt wedded to the Marxist teleology and socio-economic determinism, the particular chronology of the emergence of a public sphere, or the focus on the origins of the bourgeois public sphere in literary and private life found in Habermas's original formulation of his thesis. It has been used instead as a means of characterising and conceptually organising proliferating studies of the emergence of public opinion as a factor in political action, the efflorescence of print culture and especially the periodical press and political propaganda, and the development of new spaces of public sociability such as coffee houses, club life, and commercialised leisure spots.

When considered in this broader, if less analytically precise, sense, it is clear that studies of the Augustan public sphere have been around for quite a long time. Political writers and observers in Queen Anne's reign were acutely aware of the problems posed by the influence of public opinion on contemporary politics and they commented extensively on the growing importance of print propaganda, newspapers, coffee houses and the like

---

[2] Jürgen Habermas, *Strukturwandel der Öffentlichkeit* (Darmstadt and Neuwied, 1962); Jürgen Habermas, *The Structural Transformation of the Public Sphere*, trans. Thomas Burger (Cambridge, MA, 1989).

[3] *Habermas and the Public Sphere*, ed. Craig Calhoun (Cambridge, MA, 1992), especially the essays by Geoff Eley, Keith Michael Baker and David Zaret.

[4] David Solkin, *Painting for Money: The Visual Arts and the Public Sphere in Eighteenth-Century England* (New Haven, 1993); John Brewer, 'This, That, and the Other: Public, Social, and Private in the Seventeenth and Eighteenth Centuries', in *Shifting the Boundaries*, ed. Dario Castiglione and Lesley Sharpe (Exeter, 1995), 1–21; Lawrence Klein, 'Gender and the Public/Private Distinction in the Eighteenth Century: Some Questions About Evidence and Analytic Procedure', *Eighteenth-Century Studies*, xxix (1995), 97–109; Steven Pincus, ' "Coffee Politicians Does Create": Coffeehouses and Restoration Political Culture', *Journal of Modern History*, lxvii (1995), 807–34; Joad Raymond, 'The Newspaper, Public Opinion, and the Public Sphere in the Seventeenth Century', *Prose Studies*, xxi (1998), 109–40. Also noteworthy as an 'early adopter' of the public sphere catchphrase was Dror Wahrman, 'National Society, Communal Culture: An Argument About the Recent Historiography of Eighteenth-Century Britain', *Social History*, xvii (1992), 43–72.

© *The Parliamentary History Yearbook Trust 2009*

in their society.[5] For many historians of the 'age of Swift' or the 'age of Defoe', these were crucial aspects of understanding their political culture.[6]

This was a social and political fact of the age that did not escape Holmes's attention. The opening chapter of Holmes's classic *British Politics in the Age of Anne* includes a rich discussion of the ways in which political partisanship infused every aspect of the early 18th-century public sphere, including the clubs, coffee houses and periodical publications that were the touchstones for Habermas's public sphere, and the collection of primary sources he edited with Bill Speck, *The Divided Society*, also includes a wealth of documentation for the importance of the public sphere for understanding Augustan politics.[7] Holmes's monograph on *The Trial of Doctor Sacheverell* devotes some attention to the ways in which Sacheverell's reputation was forged and debated 'out of doors' beyond the parliamentary context of the trial.[8] And his inaugural lecture 'The Electorate and the National Will in the First Age of Party' argued that Augustan elections were more representative of public opinion than those that followed in the later 18th and 19th centuries.[9] Despite these significant caveats, it remains the case that the bulk of Holmes's prodigious labours in British political history was not devoted to exploring propaganda, print culture, or the influence of public opinion. Holmes's vision of British politics in the 'age of Anne' was overwhelmingly focused on the history of parliament and the queen's ministries.[10]

This article attributes the relative lack of attention to the 'public sphere' in Holmes's work to the pervasive influence of Lewis Namier and the Namierite conception of political history. It is ironic that Holmes is probably best remembered as the historian who decisively refuted the neo-Namierite perspective on Augustan politics; yet like so many other such 'revisionist' studies, Holmes's work remained largely stuck within the parameters of a debate established by his adversaries.[11] Even though he challenged and ultimately superseded the Namierite paradigm, Holmes could not escape the research agenda and methodological preferences implied by Namier and his fellow travellers.

It would be premature at best, and uncharitable at worst, however, to presume that Holmes's work and that of fellow historians working on 'British politics in the age of

---

[5] Brian Cowan, 'Mr. Spectator and the Coffeehouse Public Sphere', *Eighteenth-Century Studies*, xxxvii (2004), 345–66.

[6] David H. Stevens, *Party Politics and English Journalism 1702–42* (Chicago, 1916); William Laprade, *Public Opinion and Politics in Eighteenth Century England* (New York, 1936); Michael Foot, *The Pen and the Sword: Jonathan Swift and the Power of the Press* (1957); in G.M. Trevelyan, *England Under Queen Anne* (3 vols, 1930–4), consideration of these public sphere institutions is largely relegated to vol. 1, ch. 4.

[7] Geoffrey Holmes, *British Politics in the Age of Anne* (1967, rev. edn 1987), ch. 1, esp. 20–4, 28–33; Geoffrey Holmes and W.A. Speck, *The Divided Society: Party Conflict in England 1694–1716* (1967), esp. 40–5, 66–76, 124–31.

[8] Geoffrey Holmes, *The Trial of Doctor Sacheverell* (1973); the social context was further detailed in Geoffrey Holmes, 'The Sacheverell Riots: The Crowd and the Church in Early Eighteenth-Century London', *Past and Present*, no. 72 (1976), 55–85.

[9] Geoffrey Holmes, *Politics, Religion and Society in England, 1679–1742* (1986), 1–33.

[10] Holmes's significant contributions to social history in *Augustan England: Professions, State and Society 1680–1730* (1982) should not be ignored, but remained separate from his political histories. Geoffrey Holmes, 'The Achievement of Stability: The Social Context of Politics from the 1680s to the Age of Walpole', reprinted in Holmes, *Politics, Religion and Society*, 249–80, was a sole attempt to assimilate his political and social histories.

[11] For discussion of a similar dilemma faced by revisionist historians of early Stuart England, see Peter Lake, 'Retrospective: Wentworth's Political World in Revisionist and Post-Revisionist Perspective', in *The Political World of Thomas Wentworth Earl of Strafford 1621–1641*, ed. J.F. Merritt (Cambridge, 1996), 252–83.

Holmes' entirely ignored the political culture of publicity.[12] The article thus concludes with a discussion of the ways in which Holmes's successors began to build on his work in ways that can help explain why the Habermasian public sphere paradigm emerged to the foreground of current scholarship in a field where it had been ignored for three decades after the first publication of *Strukturwandel der Öffenlichkeit* in 1962. It will be argued that Holmes's demolition of the Namierite view of Augustan politics also opened up new possibilities for further research; it ultimately widened our understanding of the 'political' and it prepared the ground for the remarkable inter-disciplinary dialogue between literary historians, intellectual historians, and political historians that has characterised the study of Augustan politics in our current 'age of Habermas'.

1

The first thing to note when considering the impact of 'Namierism' on Holmes's history is that there was always some difference between the published histories of Sir Lewis Namier and the many other works often labelled as 'Namierite'. Like most such 'isms', there have always been many varieties and styles of Namierism, but the word and the concept took off because they managed to describe in a rough and ready way a distinctive manner of thinking about the past.[13] And like these other 'isms', there has often been a great deal of confusion and debate surrounding the precise meaning of the term and the relationship between the work of the master and his disciples. Namierism has been variously associated with a variety of different historical arguments and research methods: a challenge to an older, triumphalist 'whig' interpretation of British history; a narrow focus on high politics, especially the history of parliament and the ministries of the crown; a rejection of the role of ideas and/or principles in political action; a predilection for the study of the private papers and correspondence of elites as primary source materials; a methodological preference for individualism and prosopography; and perhaps most curiously with both static structural history and detailed narrative *histoires événmentielles* of high political vicissitudes. The last of these historical methods was attacked most famously by Lawrence Stone who denounced revisionist historians of the 17th century as practising 'pure neo-Namierism, just at a time when Namierism is dying as a way of looking at eighteenth-century English politics'.[14] There is a basis for all of these associations in Namier's own work, although his attempt to write a detailed narrative of English politics in the age of the American revolution was famously a non-starter: the narrative of *England in the Age of the American Revolution* ends just before 1763, thus missing the outbreak of the American war by over a decade.[15] Despite the prominence of concepts such as 'structure' and 'society' in Namier's work, his zealous

---

[12] Stephen Taylor, 'British Politics in the Age of Holmes', *Parliamentary History*, viii (1989), 132–41.

[13] Linda Colley, *Namier* (New York, 1989).

[14] Lawrence Stone, 'The Revival of Narrative: Reflections on a New Old History', *Past and Present*, no. 85 (1979), 21.

[15] Colley, *Namier*, 32.

© *The Parliamentary History Yearbook Trust 2009*

focus on elite politics has often obscured the similarities between his largely synchronic historical vision and that of his French contemporaries in the *Annales* school. Lucien Febvre was born a decade before Namier in 1878, and Marc Bloch only two years before in 1886.[16]

It is in the work of Namier's followers and fellow travellers where his impact was really felt. Namier's challenge to the whig view of 18th-century British history was hardly novel, and this in fact accounts for the strength and popularity of his work, and ultimately for the transformation of his work into 'Namierism' – a distinctive style of methods, priorities and prejudices behind historical research that flourished in the middle decades of the 20th century.[17] This was the climate in which Robert Walcott composed his now much maligned study of *English Politics in the Early Eighteenth Century*. 'It is surely unjust to Sir Lewis Namier to father upon him Professor Walcott's failure to grasp the full dimensions of the political crisis of Anne's reign', wrote Gareth Bennett in a positive review of Holmes's *British Politics*. This may be true enough, although there is no doubt that Walcott thought Namierism offered the best means of understanding Augustan politics, and Namier himself certainly welcomed the extension of his methods and interpretative framework back into the pre-Hanoverian age.[18]

While the sustained criticism of Walcott's work from not only Holmes but also J.H. Plumb, Bill Speck, Henry Horwitz, and just about every other political historian of the period would leave one to think that Namierism was dead on arrival in the study of Augustan politics, its influence was far more pervasive than one might think at first glance. The substance of the challenge to Walcott's 'Namierite' interpretation of the period really focused on only one aspect, albeit a crucial one: his denial of the usefulness of 'party' as a means of understanding the political divisions and actions of Anne's reign. And in order to make this case, Holmes had to challenge Namierism on its home ground, the history of parliament.[19]

In choosing to meet the Namierite challenge head-on as it were, Holmes's own history remained largely parliament centred, and alternative sites of political action were largely relegated to the sidelines. The chapter on 'the managers, the queen, and the royal closet' in *British Politics* surely gives the queen her due mention – she is not a cipher in Holmes's account – but it does tend to downplay the importance of the royal court and 'bedchamber politics', particularly outside of its need to maintain parliamentary 'managers', in Anne's reign.[20] The most strident challenge to Namierite parliament-fixation came from historians such as J.C.D. Clark who believed that the court remained a vibrant political locus in the 18th century.[21] While initially dismissive of the importance

---

[16] Peter Burke, *The French Historical Revolution: The Annales School 1929–1989* (Stanford, 1990).

[17] Colley, *Namier*, 47–50; Linda Colley, 'The Politics of Eighteenth-Century British History', *Journal of British Studies*, xxv (1986), 364–5.

[18] *English Historical Review*, lxxxiv (1969), 359, referring to Robert Walcott, *English Politics in the Early Eighteenth Century* (Oxford, 1956); Lewis Namier, *Personalities and Powers: Selected Essays* (New York, 1965), 32.

[19] Holmes, *British Politics*, 33.

[20] Holmes, *British Politics*, 209, 210, 216, 414–15.

[21] J.C.D. Clark, *Revolution and Rebellion: State and Society in England in the Seventeenth and Eighteenth Centuries* (Cambridge, 1986), and contrast Robert Bucholz, *The Augustan Court: Queen Anne and the Decline of Court Culture* (Stanford, 1993).

of public sphere politics as 'shallow' and 'constricted,' the revival of interest in court culture has recently been reconciled with the public sphere.[22]

The contrast between Holmes's parliament-focused concept of politics with an older account of the crucial last four years of Anne's reign, and one entirely unconcerned with the Namierite challenge, is telling. Michael Foot's *The Pen and the Sword* (1957) offered an account of Augustan politics which revolved around two pivots, the royal court and the 'court' of public opinion. Foot's narrative is hardly as sophisticated as Holmes's work, based as it is on a much smaller and selective base of primary source materials, but it is remarkable how little Holmes's *British Politics* resembles Foot's and how much, in fact, it resembles Namier's. Swift and Defoe are bit players in Holmes's account of the Augustan political scene, and virtually no attention is given to the workhorse partisan journalists of the age such as Abel Boyer and Charles Leslie for the tories, or John Tutchin and George Ridpath for the whigs. Whereas Foot managed to make Jonathan Swift a key player in the downfall of the duke of Marlborough, he appears in *British Politics* as either a wry observer on partisan politics or occasionally as a pithy encapsulator of tory views on the war and finance. To the extent that there is anyone like a 'protagonist' in Holmes's structural history, it could only be a parliamentary manager like Robert Harley, with perhaps Sidney Godolphin, and to a lesser extent the whig junto lords, in supporting roles.

British Politics is also distinctive, and rather Namierite, for its lack of narrative. Like Namier's pathbreaking early studies of *The Structure of Politics at the Accession of George III*, which were thought to be necessary to clear the ground for writing the full history of the British imperial problem in the age of the American revolution, Holmes's *British Politics* was conceived as a prolegomena to a detailed 'history of domestic politics during the life of Robert Harley's ministry of 1710 to 1714', a work which remained famously unpublished.[23] Holmes's *characterisation* of the structure of Augustan politics could not have been more different from Namier's, but the way in which he chose to study what he called 'the character' and 'the workings' of politics owed a lot to the Namierite vision of the historian's task. There was perhaps more truth than originally intended to J.P. Kenyon's pronouncement that Holmes's *British Politics* stood out as the 'only historical work of our time comparable with Namier's *The Structure of Politics*'.[24]

British Politics can be understood as a product of what might be called the revisionist's dilemma. Because the main thrust of the argument of this work was to challenge the Namierite interpretation of the structure of politics in Anne's reign, Holmes could not fail but to replicate the structures of the original Namierite paradigm. There is a similarity here in the problems faced by revisionist historians of the early Stuart era.[25] The work of Conrad Russell, who was born in 1937, less than a decade after Holmes,

---

[22] J.C.D. Clark, *The Memoirs and Speeches of James, 2nd Earl Waldegrave 1742–1763* (Cambridge, 1988), 18; J.C.D. Clark, 'The Re-Enchantment of the World? Religion and Monarchy in Eighteenth-Century Europe', in *Monarchy and Religion: The Transformation of Royal Culture in Eighteenth-Century Europe*, ed. Michael Schaich (Oxford, 2007), 67; Hannah Smith, *Georgian Monarchy: Politics and Culture, 1714–1760* (Cambridge, 2006).

[23] Holmes, *British Politics* (rev. edn), p. lxvii. Holmes later turned to narrative history in *The Trial of Doctor Sacheverell*. Holmes's typescript draft for his study of Harley, 'The Great Ministry' is on deposit at the Institute of Historical Research.

[24] J.P. Kenyon, 'Honouring an Inspiration', *Times Literary Supplement*, 4–10 Mar. 1988, 252.

[25] Compare Peter Lake, 'Retrospective', and Brian Cowan, 'Refiguring Revisionisms', *History of European Ideas*, xxix (2003), 475–89.

and was thus part of the same generation of historians that came of age in the immediate aftermath of the Second World War, was also self-consciously revisionist with regard to the established wisdom regarding his primary field of research – the political history of early 17th-century England. Like Holmes, Russell's brand of revisionism ended up contending with its opponents on its home ground, as it were, and like Holmes, that home ground was parliamentary history. For all of his insistence that parliament was an event and not an institution, and that the court, the counties, and the 'British problem' were the main loci for politics in the early Stuart era, Russell devoted most of his career to early Stuart parliamentary history.[26] While our understanding of early Stuart politics will never be the same as a consequence of Russell's unrelenting revisionist critiques, his main historiographic legacy may well be remembered as having provided the demolition work necessary in order to begin the construction of richer, 'post-revisionist' histories of court culture and politics; of relations between the London metropolis and local communities throughout England and, indeed, the rest of Britain and Ireland; and of the political consequences of the religious debates and divisions that wracked pre-civil war England.[27]

Holmes's *œuvre* was rather more wide-ranging in its scope than was Russell's. Unlike Russell, he managed to move beyond parliamentary and even political history; indeed his later work witnessed what might be called a turn to social history.[28] But his political history writings never fully realized, or developed much further, the expansive vision of the topic Holmes laid out in his impressive first chapter of *British Politics*.

The political significance and workings of the Augustan public sphere remained underdeveloped in Holmes's writings, even when he turned his attention to what was perhaps the most prolific, albeit short-lived, public controversy of the 18th century, the Sacheverell affair. Whereas Holmes remarks upon the published version of Sacheverell's famous 5 November sermon as 'a short-term best-seller' with 'no equal in the early eighteenth century' – it is likely to have had a print run of at least 100,000 copies – he devotes little attention in his monograph to the pamphlet and periodical wars provoked by the sermon itself.[29] One cannot say that Holmes was unaware of the public sphere in the age of Sacheverell: his account draws heavily on the newspapers and periodicals, the pamphlets and treatises, and the public prints and ephemera generated by the Sacheverell controversy. For example, Holmes read carefully the regular reports of the Sacheverell affair provided by John Dyer in his manuscript newsletters which provided an account of the proceedings to readers throughout England. But these products of the Augustan public sphere were used as *contextual* sources to draw upon as Holmes narrated the rise and fall of the Sacheverell controversy, and as such they recede into the background of his book. There is very little direct engagement with, or analysis of, Sacheverell era

---

[26] For an incisive critique, see Peter Lake, 'Review Article', *Huntington Library Quarterly*, lvii (1994), 167–97. Russell's brand of parliamentary history owed much to the Namierite tradition.

[27] See *Politics, Religion and Popularity in Early Stuart Britain: Essays in Honour of Conrad Russell*, ed. Thomas Cogswell, Richard Cust and Peter Lake (Cambridge, 2002).

[28] Holmes, *Augustan England*, and Holmes, *Politics, Religion and Society*, chs 10–12.

[29] Holmes, *Trial of Doctor Sacheverell*, 75. Much of Holmes's understanding of the bibliographic context derived from the research of William Speck, later published as Henry Sacheverell, *The Perils of False Brethren*, with bibliographic note by W.A. Speck (Exeter, 1974), and F.F. Madan, *A Critical Bibliography of Dr. Henry Sacheverell*, ed. W.A. Speck (Lawrence, KS, 1978).

propaganda as *texts* themselves, each with their own particular political arguments and requiring historical explanation. The public sphere can be found in the endnotes, but rarely in the text itself, of Holmes's *Trial of Doctor Sacheverell*.

2

It is worth comparing Holmes's careful criticism of the Namierite interpretation of politics in Anne's reign with the rather more thorough-going challenge to Namierite history in John Brewer's *Party Ideology and Popular Politics at the Accession of George III*, a work published just a few years after Holmes's *Sacheverell*. As its title suggests, this book put the popular press and political ideology at the centre of its understanding of political structures in a period which was most obviously Namier's home ground. Brewer's work directly challenged Namier's and Namierite histories with their 'strong preoccupation with the workings of Westminster and a singularly narrow view of politics'.[30] Here was a work in which pamphlets, broadsides, newspapers, ballads, prints and cartoons, clubs and coffee houses, riots and demonstrations, all took centre stage. In other words, this was a history which revolved around explaining how political arguments were constructed and construed in the 'public sphere'. Brewer demonstrated just how different a 'post-Namierite' history of 18th-century Britain might look in a way that Holmes's studies of Anne's reign never quite achieved, and it is striking just how Habermasian that history looked well before the notion of a public sphere had become a catchphrase in the standard scholarly vocabulary.

Historians of Britain's 'long 18th century' did not need to read Habermas in order to discover, discuss and explain the public sphere, as Brewer's early work attests.[31] One could argue that this, in fact, accounts for much of the recent success of the Habermasian public sphere notion in recent work on the 18th century. The Habermasian public sphere gave a name to something that post-Namierite historians were already familiar with, and indeed had already begun to explore and analyse intensively. This is especially true since most historians who have used the concept have tended to modify its meaning and theoretical framework well beyond that originally articulated by Habermas himself. Peter Lake and Steven Pincus have recently argued that much of the reason for the growing popularity of the public sphere concept in Tudor and Stuart histories can be attributed to attempts to argue against and beyond the paradigms and preferences of revisionist historians of the early modern period, and their definition of this revisionism is decidedly Namierite – it focused on high politics above all and privileged the study of manuscript rather than printed sources, much like Namier did.[32] This argument could be extended

---

[30] Brewer, *Party Ideology* (Cambridge, 1976), 9. Brewer's supervisor, J.H. Plumb, had earlier criticized the Namierite view of politics on the same grounds in his 'Political Man', in *Man Versus Society in Eighteenth-Century Britain: Six Points of View*, ed. James Clifford (Cambridge, 1968), esp. 12.

[31] Brewer's later work developed seamlessly into a more obviously Habermasian view of the 18th century, see his ' "The Most Polite Age and the Most Vicious": Attitudes Towards Culture as a Commodity, 1660–1800', in *The Consumption of Culture 1600–1800: Image, Object, Text*, ed. Ann Bermingham and John Brewer (1995), 341–61; and *The Pleasures of the Imagination: The Emergence of English Culture in the Eighteenth Century* (1997).

[32] Peter Lake and Steven Pincus, 'Rethinking the Public Sphere in Early Modern England', *Journal of British Studies*, xlv (2006), 270–92, esp. 271–2; see also, *The Politics of the Public Sphere in Early Modern England*, ed. Peter Lake and Steven Pincus (Manchester, 2007). I am grateful to Alex Barber for discussions on this matter.

© *The Parliamentary History Yearbook Trust 2009*

to the historiography of the 18th century as well: as discontent with the Namierite interpretation of history grew amongst historians working on his home ground, they increasingly turned their attention to studying the organs of public opinion and the sites of civil society that Habermas had identified as the primary institutions of his bourgeois public sphere. Namier, or more accurately, the reaction to Namier's historical vision, laid the groundwork for studying the 18th-century public sphere.

One of the most remarkable developments in 18th-century studies has been the blurring of boundaries between histories of high and low politics – what Holmes at one point referred to as the 'political' and 'sub-political' nations, as well as between studies of literary culture and intellectual histories of the highly articulate works of 'political thought'.[33] Augustan historiography after the publication of Holmes's major works has been transformed by an interdisciplinary revolution that made the public sphere a major object of concern well before the Habermasian notion became a scholarly catchphrase in the late 1980s and early 1990s. Much of this can be attributed to the rise of the self-consciously interdisciplinary new cultural history in this era as a paradigm for virtually every subfield of historical study.[34]

Publications in literary and intellectual history in particular began to open up new ways of viewing the public sphere in the age of Anne. In his 1972 book on *Grub Street*, the literary historian Pat Rogers chided Holmes for mistakenly thinking that Augustan Grub Street was fictional, whereas the street really did exist in London, although it operated more often than not in the discourse of the time as a synecdoche for the whole world of early 18th-century print culture.[35] Rogers's *Grub Street* was designed to illuminate the social conditions of authorship that obtained during the life of Alexander Pope, but it also signalled the beginning of an era of substantial interdisciplinary collaboration between scholars in departments of literature and history that would produce an image of 18th-century politics quite different from the Namierite version.[36] Harry Dickinson's 1974 collection of primary sources for the Everyman's University Library was framed in explicit opposition to the Namierite approach. The century witnessed, Dickinson argued, a 'battle to inform, educate and harness public opinion', and for this reason 'any attempt . . . to understand eighteenth-century politics must involve more than just a study of the structure of politics. It needs to examine both the content of the political debates of the period and the ways in which the public participated in these debates.' Dickinson's subsequent survey of 18th-century political thought, *Liberty and Property*, delivered an extended account along these lines.[37]

One of the most important works of this era to demonstrate the importance of the public sphere in the age of Anne was Alan Downie's *Robert Harley and the Press*, a work

[33] Holmes, *Politics, Religion and Society*, 271–2.

[34] *The New Cultural History*, ed. Lynn Hunt (Berkeley and Los Angeles, 1989). For the impact on intellectual history, see Brian Cowan, 'Ideas in Context: From the Social to the Cultural History of Ideas', in *Palgrave Advances in Intellectual History*, ed. Brian Young and Richard Whatmore (Houndmills, 2006), 171–88; compare Peter Burke, *What Is Cultural History?* (Cambridge, 2004).

[35] Pat Rogers, *Grub Street: Studies in a Subculture* (1972), 18–19.

[36] Two important recent revisions of Rogers's work include Brean Hammond, *Professional Imaginative Writing in England 1670–1740: 'Hackney for Bread'* (Oxford, 1997); and Christine Gerrard, *Aaron Hill: The Muses Projecto 1685–1750* (Oxford, 2003).

[37] *Politics and Literature in the Eighteenth Century*, ed. H.T. Dickinson (1974), p. xxii; H.T. Dickinson, *Liberty and Property: Political Ideology in Eighteenth-Century Britain* (1977).

which in many ways fulfils the unrealized promise of Holmes's first chapter of *British Politics*. Holmes himself did not disparage this line of research. On the contrary, he encouraged and welcomed it.[38] Here was a study in which Holmes's establishment of the centrality of partisan whig/tory divisions could be taken as read and thus used as the basis for exploring the ways in which the politician Robert Harley managed to use the popular press for partisan advantage.[39] In his own professional turn from the study of unadjectival 'history' to literature, Downie's career has mirrored the growing interdisciplinarity of 18th-century studies in the past quarter century.[40] It is not entirely ironic that Professor Downie has gone on to become, in recent years, one of the most vociferous critics of the use of the Habermasian 'bourgeois public sphere' concept in 18th-century studies. For Downie, there is no need for a theory so divorced from state-of-the-art research on Augustan state and society, especially when so much non-Habermasian, but post-Holmesian, work on 'the emergence of public opinion as a force in the state' has already laid the ground for an alternative model for understanding the public sphere.[41] Scholars hardly need Habermas to discuss the impact of public opinion on politics, when post-Namierite scholars have been engaged in developing a far more nuanced model.[42]

It is in the work of Holmes's successors that one can see the full fruition of his refutation of the Namierite characterisation of 18th-century politics, and it is here where the historical study of the public sphere *avant la lettre* began to take off. The 1980s and 1990s saw a rush of publications exploring the role of the crowd, the press, and public opinion in shaping 18th-century political culture. Works by Marie Peters, Nick Rogers, Paul Monod, Christine Gerrard, Bob Harris, and Kathleen Wilson established an understanding of 18th-century politics beyond Westminster in which public politics figured prominently.[43] By and large, these works were published well before the public sphere concept took hold in scholarly discourse, yet it could be argued that it was the expanded concept of politics and political culture expounded in works such as these that allowed for the idea of a developing 'public sphere' to take hold with such ease.

[38] See, e.g., his review of J.A. Downie, *Robert Harley and the Press* (Cambridge, 1979) in 'The Politics of Persuasion', *Times Literary Supplement*, 18 Apr. 1980, 428.

[39] J.A. Downie, *Robert Harley and the Press: Propaganda and Public Opinion in the Age of Swift and Defoe* (Cambridge, 1979); see also, James Richards, *Party Propaganda Under Queen Anne: The General Elections of 1702–1713* (Athens, GA, 1972).

[40] After studying early 18th-century history with Bill Speck at Newcastle in the early 1970s, Downie says he 'found the questions [he] was wanting to ask about the political literature [of the period] were not being asked by historians' (personal communication). He began his post-doctoral career with a research fellowship in the English department at the University of Wales, where Pat Rogers was also a professor. I am grateful to Professor Downie for discussing his early career trajectory with me.

[41] J.A. Downie, 'The Myth of the Bourgeois Public Sphere', in *A Concise Companion to the Restoration and Eighteenth Century*, ed. Cynthia Wall (Oxford, 2005), 77; J.A. Downie, 'How Useful to Eighteenth-Century English Studies is the Paradigm of the "Bourgeois Public Sphere"?', *Literature Compass*, i (2003), 1–19.

[42] J.A. Downie, 'Public Opinion and the Political Pamphlet', in *The Cambridge History of English Literature, 1660–1780*, ed. John Richetti (Cambridge, 2005), 549–71.

[43] Marie Peters, *Pitt and Popularity: The Patriot Minister and London Opinion During the Seven Years War* (Oxford, 1980); Nicholas Rogers, *Whigs and Cities: Popular Politics in the Age of Walpole and Pitt* (Oxford, 1989); Paul Monod, *Jacobitism and the English People, 1688–1788* (Cambridge, 1989); Christine Gerrard, *The Patriot Opposition to Walpole: Politics, Poetry and the National Myth 1725–1742* (Oxford, 1994); Robert Harris, *A Patriot Press: National Politics and the London Press in the 1740s* (Oxford, 1993); Kathleen Wilson, *The Sense of the People: Politics, Culture and Imperialism in England, 1715–1785* (Cambridge, 1995).

© *The Parliamentary History Yearbook Trust 2009*

3

The study of British politics in the age of Anne today could hardly be more different than it was when Holmes composed *British Politics*. Whereas Holmes felt compelled to engage with Namierite historiography on its home ground, and to a large degree on its own terms, historians working after Holmes's achievements have expanded their concept of the political to include not just public sphere institutions such as print culture, urban coffee houses and village parish pumps, but they have also reinvigorated the study of other sites of political action neglected by Namierite histories such as the established church and dissenting meeting-houses. Nevertheless, there remains a number of important unanswered questions that have not been adequately addressed by these post-Holmesian histories of the Augustan public sphere.

Perhaps the most important has been the question that loomed large in Holmes's day. J.H. Plumb and Holmes phrased the problem in terms of the 'origins of political stability'. Plumb noted a 'contrast between political society in eighteenth- and seventeenth-century England. In the seventeenth century men killed, tortured and executed each other for political beliefs; they sacked towns and brutalized the country-side. They were subjected to conspiracy, plot and invasion . . . by comparison, the political structure of eighteenth-century England possesses adamantine strength and profound inertia.'[44] One need only compare the striking difference between the fates of Algernon Sydney and that of Henry St John, Viscount Bolingbroke, to observe the difference. Sydney was executed for treason in 1683, while Bolingbroke died of cancer having had the luxury of working on editing his voluminous writings for the benefit of posterity in old age.[45] The contrast is as vivid today as it was 40 years ago; the question: 'how did this transformation happen?' remains a good one, and it remains incompletely answered.

Plumb tried to explain the change in terms of the rise and consolidation of a whig oligarchy, particularly under the adept management of Sir Robert Walpole. Holmes sought the answer in terms of changes in the demographic and economic structures of English society, although he agreed with Plumb that the 1720s seemed to mark a watershed moment of transition. Neither of these propositions has managed to withstand extended scrutiny, and historians as diverse as Stephen Taylor, John Brewer, Jonathan Scott, Tim Harris, and Steven Pincus have all preferred to emphasize the transformative impact of the Glorious Revolution of 1688–9 on British political society.[46] The

[44] J.H. Plumb, *The Origins of Political Stability: England 1675–1725* (Boston, 1967), p. xviii; compare Taylor, 'British Politics', 137–8, which has also inspired the reflections in the following paragraphs. See also the debate on Plumb's arguments by Clayton Roberts, Stephen Baxter and Norma Landau in *Albion*, xxv (1993), 237–77. Plumb's own liberal prejudices are set in context in David Cannadine, 'Historians in the "Liberal Hour": Lawrence Stone and J.H. Plumb Re-Visited', *Historical Research*, lxxv (2002), 316–54.

[45] Jonathan Scott, 'Sidney, Algernon (1623–1683)', *Oxford Dictionary of National Biography* at http://www.oxforddnb.com/view/article/25519 (accessed 25 Nov. 2007); H.T. Dickinson, 'St John, Henry, Styled First Viscount Bolingbroke (1678–1751)', *Oxford Dictionary of National Biography* at http://www.oxforddnb.com/view/article/24496 (accessed 25 Nov. 2007).

[46] Taylor, 'British Politics'; Stephen Taylor, '*Plus Ca Change* . . . ? New Perspectives on the Revolution of 1688', *Historical Journal*, xxxvii (1994), 457–70; John Brewer, *The Sinews of Power: War, Money and the English State, 1688–1783* (Cambridge, MA, 1990); Jonathan Scott, *England's Troubles: Seventeenth-Century English History in European Perspective* (Cambridge, 2000); Tim Harris, *Revolution: The Great Crisis of the British Monarchy 1685–1720* (2006); Steven Pincus, *England's Glorious Revolution: A Brief History with Documents* (New York, 2006). While still insisting on the important turning point marked by 1688, Pincus's *First Modern Revolution*

establishment of the protestant succession and the consequent transfer of the rhetoric of anti-popery from a domestic to an international stage; the institutionalisation of parliamentary government and a fiscal-military state; and ultimately the Anglo-Scottish union and the rise of an Irish protestant ascendancy in these accounts were the real watershed developments in British politics, and they were all dependent upon the changes wrought by the Glorious Revolution. The work of Walpole and his whig oligarchs was just a matter of tidying up after the revolutionary decades between the 1690s and 1720.

One recent exception to this trend has been Mark Knights's remarkable study of *Representation and Misrepresentation in Later Stuart Britain*, which cautions against exaggerating the Glorious Revolution as a key turning point.[47] Knights posits instead the existence of a 'later Stuart' political culture which persisted from the Restoration until the rise of Walpole in the 1720s. Knights's work is significant, then, in reviving the chronology for the development of a distinctively different 18th-century political culture from that which had been posited by Plumb and Holmes.

While Knights relies on the works of Plumb and Holmes on the importance of partisanship on parliamentary elections and the electorate after the Glorious Revolution, his account of the structure of later Stuart politics is substantially different, and so is his explanation for the emergence of a rather different, relatively more stable, and ostensibly more 'polite' political culture in the age of Walpole and his successors. Unlike Holmes's *British Politics*, Knights's study puts the public sphere at the centre of his analysis. His book tells the story of the emergence of both a quantitatively larger and more extensive public sphere of politics in the later Stuart era. The rise of this 'practical' public sphere substantially and permanently altered the ways in which British politics would be conducted in the 18th century. But Knights simultaneously explores the anxieties and concerns raised by the emergence of the public 'as a collective fiction with an enlarged role as a legitimizing power and as an umpire'. This 'normative' public sphere was far less readily accepted, and indeed the continued intensity of later Stuart partisanship, Knights suggests, ultimately provoked attempts to contain and restrain it. In this way, 'the practice of politics . . . helped to establish the languages of politeness, reason, interest and sociability' that have been a major concern for historians of 18th-century thought and culture.[48] It also helped pave the way for the oligarchical practices of the Walpolean whigs in the years after the passing of the Septennial Act in 1716. The 'origins of political stability' in the age of Walpole, such as it was, lay in the fears of excessive partisanship provoked by the ferocious debates that raged in the later Stuart public sphere.[49]

---

[46] *(continued)* (forthcoming) will also argue *in extensa* for the continually contested nature of the meaning of the Glorious Revolution in 18th-century political culture. I am grateful to Steve Pincus for discussing his work in press.

[47] Mark Knights, *Representation and Misrepresentation in Later Stuart Britain: Partisanship and Political Culture* (Oxford, 2005), 3.

[48] Knights, *Representation*, 5, 336; on politeness, see Lawrence Klein, 'Politeness and the Interpretation of the British Eighteenth Century', *Historical Journal*, xlv (2002), 869–98. On the distinction between a normative and a practical public sphere, see Brian Cowan, 'Publicity and Privacy in the History of the British Coffeehouse', *History Compass*, v (2007), 1180–213, and Brian Cowan, *The Social Life of Coffee: The Emergence of the British Coffeehouse* (New Haven, 2005).

[49] Knights is, rightly, less sanguine about the actual stability of 18th-century politics than Plumb was; see Knights, *Representation*, 336 n. 4.

© *The Parliamentary History Yearbook Trust 2009*

With studies such as Knights's, we are now beginning to build a detailed post-Habermasian understanding of the ways in which the public sphere affected the structures of politics in later Stuart Britain. Furthermore, this work has developed a much more convincing explanation for the transformation of the political world of Algernon Sydney into that of Henry St John, Lord Bolingbroke. Nevertheless, Knights is better at explaining the failings of, and reactions to, the partisan public sphere than he is at developing a positive account of the emergence of polite culture in the 18th century. While some progress has been made in that direction, primarily by intellectual historians focusing on politeness as a discourse, the rise of an 18th-century 'culture of politeness' itself remains as elusive, and as ill-defined, as the supposed achievement of political stability.[50]

Finally, it is worth remarking that the narrative history of early 18th-century Britain has remained seriously underdeveloped in the decades since Holmes wrote his major works. The promise of the foundation work laid in *British Politics* has gone largely unfulfilled in the succeeding decades. There is no doubt that Holmes's unpublished history of the Harley ministry would have made a significant contribution in this respect, and indeed his own work on the Sacheverell trial remains one of the most detailed political narratives of the period to date.[51] We still need detailed studies of important early 18th-century crises and debates such as the 1701 'Kentish petition', the convocation controversies, and the debates over occasional conformity.[52] With regard to the public sphere, most political histories of Anne's reign have tended to be either biographical or thematic in approach; while these genres have their merits, they are no substitute for a revised narrative of the ways in which politicians, both high and low, and their various publics interacted. This new narrative, or perhaps a series of related narrative histories, would offer the best means by which future historians might begin to explain the ways in which the end of the long and revolutionary 17th century also marked the beginnings of the long and fraught, but resiliently oligarchic 18th century.

---

[50] Compare Lawrence Klein, *Shaftesbury and the Culture of Politeness: Moral Discourse and Cultural Politics in Early Eighteenth-Century England* (Cambridge, 1994); Nicholas Phillipson, 'Politics and Politeness in the Reigns of Anne and the Early Hanoverians', in *The Varieties of British Political Thought 1500–1800*, ed. J.G.A. Pocock, with the assistance of G.J. Schochet and L.G. Schwoerer (Cambridge, 1993), 211–45; and see Markku Peltonen, 'Politeness and Whiggism, 1688–1732', *Historical Journal*, xlviii (2005), 391–414.

[51] See, however, Victor Stater, *High Life, Low Morals: The Duel that Shook Stuart Society* (1999) and Daniel Szechi, *1715: The Great Jacobite Rebellion* (New Haven, 2006).

[52] Andrew Starkie, *The Church of England and the Bangorian Controversy, 1716–1721* (Woodbridge, 2007) attempts a study of this sort for one great early Hanoverian fracas.

© *The Parliamentary History Yearbook Trust 2009*

NOTES

Party Affiliation in the House of Lords in 1710: A Contemporary Assessment*

CLYVE JONES

A copy of a printed list of members of both the house of lords and the house of commons published in 1708 has been annotated with manuscript markings of the party affiliations of the members, probably dating from 1710. This note looks at the this contemporary assessment of the affiliations of the peers and bishops in the Lords and compares it with the party affiliations published by Geoffrey Holmes, mainly in his seminal work, *British Politics in the Age of Anne*.

Keywords: house of lords; party affiliation; Geoffrey Holmes; *British Politics in the Age of Anne*; whig junto; Robert Harley; Henry Sacheverell

Modern historians of party in parliament have mainly relied on the voting record of an MP in the Commons or a peer or bishop in the house of lords to determine their party affiliation. Other sources have been used, such as correspondence, as well as other parliamentary lists – forecasts and management lists – to flesh out such deductions. It is rare that the historian is presented with a contemporary listing of such party affiliations. We are fortunate that such a contemporary list exists for the reign of Queen Anne. We are doubly fortunate that this list was probably drawn up in early 1710 at a time when party affiliations were on a cusp towards the end of the administration led by the duumvirate of Godolphin and Marlborough, backed by the whig junto, and just before the emergence of the new, largely tory government of Robert Harley (from 1711, the earl of Oxford), whose administration from 1710 was to lead to fissures in the tory party and to some realignment of party affiliations amongst its followers in both the Commons and the Lords. Thus this list gives us a snapshot of party following in both houses of parliament immediately before the momentous changes wrought by the coming of peace at the end of the long war of the Spanish Succession and the struggle in Britain for the Hanoverian succession to Queen Anne.

It is the purpose of this note to concentrate on party affiliation in the house of lords, as presented by this contemporary list, and to compare the list's assessment of party with that of a modern historian, Geoffrey Holmes, whose work, particularly in his *magnum*

* I would like to thank Robin Eagles for reading an early draft of this note and for making useful suggestions regarding the party affiliations of some of the peers, particularly Cardigan and Shrewsbury.

© The Parliamentary History Yearbook Trust 2009

opus, British Politics in the Age of Anne (published in 1967, with a revised edition in 1987), forms the basis of today's understanding of party in the early 18th century. Holmes's book contained a seminal chapter on the upper House of parliament, which was the beginning of a modern revival of interest in the history of the Lords, which has flowered in the 40-odd years since its publication.

1. *The List and its Dating*

The contemporary list of party affiliations is in the form of manuscript annotations to a printed pamphlet entitled *A True LIST of the Lords Spiritual Temporal, Together with the Members of the House of Commons, constituting the First Parliament of* Great Britain, *as they stand Returned on the Part of* England *in the Office of the Clerk of the Crown in* Chancery, *and were Chosen on the Part of* Scotland *by the late Parliament of that Kingdom. 1707.*[1] The sub-title indicates that '*What Alterations have been made to the 30th of March 1708 are here Corrected.*' There is no publisher, place of publication, nor date given on the pamphlet, but one can surmise that it was probably published in 1708. Thus circa May 1708 is the date that has been taken, up till now, as the time of the annotations. This dating is given some credence by the fact that the Commons' section has the returns from the general election of May 1708 added in ink with party classifications and also marking those who lost their election in 1708. [2] However, besides the manuscript annotations of party allegiance for members of the Lords, there are further annotations to the peers and bishops consisting of '+' and '−' against some of the names, which turns out to be an indication of that person's vote in the division on 20 March 1710 on the impeachment in the house of lords of Dr Henry Sacheverell. The assumption has been made here that the two sets of annotations for the members of the Lords are contemporary, thus making the party affiliation annotation post mid March 1710.[3] Two of the annotations indicate that Bishops Hall of Bristol and Bull of St David's are deceased (see the Appendix below): Hall died on 4 February and Bull on 17 February 1710, thus strengthening the case that the annotations for the Lords at least are later than the middle of March 1710.

The annotations for both the Lords and Commons are in the same hand, but they may not have been made at the same time; if so, then the manuscript annotations to the list could have two dates – May 1708 for the Commons and March 1710 for the Lords, assuming the party affiliations for the Lords were marked at the same time as the markings for the vote of 20 March 1710 on Sacheverell's trial. An intriguing possibility, however, does arise that all the annotations are of the same date, namely sometime in 1710 and that the purpose of the annotation was to prepare a new updated edition of

---

[1] The section on the peers and bishops is printed below in the Appendix.

[2] See *British Parliamentary Lists, 1660–1800: A Register*, ed. G.M. Ditchfield, David Hayton and Clyve Jones (1995), 39, 120–1; *The History of Parliament: The House of Commons, 1690–1715*, ed. Eveline Cruickshanks, Stuart Handley and D.W. Hayton (5 vols, Cambridge, 2002), i, 839. During the research for the History of Parliament this list was discovered in private possession and a photocopy was deposited in the archive of the History. I am grateful to the History of Parliament for allowing me access.

[3] For a detailed description of the annotations see the introduction to the Appendix. Several of the peers in the list are annotated as being papists. Cardigan is not one of them though he only converted to the Church of England and first took his seat in the Lords in Jan. 1708. He is marked as being a whig, so he must have been sitting in the Lords for some time before his politics could have been revealed to contemporaries.

the list for publication in 1710, possibly in time for the general election in October or immediately after. One such list of the parliament after the general election is known to have been published by John Nutt, entitled *A true list of the Lords spiritual and temporal: As also a list of the Knights and Commissioners of Shires, Citizens and Burgesses, chosen to serve in the Parliament of Great Britain, summoned to meet at Westminster the Twenty fifth of November-. . . Note: Those which have this Mark ★ before them were Members of the last Parliament.* A similarly-titled pamphlet was also published in 1710 by J. Baker. However, a pamphlet with virtually the same title as the one dealt with in this note was published in 1708 by one M. Jones, and two others at least were also printed in 1708. The pamphlet under discussion here could have served as an updated text for any of these if the Commons' annotations are in fact from 1708, with the Lords' annotations added later in 1710.

It is unfortunate that we do not know the author of these annotations. We can only surmise, based on the analysis that follows, that whoever it was was politically literate, for he or she, after a comparison with the work of Geoffrey Holmes on party, are found to be largely in agreement with modern assessments of party affiliations. Leaving aside the unlikely possibility that both the annotator and Holmes got their assessments wrong, this comparison does raise the intriguing question, which continues to plague historians: could a contemporary observer, possibly with access to the persons involved, be more accurate in his assessment of his own times than a modern historian who has access to a much wider range of sources than a contemporary observer is ever likely to have had knowledge of, thus to some extent giving the modern historian an 'overview' that could not have been had by a contemporary on the ground? Or is the modern historian's hindsight distorted by his sources which are almost certainly selective, being limited by the accidents of survival? Both the contemporary and the modern historian are unable to see the complete picture, so who is best placed to give the truest answer?

2. *Geoffrey Holmes's Listing of Party Affiliation*

Geoffrey Holmes published two party listings of the member of the house of lords. The first was in 'Appendix A: Party Allegiance in the House of Lords, 1701–14', in *British Politics in the Age of Anne*, 421–35. This listing was based on the voting of the peers and bishops recorded in five divisions lists between 1701 and 1711,[4] and two estimates of future possible voting.[5] At the time of writing *British Politics* these were the only full lists of the House available to historians; that is, full in the sense that they included all the lords voting or considered worthy of estimating on both sides of the question, not the full membership of the Lords. The second of Holmes's lists appeared six years later in *The Trial of Doctor Sacheverell* (1973), 283–7, 'Appendix B: The Judgment of the Lords'.[6]

---

[4] On the impeachment of Lord Somers, 1701; the 1st Occasional Conformity Bill, 1703; the 2nd Occasional Conformity Bill, 1703; the impeachment of Henry Sacheverell, 1710; and the duke of Hamilton's case, 1711.

[5] The earl of Oxford's estimate of the possible voting on the French Commerce Bill, 1713; and the earl of Nottingham's estimate of the future voting on the Schism Bill, 1714.

[6] This appendix consists of two lists: 1. the 'guilty' vote of 20 March 1710, which is the official version published after the trial (which is the list used in this note); and 2. the 'No preferment' vote of 21 March 1710, for which there is no known contemporary list, and which Holmes reconstructed from other contemporary evidence.

© *The Parliamentary History Yearbook Trust 2009*

This list to some extent repeated the version in *British Politics*, but was fuller as it included some lords not in the first list. The omissions in the first list were those peers and bishops who appeared in only one of the seven lists. Holmes's thinking was perhaps that a single appearance in the listings did not necessarily give an indication of party affiliation over a longer period. The party affiliations given in the two lists in *Sacheverell* were based on his earlier listing in *British Politics*, and enabled Holmes to indicate where cross-party voting had occurred.

Both of Holmes's *Sacheverell* lists share one drawback when compared with the contemporary 1710 annotated list: they are less complete. The 1710 list, while not annotating the party affiliation of every single peer or bishop on the basic printed list,[7] has more names than either of Holmes's lists. The listings in *British Politics* and in *Sacheverell* give only those peers and bishops who appear on the original lists, thus there are a number of lords who appear on the 1710 list, which is based on a full list of peers and bishops, who are not covered by Holmes.[8]

3. *1710 Annotator* v. *Geoffrey Holmes*

The following assessment is divided into three parts: 1. those who in the 1710 contemporary list have party markings where Holmes has exactly the same assessment of party; 2. those where Holmes has a similar assessment as the 1710 list; and 3. those where the 1710 list and Holmes differ. (The comparison in the following calculations is between columns 1 and 5 in the Appendix.) In the first category there are 71 peers and 21 bishops where the two sets of party markings agree exactly. In the second category similar markings are found for 24 peers, but for no bishops. While in the category where the Holmes and the 1710 list differ there are 20 peers and one bishop. It is the last two categories which hold the most interest for the historian of today.

Where Holmes and the 1710 list have similar party classifications, it is the case that Holmes's party marking represents a more subtle interpretation of a person's political standing; for example Newcastle is marked in the 1710 list as whig with which Holmes, in his *Sacheverell* list, agrees, but in *British Politics* he is classified as a court whig. The same change is made for Somerset, Richmond, Grafton, St Albans and Schomberg just amongst the dukes. Others follow amongst the marquesses and earls, whilst amongst the barons a similar change is made from tory to either court tory or Hanoverian tory. These changes by Holmes based, as they are, largely on the activities of the peers concerned post 1710 (which for obvious reasons were not known to the 1710 annotator) do not necessarily reduce the usefulness of the 1710 contemporary assessment. The latter were probably largely based, where relevant, on the voting of the peer or bishop in the Sacheverell trial. Indeed, where Holmes gives the classification in his *Sacheverell* it matches that given by the 1710 marker when he is dealing with the whigs, but with the tories it is a case of changing from court to court tory (Delawarr), court tory in both assessments (Byron), court tory to tory (Dartmouth), or tory to Hanoverian tory (Abingdon and Guernsey).

---

[7] Party annotation is missing from 16% of the list.

[8] There are 20 peers and three bishops in the 1710 contemporary list which have party markings and which are not covered by Holmes (15%).

For the modern historian, the real interest lies, however, in the differing interpretations of party allegiance between the 1710 marker and Holmes. Some of these might be put down to mistakes on the 1710 annotator's account, for an examination of the marks in some cases shows that he made mistakes which were at some later stage corrected or erased: Essex, marked a whig (a tory by Holmes) is crossed out; Audley's marking as a whig is crossed out (though Dudley and Ward's marking as a whig, which must be a mistake as he did not take his seat until 1726, is not crossed out); and Bishop Tyler of Llandaff was originally marked as a tory, but that was replaced by a 'W', the same classification as given by Holmes. The differences that remain pose many questions: Shrewsbury from a whig to a tory (though Holmes gives him as a whig based on the Sacheverell vote);[9] Marlborough from whig court (see Appendix for explanation) to tory; Cardigan from whig to tory;[10] Feversham from court whig to court tory; Scarbrough from tory to whig; Mar from whig to tory; Loudoun from whig to Hanoverian tory; Ferrers from whig to tory; Raby from whig to court with tory leanings; Lexinton from whig to tory; Berkeley of Stratton from whig to court tory; Cornwallis from tory to whig; Ossulston from tory to whig; and Barnard from whig to tory. Some of these may again have been mistakes on the 1710 annotator's part, which were not spotted and neither crossed out nor corrected. Some may be genuine assessments on the part of the 1710 annotator but which were of a temporary nature. If so, they are all the more valuable. He was spot on with his assessment of Peterborough as both a tory and a whig, as the earl was previously a whig but went over to Harley in 1710 – but when did he move over? Is the 1710 annotator's assessment of this change earlier than previously reckoned? Without further evidence emerging, the 1710 assessment when in contrast to Holmes's may have to be taken into account provisionally until further work is carried out. This is where the Lords' section of the History of Parliament covering 1660–1832 may be able to assist. When the section of biographies covering 1660–1715 is published we will possibly have some answers to these apparent contradictions.

Whatever answers the historian eventually finish up with, these 1710 contemporary party markings for the house of lords will remain interesting and thought-provoking. Like all other similar assessments they can give no more than a snapshot of political loyalties which may be, for some of the lords on the list, no more than a record of their party position at one point in time, which changed as time and events at a very critical period in British history moved on.[11]

---

[9] Shrewsbury had been a staunch friend of the whig junto in the 1690s, but had attracted their extreme annoyance by the time of his departure for the continent at a time when they felt under threat. When he returned from Europe in 1706 he was perceived to be something other than a pure whig, and his later alliance with Harley seemed to make him very much a courtier or 'government' rather than a party man.

[10] Cardigan had been brought up a catholic, but he was close to Shrewsbury, who was one of the trustees during his minority, and the man who helped to convert him from Rome (Cardigan formally abjured on 11 Jan. 1708, and first sat in the Lords on the following day). This explains why his allegiance mirrors that of Shrewsbury.

[11] Compare the other similar personal assessments recorded in 1713 by Swift (aided in some cases by Lord Oxford), though we know that Swift was close to the centre of politics, whereas the political expertise of the 1710 compiler is likely to remain unknown: see Clyve Jones, 'Swift, the Earl of Oxford, and the Management of the House of Lords in 1713: Two New Lists', *British Library Journal*, xvi (1990), 117–30.

© *The Parliamentary History Yearbook Trust 2009*

Appendix

A True LIST of the Lords Spiritual and Temporal, Together with the Members of the House of Commons, constituting the First Parliament of Great Britain, *as they stand Returned on the Part of* England *in the Office of the Clerk of the Crown in* Chancery, *and were Chosen on the Part of* Scotland *by the late Parliament of that Kingdom.* 1707. *What Alterations have been made to the 30th of March, 1708, are here Corrected*

(The names in the following list are arranged in the same order as printed in 'A True LIST', that is in order of rank and then by precedence. The following abbreviations, which appear in manuscript on the original printed list, have been used: C = court, T = tory, CT = court tory, CW = court whig, W = whig, Pap = papist, (* = under age, this mark is printed on the list); the following are not marked in the original document: HT = Hanoverian tory, SR = Scottish representative peer.)

Column 1 = party classification contemporary with *A True LIST.*

Column 2 = title.

Column 3 = contemporary listing of the vote of 20 March 1710 on Sacheverell's guilt (+ = guilty, − = not guilty).

Column 4 = Geoffrey Holmes's party classification in 1710.

Column 5 = Geoffrey Holmes's party classification based on full voting record (available in 1967) for Anne's reign.

(1)	(2)	(3)	(4)	(5)
Dukes and Great Officers of State				
	Cumberland[1]			
W	B. Cowper [Lord Chancellor]	+	W	W
CT	E. Godolphin [Lord Treasurer]	+	C	T(W)
TC[2]	E. Pembroke [Lord President of the Council]	−	CT	CT
W	Newcastle [Lord Privy Seal]	+	W	CW
Pap	Norfolk			
W	Devonshire [Lord Steward]	+	W	W
W	Somerset		W	CW
W	Richmond	+	W	CW
	Southampton [Cleveland][3]	+	W	CW
W	Grafton	+	W	CW
T	Ormond	−	T	T
T	Beaufort	−	T	T
T	Northumberland	−	CT	CT
W	St Albans	+	W	CW
W	Bolton	+	W	W
W	Schomberg	+	W	CW
W	Shrewsbury	−	W	T
T	Leeds	−	T	T
W	Bedford	+	W	T/W[4]
WC[5]	Marlborough			T

© *The Parliamentary History Yearbook Trust 2009*

T	Buckingham and Normanby	–	T	T
W	Rutland			
	Hamilton[6] [SR]	–	CT	
W	Montagu		W	
W	Cambridge[7]			
W	Queensberry [Dover][8]	+	C	
W	Montrose [SR]	+	W	
W	Roxburghe [SR]	+ :	W	

Marquesses

W	Lindsey			T/W[9]
W	Kent	+	W	CW
W	Dorchester	+	W	W
	Tweeddale [SR]			
W	Lothian [SR]	+[10]		

Earls

W	Derby	+	W	W
★	Huntingdon[11]			
	Lincoln	+	W	CW
W	Suffolk	12	W	W
W	Dorset and Middlesex	+	W	CW
★	Salisbury[13]			T
T	Exeter			T
C	Bridgwater	+	W	CW
W	Leicester	+	W	W
T	Northampton	–	T	T
★	Warwick and Holland[14]			
T	Denbigh	–	T	T
W	Bolingbroke			
W	Westmorland	+	W	W
W	Manchester	+	W	CW
T	Berkshire	–	T	T
W	Rivers	+	W	W[15]
T&W	Peterborough and Monmouth			T/W[16]
W	Stamford	+	W	W
T	Winchilsea	+	CT	T
	Carnarvon			T
T	Chesterfield			
T	Thanet	–	T	T
W	Sunderland	+	W	W
T	Scarsdale	–	T	T
T	Sandwich		T	T
T	Clarendon		T	T
W	Essex[17]			T
W	Cardigan[18]			T
T	Anglesey	–	T	T

© *The Parliamentary History Yearbook Trust 2009*

★	Bath[19]			
W	Carlisle	+	W	W
T	Ailesbury			
★	Burlington[20]			
W	Shaftesbury			W
T	Lichfield			
T	Sussex	–	T	T
CW	Feversham			CT
W	Radnor	+	W	CW
T	Yarmouth	–	T	T
W	Berkeley	+	W	W
T	Nottingham	–	T	T
T	Rochester	–	T	T
T	Abingdon	–	T	HT
W	Gainsborough			
W	Holderness	+	W	CW
T	Plymouth	–	T	T
Pap★	Derwentwater[21]			
Pap	Stafford			
W	Portland	+	W	W
W	Torrington			CW
T	Scarbrough	–	W	W
W	Warrington	+	W	T/W
W	Bradford	+	W	W
W	Rochford			
W	Albermarle			
W	Coventry			W
W	Orford	+	W	W
T	Jersey	–	T	T
W	Grantham	+	W	CW
W	Greenwich (Argyll)	+	W	W
W	Wharton	+	W	W
T	Poulett	–	T	T
W	Cholmondeley	+	W	CW
W	Bindon			
W	Crawford [SR]	+	W	
W	Sutherland [SR]			
W	Mar [SR]	–	CT	T
W	Loudoun [SR]	+	CT	HT
W	Weymss [SR]	–	CT	
W	Leven [SR]	+	C	
W	Seafield [SR]	+	C	W/T
W	Stair [SR]			
T	Rosebery [SR]	+	CT	T
	Northesk[22] [SR]	–	CT	T
	Orkney[23] [SR]	+	CT	C

© *The Parliamentary History Yearbook Trust 2009*

W	Glasgow [SR]	+	C	
W	Ilay[24] [SR]	+	W	W

Viscounts

T	Hereford			T
Pap	Mountacute			
W	Say and Sele	−	T	T[25]
T	Falconberg			
W	Townshend	−	W	
T	Weymouth	−	T	T
T	Hatton			T
★	Longueville[26]			W
★	Lonsdale[27]			

Barons

W	Abergavenny			W
W[28]★	Audley[29]			
T	Delawarr	+	C	CT
W	Berkeley			
W	Ferrers	−	T	T
W	Fitzwalter	+	W	W
W★	Dudley and Ward[30]			
Pap	Stourton			
	Willoughby of Broke	−	T	T
W	Willoughby of Parham			
W	Paget	+	C	W
Pap	Howard of Effingham			CW
T	North and Gray	−	T	T
T	Chandos	−	T	T
	Hunsdon	+	C	C
Pa[p]	Petre			
Pa[p]	Arundel of Wardour			
WPap[31]	Teynham			
T	Brook			T
W	Lovelace			W
W	Maynard			T
	Howard of Escrick	−	T	T
W	Mohun	+	W	W
W	Raby[32]			C(T)
T	Leigh	−	T	T
Pap	Jermyn and Dover[33]			
T	Byron	+	CT	CT[34]
P[ap]	Widdrington			
W	Colepeper	+	W	W
W	Rockingham	+	W	W
W	Lexinton	−	CT	T
P[ap]	Langdale			

© *The Parliamentary History Yearbook Trust 2009*

W	Berkeley of Stratton	–	CT	CT
T	Cornwallis	+	W	W
T	Crew[35]	[–][36]	T	T
P[ap]★	Arundel of Terrice			
T	Craven	–	T	T
	Clifford of Chudleigh			
	Osborne	–	T	T
★	Carteret[37]			HT
T	Ossulston	+	W	W
T	Dartmouth	–	CT	T
T	Stawell	–	T	T
T	Guilford	–	T	T
P[ap]	Waldegrave			
T	Ashburnham		T	T
T	Lempster	–	T	T
T	Butler of Weston[38]	–	T	T
W	Herbert of Chirbury	+	W	W
T	Haversham	–	T	T[39]
W	Somers	+	W	W
W	Barnard			T
W	Halifax	+	W	W
T	Guernsey	–	T	HT
T	Gower	–[40]		
T	Conway	–	T	T
W	Hervey	+	W	
W	Pelham	+	W	

Archbishops and Bishops

W	Canterbury (Tenison)			W
T	York (Sharp)	–	T	T
T	London (Compton)	–	T	T
T	Durham (Crew)	–	T	T
CT	Winchester (Trelawny)			T
W	Worcester (Lloyd)			W
T	Rochester (Sprat)	–	T	T
W	Salisbury (Burnet)	+	W	W
W	Hereford (Humphreys)			
W	Lichfield and Coventry (Hough)	[41]	W	W
W	Ely (Moore)	+	W	W
W	Peterborough (Cumberland)	+	W	W
W	Gloucester (Fowler)		W	W
W	Bristol (Hall)[42]			
W	Chichester (Manningham)	[43]		
W	Oxford (Talbot)	+	W	W
W	Bangor (Evans)			W
W	Carlisle (Nicolson)			W

© *The Parliamentary History Yearbook Trust 2009*

T	Bath and Wells (Hooper)	–	T	T
W	St Davids (Bull)[44]			W
	Lincoln (Wake)	+	W	W
W[45]	Llandaff (Tyler)			W
T	Exeter (Blackall)			T
T	Chester (Dawes)	–	T	T
W	Norwich (Trimnell)	+	W	W
W	St Asaph (Fleetwod)[46]	+	W	W

Notes

1. Prince George of Denmark, husband of Queen Anne, who died on 28 Oct. 1708.
2. This is the only time the annotator uses the abbreviation TC. See below n. 4 for possible explanations for this marking.
3. Succeeded his mother as duke of Cleveland on 9 Oct. 1709.
4. Temporary convert to T; returned to W in 1708 (Geoffrey Holmes, *British Politics in the Age of Anne* (1967), 425).
5. This is the only time the annotator uses the abbreviation WC. This, and the TC above, may just be scribal errors for CW and CT, but they could be indications of a more subtle analysis of Pembroke's and Marlborough's political positions: e.g., the duke of Marlborough was more whig with a court leaning than a lord marked CW, who was more a court orientated lord with a whig leaning.
6. Added in MS in margin.
7. The electoral prince of Hanover, later King George II. He never sat in the Lords under this title, but sat first as prince of Wales in March 1715.
8. He first sat as a Scottish representative peer, and then upon his creation in the post 1707 union British peerage on 26 May 1708 as duke of Dover (see n. 32 below).
9. T convert to mild W (Holmes, *British Politics*, 430).
10. Crossed out.
11. Born in 1696, he first took his seat in the Lords in 1723.
12. Absent from the vote (Geoffrey Holmes, *The Trial of Doctor Sacheverell* (1973), 285).
13. Born in 1691, he first took his seat in the Lords in 1712.
14. Born in 1698, he first took his seat in the Lords in 1719.
15. Went over to Harley (T) in 1710 (Holmes, *British Politics*, 431).
16. Went over to Harley (T) in 1710 (Holmes, *British Politics*, 431).
17. Crossed out.
18. Cardigan had converted from being a Roman catholic to the Church of England in Jan. 1708 and first sat in the house of lords on 12 January (Huntington Library, San Marino, CA, Hasting Papers, HM 30659 (95): newsletter, 15 Jan. 1708).
19. Born in 1692, he died under age in 1711.
20. Born in 1694, he first took his seat in 1715.
21. Born in 1698, he never took his seat.
22. Added in MS in margin.
23. Added in MS in margin. He was the brother of the duke of Hamilton.
24. Brother of the duke of Argyll.

© *The Parliamentary History Yearbook Trust 2009*

25. The 4th viscount, who was a whig and who may account for the annotator's marking of 'W', died in Jan. 1710; the 5th viscount was a tory and voted Sacheverell not guilty.
26. Born 1690, he first took his seat in Feb. 1713.
27. The 2nd viscount was born in 1692, and succeeded as a minor in 1700; he first took his seat in Apr. 1713 and died in Dec. 1713. The 3rd viscount was born in 1694; he first took his seat in 1715.
28. Crossed out as presumably making him as 'W' was an error as he never took his seat.
29. The earl of Castlehaven in the Irish peerage; his date of birth is unknown.
30. Born in 1704, he first took his seat in 1726. Presumably marking him as 'W' was an error as with Audley (see n. 27 above), but never corrected.
31. Partly crossed out and not very legible. Teynham conformed to the Church of England and took his seat in 1716. According to G.E.C., *Complete Peerage* (xii/i, 683) he was a whig when appointed a lord of the bedchamber in 1723. However, in 1717, concerning the end of the impeachment of Lord Oxford he has been listed as a 'T?', though he was granted a pension from the government on 26 July 1717 (Clyve Jones, 'The Impeachment of the Earl of Oxford and the Whig Schism of 1717: Four New Lists', *Bulletin of the Institute of Historical Research*, lv (1982), 85).
32. Created earl of Strafford in Sept. 1711.
33. Name crossed out followed by 'Pap'. This Dover title died out on 6 Apr. 1708 (see n. 7 above).
34. But very 'Whimsical' (Holmes, *British Politics*, 426).
35. Baron Crew was also bishop of Durham.
36. So marked as bishop of Durham.
37. Born in 1690, he first took his seat on 25 May 1711.
38. Earl of Arran in the Irish peerage, he was the brother of the duke of Ormond.
39. W converted to T. He died in Nov. 1710 (Holmes, *British Politics*, 428).
40. Gower did not vote on 20 Mar. 1710 (not in the list in Holmes, *Sacheverell*, 283–5); he is not listed as present in the Lords on 20 Mar. 1710 (*LJ*, xix, 114).
41. Absented from the vote (Holmes, *Sacheverell*, 285).
42. Name crossed out, followed by 'dscd' (deceased). Hall died on 4 Feb. 1710.
43. Absented from the vote (Holmes, *Sacheverell*, 285).
44. Name crossed out, followed by 'dscd' (deceased). Bull died on 17 Feb. 1710.
45. Replaced T crossed out.
46. Name not printed, gap filled in MS.

© *The Parliamentary History Yearbook Trust 2009*

The Debate in the House of Lords on 'No Peace without Spain', 7 December 1711: A New Source

CLYVE JONES

The debate in the house of lords on 'No Peace without Spain' in December 1711 was the first test of the strength of the administration of Robert Harley, earl of Oxford, in the upper House. Though there are more sources for this debate than is normal for proceedings in the Lords, few can claim to be by eyewitnesses. A newly 'discovered' anonymous letter from an eyewitness found in the papers of the lord great chamberlain's office in the Parliamentary Archives gives a detailed account of this important debate.

Keywords: house of lords; parliamentary debates; No Peace without Spain; Robert Harley; W. Dorset Fellowes; marquess of Lindsey; Jonathan Swift

Geoffrey Holmes published his first article in 1960 on 'The Commons' Division on "No Peace without Spain", 7 December 1711'.[1] It was based on a list of 106 MPs representing half the Commons' division, those who voted in favour of Robert Walpole's amendment to the address thanking Queen Anne for her speech opening the session of parliament 'announcing the imminence of a general peace conference', asking that care be taken to prevent Spain and the West Indies from remaining in the possession of Philip V, grandson of Louis XIV of France. This list was in the Harley Papers, part of what was then called the Portland Loan, or Loan 29, in the British Museum.[2]

In the house of lords, the earl of Nottingham on the same day moved the same amendment to the address and this note is concerned with a recently discovered new account of the ensuing debate (which also contains information on the Commons' debate) to be found in the Parliamentary Archives (previously known as the House of Lords Record Office), which is printed below in the Appendix.

1

The letter opens: 'As severe a Closeting as has been known in England was put in Practice last week. It intimidated some but not quite enow [enough] to carry it in the House of Lords for Supporting the Steps wch have been made towards a Peace.' The historian is fortunate that Robert Harley, earl of Oxford, as well as being a political

---

[1] *Bulletin of the Institute of Historical Research*, xxxiii (1960), 223–34.

[2] This collection, now in the British Library, has since been catalogued and numbered as Additional Manuscripts.

© *The Parliamentary History Yearbook Trust 2009*

manager of the first rank, was also an inveterate compiler of lists, some of which are a record of his management. Four such lists have survived in his papers for December 1711 which deal with the debate on 7 December, two of which are concerned with Oxford's 'severe a Closeting as has been known', and two which partly record how successful that closeting was. First, there is an undated list, partly in Oxford's hand, which is probably a calculation of support in early December 1711; second, a list dated 2 December of peers and one bishop to be canvassed before the debate on the 7th; and third, two lists dated 10 December, firstly of those officeholders and pensioners who voted against the ministry on the 7th, and secondly a list probably of loyal peers who voted for the ministry.[3]

The list of support from early December has 41 names (including seven bishops), three of which have a 'q' marked next to the names, presumably indicating a 'query', while the later canvassing list has 39 names (including one bishop), one of which is marked 'q'. Only 14 names (none of them bishops) are common to both lists, and one – Maynard – has a query mark on the canvassing list but not on the list of supporters. Comparing these lists with the two indicating how peers and bishops who were officeholders or pensioners voted on 7 December shows that on the list of supporters, 11 (including one query) supported the ministry, with six against, while on the list of those canvassed, five voted with the ministry and six against. There would have been others on the first two lists of supporters and those canvassed who did not hold an office or a pension from the ministry and who voted on 7 December, but as we do not have a division list for that day we do not know who these peers and bishops were. So any analysis of how successful Oxford's closeting was can only be a partial assessment, confined to officeholders and pensioners whom Oxford chose to list. Such an assessment does, however, bear out the opinion expressed in this new letter that if some were 'intimidated', not enough were persuaded to support the ministry's peace policy.

A comparison of Oxford's list of supporters of December 1711 with those who were present at the opening of the session on 7 December shows that 24 of the 41 who were listed attended (that is 58.5%), while 29 of the 39 (or 74.4%) of those on Oxford's canvassing list attended. It is not clear how many on each list were actually approached by Oxford, but the level of attendance of those on the canvassing list is high, though there is no way of knowing if those who attended did so as a result of being canvassed. A small number of proxies can be added to these attendance figures: seven to the list of supporters and four to the canvassed list, though one peer's proxy, that of Lord Maynard, is in both totals.

The bulk of the names on both lists were tories (30 out of 41 or 73% on the supporters list; and 17 out of 39 or 43.6% on the canvassing list)[4] and thus could be considered as natural supporters of the ministry, particularly in its early days. The other names on the lists, particularly those on the canvassing list, were court (Orkney) or

[3] BL, Add. MSS 70331–2 (unfoliated), printed in Clyve Jones, ' "The Scheme Lords, the Neccessitous Lords, and the Scots Lords": The Earl of Oxford's Management and the "Party of the Crown" in the House of Lords, 1711–14', in *Party and Management in Parliament, 1660–1784*, ed. Clyve Jones (Leicester, 1984), 152–60.

[4] On the canvassing list there were also one court tory (Northumberland) and one Hanoverian tory (Pembroke). Also Viscount Hatton had been a whig but was moving towards becoming a Hanoverian tory at this time.

court whigs (11 out of 39, or 28%), with the odd whig thrown in (6 out of 39, or 15%).[5]

2

The opening of the new session of parliament in December 1711 was in the early days of Oxford's management of the Lords. He had only been raised to the peerage in May 1711 and had sat very few times in the upper House before it was prorogued in July. Though there is some evidence that even as early as the mid 1690s Oxford, whose management expertise was almost solely confined to the Commons, had begun to take an interest in the workings of the upper House,[6] his management techniques and acute eye for assessing an opponent's and a supporter's political position needed some refining to cope with the Lords. This is attested to by the blunder of hot-headed, senior tories on 8 December, which Oxford failed to prevent, and may even have supported, when an unsuccessful attempt was made to reverse the vote of the previous day.[7] The fiasco, which resulted, in an even greater desertion of the ministry by erstwhile supporters, rebounded on Oxford. However, by the end of the year, his sure political touch, strengthened by his experience on 7 and 8 December, had returned and he had regained the initiative in the Lords, by persuading Queen Anne to create 12 new peers[8] and to dismiss the dukes of Marlborough and Somerset, and he had gained support for his peace initiatives.

3

The author and recipient of this newly discovered letter are unknown as the letter is neither addressed nor signed, but the author probably was in the House during the debate in the Lords, and may even have been a member, as W. Dorset Fellowes, in whose

---

[5] Seven of the court whigs had pensions as did the one court tory. One of the whigs (Herbert of Cherbury) was moving towards becoming a court whig. The party classifications are the ones given by Holmes in *British Politics in the Age of Anne* (1967, rev. edn 1987), 425–35. Two peers have not been classified by Holmes: Earl Marischal (a Scottish Representative peer) on the supporters' list, and the earl of Rochford (on both lists): Robert Harley considered Marischal a supporter in early Dec. 1711; and Harley thought the 3rd earl of Rochford, who had succeeded to the tile in July 1710, as doubtful in Oct. 1710, and in Dec. 1711 as a 'query' supporter and one to be canvassed before the vote on the 7 December debate (Jones, ' "The Scheme Lords, the Neccessitous Lords, and the Scots Lords" ', 157–8). There were also two 'independent' peers: the marquess of Annandale on the supporters' list, who probably leaned to the tories (and has been counted with the tories), and the earl of Warrington, who though essentially a whig, did fitfully support Oxford at this time when he was in negotiations for his unpaid pension; for whom see J.V. Beckett and Clyve Jones, 'Financial Improvidence and Political Independence in the Early Eighteenth Century: George Booth, 2nd Earl of Warrington (1675–1758)', *Bulletin of the John Rylands Library*, lxv (1982), 8–35.

[6] Clyve Jones, 'Robert Harley, Christmas and the House of Lords' Protest on the Attainder of Sir John Fenwick, 23 December 1696: The Mechanism of a Procedure Partly Exposed', *eBLJ* (*electronic British Library Journal*) (2007).

[7] Clyve Jones, 'The Division That Never Was: New Evidence on the Aborted Vote in the Lords on 8 December 1711 on "No Peace without Spain" ', *Parliamentary History*, ii (1983), 191–202.

[8] Clyve Jones, 'Lords Oxford's Jury: The Political and Social Context of the Creation of the Twelve Peers, 1711–12', in *Partisan Politics, Principle and Reform in Parliament and the Constituencies, 1689–1880: Essays in Memory of John A. Phillips*, ed. Clyve Jones, Philip Salmon and Richard Davis (Edinburgh, 2005), 9–42.

© *The Parliamentary History Yearbook Trust 2009*

collection the letter was found, conjectured in a note written at the end of the final page of the letter. But it is not likely that the author of the letter was, as Fellowes thought, 'probably one of the ministers'. The opening tone of the letter is one that would be expected to come from an opponent of the ministry. Also by this stage Lord Lindsey, whom Fellowes thought to be the recipient of the letter, had abandoned his tory stance and had adopted 'mild Whiggery',[9] and had moved into opposition to the administration and possibly to the court. Fellowes's conjecture on the identity of the recipient was based on two facts: 'This Paper must have been written by some Nobleman, probably one of the ministers, to the Earl of Lindsey [the 4th earl, who had been created marquess of Lindsey in 1706] – one of the Duke of Marlborough's friends from the concluding point – "I have reason to believe the Duke of Marlborough would employ your Proxy, if you would honour him with it." ' It is true that Lord Lindsey's proxy dated 26 December was entered into the Lords proxy book in favour of Marlborough (and according to the book it was not vacated by Lindsey's presence in the House until 28 April 1712).[10] Besides this fact, Fellowes may have thought the letter was written to Lindsey, the hereditary lord great chamberlain of England, because he probably found it in Lindsey's papers as lord great chamberlain, being himself secretary to a later lord great chamberlain.

Lindsey is not recorded in the *Lords Journal* as attending the house of lords on 7 December 1711.[11] However, he did sit on 20, 21 and 22 December,[12] and this letter may have been the reason he attended the House before he probably left London for the Christmas recess, probably returning to the family home of Grimethorpe in Lincolnshire, from whence he dispatched a proxy dated 26 December.[13] According to the *Lords Journal* Lindsey returned to the House on 2 January 1712[14] (in contrast to the proxy record which states he did not attend again until 28 April). However, there are two pieces of evidence which place Lindsey in the Lords' chamber on 11 December. First, Queen Anne, after opening parliament by delivering her speech in her robes with full regalia, then attended the debate incognita, that is, sat on the throne but without her robes and regalia and so by convention was officially ignored by the House. At the end of the proceedings 'when the queen was going from the house, where she had sat to hear the debate, the duke of Shrewsbury lord chamberlain [of the household] asked her, whether he or the great chamberlain Lindsay ought to lead her out; she answered short, Neither of you, and gave her hand to the duke of Somerset, who was louder than any in the house for the Clause against Peace'.[15] Second, in an unofficial presence list probably compiled by a clerk for the Scottish representative peer, the earl of Loudoun, headed

---

[9] Holmes, *British Politics*, 430.

[10] Parliamentary Archives, HL/PO/JO/13/7. The next proxy registered as held by Marlborough, from 4 to 20 Mar. 1712, was that of the earl of Berkeley.

[11] *LJ*, xix, 335. Lindsey is also not recorded as attending the House in the manuscript minutes of the Lords, from which the presence list in the *Lords Journal* is derived.

[12] *LJ*, xix, 345, 347–8.

[13] As far as the incomplete proxy record allows, we can say that Lindsey was not often involved in leaving or holding proxies: between 1689 and 1714 he only held three proxies in 1689, 1696 and 1698 and only left his proxy five times, twice with his brother Abingdon in 1693 and 1711, once with Marlborough in 1711, and twice with Nottingham in 1714 (Parliamentary Archives, HL/PO/JO/13/7). Thus his leaving his proxy with Marlborough in 1711 may strengthen the case that he was indeed the recipient of this letter.

[14] *LJ*, xix, 352.

[15] Jonathan Swift, *Journal to Stella*, ed. Harold Williams (2 vols, Oxford, 1974), ii, 433.

'Lords Present the 7th December 1711', the 'L. Great Camberlain' is placed at the bottom of list of barons, together with four other peers (three barons and one earl) who were also not listed officially in the Journal as present on 7 December.[16] The positioning of these four peers and Lindsey at the end of the presence list strongly suggests that they may have arrived late after the rest of the list had been compiled by a clerk, and this may account for them not being on the official list. Lindsey arriving late may also account for the letter, the author perhaps assuming that Lindsey had missed the bulk of the debate.

The information about Shrewsbury's question to Queen Anne was given to Jonathan Swift the following day, 8 December, by Abigail Masham, a woman of the bedchamber (in effect the queen's dresser) since 1702, and from January 1711 the keeper of the queen's privy purse, and the queen's then favourite. Unlike the ladies of the bedchamber, the higher-ranking attendants on the Queen, an office held by peeresses, Mrs Masham would not have formally attended the queen into the house of lords and would not have stood behind her on the dais where the throne was situated while the queen read out her speech. However, as the queen's dresser she may have gone with the queen to Westminster to help her robe and disrobe in the Prince's Chamber next to the House. If so, Mrs Masham may have witnessed the scene she described to Swift,[17] or possibly have been told of it by an eyewitness – one of the ladies of the bedchamber or by the earl of Oxford, her cousin, friend and confident whose influence with the queen she promoted.[18]

Thus it is possible that Lindsey was present, and his office would probably have obliged him to be present (as lord great chamberlain he was in charge of the palace of Westminster, officially a royal residence). However, his attendance in Anne's reign at the opening of parliament was not good: six times out of 11. But the official record of the House – the Journal (which is not infallible) – and the letter reproduced here would seem to contradict this, unless, of course, he was not the recipient of the letter, but no other peer registered their proxy with Marlborough around this time.

The debate in the house of lords on 7 December 1711 is one of the better recorded debates in Anne's reign. We cannot be sure, however, if any – apart from the letter reproduced here – were by eyewitnesses. As Geoffrey Holmes wrote in his unpublished account of the Harley ministry: 'Of the debate as a whole L'Hermitage, though not personally present, gives a valuable account. The accounts of Boyer and Pittis are also useful.'[19] L'Hermitage, the Dutch resident in London, sent his report back to the States General, and a copy can be found in BL, Add. MS 17677EEE, ff. 388ff. Abel Boyer published his account in his *History of Queen Anne*, but not until 1735. William Pittis's account appeared in print in 1712 as *The History of the Proceedings of the Second Session of*

[16] Jones, 'The Division That Never Was', 199.

[17] She may have been standing during the debate at the door in the south-west corner of the house of lords which lead to the Prince's Chamber which was partly covered by one of the Armada tapestries which lined the walls of the chamber. See a description of two lords in 1689 'retiring between the hangings [the tapestries] and the door next to the bishops' room' in the south-east corner of the chamber: *Memoirs of Thomas, Earl of Ailesbury* (2 vols, Westminster, 1890), i, 230.

[18] R.O. Bucholz, *The Augustan Court: Queen Anne and the Decline of Court Culture* (Stanford, CA, 1993), 119, 163–6.

[19] Geoffrey Holmes, 'The Great Ministry', 163 n. 122. This is a typescript of an unpublished monograph by Geoffrey Holmes. A copy is deposited in the library of the Institute of Historical Research, University of London.

the Present Parliament. Other contemporary sources also provide valuable information, particularly *Bishop Burnet's History of His Own Times*, first published 1724–34 (two volumes), though the standard edition to date is that published in 1833.[20] Burnet, bishop of Salisbury, was present in the Lords on 7 December.[21] Individual letters in contemporary correspondence also provide the occasional insight, though how many were eyewitnesses is an open question. Some of the better reports of the debate in letters were written by the brothers John and Ralph Bridges to their uncle, Sir William Trumbull. Their information was undoubtedly from Henry Compton, bishop of London, whose chaplain was Ralph Bridges. Compton was present in the House on 7 December.[22] Jonathan Swift had good contacts at court and in parliament, not least of which was the lord treasurer himself, Robert Harley, earl of Oxford.[23] Nonetheless, the value of the present letter is that it almost certainly was written by an eyewitness and as such is one of only a very few such sources and contains evidence which corroborates much of what is in the other sources.

Appendix

Parliamentary Archives, HL/PO/LB/1/30, 'Illustrations and Notes Relative to the Duke of Marlborough in 1711', by W.D. Fellowes, [pp.] 20–5: ? to [? the marquess of Lindsey], 10 December 1711.

As severe a Closeting as has been known in England was put in Practice last week. It intimidated some but not quite enow [enough] to carry it in the House of Lords for Supporting the Steps wch have been made towards a Peace. The Struggle there was upon my Ld Notting[ham']s[24] motion; That to the address of thanks for the Q[ueen']s Speech,[25] the humble opinion of the House shou'd be added, That such a Peace, as shou'd leave Spain and the Indies to any Prince of the House of Bourbon, cou'd not be safe for the Liberty of Europe. This the Court oppos'd with all its force chiefly urging, that it did not look like having an entire confidence in the Queen, who did not ask their advice in her Speech, but assur'd them she wou'd take care of every thing. 'Twas said on the other side, That for that very reason, that in such a Juncture she did not please to ask their advice, it Seem'd the more necessary to offer it. That this was far from touching upon her Prerogative, since nobody disputed Peace & Warr were entirely in Her, but that since it was always supposed, no English Prince did any thing but with the advice of their ministers, The opinion of the Great Council, the House of Lords, might probably have some weight with those ministers, especially such as might be appointed to negociate this Peace.

---

[20] Gilbert Burnet, *Bishop Burnet's History of His Own Times* (6 vols, Oxford, 1833). Lionel Glassey of Glasgow University, and a friend of Geoffrey Holmes is presently engaged on a new edition of Burnet.

[21] *LJ*, xix, 335.

[22] *LJ*, xix, 335.

[23] See Swift, *Journal to Stella*, i, 432.

[24] Daniel Finch (1647–1730), 2nd earl of Nottingham.

[25] For the queen's speech, see *LJ*, xix, 335–6.

© *The Parliamentary History Yearbook Trust 2009*

My Ld Notting[ha]m Spoke a great while, and with great earnestness, to show, That if Spain & the Indies, were given up to France, Europe was undone, Britain enslav[ed][26] and the Queen unsafe upon her Throne. This he said appeared to him so much beyond a doubt, That altho' he had so numerous a Family to provide for,[27] that some men had more reason to wish an end of Taxes; yet he thought this a point of that dreadfull consequence that shou'd the Government find it necessary in order to carry it, to take his whole Revenue to apply to the war, leaving him only some small branch to keep him and his Children alive, he call'd God to witness he wou'd most chearfully submit to it. The other side pleaded hard for a delay of some days before they gave the Queen their advice, saying they were not prepar'd for so great a decision. But they were ask'd whether this was not long ago decided, when 'twas on this acc[oun]t and no other the War had been begun, and continu'd ten years.[28] That therefore to talk of being unprepar'd was a poor pretence. And my Ld Godolphin[29] said, there was no time to be lost, that Europe lay gasping, without any other hope, than that this Parliam[en]t now met might possibly rescue them from the utter destruction they saw at their doors; That the alliance was shaken almost to pieces, that 'twas with difficulty they even held together 'till they cou'd know what this Parliam[en]t wou'd do, That it was post night for Holland, and that he desir'd the Post might not go away without this for their comfort, that the House of Lords had with distain declar'd against a Peace, that wou'd make them and all their Posterity the Vilest Slaves.

My Ld Wharton[30] said, Those who cry'd[?] we cou'd go on no longer ought to declare themselves in still plainer Terms & say we are Conquer'd, we must Submit to what out Lord the King of France[31] will please to lay upon us.

My Ld Anglesey[32] arraign'd in general Terms, those who had carry'd on the Warr & said they might have had a Peace a good one too, after the battle of Ramellies.[33] Upon wch the D[uke] of Marlborough[34] got up and Spoke like a Roman Gen[era]ll. Begun with a defiance to Him and all the World to charge him with having conceal'd the most minute thing that past on that occasion from the Queen. He said he spoke it before God, and before Her who then heard him. [that wch: crossed out] and as she knew that what he said was true he did not doubt but she wou'd add to her other Goodness towards him, that of doing him this justice. He then said, he was Old and Tyr'd with the Fatgues of Warr, as well as with the daily affronts & Schocks he had of late been expos'd to while he was doing all that God had given him Power to do, in the Service of his Queen & Country. That he was so far from wishing to prolong the Warr that he wou'd crawl on

---

[26] Edge of letter obscured by binding.

[27] Nottingham's surviving children consisted of one daughter by his first wife, and five sons and eight daughters by his second wife (his second wife also bore him ten other children who died young and seven stillborn): *Collin's Peerage of England*, ed. Egerton Brydges (9 vols, 1812), iv, 401.

[28] The War of the Spanish Succession had started in 1702, and was to finish in 1713 with the Treaty of Utrecht; before that England had been at war against France in the War of the League of Augsburg 1689–97.

[29] Sidney Godolphin (1645–1712), cr. 1st earl of Godolphin 1706; formerly lord treasurer, 1700–1, 1702–10.

[30] Thomas Wharton (1648–1715), cr. 1st earl of Wharton 1706, a member of the five-man whig junto.

[31] Louis XIV, king of France 1643–1715.

[32] Arthur Annesley (*d.*1737), succ. 1710 as 5th earl of Anglesey.

[33] The second of Marlborough's great victories over the French, 23 May 1706.

[34] John Churchill (1650–1722), cr. 1st duke of Marlborough 1702; captain general of the English forces, generalissimo of the allied forces, and master general of the ordnance 1702–30 Dec. 1711.

© *The Parliamentary History Yearbook Trust 2009*

all four[s] to the Queen's feet to beg she wou'd consent to Peace, but not a Peace that must Ruin both her Self her Subjects & all the World about her.

The Queen was by all the Debates, and at last it was Carry'd by two,[35] for the advice.

The Court however thought they cou'd reverse it next day, upon the Question of agreeing with the Committee that was to draw up the address[36] but they were deceiv'd, for my Lord Guernsey,[37] Lord Weymouth,[38] Ld Cartwright[39] & others went over from the Court, so that they lost it by sixteen.[40]

In the House of Commons the debate was upon the Same foot: And tho' it went there on the Court Side, Yet such things were said, and such hints given to the Ministers to have a care of a bad Peace, that 'tis reckon'd they will look Upon themselves on the matter, as much pin'd downe by the Com[mon]s as the Lords

Mr Aislesby[41] Spoke against the Court in the Warmest manner. One thing past in the debate, that is much talk'd on in the Towne. They call'd upon Secreatary St John[42] to tell them whether the Dutch had willingly agreed to the measures propos'd to them from our side; He said they had their answer in the Queens Speech which assured them of it. Sr Peter King[43] then ask'd him, Whether before they agreed to what was proposed to them, they did not make all those objections which he heard then made in the House to which he would Answer nothing.

Unless your L[ord]ship has chang'd your Eyes and Inclinations both, you will easily see through all this Scheme, and wish it confounded. There is then but one thing more, which is to help. The Question is not to get on horseback as at the Revolution,[44] I hope it won't come to that; but the way to prevent it, is to Vote. If you do not come up your self I have reason to believe, the D[uke] of Marlb[orough] wou'd employ your Proxy (if you wou'd hon[ou]r him with it) for the Queen's Safety, your own, your Country's, and all Europe's.

---

[35] The majority was in fact one: Contents 61 plus 6 proxies, 67; Not Contents 55 plus 11 proxies, 66.

[36] For this ill-judged attempt to reverse the vote of the previous day in the Lords, see Jones, 'The Division That Never Was', 190–202.

[37] Heneage Finch (c.1649–1719), cr. 1st Baron Guernsey 1703; younger brother of the 2nd earl of Nottingham.

[38] Thomas Thynne (1640–1714), cr. 1st Viscount Weymouth 1682.

[39] This spelling was a common way of recording Lord Carteret's name and possibly reflected the pronunciation of the name. John Carteret (1690–1763), 2nd Baron Carteret.

[40] There was no formal division on 8 Dec. 1711 in the Lords as the attempted vote turned into a fiasco. Various observers estimated the majority for keeping the amendment to the address if there had been a full division as 11, 17 or 18, while contemporary printed sources later reported 20 or 22 (see Jones, 'The Division That Never Was', 191–4, 199 n. 5).

[41] John Aislabie (1670–1742), MP for Ripon 1695–1702, 1705–22, for Northallerton 1702–5, a lord of the admiralty 1710–14; a tory who co-operated with the whigs more openly than any other 'whimsical tory' ('whimsicals' were tories who were dissatisfied with the government's policies); he was one of the proposers of the amendment to the address on 7 Dec. 1711 (*The History of Parliament: The House of Commons, 1690–1715*, ed. Eveline Cruickshanks, Stuart Handley and D.W. Hayton (5 vols, Cambridge, 2002), iii, 14, 18).

[42] Henry St John (1678–1752), MP for Berkshire; secretary of state 1710–14; cr. 1st Viscount Bolingbroke 1712.

[43] Sir Peter King (c.1669–1734), MP for Bere Alston 1701–15; recorder of London 1708–15; later Baron King and lord chancellor 1725–33.

[44] The 'Glorious Revolution' of 1688–9.

The Duke of Somerset[45] has been warm & active against the Court in this Struggle. The Duke of St Albans[46] (who must starve if turn'd out)[47] came up to Towne on purpose to Vote against the Court. My Ld Cholmondeley[48] voted the same way the Duke of St Albans did.[49]

[45] Charles Seymour (1662–1748), 6th duke of Somerset; master of the horse 1702–Jan. 1712.

[46] Charles Beauclerk (1670–1726), cr. 1st duke of St Albans 1684; illegitimate son of King Charles II.

[47] His only office of profit was captain of the Band of Gentlemen Pensioners which he occupied from 1693 to Jan. 1712.

[48] Hugh Cholmondeley (c.1662–1725), cr. 1st earl of Cholmondeley 1706; treasurer of the royal household 1708–13.

[49] Both were recorded as voting against the ministry by the 'prime minister', the lord treasurer, the earl of Oxford, and possibly by the Scottish representative peer, the earl of Loudoun (see Jones, 'The Division that Never Was', 192, 197–8). Both were court whigs, who normally supported the tory ministry.

© *The Parliamentary History Yearbook Trust 2009*

Index

© *The Parliamentary History Yearbook Trust 2009*

© *The Parliamentary History Yearbook Trust 2009*

© *The Parliamentary History Yearbook Trust 2009*

Printed and bound by CPI Group (UK) Ltd, Croydon, CR0 4YY

13/04/2025

14656465-0004